PRAISE FOR *Bad Software*...

"This book is worth buying for the first chapter alone. In *Bad Software*, Cem Kaner and David Pels provide consumers with simple steps for dealing with defective software—a how-to book for consumer protection in the information age. In addition to practical advice, they discuss an important legislative threat to consumers: Article 2B of the Uniform Commercial Code. Kaner and Pels are right on target in their scathing critique of this regressive draft law that will allow software companies to insulate themselves from liability for defective products."
—Ralph Nader
  Consumer Advocate
  July, 1998

"No software customer, be they home user or corporate CIO, should be without this book. If you're tired of dealing with buggy programs and poor technical support, this is the place to find out what you can do about it."
—Ed Foster
  InfoWorld, "Gripe Line" Columnist

"A masterful job."
—Watts Humphrey
  Fellow
  Software Engineering Institute
  Carnegie Mellon University

"*Bad Software* is a wake-up call to software consumers to stop putting up with poor-product quality. The authors did an excellent job of navigating controversial issues. Consumers are told in no uncertain terms what the law entitles them to and what it does not. Examples of good and bad publishers are given, and both definitely *do* exist. The overall explanations of how software producers evaluate the requests of consumers and how consumers evaluate the trustworthiness of producers are superb. Every software consumer should own *Bad Software*."
—Jeffery E. Payne
  President
  Reliable Software Technologies

"An expert analysis of the serious problems that Article 2B will create for the general public and for writers."
—Jonathan Tasini
  President of the National Writers Union
  Lead plaintiff in the lawsuit, *Tasini v. New York Times*

"Software purchasers are often perplexed when confronting problems with packages. *Bad Software* was written for those disappointed and confused purchasers. It provides practical help in dealing with problems with software. *Bad Software* is instructive and readable for consumers and computer professionals alike. It's a required resource for anyone using software packages."
—Sharon Marsh Roberts
  Chairman
  Independent Computer Consultants Association

"An important contribution to improving the quality of a product by creating more knowledgeable consumers."
— Dr. Frederick C. Van Bennekom, Senior Consultant, Service Management
    International; Lecturer, Northeastern University College of Business Administration.

Bad Software

What To Do When Software Fails

Cem Kaner
David Pels

WILEY COMPUTER PUBLISHING

John Wiley & Sons, Inc.
New York • Chichester • Weinheim • Brisbane • Singapore •Toronto

This book is dedicated to my father, Harry Kaner, who raised me in his businesses. He taught me that it is good to succeed in business and that, along with money, true commercial success involves integrity, fair dealing, and a commitment to the dignity of the people who work with you.

—*Cem Kaner*

This book is dedicated to my parents, Richard H. Pels and Carolyn M. Pels, who taught me the inherent value of people and the importance of honoring your word and following through on commitments.

—*David L. Pels*

Disclaimer Note:
This book (including its sample letters) provides general information and does not constitute legal advice about your particular situation. Conmputer-related laws are changing rapidly, they vary from State to State, and the application of the law may depend on specific facts that arise in your situation but were not considered in this book. Please use all letters at your own risk. Also, unless you make arrangements directly with his firm, Cem Kaner is not your attorney. He has no laywer-client relationsip with you. Please tell the person to whom you send any sample letter that you copied it from a book, and don't say that it is a letter from your lawyer. It is not.

Designations used by companies to distinguish their products are often claimed as trademarks. In all instances where John Wiley & Sons, Inc., is aware of a claim, the product names appear in initial capital or ALL CAPITAL LETTERS. Readers, however, should contact the appropriate companies for more complete information regarding trademarks and registration.

This book is printed on acid-free paper.

Published by John Wiley & Sons, Inc.

Published simultaneously in Canada.

This publication is designed to provide accurate and authoritative information in regard to the subject matter covered. It is sold with the understanding that the publisher is not engaged in professional services. If professional advice or other expert assistance is required, the services of a competent professional person should be sought.

Library of Congress Cataloging-in-Publication Data:
Kaner, Cem.
    Bad software : what to do when software fails / Cem
Kaner, David Pels.
      p.   c.m.
    Includes bibliographical references and index
    ISBN 0-471-31826-4 (paper : alk paper)
    1 Software failures.   I Pels, David 1962–
II. Title.
QA76.76.F34K36   1998   98-34426
005--dc21   CIP

Printed in the United States of America.

10 9 8 7 6 5 4 3 2

Contents

Preface

You buy an interesting new computer program. You try to use it, but it is too awkwardly designed. And, some basic features are missing. Others don't work. You telephone the *publisher* (the company that made the program); its telephone answering system puts you on hold for an hour. Finally, you speak to the publisher's technician, who tells you that everyone else *loves* the program. "Maybe you just don't understand how to use it—*how carefully have you read the manual?* As to those problems you're *claiming* that the program has, no one else has *ever* reported *anything* like them. There must be something wrong with your computer. Who made your computer's video card? Oh, *them*. Yes, you should call *them*. It's probably *their* fault."

Sound familiar?

In 1995, the Better Business Bureau received more complaints involving computers than they received about used car dealers. For the first time, computer sales (including software) was among the 10 most complained about types of businesses in the BBB records, rising from 20th place in 1994 to 8th place in 1995 (Better Business Bureau, 1995). (In 1996, complaints about computer sales rose to 7th place.)

You Don't Have to Put Up with This

Some publishers take great pride in their products and their customer relations, but others treat their customers like suckers. They know that most Americans who buy a defective program don't call for help or demand a refund. These publishers also know that most of the people who do call to complain or ask for help probably won't call back if they can be made to feel guilty or stupid or if they know that the next call will be a pain in the neck. Instead, they'll throw the program away or leave it, unused, on their bookshelf to collect dust. Therefore, these companies spend a pittance designing and testing their products, and then they brush you off when you have a complaint.

You Don't Have to Be a Sucker

This book is about getting your money's worth:

- You probably want the program to work. (Why else would you have bought it?) *This book will help you figure out what questions to ask the publisher's technical support staff and what to tell them, to help them help you get your program working.*

- If the program just won't work, you'd probably like a replacement program that will work. *This book will help you find out if a replacement is available and will suggest ways to ask for it.*

- If you can't get a replacement, you probably want a refund. But maybe you should ask for more than a refund. For example, if you had to call the publisher's 900 number to report an error in their program, who should pay for that call? It is *their* error. Maybe, you should ask *them* to pay for the call. *This book will help you decide what to ask for.*

- If the publisher just wants to treat you like a sucker, keep your money, and let you go away unhappy, this book will help you change its mind. You have rights. *This book will help you understand, communicate, and exercise your rights.*

- Most publishers don't think of you as a sucker, but you can still have bad experiences with their products. Some people treat honest companies' staff as though they were incompetent liars. This isn't the best strategy. If you were to personally offend honest people, they might not work very hard to solve your problem. *This book will help you get satisfaction from good publishers as well as from bad ones.*

What's the Problem?

The odds are that you're reading this book because you're having a bad experience with a software company. Many of the companies that give their customers bad software are bad companies. But not all of them. No computer program is perfect. You can have bad experiences with software from an honest, decent, reasonable publisher.

One underlying problem is that publishers are pushing themselves and each other to ship products faster and faster. As a result, some software is only minimally tested. So, when you buy it, it might or might not work.

Software companies knowingly ship defective products every day. *Almost all companies ship programs with known bugs.* (We provide references for this and for the customer support/dissatisfaction statistics in Chapter 2, "Introduction.")

When you call to complain or to ask for help

- Some companies will provide excellent assistance.
- Some will hide behind a warranty disclaimer (a piece of paper they stuck in the box that says that they are selling the software "as is") and refuse any help.
- Some will put you on hold and leave you there for a ridiculously long time (after an hour, most callers hang up and don't call for help again);.
- Some will help you only if you pay additional money for the support.

A typical call to customer support costs the company about $23. So, software companies are working hard on what they call "call avoidance"—if you ever sat on hold for an hour waiting to talk to a software support technician, you know what we're talking about.[1] Customer satisfaction with software customer support has declined for 10 straight years.

A Famous Example: The Pentium Bug

In the summer of 1994, Intel discovered a defect in its Pentium chip. Under some circumstances, the chip didn't do certain arithmetic calculations correctly. (The notes in this section are taken from the Santa Clara County Superior Court's case file for *In re Pentium Processor Litigation*.)

Intel continued to ship the chip for several months, without telling customers about the problem. Then, in late 1994, a university professor discovered the bug and published a report on it.

From a technical viewpoint, we don't know how severe the underlying bug was. Intel estimated that a customer would encounter the bug once every 27,000 years. Others estimated that customers would encounter the bug within days, weeks, months, or years. (*PC Week*, 1994.)

In practice, this was a serious bug. On the basis of the failure, the Food and Drug Administration replaced its own chips and suggested that companies submitting data to the FDA should conduct their analyses on computers that didn't have the Pentium bug. A major stock broker swapped out all of its chips,

---

[1]Call avoidance involves more than just hiding from calls. It's a philosophy of call cost reduction. The idea is to either prevent calls (by reducing the number of bugs that reach customers), to divert calls to nonhumans (such as voice message trees or knowledge bases, Internet-based data, and BBSs), or to reduce the amount of time required to fix the customer's problem (perhaps by including diagnostic wizards with the shipping product, which do 80 percent of the work that a live support person would otherwise do) or by discouraging people from calling. We talk about the different practices in Chapter 3; some companies are more customer-sensitive than others. But sadly, one of the most visible results of the call avoidance movement is that the customer-on-hold times in our industry are outrageous.

fearing miscalculation-related liability. Scientific researchers and their graduate students had to redo work, losing months of research.

Initially, Intel refused to swap out defective chips unless the customer could prove, to Intel's satisfaction, that she was likely to be a victim of the bug. The response on the Internet and in the press was a public relations nightmare. For example, an article in the *Wall Street Journal*, was titled "Intel isn't serving millions who bought its Pentium campaign."(Mossberg, 1994) Several customers filed lawsuits against Intel.

On December 20, 1994, Intel announced a "no questions asked" returns policy (*Wall Street Journal*, 1994).

This took care of much of the criticism in the press, but according to the customers' lawyers, customers who called for replacement chips still ran into significant obstacles:

- Customers who ordered a replacement chip during the first phone call had to leave a phone number and wait for a callback by an Intel technician, who would explain the "real" story about the Pentium flaw.

- Installation arrangements were not well worked out. In some cases, customers were told that they had to bring the computer to an authorized service center for installation, but there weren't any service centers near them.

- In general, Intel was willing to provide the chip, and possibly to swap chips at a service center, but was not willing to pay other costs associated with downtime and retesting of the computer after the chip had been swapped. Common estimates of these costs were $300[nd]400 per computer.

- Customers had to pay for their own insurance and postage to return the processor to Intel. (We're unclear about whether Intel was actually willing to pay insurance or postage, but if you were a consumer and you didn't ask for reimbursement, no one was offering it to you.)

- Finally, Intel required customers to provide a credit card number for up to a $1,500 "security deposit" before sending out the replacement chip. Some customers understood that their card would be charged immediately, even though the replacement chip would be sent when available (subject to a backlog of as much as 90 days). Others understood that their card would be charged only if they didn't return the defective chip. The rationale in both cases was that this would encourage customers to return their old chips after receiving the new one (important to deter fraud). But, according to plaintiffs' counsel, the street price of these chips was only $200 to $400.

Taken together, these obstacles made it difficult to obtain even a simple replacement for the chip, let alone repayment of money lost because of the chip's bugs.

Lawyers for the customers refused to settle these lawsuits until these problems were dealt with. Eventually, there was a settlement: Intel established a true no-questions-asked return policy for the chips, under the supervision of the customers' attorneys. Intel paid for shipping and other incidental expenses associated with replacing the defective chips, and it repaid individual plaintiffs for consequential losses that they could satisfactorily prove.

The Intel case was famous, but the problems it illustrated were not unusual. What was unusual was that Intel's customers refused to put up with the problem. The result was that they successfully held Intel accountable and got what they'd paid for.

By the way, the Intel case illustrates another point: A lot of software that you buy comes embedded on computer chips. As another example of the same point, think of a computer card whose onboard software makes it incompatible with something that it claims to be compatible with. This is just as much an example of bad software as a program on a disk that is falsely advertised as being more compatible than it is.

The Goal of This Book

This is a pragmatic book. We know that you thought you were buying a program, not a headache. We've organized the book to help you get satisfaction as quickly as possible.

- The first chapters of this book are written to help you in your negotiations with the sales or support staff of the software publisher and the company that sold you the software. Most people will be able to resolve most disputes at this level.

- The next chapters explain how to bring additional pressure to bear, by filing complaints with the company's senior management, by publicizing your complaints, or by taking your complaints to appropriate consumer protection agencies.

- If those steps don't work, you should think carefully about your rights. We review the laws applicable to consumer software in Chapter 7, "Software and the Law."

- If the law is on your side, and the software publisher and retailer won't work with you, you can bring legal action. Later chapters look at your options for this, explaining class actions, consumer protection actions, and small claims court.

- In the last chapter, we suggest ways to shop for software that will reduce your chance of being cheated the next time you buy software. Along with tips for traditional purchases, we look at new problems in buying products over the Internet. New laws governing these purchases have serious loopholes that could cost you thousands of dollars.

If you're in the right, this book is your roadmap to relief.

How to Use This Book

This book is a tool.

We know that many readers will find the details of this book interesting because they are professionally interested in software development and support, in computer law, or in consumer protection. We're glad they're reading the book, and we hope that they find it useful.

But most readers bought this book because they've been having trouble with bad software, and they want to learn how to deal with it better next time. These readers are who we will speak to most directly (as "you") in this book.

This book covers a wide range of problems and situations. Some of what we say will apply to you, and some of it won't. We've tried to present the material in an order that lets you deal with your problem and quit reading. Our ordering won't be perfect for everyone, though, so here's a suggestion. Don't worry about reading everything in order. If you get to a section that doesn't seem useful, skip it. If you realize later that it will be useful, read it then.

Terminology

Here are some words that we use frequently:

Bug.   A *bug* is a *defect*, an error in the program or in the documentation (instructions) that came with the program.

BugNet.   This online information service is about bugs and workarounds. You can find it at www.bugnet.com.

Return Merchandise Authorization (RMA).   The publisher agrees to let you return a product that you bought (probably for a refund) and gives you a number or code (the RMA) that will identify the product and the agreement for the publisher's warehouse and accounting staff (so that you'll get your refund check).

Software publisher.   A *software publisher* is a company that publishes and sells computer programs. For example, Microsoft, Adobe, Lotus, and Learning Company are software publishers. Some publishers develop their own software; some buy existing programs and repackage them; and some buy software that is under development, do the testing, write the documentation, and then package and sell the finished product. A publisher is a company, not a human, and so we refer to a publisher as *it*, rather than as *he* or *she*.

Technician.   A *technician* is the person employed by the publisher or retailer, who tries to help you when you have a problem. Most publishers call these people Customer Service Representatives (CSRs) or Technical Support Representatives or support staff. But when we used those words with some consumers (who read early drafts of this book), some of them said, "Who? You mean the technician?" *Technician* seems to be the more common word in popular vocabulary that refers to a person who helps you to get technical things fixed, so we use that word instead of CSR, which is our natural jargon.

Warranty.   A *warranty* is a promise inside a contract. In the sale of a product, it is either a statement that describes or defines the product (the promise is, "this statement is true") or a promise of something in the future ("We promise to fix this product if it ever fails."). Some warranties are *implied warranties*—the law writes them into the sales contract whether the seller mentions them or not.

Disclaimer.   A *disclaimer* is a statement by the publisher that it is not taking responsibility for something. When a publisher makes a *warranty disclaimer*, it is denying that it has made any promises that the program will work or will do anything useful. There are legal limits on publishers' ability to disclaim liability.

Workaround.   A *workaround* is some alternative way of doing what you want to do. You are "working around" a bug in the program that stops you from doing your task in the obvious way.

Style

Here are some notes on the style and layout of the book.

REFERENCES

Along with drawing on our own experience in this field, we've been actively researching this book since 1993—five years of work that have taken us to legislative drafting meetings, to courthouses reading unpublished documents in case files, to many libraries (online and traditional ones), and to professional meetings of software developers, software support staff, software quality control staff, software publishers, consumer psychologists, writers, lawyers who specialize in computer law, lawyers who specialize in consumer protection law, and lawyers who specialize in general business law. We've gathered a lot of source material over the years, and much of it is very useful.

We know that popular books are often written in a believe-it-or-leave-it style that provides the insight of the author but skips the distracting and sometimes tedious footnotes that point you to the reference material used by the author. The style sometimes makes the book easier to read, but you're out of luck if you need information or want to check our sources for some other reason. For example, a publisher or lawyer might be more impressed if you refer them to a study conducted by the Software Publishers Association than if you say you read something in our book. And, you might find it useful to read some of the court cases that we describe here. Many of them are well written and insightful, as well as being useful as official statements about the law.

Because this book is a tool, and we believe that our sources will be useful to several readers, we point to references to a greater degree than usual for popular books. We've tried to keep these references out of your way:

- Rather than using footnotes, we usually refer to a book or paper by the name of its authors. For example, when we say that *Schreiber (1997)* said something, you'll find complete bibliographic information in our references section at the back of the book.

- We also cite court cases. *Princeton Graphics v. NEC Home Electronics* (1990) refers to a decision that was published by the court in a lawsuit between Princeton Graphics and NEC. You'll find the full bibliographic reference in the References section. The traditional legal reference style is too abbreviated for nonlawyers. Rather than say "739 F.Supp. 1258 (SDNY)," our references section spells it out: "Federal Supplement, volume 739, p. 1258 (United States District Court, Southern District of New York.)." With this information, you can call your public library to find out how to get a copy of the decision. (By the way, lawyers usually call these "cases" even though a single court case might be the subject of many decisions.)

- Sometimes, we still use traditional footnotes. Typically, these provide additional technical references that we expect to interest only some readers.

QUOTES

We indent long quotes and show them in a separate typeface, like this:

> This is a quote. Most quotes will run several lines long.

HEADINGS

We change the style of the heading of sections to tell you what we're doing when we switch from one section to another. When we start a subsection, we're writing about the same issue as before but in more detail. When we start a new section (not a subsection), we're changing to a different topic. Here's what our headings look like:

This Type of Heading Shows That We're Starting a New Main Section

THIS TYPE OF HEADING STARTS A NEW SUBSECTION OF A MAIN SECTION

This Heading Starts a Subsection of a Subsection

This Heading Starts a Subsection of a Subsection of a Subsection.

GENDER

It is sexist to always refer to people as "he" and very clumsy to say things like "she/he." Instead, we assign different genders to different people and vary the assignments across chapters. For example, in Chapter 1, customers are male and support technicians are female. In Chapter 2, customers are female, and technicians are male.

Examples

We've included examples in several chapters. Many come from our direct, personal knowledge of the events described. Other cases have been reported to us in detail by more than one person who was in a position to know the internal situation. The information came to us with the expectation that all company-identifying details would be kept confidential. This book is about learning to work with the industry. We have no interest in embarrassing individual companies. Therefore, unless we are talking about a public lawsuit, we have disguised the products and the publishers in these examples.

Acknowledgments

Many people have helped us in the development of this book by discussing the issues with us, by providing us with data, by helping us do the research, or by criticizing one or more of the many drafts of the chapters. We extend our thanks to the following people: James Bach, Robert Bauer, Dick Bender, Dave Broenen, Dave Bunnell, Dan Coolidge, Joel Dejardin, Danny Faught, Karla Fisher, Heather Florence, Ed Foster, Dan Gallipeau, Dale Gipson, Sharon Hafner, Mark Harding, Gail Hillebrand, Doug Hoffman, Watts Humphrey, Ginny Kaner, Phil Koopman, Craig Kubey, Brian Lawrence, John Lyons, Stan Magee, Bruce Martin, Anita Metzen, Derick Miller, Judah Mogilensky, Julie P. Neilson, Noel Nyman, Todd Paglia, Bill Pardee, Jeff Payne, Bret Pettichord, David Powell, Drew Pritsker, David Rice, Sharon Marsh Roberts, Johanna Rothman, Jeanne Sheldon, Steve Starr, Jane Stepak, Melora Svoboda, Donna Tosh, Clark Savage Turner, Emmanuel Uren, Fred Van Bennekom, J. Allen Wessels, Miryam Williamson, Ralph Wilson, Tamar Yaron, and Harry Youtt.

We particularly thank Ginny Kaner for her work as a research assistant, which included library research, survey administration and other clerical work, content and copy editing, and many critical discussions of the tone and approach of the material.

We also thank the West Publishing Corporation for granting us access to WestLaw for the initial research for this book.

Chapter 1

Read This First

Chapter Map
If you just bought a software program and it doesn't work, your wisest choice might be to ask for a refund, and the sooner after buying the product you do this, the easier it will be to get the refund. This is so important that we put this chapter first, even before the Introduction, so that you won't delay getting your refund by spending unnecessary time reading. We'll see you in Chapter 2 if you have a problem getting that refund.

Warning
This book discusses your rights under current (1998) American law. We expect a new law to be proposed to state legislatures in 1999. This 200-plus page amendment to the Uniform Commercial Code, backed by software publishers and computer manufacturers, is called Article 2B. This amendment will completely rewrite the laws governing software quality and significantly limit your rights. We talk more about Article 2B in the Appendix.

Asking for a Refund

If you just bought the program and it has obvious *bugs* (defects), stop using it. Take it off your hard drive before it does something bad. Maybe it won't, but why take the risk? Even if the program isn't obviously defective, you should ask for a refund if you realize immediately that it doesn't meet your expectations. Don't try to push it beyond its capabilities. Just take it back.

If the program has already failed in a way that cost you a lot more than the price you paid for it (for example, the program erased your hard disk), then you want more than a refund. The rest of this book can help you demand fair compensation. But, if the program hasn't yet hurt you, damaged your files, lost your work, cost you your job, ruined your reputation, or made you screaming mad, then asking for a refund is probably your best recourse.

DO YOU HAVE THE RIGHT TO A REFUND?

Maybe.

The company that sold you the program may have a sales policy that entitles you to a refund. Here are some examples:

- *Most stores will give a refund within a week* if you come back with a receipt and an explanation of why you're unhappy with the program.

- *Several stores and mail-order companies give a 30-, 60-, or 90-day satisfaction guarantee.* If you buy the program and don't like it, they'll give you a refund with no questions asked.

- *In most states, you don't have a right to a refund for a nondefective product.* However, some states (and cities) have laws that require merchants to give refunds to customers who bring back merchandise within a certain number of days (perhaps 3, 7, or 21) of the purchase. A merchant can escape this requirement only by posting a notice that its return policy is shorter. If the merchant doesn't post a notice, you have the full number of days to get your refund.

- *Even if the store posts a notice that reads, "No refunds on opened packages," you probably can get a refund if you find an obvious defect and if you bring the product back very quickly.* We discuss this at the end of the chapter, in the section on "Uniform Commercial Code Rejection Rules."

The publisher might have a sales policy that entitles you to a refund.

- *Some software publishers offer their own satisfaction guarantee.* You'll see it on the box or in the manual. The guarantee applies whether you bought the product from the store or directly from the publisher. If you decide, within the guarantee period (30, 60, or 90 days, or even a year in some cases), that the program is not what you wanted, send it back to the publisher, with your receipt, and the publisher will send you a refund. In many cases, you have to call first to get a *return merchandise authorization* (RMA) number.

- *Many other publishers have an unofficial refund policy.* If you call within a few days or weeks of buying the software and explain why you don't like the program and therefore want a refund, many publishers will give it to you.

- *Publishers often will tell you to take the product back to the store where you bought it—with good reason.* You paid a retail price to the store, but the store bought the product from the publisher (or distributor) at a much lower price. If the publisher gives you a full refund, that company is giving you more than it received from the retailer.

> ### Note
> *Unfortunately, many software retailers refuse to take back opened software packages. If the publisher's technician tells you to take the product back to the store, get the technician's full name and tell her that you'll call back if the store won't accept the return. Ask for her phone number as well, so you can call back directly, instead of wading through the automated leave-you-on-hold-forever phone system. Make a note of your conversation, including the date and time that you talked to the technician and specifically what you talked about. If you do have to call back later, you'll have a solid response to anyone who says that you should have tried to return the program sooner.*

You might be entitled to a refund under the *Uniform Commercial Code* (UCC) rules for rejection and revocation.

- The Uniform Commercial Code applies across the United States (except in Louisiana, where similar rules apply). You have the right to inspect merchandise before you accept it. You can inspect most types of merchandise at the store, but it's usually impossible to inspect software until you take it to your home or office and install it on your hard drive. If you find defects during the inspection period, you have the right to reject the software. We'll say more about this later in the section, "Uniform Commercial Code Rejection Rules."

If the program was misrepresented to you, you are entitled to a refund.

- The software publisher isn't allowed to mislead you about what the program can and cannot do; neither is the salesperson who sold you the program. In the United States, federal and state laws ban unfair and deceptive trade practices. If you were misled and if neither the publisher nor the store or mail-order company that sold you the program will give you your money back, read Chapter 3, "Preparing to Make the Call," which discusses ways to gather evidence to prove misrepresentation, including evidence of spoken misrepresentations; Chapter 4, "Knowing What to Ask For," which helps you decide how much additional money to ask for; Chapter 6, "Consumer Protection Agencies," which helps you decide to which government agencies to report these businesses; Chapter 7, "Software Quality and the Law," which summarizes your legal rights; and Chapter 9, "Lawyers," which tells you how to hire a lawyer.

If the program doesn't work, then you are entitled to a refund.

- Every product that you buy comes with an implied warranty of merchantability. This warranty is not a promise that the program is perfect; it is a promise that the program works reasonably well and can actually do the things that the publisher has said it can do.

- Some companies try to tell their customers that software has no warranties, that software is like those unsavory-looking used cars with the big sign that reads, "AS IS. THIS VEHICLE IS SOLD WITH NO WARRANTY OF ANY KIND." If you find one of these notices inside the box after buying a program, ignore it. It has no legal force. It just keeps people who don't know any better from calling (see the section, "Warranty Disclaimers in Software Packages" in Chapter 7).

Furthermore, you have every reason to ask for a refund if you haven't had the product for very long and you already hate it, even if you aren't legally *entitled* to a refund. Many publishers, stores, and mail-order houses will give you a refund whether their published policies promise one or not. It doesn't hurt to ask. Again, the sooner you ask after you get the program, the more likely they are to agree.

HOW TO GET A REFUND

You can get refunds from several places: from the store or mail-order business that sold you the software, from the publisher, even from your credit card company if the store or publisher gives you a runaround. Because your approach should differ slightly in each case, we consider the alternatives one at a time. Here are some pointers common to each of the alternatives:

- Once you realize that the program is giving you trouble, start making notes. Use a notebook or a pad of paper that keeps your notes together. Make a note to describe every misbehavior of the program. And, take notes during every communication that you have with the store or the publisher, whether it is face to face or over the phone. Keep copies of all the letters that you send (to anyone) about this product.

When you send the publisher, retailer, or a credit card company a letter or a returned product, use a form of delivery that provides proof of delivery, such as certified mail, return receipt requested, or UPS or Federal Express. That way, the company can't claim that they never received it.

If you can't get a refund, consider asking a consumer protection agency for help. For example, your county or state might have a Consumer Affairs Department that helps resolve disputes between businesses and consumers. The Better Business Bureau is a private consumer assistance agency funded by businesses. See Chapter 6, "Consumer Protection Agencies," for a discussion of these agencies.

The Uniform Commercial Code's rules on acceptance and rejection are quoted and discussed at the end of this chapter, where we also include a letter that might help you convince someone that you are entitled to a refund.

The following sections are often similar, so read those that apply to your situation and skip the others.

Asking the Store for a Refund

If you bought the program at a store, go back there and ask for a refund. If the salesperson refuses, ask to speak to the store manager. If the manager is unavailable, ask to speak to the store's assistant manager (and if necessary, ask her to let you speak to the store's manager).

If the manager won't authorize the refund, quote the Uniform Commercial Code rules on acceptance and rejection. Few retailers are aware of these rules, so it will help you to have them handy.

If you can't get to the manager or if he won't give you a refund, ask for the address of the store's head office, the name of the president of the company, and the name and phone number of the person at the head office who is in charge of handling customer complaints. Write this information down. As you're writing it down, look the person you're talking to in the eye and ask, "Are you sure that you don't just want to take care of this now? Why not just give me a refund, and we can both be finished with it?"

- Before spending time writing a complaint letter, call the software publisher. It might agree to take the product back. See the section, "Asking the Publisher for a Refund," later in this chapter.

If you bought the program with a credit card, call your credit card company's customer service department. Ask whether they'll give you a refund if you return the program to the store and the store refuses to give you a refund. If they agree to this, ask for instructions. They'll probably direct you to mail the program back to the store, certified mail, return receipt requested. You'll then have to send a letter to the credit card company with a copy of the return receipt. Read the section, "Getting Help from Your Credit Card Company," later in this chapter.

Asking the Mail-Order Company for a Refund

Call the company. Have the program and your receipt handy so that you can answer a few quick questions. Explain that you don't like the program and that you don't want to keep it. Ask for the full name of the person to whom you're talking. If this person won't authorize a refund, ask for the manager, and if necessary, ask for the manager's manager. Don't take "No" for the answer until you run out of people to talk to. Ask for each one's name and title and write the information down.

If the person that you're talking to won't authorize the refund, quote the Uniform Commercial Code rules on acceptance and rejection. Few salespeople are aware of these rules, but they apply directly to mail order. It will be useful to have them handy.

- If the company agrees to take back the program, send it back with a simple letter explaining why you're returning it.

If the mail-order company won't give you the refund, call the software publisher. Maybe the publisher will agree to take the product back. See the next section, "Asking the Publisher for a Refund."

- If you used a credit card to buy the program, and you bought it within the last 90 days, you probably can get a refund through your credit card company. Read the section, "Getting Help from Your Credit Card Company," later in this chapter.

Asking the Publisher for a Refund

If you're unhappy with the program because it crashes or because it doesn't deliver all the benefits promised in the publisher's advertisements, in the manual, or on the box, then you have every reason to expect the publisher to stand behind the program. Call the publisher. Have your receipt and the program with its packaging handy, to help you answer questions about exactly what you bought. If you just want a refund, you don't have to be sitting by your computer when you call. If, however, you want help *with the program*, it's a good idea to have your computer running and ready to use when you call. See Chapter 5, "Making the Call."

> **Tip**
> *The publisher's staff might want you to give details about your computer and all of its components. If you know them, by all means oblige, but don't let the staff talk you into spending time investigating your equipment. This is part of their effort to motivate (or intimidate) you into keeping the program. Don't lose sight of the fact that you don't want to keep the program; you just want a refund. Say so. Say it in a friendly tone of voice but be direct and be firm. Ask what the quickest way is to get the refund.*

If the person you're talking to won't authorize the refund, quote the Uniform Commercial Code rules on acceptance and rejection. Few technicians are aware of these rules, so it will pay to have them handy. If you still can't get the refund authorized, ask for the technician's full name and ask to speak to his manager. Continue taking names and titles and speaking to "higher-ups" until you get someone who says, "Okay, we'll give you the refund," or until you run out of people.

- If the publisher agrees to take back the program, send it back with a simple letter. All that you have to say is that you talked with (whomever you talked with) and that he authorized you to return this program for a full refund. If the technician gave you a return merchandise authorization number, an incident number, or some other number that helps them track your letter back to a specific discussion in their records, include that number in your letter.

If the publisher won't give you the refund, call the retail outlet that sold you the program. Maybe they'll take it back. Refer to one of the preceding sections, "Asking the Store for a Refund" or "Asking the Mail-Order Company for a Refund."

- If you used a credit card to buy the program and if you bought it within the last 90 days, you probably can get a refund through your credit card company. Read the next section, "Getting Help from Your Credit Card Company."

- Finally, consider doing more research about the program and its faults and call the publisher again. Read Chapters 2 through 4 for information on how to prepare for the call, paying special attention to Chapter 4, "Knowing What to Ask For." If the publisher makes you work to get your refund, ask to be reimbursed for all of your expenses. Read Chapter 7, "Software Quality and the Law," for an explanation of some of your legal rights.

Getting Help from Your Credit Card Company

If you used your credit card to buy the program by mail, you can send the program back to the *seller,* the company that sold you the program, and dispute your credit card bill. The rules for disputing your bill are usually printed on the back of your monthly credit card statement. If you're not sure you understand them, call your credit card's customer service number and ask for both a verbal and a printed explanation of the rules. Here is a summary of the typical rules:

- You must dispute the transaction within 60 days of the date of the statement that included the transaction.

To dispute the transaction, you must write a letter to your credit card company explaining why you sent back the program. Keep it short. For example, "I am returning this program because it didn't work. It kept crashing on my computer." Keep it polite and calm. Remember, it's not your credit card company's fault that the program doesn't work. You want them to help you.

> **Note**
> *The address for writing this letter to your credit card company is probably different from that to which you send your payments. Your monthly statement probably includes this address. If, however, you're not sure of the address or can't find it on your statement, call your credit card company's customer service number.*

- The credit card company might also want to see a copy of your complaint letter to the store or publisher. If you sent such a letter, include it.

In the letter, include your credit card number and a photocopy of the statement (keep the original) that lists the purchase you're disputing. Circle the transaction, highlight it, or in some other way make it stand out to show the credit card company which purchase you're talking about.

- You must have sent the product back to the seller, and you must be able to prove it. Thus, send it by certified mail, return receipt requested, or use a comparable proof-of-delivery service. Send a photocopy of the return receipt or mailing receipt (keep the original) to your credit card company.

UNIFORM COMMERCIAL CODE REJECTION RULES

The *Uniform Commercial Code* (UCC) is the law in every state (except in Louisiana, which has not adopted all sections of the code; nevertheless, its laws for sales are similar in effect). Unfortunately, the rules for acceptance and rejection of merchandise are less widely known than they should be. We explain them here because they are powerful tools for consumers. Under the right circumstances, you can use them effectively to get a refund.

The first UCC rule, the *Perfect Tender Rule*, says that you are entitled to reject a product for any defect. Here it is (the most important part appears in bold):

> ## Section 2-601. Buyer's Rights on Improper Delivery
>
> *Subject to the provisions of this Article on breach in installment contracts (Section 2-612) and unless otherwise agreed under the section on contractual limitations of remedy (Sections 2-718 and 2-719),* **if the goods or the tender of delivery fail in any respect to conform to the contract, the buyer may**
>
> (a) **reject the whole,** *or*
>
> (b) accept the whole, or
>
> (c) *accept any commercial unit or units and reject the rest.*

In the typical retail sale, you have the opportunity to inspect the merchandise before you buy it. For example, when you buy a leather jacket, you can try it on, check the seams, and generally look it over before you take it to the cash register. If you see a flaw, even if it's just a little scratch in the leather, you don't have to buy it. In other retail situations, you pay for the merchandise first and inspect it later. For example, when you special order a leather jacket, you pay first, and the jacket is delivered to the store. When you come to the store, you can look it over. If the jacket is ripped or has a slight stain or scratch, you don't have to accept the jacket. If, however, you choose *not* to inspect the jacket and you discover the flaw much later, you are stuck with it.

Section 2-606. What Constitutes Acceptance of Goods

(1) *Acceptance of goods occurs when the buyer*

(a) **after a reasonable opportunity to inspect the goods** signifies to the seller that the goods are conforming *or that he will take or retain them in spite of their nonconformity; or*

(b) *fails to make an effective rejection (subsection (1) of Section 2-602,* **but such acceptance does not occur until the buyer has had a reasonable opportunity to inspect them;** *or*

(c) *does any act inconsistent with the seller's ownership; [rest of section omitted]*.

But now suppose that the jacket is delivered to your home. You sign for the delivery and then open the package and look at the jacket for the first time. You see a rip. Did you accept the jacket when you signed that you had received it? No. You haven't accepted it, under the law, until you've had a chance to inspect it and then have kept it, or until you have said that you accept it. If you find a problem during your inspection of the jacket, you can still reject it. Rejecting it means that you can take it back, or send it back, to whomever sold it to you, and the seller must give you a refund.

Section 2-602. Manner and Effect of Rightful Rejection

(1) **Rejection of goods must be within a reasonable time after their delivery** *or tender. It is ineffective unless the buyer seasonably notifies the seller... [rest of section omitted]*.

How long do you have to inspect and reject a product if it is defective? The time limit depends on the circumstances. The more complex the product and the more difficult the defect is to discover, the more time you probably have. White & Summers (Volume 1, Section 8-3, 1995), the leading treatise on the UCC, cites several cases on this. For example, a court refused to allow a rejection just 24 hours after delivery of a horse because its injury normally would have been discovered by an inspection at the time of sale (*Miron v. Yonkers Raceway, Inc.,* 1968). In contrast, another court allowed rejection several months after a customer purchased dump truck underbodies because it was impossible under the circumstances to finish a proper inspection sooner (*Sherkate Sahami Khass Rapol v. Henry R. Jahn & Son, Inc.*, 1983).

Six Simple Principles

To our knowledge, no courts have decided how long you have to inspect prepackaged, noncustomized computer software; nevertheless, the legal principles are clear:

1. **You have the right to inspect the product before you accept it.** This is UCC Section 2-606(1)(a).

2. **To inspect a program, you have to be able to install and run it on a computer.** You need enough inspection time to enable you to determine how the program works and to have a reasonable opportunity to notice obvious bugs.

3. **If it is impractical for you to inspect a product before you take it home or to the office, then you have the right to inspect the product there.** This is UCC Section 2-606(1)(b).

4. **You have the right to a product that works the way that the seller (publisher or retailer) said that it would.** The publisher's and seller's statements may be found in advertisements, on the box, in the user manual, in online help, on the publisher's Web site, and in your oral discussion with the publisher's or store's staff. (We talk about this further in Chapter 3, in the section "Background for Negotiating," and again in Chapter 7, in the section, "Warranties.")

5. **If the product doesn't conform to the contract, you can refuse to accept it (your refusal is a rejection).** This is UCC Section 2-601. The product fails to conform to the contract if it doesn't meet the publisher's and seller's promises or if it has other defects. Any defect, no matter how minor, is good reason for you to reject the product.

6. **You don't have much time to inspect the product.** If you haven't rejected the product within a reasonable time after taking it home, the law says that you've accepted it. This is in UCC Sections 2-606(1)(b) and 2-602(1). For a software program, you probably have a few days; you might be able to justify needing a few weeks, or for a very complex program, a few months.

People who tell you that you can't bring a software product back if you have opened the package and installed it on your hard disk are mistaken. They probably don't understand the Uniform Commercial Code.

Law Office of Cem Kaner
P.O. Box 580, Santa Clara, CA 95052-0580

Dear Vendor:

The customer who is giving you this letter has asked you for a refund because he believes that the program that you sold him is defective. If he bought the program just a few days ago, and if the program is defective, then you probably owe him a refund.

The Uniform Commercial Code (UCC) is the law in every American state except Louisiana (whose laws are similar). Article 2 of the UCC is the Law of Sales. American courts have consistently applied Article 2 to off-the-shelf software (software that is not customized).

Section 2-601 of the UCC says that *"if the goods or the tender of delivery fail in any respect to conform to the contract, the buyer may reject"* them. This is called the Perfect Tender Rule. The customer can refuse to accept a product that has even a small defect, just as, when you go shopping for clothes, you can refuse to accept a shirt that has a loose thread or a small stain.

The difference between shopping for clothes and shopping for software is that you can inspect the shirt at the store, to see whether there is a defect. If you didn't give the customer an opportunity to sit at your computer and check the program at your store (a task that might take a customer several hours), then he did not have a reasonable opportunity to inspect the program. His inspection happens after he takes the program to his home or office, where he can see if the program works on his machine. If this is the only opportunity for him to inspect the product, he can break the shrink-wrapping around the disks, install the program on his computer, and return it if he finds defects during this initial try-out.

A customer can't keep a program for a long time and then bring it back because it has a small defect. He has only a "reasonable time" to inspect it, long enough to walk through the features and the manual to see whether there are noticeable problems. The Perfect Tender Rule does not apply after the inspection/acceptance period. Section 2-606(1)(a) says that *acceptance occurs after the buyer has had "a reasonable opportunity to inspect the goods."* And 2-606(1)(b) says that *"acceptance does not occur until the buyer has had a reasonable opportunity to inspect them."*

Court decisions differ on how long a "reasonable inspection period" lasts. It depends on the specific circumstances. In some cases, the court has refused to allow even a few hours to the customer. In others, involving complex products and difficult circumstances, courts have allowed up to six months. I believe that most courts would be sympathetic to a software customer who, within a few days or perhaps even a week after buying the software, comes back to your store to ask for a refund or calls you (see UCC 2-602(1)) to tell you that the software is defective and that he wants a refund.

Yours truly,

Cem Kaner, J.D., Ph.D.

June 1, 1998

Warning

If you do return a software product for a refund, erase it from your computer and don't keep any copies. It would be completely unfair—as well as a violation of the Copyright Act—to buy a program, make a copy, take the original back for a refund, and then keep and use the copy.

You might not find it easy to explain the law and your rights to a retailer or a publisher, so we have included a letter from Cem Kaner to a retailer that explains the customer's right to inspect and return defective products. Feel free to photocopy this letter and take it with you to the store or mail it with your letter to the publisher, mail-order company, or consumer protection agency you intend to address.

Note

This letter provides general information and does not constitute legal advice about your particular situation. It is up to you to decide whether this letter is appropriate for your circumstances. You should also realize that the law might have changed by the time you use this letter and that different courts interpret the same laws differently. Cem Kaner is not serving as your attorney by supplying this letter in this book.

Action Plan

Every chapter in this book has an action plan. The one in this chapter is very simple:

- Hurry up and ask for that refund.

- If it's too late, if the program has done too much damage, if you are too mad, or if the publisher has refused (or if you're reading this book because you want to, not because you're trying to deal with some worthless program), then read on. Enjoy Chapter 2. "Introduction."

- If the program has a warranty, you must notify the publisher of defects within the warranty period. See Chapter 5, "Making the Call."

Introduction

 Basic Messages of this Chapter
Some people are made to feel stupid when they call for technical support. You are not stupid. It's not your fault that the program doesn't work. It's not your computer's fault that the program doesn't work on your computer. You spent good money to get a program that works, not to get a new hobby called *Troubleshooting 101*.

The customer support technician that you're talking to is an innocent victim. Most of these technicians genuinely want to help you, but their hands might be tied. Don't fight with them; find a way to cooperate.

This chapter looks at the business decisions that go into making software programs. Asking for proper service from the publisher will be easier once you understand that problems probably result from decisions the publisher made with its eyes wide open. Some service technicians make people who call for help feel stupid; sometimes this is a deliberate tactic, sometimes not. Don't take it personally. The problem you're facing is a business problem; deal with it at that level.

This chapter also starts our effort to help you evaluate whether you're getting good service from the publisher. At some point, you may have to decide whether the publisher is treating you fairly. If not, your strategy might be much harsher than if you think the publisher is making honest mistakes.

THE CHAPTER ADDRESSES FOUR KEY QUESTIONS:

1. How are problems handled? (Are you getting service or excuses?)

2. What's the business situation? (Publishers make trade-offs knowingly.)

3. Is it "shelfware?" (Are you being played for a sucker?)

4. What are your rights? (Quick overview of some law.)

How Problems Are Handled

Imagine that you buy a radio only to discover when you try to use it that one of its buttons doesn't work. Naturally, you'd take it back. The people at the store would say, "Oops, sorry," and either fix it immediately or give you a new one. Let's further imagine that this model is bad, that all these radios have this button that doesn't work. You'd ask for a different model or for a refund. And, the people at the store would say, "Certainly."

Suppose, however, that the people at the store didn't want to give you a refund. Instead they said, "The radio works. Just hold it upside down and press these other two buttons. Then this button will operate. This feature helps you stay in shape by exercising your hands and fingers." You'd say, "You must be kidding. Give me that refund." If they still wouldn't give you a refund, you'd feel perfectly justified in complaining to the store manager, the Better Business Bureau, the manufacturer of the radio, the newspaper, all of your friends, and your county or state's consumer protection department.

When you buy a computer program and one of its "buttons" doesn't work, life can be just that challenging. Here are some of the key problems that you and the industry face:

It is impossible to write defect-free software.   (Software defects are called *bugs*.) It is also impossible to fully test a program. No one can find and remove all the bugs.[1] So, every program has bugs; in theory, you could demand a refund for every program you own.

Many retailers actively discourage customers from returning software, even if it is defective.   Some companies even publish a policy that says they *can't* take returns because that would violate the Copyright Act. But, there's nothing against taking returns in that act. The Copyright Act restricts software *rentals*; giving a refund to a dissatisfied customer is not a rental situation. (See the analysis in *Central Point Software, Inc. v. Global Software & Accessories, Inc.,* 1995).

Retail salespeople rarely know how to help you make the program work.   Face it, these underpaid salespeople are rarely computer experts. And, even the savvy ones have a hard time keeping up with all of the programs that the store sells. Result: You'll have to direct most of your questions and complaints to the publisher rather than to your local retailer.

Software problems can be subtle and, thus, difficult to troubleshoot. For example, a normally reliable program might crash only if you use it with a

---

[1] *See* Kaner (1997f) and Kaner, Falk, and Nguyen (1993), especially Chapter 2, for a discussion of the problems of finding all the bugs. Some of our colleagues think that it is, or will become, possible to write defect-free code. They cite evidence that the best programming organizations have gotten *much* better at preventing bugs. See Humphrey (1997) and Ferguson, Humphrey, Khajenoori, Macke, and Matuya, (1997).

particular mouse, video card, and certain versions of the programs (*drivers*) that make the mouse and video card work. Use a different card, mouse, or driver, and you won't have the problem. A problem that is obvious on your computer might seem odd to the publisher's technician. Skilled technicians make it a practice to learn everything they can about your computer's components because their advice to you could depend on what you have.

Excuses, Excuses

People tend to use the same lame excuses time after time. Here are some of the common ones you'll hear when you try to return bad software.

At the Store

- The Copyright Act forbids us from taking back software from dissatisfied customers.

- We can't take the software back because your computer might have given it a virus.

- We don't understand your problem. You have to call the publisher. If they authorize the return, in writing, we'll take it back.

- Sorry that we can't answer your questions. You have to call the publisher for technical support.

- Our policy says we can replace only defective media.

From the Publisher

- This is the first time we've heard of this problem.

- Maybe you just don't understand the program. How carefully have you read the manual?

- What kind of video card (mouse, memory, printer, CD-ROM drive, disk drive, monitor, joystick, modem, and so on) do you have? Oh, that. Maybe that's why your computer doesn't work properly. Call them.

- That's not a bug; it's a feature.

- Oh, you're right. This feature doesn't work. But, we have a workaround. Just do this (inconvenient or bizarre thing) and you can get the result you want.

- We're working on a new version to fix this problem. Call back in six weeks.

- We have a new version that will fix your bug. Of course, you have to pay $89 for this version because we added lots of features. You don't really think you should get all those features for free, do you?

- A refund? You have to get that at the store that sold you the program.

- Of course you can't do that with this version of the program. You have to buy our professional version to do that. With your preferred customer discount, it's only $129.99. Would you like to order it now?

Few people know how to investigate or describe software problems systematically. This makes it difficult for even a conscientious technician to help you, because she has to figure out what you're complaining about.

When you call a software publisher, you eventually will speak to a customer support technician. She has to make several judgment calls during the phone call. Here are some of the questions that an ethical technician might be considering:

- Have I heard of this problem before? If so, what have we tried before to solve it? If not, what questions can I ask to find out what is causing it and how serious it might be?

- Is it possible that something is broken in the customer's machine? (A surprising number of people forget to plug in or turn on the computer.)

- Could I solve this customer's problem by teaching him something about how the program works or by pointing him to a useful place in the manual?

- Would a reasonable customer be upset about this problem? If not, what's the company's policy on dealing with unreasonable people?

- Is this likely to be a hardware-specific bug? If so, what is the customer's configuration? Can I help the customer make the program work on that system?

- How can I find out if some other program is also in memory on the customer's machine and is interfering with this one?

- What would it take to satisfy this customer?

Note the tone and objective of these questions. Their goal is to get enough information to solve the problem and then to solve it. Many of these questions sound like the excuses in "Excuses, Excuses" (page 15). The difference is in the use of the information. The conscientious technician tries to solve the customer's problem. If she can't find a technical solution, she'll look for some other way to satisfy the customer (refund, exchange for a different product, upgrade to the next version, enrollment in the beta test program, whatever). At excuse-making companies, the technician might still try to find a solution for the customer's problem, but if she can't find one quickly, or if she feels offended by the customer (poorly trained technicians are more easily offended by people who are, often legitimately, upset), then she'll use the information she gets from you to push the problem back at you.

Here's a practical illustration of the difference. Suppose that the technician realizes that you don't understand how one of the features works:

The helpful technician asks whether you have the manual handy.   If you do, she directs your attention to the relevant section. She might even save you from being embarrassed by reassuring you that a lot of people miss this section. She then gives you an overview of the section or gives you time to scan it and ask questions, or she gives you a direct-dial number to call her back if you have questions. When you hang up, you and she are both confident that you'll understand this material.

The not-so-helpful technician asks whether you have read the part of the manual that explains this feature.   If you admit that you haven't, she'll suggest that you do so now. Then she'll say good-bye and hang up. If you say you can't find this feature in the manual, she'll "win" because she can tell you the relevant page number to look on. If you tell her that you did read it but you didn't understand it, she'll say, "Oh" in that tone of voice that implies she has known rocks that are smarter than you. You might or might not understand the feature when you hang up, but you definitely get the message: *This is your problem, not ours. You deal with it. What do you expect for $100? Quit bothering us!*

No matter who you get on the phone, keep your perspective. Be polite, friendly, and reasonable. Don't be embarrassed if you are not an expert at describing and analyzing the program's problems. This is a technical skill that often requires special training to develop. But, be willing to conduct basic troubleshooting, because if you aren't, no technician can help you. Don't let yourself be intimidated. Let the following reminder guide you.

> ### *Reminder*
> *You are not stupid. It is not your fault that the program doesn't work. It is not your computer's fault that the program doesn't work on your computer. You spent good money to get a program that works, not to get a new hobby called* Troubleshooting 101.

 ## Example: A Faulty Interface Card

A few years ago, a company sold a computer interface card that did input/output functions. Let's call this company Brand X. We can't tell you what card this was, so imagine that this card had video display, video animation, sound, or some other capability that people could see or hear.

Brand X advertised its card as being "fully compatible with" (which means, working just like) another manufacturer's card, the industry best-seller. Unfortunately, even though Brand X's card usually worked pretty much like the standard card, the Brand X card's output was distorted, sometimes obviously and annoyingly.

Unfortunately, Brand X had laid off key engineering staff and so could no longer upgrade this card. Oops. As a result, customers who had problems had to live with them or take a refund. No cost-effective solution to the incompatibilities was available, and Brand X had no intention of upgrading the card.

Not knowing how else to respond to the crisis, Brand X's Marketing Department decided to contain it. They specifically ordered the support staff to discourage customers from asking for refunds. They said that the distortion was usually pretty minor and that the complaining customers were just nitpickers.

Furthermore, Marketing ordered the support staff to say that they'd never heard of this problem before, to promise to investigate it, to take the customer's name and phone number, and to promise to call the customer back if they found a solution. Marketing even supplied a form letter to send to complaining customers.

The support technicians were furious about this. They knew full well that they would never call back with a solution. They were just stalling customers, not helping them. Morale suffered. Brand X's middle managers had heated meetings about this problem. Unfortunately, nobody knew how to solve it. Some wanted to do more for the customers (such as offer refunds). Others wanted to stop making the technicians lie to customers. Still others wanted to stop selling the product or at least to stop manufacturing new cards and just sell the last of the stock on hand. In the end, most of the managers weren't willing to just give up on the product and take a loss. So for a while, Brand X kept making and selling these defective cards.

If you had called Brand X with a complaint about this problem, the technician you talked to would have lied to you. If you had escalated the discussion (talked to the technician's supervisor), that person would have lied to you, too. To get a refund (and plenty of people gave up along the way), you had to work your way up the ladder until you finally got to someone with the authority to give you a refund (who might not be able to tell you the truth but could send you a check.)

Until the company finally decided to stop making these cards, the support technicians could follow the company's orders, or they could quit.

They had no other choices. You would never have suspected that they were furious about being ordered to do this. You would have done absolutely no good by shouting. On the other hand, you wouldn't have served yourself well by believing these people and putting up with a card that was obviously defective. Too many people accepted this stalling and evasion. Because tactics like these are effective, companies continue to use them.

The Business Situation: Publisher Trade-Offs

Publishers make decisions that affect quality, service, and revenue with their eyes open. The odds are good that the problem you're facing is the result of a deliberate decision made during the program's development or during the planning for its technical support. This section identifies and explains some of those types of decisions.

> *Tip*
> *By the time you buy the program, call the publisher, and speak to the technician, quality and service decisions are history. There's nothing the technician can do about them; she probably wasn't consulted about them when the decisions were made, and she probably has been forbidden by the company (which considers its internal decisions to be secret) to even tell you about them. People like you complain because of these decisions, and people like her have to listen to all of these complaints because of these decisions. She's probably as frustrated with some of those decisions as you are, maybe much more so. Don't take out your frustrations on the technician. All you achieve is to hurt her feelings and make her less interested in helping you.*

When the publisher makes a deliberate trade-off, it expects complaints. The publisher has accepted that the product will not serve the needs of certain customers. It gambles that not many people will complain. The lesson here is: If you want the publisher to make better products in the future, you *should* complain.

THE NEED FOR TRADE-OFFS

Quality-related decisions are difficult because the publisher has to face difficult trade-offs. The first problem is that time-to-market can be a critical factor for the success of the product. The first product in a category often dominates that category's market, even when a later release is better. After a product is regarded by customers as a standard, which can happen pretty quickly with a first-to-market product, later competitors might have an extremely difficult time gaining a viable share of the market. (Arthur, 1994, discusses the natural development of monopolies in industries like software.) The publisher also has to trade off money, which it might not have, against customer satisfaction. Every decision about quality or customer service involves trade-offs.

Software publishing has become a tough business with established, entrenched competitors. The following numbers, from the early days of CD-ROM-based mass-market software, show how hard it is to market and sell new software products:

- By early 1995, at least 11,837 CD-ROM titles had been published; many of them were new, published in 1994 (InfoTech, 1995; Swisher, 1995).

- In 1994, the typical traditional software store carried only about 300 titles, and mass-market retailers carried only about 30 (Steinberg & Sege, 1995).

- Of an estimated 1,700 CD-ROM titles being released for the 1994 Christmas season, estimates were that only 200 would turn a profit (Steinberg & Sege, 1995).

For many software publishers, distribution has become less certain, and margins have thinned (Software Publishers Association, 1996). Several publishers are making less money and struggling to stay in business. Looking at numbers like these, you can understand why several software publishers have been trying to reduce their per-customer investment in customer care during the past few years.

On the other hand, the market has become huge. In 1994, sales of personal computers ($8 billion) exceeded sales of ordinary televisions (Associated Press, 1995). The computer has become a common consumer purchase. Software publishers have chosen to stay in this market, and many of them are faring quite well (Software Publishers Association, 1996).

EYES-WIDE-OPEN DECISIONS

Against this background of uncertain returns on their investments, publishers make deliberate decisions to trade off costs against customer satisfaction, with their eyes wide open to the effects. Some product failings are due to blunders or to poorly organized software-development processes. But, in many cases, publishers consciously decide to save money on the product now and to deal with customer dissatisfaction later. The following sections offer some examples in a variety of categories.

During Product Planning and Design

Why is the program missing obvious, essential features?   Publishers know how to research the market. (Those who don't hire consultants who do.) It's not hard to survey the capabilities of competitive products, to read product reviews, and to talk to customers. So, the question is, when a publisher releases a product that is missing obvious, essential features, did it know those features were needed but chose not to spend the money developing them, or did it just skimp on the basic market research? Either way, the publisher saved money at your expense.

Why is the program hard to use?   It costs money to design products that are easy to use. Publishers *choose* whether to hire usability specialists, to build and test prototypes of their products, or to test a product's usability during the design stages.

Why does the program crash?   A publisher can use fault-tolerant design methods to create programs that cope gracefully with unexpected or invalid data, broken computer components, and even with serious logic errors. But, those methods take money, time, effort, and careful analysis.

Why do the same bugs infest version after version?   Some publishers don't study their customer complaint records when they design a new version of a product. Result: Old problems don't get fixed. Other publishers know what needs fixing, but they introduce so many new bugs into new versions (and have to fix those in crisis, panic mode) that they run out of time to fix the old ones. Overly optimistic schedules destroy many fine products.

During Programming

Why does the program have so many bugs? Because the programmers made a lot of mistakes. Why? Because they didn't have the time, resources, or leadership to do the job well. Here are some common examples:

Some publishers don't plan realistically.   Many schedules are based on an executive order, not an analysis of the amount of time and staff it will take to do the job. The project becomes a rush job, and the customer is stuck with the result.

Some programmers are so overworked they don't get enough sleep. We're not kidding. This is a problem. Some publishers drive their (salaried, not eligible for overtime) staff for long, long hours. Tired programmers produce buggy programs.

Some publishers won't invest in good tools for their staff.   Imagine trying to build a house without a level. That's what it's like to build a program without a great debugger, a source-control program, a top-notch debugging compiler, a run-time memory management checker, and so on.

Some publishers reward staff for speed instead of reliability.
Example: Joe and Sandy started comparable tasks in July. Joe finished programming in August, but his code was so unreliable that the testing group kept finding bugs in it until December. Sandy took until September to code *and check* her work; she got it right, and her program cleared testing in October. Many companies would reward Joe instead of Sandy, because he *appeared* to be a faster programmer. Not surprisingly, those publishers' programs have lots of bugs.

Why can't you understand the program's error messages? Why doesn't the program warn you before you do something that has serious repercussions (such as erasing all your work)?   It's tedious and time-consuming (and therefore expensive) to predict the mistakes that people are likely to make, then to deliver an understandable warning or error message for each, and finally provide documentation or online help that further explains each message. The attitude of some publishers is that if it's your mistake, you can't blame the publisher for it. So why should the publisher help you deal with it?

Note

Watts Humphrey was a senior manager of software development at IBM; then he founded the Software Engineering Institute. He is also a well-known author. He wrote us to object strongly to our use of the common buzzword "bug." He made the point so well that we are including most of that letter here:

> [Bug] trivializes an important issue. When programs have "bugs," we tend to think of them as annoyances. While many may be annoyances, some will be much more serious. I contend that they are not bugs but defects. Any program with one or more defects is defective. While we cannot guarantee that programs are defect-free, we cannot guarantee that 747's are defect-free either. But that does not stop Boeing from striving for defect-free work. It should not stop the software community from striving for defect-free work either.

> Unfortunately, with a trivializing term like bug, programmers tend to think of quality as unimportant. It is nothing of the kind! When developers say their program is fully tested and only has a few bugs, people think that is okay. If we called them "land mines" or "time bombs," the statement that the program was pretty well tested and only has a few time bombs would get a different reaction. We must face it, out of the millions of software defects, some really are time bombs.

While the Program Is Being Tested

It's impossible to *fully* test a program (Kaner, 1997f); therefore, it is probably impossible to find all the bugs in the program; and it is certainly impossible for the publisher to know whether it has found all the bugs. But short of the infinite amount of time required for *complete* testing, there are wide differences among publishers. One might budget four to six months to test a product; another might spend four weeks testing the same product, or a publisher might do virtually no in-house testing and rely on their customers to do their testing for them. They think, usually incorrectly, that this type of testing is nearly cost-free. But, even if the costs are low, the real problem is that customers are not systematic, trained testers, and they miss a lot of bugs. When a publisher says, "We've never heard of that bug," it might mean, "We didn't find that bug because we did almost no testing."

It is possible, however, to find almost all of the bugs in a program. Software test managers have told us of products in which all but five bugs reported by customers actually had been found first in the test lab. (We assume that they are not including reports of incompatibility between their software and various types of equipment.) One large software publisher tracked this type of performance over a two-year period. The head of its software testing organization said that customers reported only 10 new bugs (bugs that hadn't been found in the test lab before release of the product to customers) in one product. In all of the other products, customers reported even fewer new bugs. Software testing (or *quality control*) managers and consultants sometimes measure the effectiveness of their software testers in percentage terms. They add all the bugs that were either found presale (usually by in-house testers) to all new bugs reported post-sale by customers. What percentage of the total were found by the testers? In the mass-market software world, percentages like 95 percent seem to be common, and percentages like 99.5 percent might not be out of line.[2]

Even though well-run publishers *do find* most of their problems during their testing process, they *don't fix* them all. Early bug-fixing takes time away from coding new features. Late bug-fixes can delay the release of the product and cause even more bugs. Publishers consider some bugs minor and irrelevant. They decide that probably no one is going to complain about these bugs or that no one's work will be affected by them, so they don't bother to fix them

---

[2]These estimates are based on verbal reports from the following: testing/quality-control managers who take pride in their group's work; from a few sets of numbers sent to us; and from a reputable independent test lab that keeps such statistics as a matter of contractual responsibility. These numbers are not widely published nor easy to obtain, and we do not know how representative they are. Relatively few publishers track this number or any other measure of testing effectiveness. We suspect that not all mass-market software publishers obtain results like these. In these fast-to-market times, several companies have cut back on their quality-control budgets. They probably find and fix fewer problems. We caution readers that different numbers occur in different market segments. For some very expensive, large systems, it seems common and acceptable to put a product in service with a much lower percentage of bugs found. The vendors in these cases handle the problems on a customer-by-customer basis, with a much higher level of service. The net result seems acceptable to those customers.

(Bach, 1996; Yourdon, 1996). For example, it is widely reported that Windows 3.1 shipped with 5,000 known bugs. (This sounds like a big number, but don't infer a criticism of Microsoft that we don't intend. We believe that Microsoft's staff members are careful in their risk analyses and that they try hard to ensure that the bugs they knowingly ship with a product will not impact consumers' use of their products. We aren't saying that we agree with all of their decisions. We are saying that we think that they're ethical.)

Similar to the Microsoft numbers, here is a report from Apple, "Apple shipped the first version of Hypercard with about 500 known bugs in it...I was working at Apple when Macintosh System 7.0 shipped, and it went out with thousands of bugs." (Bach, 1996)

Some companies exercise care and wisdom in their risk analyses, but others' practices are much sloppier. As a result, some publishers release products with inappropriate errors, which were known (if not necessarily fully appreciated) at the time of release. Customers' complaints are often about *known* bugs, even if an individual customer support technician has not heard of the bug or pretends to have never heard of it.

> ### Note
> *This does not mean that software publishers are aware of every bug when they ship a product. It is dismayingly common to be surprised by repeated customer complaints about one or two serious bugs that were never imagined in the lab. But, once publishers start getting reports of these bugs, they know about them. Certain publishers will continue to manufacture and sell products that contain serious errors for longer than others.*

Finally, what if the program won't work on *your* computer, but it works on other computers? Don't let the publisher's technicians intimidate you by saying that your computer's configuration is weird or unusual. Never forget that the publisher *chooses* the amount and extent of configuration testing that it does. (Configuration testing includes testing the program with other programs, different types of computer equipment, different versions of the operating system, etc.) Configuration testing is expensive, and it can be an overwhelming job. To keep within their budget, publishers limit their testing to specific hardware and software; as a result, they ignore many products that they know customers will use in conjunction with their software. For example, even though a publisher can't afford to test the program with *every* video card, that doesn't excuse the program's incompatibility with *your* video card, and it doesn't necessarily mean that your card is weird or unusual. (On the other hand, if you do have unusual equipment, don't be surprised if programs have trouble with it.) Conscientious publishers will list the supported or tested configurations on the outside of the box or at their Web site. Others hope that their software will work on configurations that they never tested, and then they blame you when it doesn't.

One kind of configuration problem makes unwilling victims of both you and the publisher. If the device, such as a video card, was designed *after* the publisher started selling its product, you can't expect the publisher to have found incompatibility with this device before it released the software. The same type of problem arises when you try to run a new program with an old one. The old one might no longer work because of odd behavior by the new one. You can't (usually) blame that on the old one.

About the Documentation

A favorite complaint of customer support technicians is that customers don't read the manual. So, they tell you to read it. (Under their breath, they say RTFM, Read the Fine Manual.) So you try. But, if you don't understand it, a manual isn't very useful. Is it you? Are you stupid? Is it because you aren't experienced enough with computers? Probably not.

Good writing costs money. A well-written, comprehensive software manual for a consumer audience costs about eight hours of work per page.[3]

Publishers often choose not to invest enough to write a manual that its customers can understand. Writers often are budgeted for as little as an hour per page. In many companies, such decisions are rationalized with statements that there's no point spending much money on the documentation because no one reads it anyway. (So, why do these companies whine "RTFM" when people don't learn anything from their lousy documentation?)

Some publishers believe the myth that no one reads their manuals because so many of the people who call for support seem not to have read (or not to have understood) the manual. What they don't realize is that most people solve their own problems without calling for support. Research by Dataquest (Johnson, 1995) illustrates the point. Most customers (more than 80 percent) solved their own problems by looking up information in the manual, through online help, or by using other electronic documentation. People were less successful at *finding* information in these documents than they wanted to be. With better documentation, more people would have solved more problems.

Kaner recently studied this issue for a client. When customers called for support, we asked whether they had checked their manuals before calling. They usually said, "Yes," so we followed up by asking what they had found. Nearly

---

[3]These estimates include planning, researching, writing, editing, layout, and indexing. Hackos (1994) gives slightly lower estimates, but we are allowing for the extra time it takes to include good troubleshooting info, which takes longer to research per page, and for a better-than-average index.

90 percent of the callers could specify why the manual or online help hadn't answered their question. The problems they cited were unsurprising. They couldn't find what they needed because of the following reasons:

- The index was incomplete, or wrong, or pointed to irrelevant information.
- The table of contents provided no hint as to where to find the information.
- The information was wrong, incomplete, incomprehensible, or spread across too many places in the book to be useful.

Sound familiar?

If the manual and help were correct, useful, and understandable, how many support calls would never be made, and how many others could be handled much more quickly?

 Some publishers try to save money on documentation by putting the manual online. This saves them the cost of printing a manual. Unfortunately, material that is structured for the printed page doesn't work as well on screen. (Hackos, 1997, explains the differences well and concisely.) Good help systems take longer to create and test than excellent manuals. As a result, help systems that come with mass-market products are usually incomplete and hard to use.

Other problems with documentation include the following:

Errors.   In a recent survey, 50 percent of the responding companies admitted that they don't put their documentation through quality control. (Customer Care, Inc., 1994, p. V-29; for additional references see Kaner and Pels, 1996). Thoroughly testing a manual costs about 15 minutes per page. But, some managers contend, if nobody's going to read it, why spend so much time checking whether it is accurate? In short, you get what they paid for.

Incorrectly described and missing features.   One of the frustrations of being a technical writer is that the writing must be done while the program is still changing. It takes less time to duplicate disks than to print a manual. The result of this, on a time-constrained project (which includes most mass-market software projects) is that the manual goes to the printer while the software is still being tested, fixed, and revised.

Poor (or no) index.   Readers rate a good index as a critically important feature of a manual (Grech, 1992). But, a good index should be created, reviewed, and edited as the book is written (Hackos, 1994; and see Mulvany, 1994, for an excellent discussion of techniques for developing high-quality indexes). A well-edited, thorough index costs as much as 30 to 45 minutes for each page of the manual. But, most indexes are compiled quickly at the very end of the project, when there's no time for a good job, and no time for a careful edit without slipping the book's schedule. (See Bonura, 1994, for an explanation of the quick indexing approach.)

Insufficient and/or ineffective troubleshooting tips.   Good troubleshooting is expensive. The writer must do research to determine which problems to write about and then has to master each problem's symptoms and solutions. The underlying issues are often much more technical than the rest of the book. It can take 20 (or more) hours per page to research, write, edit, lay out, and test troubleshooting material.

If the manual and online help are poorly written, disjointed, and error-ridden, and you can't find anything in them, or even if you do find something and if it doesn't try to help you get out of trouble, then the publisher has given you nowhere to go when you have problems. This doesn't mean that you're too dumb to understand the program and the manual. It means the publisher was too cheap.

About Technical Support

The software industry is facing a crisis in support costs. As products reach a broader audience, the customer base expects products that are more reliable and more capable of living up to their advertised benefits. Early adopters of products are tolerant of many practices that infuriate the mass market (Moore, 1991). Computers and software have become mass-market items during this decade, and the result has been a shock to the industry. The numbers given here illustrate the size of the problem. These are industry data, from reputable sources. We provide additional references in Kaner and Pels (1997).

- In 1996, 200 million calls were made for technical support (Johnson and Gately, 1996; Bultema and Oxton, 1997; Schreiber 1997).

- Complaints to consumer protection agencies about home computers and software have gone through the roof. According to the Better Business Bureau, in 1995, computers and software were the eighth most complained about industry. This jumped to seventh place in 1996.

- At an average of about $23 per call, the industry spent about $4.6 billion on these calls. (Tarter, 1993, $23.33; Murtagh, 1994, $20.22; Help Desk Institute 1997, $25; Customer Care Institute, 1993, $25, but the 1994 estimate was $18. The Software Support Professionals Association, 1997, document RTR0011 estimates $25 per call for PC/shrink-wrap products and much more for Unix and mainframe products.)

- According to a report by Dataquest, over a seven-year period, the ratio of support to total employees in hardware and software companies grew from 1 in 12 to 1 in 6 (Johnson and Gately, 1996). The Association of Support Professionals (1997) confirmed this, reporting that on average, customer support staff make up 15 percent of software publishers' total employees.

- Customer satisfaction with software publishers' technical support dropped steadily for 10 years. (Bill Rose, president of the Software Support

Professionals Association, 1996; Ron Schreiber, chairman of Softbank Services, 1997.) J.B. Wood, executive vice-president of Prognostics, a leading market research firm, reported in 1996 that customer dissatisfaction with support had finally bottomed out in the eleventh year.

- Publishers differ widely in the percentage of revenue that they're willing to invest in customer support (Tarter, 1993). Some publishers see the quality of their support relationship with customers as a strategic advantage and as a source of invaluable marketing and product-improvement information. (Barlow and Moller, 1996, and Van Bennekom, 1994, explain this well.) Others don't. For example, Jeffrey Tarter, editor of *Soft*Letter*, a very influential newsletter in the industry, in 1996, wrote a widely read commentary on Microsoft's investment in better technical support. Starting in 1993, Microsoft spent about $500,000,000 to improve its technical support for products such as Office. The organization improved greatly (to world-class levels, according to other data that we've seen). However, according to customer surveys, customer perceptions of Microsoft's service quality improved, but only to not much better than average. Tarter concluded that this investment would, therefore, not affect customers' buying behavior, "Despite lots of wishful thinking to the contrary, spending money to upgrade a company's service reputation remains a lousy investment."

We are horrified by thinking like this. It doesn't serve customers. And, we doubt that it serves the industry. We suspect that the main effect of bad support is not on new sales but on the probability that existing customers will buy the next version of a product or other products from the same company. The cost of losing existing customers is very high (Wood, 1996; Goodman, 1997). Good service is an important factor in helping companies build long-term relationships with customers (Anton, 1996). Sterne (1996) cites data showing that customers who complain are among the business' most loyal customers. Unfortunately, some publishers analyze the world differently. They invest less in support because they think that it won't significantly improve sales or profitability.

Why Don't They Answer the Phone?

Publishers can predict the number of customers who will call and when they will call for support. Publishers *decide* how long they want to leave the average caller on hold and how many of these callers they want to eventually talk to and help. (See, for example, Murtagh, 1993; Brown, 1996; and Khandpur and Laub, 1997). For many publishers, this number is not 100 percent. Most publishers want to talk to most callers, but some plan their staffing level to handle as few as 10 percent of the incoming calls. They correctly expect the other callers to hang up without service after being left on hold for an hour or two.

Tip
You might be on hold a long time even with a very customer-focused publisher, due to unexpected flurries of calls. But, companies that decide to leave their typical caller on hold for outrageously long periods of time do so because they don't want to talk to them. With such companies, you must show that you are serious about getting help.

About half of the calls into software publishers are left on hold for two minutes or less. (Software Publishers Association, 1995, p. 18, estimated 2 minutes; Customer Care, Inc., 1994, estimated 4 minutes.) Others get to very few of their calls this quickly. If you look at the average amount of time people are left on hold (total number of minutes on hold, divided by the number of calls), it's about 15 minutes. Average hold times have been reported as follows: 12.2 minutes (Software Publishers Association, 1995, p. 17), 15 minutes for PC/shrink-wrap products but less for Unixand mainframe software (Software Support Professionals Association, 1997, document RTR0018); 19.8 minutes (Schreiber, 1997). Many people spend more than an hour on hold. At 15 minutes hold time per call, for more than 200 million people, the industry left people on hold for about 3 billion minutes last year.[4]

Note
Service Management International (Brown, 1996) did a small study of hold times across industries and found that software companies leave callers on hold longer than any other industry studied. They were worse than government agencies, computer hardware companies, airlines, banks, utility companies, and others.

Leaving callers on hold can be expensive. For example, in 1996, software publishers who provide toll-free support paid $500 million for toll charges while customers sat on hold (Schreiber, 1997). Rather than wasting this money, many publishers now give you a busy signal when they're too busy to take your call. According to Schreiber (1997), *at peak times, 85 percent of calls into technical support groups now get busy signals.*

---

[4]Schreiber's (1997) estimate was 66 million hours—3.96 billion minutes. And, these averages are probably underestimates, because they're from companies that send back survey questionnaires. The companies that service their customers least well are probably not likely to answer these lengthy questionnaires. The SPA and the Customer Care Institute listed the companies that responded to their surveys, and we noted the absence of several companies that we regard as troubled.

Why Don't They Solve Your Problem?

Some companies put knowledgeable technical staff on every call, but others start you off with clerical-level staff who work from notes that address only the most common problems. According to the Software Publishers Association (1995), technical support staff at more than half of the publishers are given only 40 hours of training (or less) before being put on the phones to handle calls on their own. You may have to work your way through two or three levels of these people before reaching someone who knows the program *and* has the authority to make decisions. According to the Software Support Professionals Association (1997, document RTR0022), it takes an average caller half an hour to reach a technician who is appropriate for the question being asked.

Tip
Don't give up and hang up if you don't get a straight answer. Ask for the technician's boss. If he can't help you, ask for his boss.

Why Are They So Ineffective in Multivendor Situations?

If you own a word processor made by one company, a printer made by a second, and an operating system made by a third, guess what happens when your word processor won't work with your printer? The word processor company blames the printer. The printer company blames the operating system. The operating system company blames the manufacturer of your video card, who blames your word processor. You have a merry time calling each company several times until you either give up (a not uncommon result), or you finally get an answer.

Big companies often have help desks. For example, the help desk in a large hospital might support the hospital staff in their efforts to use the word processor, printer, and other equipment. These groups operate as sophisticated user representatives and will keep pushing at the manufacturers until they solve the problem. On average, however, it takes *them* 3 to 18 times as long to resolve a multivendor problem as opposed to one that can be pinned to a specific piece of software or hardware (Oxton, 1997; Schreiber, 1997). Individual consumers and small businesses don't have the luxury of a help desk to serve as their professional bloodhounds. Often, these customers' problems are never resolved. Given enough runaround, they have no alternative to throwing products away and starting over.

When publishers economize on configuration testing, they make multivendor problems even harder to support. When the publisher has no data on its compatibility with many products, the technical support technician has to work in the dark with the customer, without supporting data.

Problems Caused by Outsourcing

Many publishers arrange to have some of their support services handled by another company, called an *outsourcer* or a *third-party support service*. The practice itself is called *outsourcing*. Some publishers do partial outsourcing, using the other company to handle overflows or specific types of calls. Others eliminate their own support departments and rely exclusively on the outsourcer's staff. You won't know you've reached a third-party support technician because, when you call about Brand X, the support company's representatives will answer the phone saying "Brand X."

The quality of third-party support is sometimes excellent. The best of them regard what they do as a long-term business. They have top-notch call-handling technology and systems. But, third-party support also can be poor. Even the best third-party staff might know less about Brand X's products than Brand X staff. Khandpur and Laub (1997) discuss advantages and drawbacks of outsourced support. One problem we've seen is that publishers that use third-party support primarily to drive down their support costs, which is frequently touted as a major benefit of outsourcing, might be more likely to pick the lowest-cost providers. Their contract with Brand X might give them fewer options to take care of you. And, they probably have less of a stake in keeping you as a Brand X customer than does Brand X. But, Brand X has ways to manage these risks, and several publishers handle partial outsourcing quite well.

> ### *Note*
> *Keep in mind that many outsourcing contracts have an "escalation" clause. This means that if the outsourcer can't help you, and you continue to ask for help, you are forwarded to a senior technician or manager at Brand X, who probably has more options and more knowledge. Outsourcers may be reluctant to transfer your call to Brand X, especially if their contract with Brand X says that they shouldn't do this very often. But, that's their problem. If you have a reasonable complaint and you aren't getting the help you need, ask for a manager; if you are already talking to a manager, ask whether you are talking to an employee of Brand X or to a third-party support provider. If it's the latter, ask to be transferred to someone more appropriate for the call, at Brand X.*

Why Do They Charge for Support?

Many companies that charge you money when you call to ask for help with their product do so because they can't afford to take so many calls. They want to encourage you to read the manual or to use their other, less-expensive, methods for providing support, such as their support information center on the World Wide Web.

Many support calls are not for defects. Rose (1990) estimated that "actual code defects make up only 10 to 15 percent of customer calls." Tourniare and Farrell's (1997) estimate is even lower: 5 percent. Additional calls are caused by defects in the manual and other documentation. As Rose put it, documentation "is the single most critical area for software vendors to improve." Other estimates about the number of calls due to defects are higher. For example, Goodman, Malech, and Adamson (1988, p. 6), summarizing research in several nonsoftware industries, said, "New research indicates that two complaints out of three are caused by problems for which the customer is at least partially to blame, and which won't respond to traditional quality-control improvement methods." Bach (1995a), a leading consultant on the testing of mass-market software, offered about the same estimate (38 percent of calls for software support are due to bugs). We think these estimates often ignore the problem that many user errors are caused by the software, because it is poorly designed.

Our estimates of the extent to which phone calls come from bad software are higher than others, and they're based on good, mass-market software product data. We studied customer call records and letters in detail for a very successful product and in less detail for some other products. We were in a position to know the engineering design trade-offs involved with these products. Our conclusion was that changes that could reasonably have been made by the product development department (bug-fixes, documentation improvements, and minor design changes to make the product more understandable) could have reduced the number of incoming calls by 50 percent. Several of those changes were made, with the predicted large drop in call volume. Still, this number indicates that half of the calls aren't easily prevented by improving the product. They are often calls for advice rather than for technical support. Publishers feel justified in charging what is really a consulting fee for these types of calls.

Other companies see support charges as a way of making profit. Recently, for example, warranties for new computers were shortened, thereby providing sellers with new opportunities to sell service contracts to home users (Clancy, 1996; Christopher, 1997). Dataquest (Christopher, 1997) found a trend had developed toward giving shorter warranties for computers, which helped vendors sell more service contracts. Similarly, for software, the Association of Support Professionals (1997) reported that "few mass-market software companies have managed to make support a significant profit center," but that the ones that offered extremely short warranties, which they classed as three months or less, were "doing the best job of generating revenue" from fee-based support.

- Most publishers will give you a free support period (30 or 90 days or longer). You can call for help during this time at no charge, but when this warranty period is up, they'll charge. A few companies charge even for the first call (Bertolucci, 1996).

- Most publishers will refund their charge for your call (if you ask them to) if it turns out that you are calling about a real bug, as opposed to calling for advice that you could have gotten from the manual.

- Charging customers for support creates an unhealthy incentive to leave bugs unfixed in programs in order to encourage customers to buy support-service contracts. Few companies behave this way, but be aware that there are those that do.

Winson (1991) provides a slightly dated but customer-sensitive, thoughtful, and reasonable discussion of the trade-offs involved in charging for support.

About the Marketing Materials

Marketing materials tell you before you buy the product what to expect of it. They set your expectations, directly and via the many media reviews that parrot them. Some companies take their descriptions to the edge of false advertising (or beyond). Customers who believe these materials will be disappointed after they buy the program.

A 1997 article in *PC World* illustrates the problems we see too often. In "Software Speed-Ups: Bold Claims and Dubious Promises," reporter Michael Desmond looked at claims made by publishers of software that would, allegedly, make your computer use its memory more efficiently or speed performance of your hard disk or CD-ROM, "PC World took a close look at eight acceleration utilities for Windows 95 PCs and found that the products frequently failed to meet the claims displayed on their boxes. In fact, several products did not provide any discernible performance improvement in our tests, and in some operations, system performance even slowed."

For example, *PC World* tested one hard disk accelerator that had published the claim "makes your hard disk up to 496 percent faster." Overall, the accelerator actually improved performance by 12 percent. So, what was the basis for the 496-percent claim? The accelerator publisher's spokesperson responded, "A 500 percent improvement is the most extreme improvement that you can possibly see."

Doesn't Anyone Test the Marketing Materials?

Maybe not. Sometimes, marketing copy contains blatant errors by accident: A copywriter wasn't told that the program's design was changing or that critical bugs wouldn't be fixed. But, how understanding should we be about errors like this (especially errors that cost us time and money)? Some companies scrupulously check their materials for accuracy; others don't. When a company publishes a false statement that it *chose* not to check for accuracy, should we treat this as lying or as an innocent mistake? It's not an easy question to answer.

Why Don't They List Equipment Compatibility on the Box?

Many publishers *do* list their program's hardware requirements on the side or back of the box or visibly through the CD jewel case, as recommended by the Software Publishers Association's Software Packaging Special Interest Group (1995a, b). This listing takes up precious advertising space, but that's better than what happens when they make a too-general statement (such as "works with Windows-compatible printers") or no statement. People who own incompatible equipment and don't see any restrictions on the package will be disappointed when they buy the product and then have to complain about and/or return it.

Publishers that choose not to list their compatibility problems don't want to confuse prospective buyers with the facts. They don't want to unnecessarily lose sales to people with compatible equipment, so they put up with complaints from people who buy first and find out later they have incompatible equipment. If you're in this situation, don't be shy about demanding a refund and reimbursement for any other expenses that this program has cost you.

Why Do They Advertise Features That Don't Work?

Why do they brag about features that are too hard to use? Why do they make customers think that those features are the most important benefits of the product? Don't they understand the effect of this on customer dissatisfaction and technical support costs? We have no idea why people do these things, but they do. Read *Dilbert*.

So What Are We Saying Here?

Simply, that the publisher *must* make trade-offs. The publisher *cannot* provide all possible features, design them elegantly, code them perfectly, test them immaculately, describe them gloriously, and support them lovingly—not at prices you (or anyone else) could afford.

A reasonable, honest publisher might decide that the program doesn't have to do something that *you* need or that it doesn't have to work on a machine that *you* have. *This is just business.* But, you are not being unreasonable for wanting a program that will do a specific task (and do it without crashing or trashing your data). And, if the advertisements, the magazine reviews, or the description on the box made it sound as if this program was just what you needed, and it wasn't, that's the publisher's problem, not yours. You bought the product in good faith. Now the publisher has to deal with you in good faith.

Are You Being Played for a Sucker?

American customers rarely hound companies that cheat them. If it takes too long or is too much hassle to call for help or to demand a refund, most American customers won't bother; for example:

- Research by the National Fraud Information Center (NFIC & MasterCard International, undated) shows that fewer than 10 percent of fraud victims report their losses to law-enforcement authorities.

- John Goodman, president of the Technical Assistance Research Program, in 1997 cited data indicating that 50 percent of dissatisfied consumers never complain about a problem; 45 percent will complain only to first-level support staff; and only 5 percent will go beyond first-level support and complain to corporate management.

- According to E.T. Garman (1996), for relatively small purchases, only 30 percent of consumers will return the product, and only 3 percent will call the manufacturer (if they bought from a retailer) to complain. Even when the product costs $150 or more, about one-third of customers never complain.

Some publishers rely on the fact that most Americans who buy a defective program don't call for help or demand a refund. They also know that most of the people who do call to complain or ask for help probably won't call back if they can be made to feel guilty or stupid, or if they know that the next call will be a pain in the neck. These publishers spend almost nothing on designing and testing their products; then they brush you off when you have a complaint.

"Shelfware" is software that sits on the customer's shelf unused, usually because it's badly designed or has bugs (Plauger, 1990; Grech, 1992). It's too expensive to throw away but too much hassle to take back. Over the past few years, we've heard some marketing managers use the word in a more cynical way to mean a product that does the following:

- Is well enough advertised and packaged to sell

- Does something that is not *essential* for most customers; so, if it doesn't work, the customer won't have an urgent need to get it fixed

- Is developed and tested on such an inadequate budget that it is probably not worth using

- Is priced cheaply enough that it's not worth the customer's time to return it

Unethical people sell worthless products in every industry, so it should be no surprise that they exist in the software industry, too. We raise the point here to remind you of the following when you buy bad software:

- It might come from a publisher that cares deeply about your business and will go out of its way to support you.

- It might come from a publisher that is trying to sell a reasonable product and is trying to do an acceptable (if limited) job of supporting customers.

- It might be intentional shelfware.

You'll have to decide, in your interaction with a publisher, with what kind of people you're dealing. But, don't be afraid to conclude that you've been sold shelfware if the product is badly designed, if the publisher's customer support phone number is hard to find and the phones are always busy, or if the technicians are particularly unhelpful and intimidating. If you were sold shelfware, your negotiating stance with the publisher should be different than if you were sold a weak or faulty product by an otherwise honest company.

You Have Rights

Software publishers are subject to the law, just like all other sellers. We consider the laws in more detail starting in Chapter 7, "Software Quality and the Law." For now, keep a few points in mind:

The inside-the-box warranty disclaimer is not legally enforceable. If you find a piece of paper in the box (called a disclaimer) that says that the program was sold "as is" without any warranty and that the publisher cannot be held liable for any damage caused by the program, don't believe it. No publisher can disclaim its express warranties, and any statement of fact that the publisher makes about the product or its capabilities can be interpreted as an express warranty under the Uniform Commercial Code (UCC). The publisher *can,* however, disclaim implied warranties. These are warranties that purchasers are entitled to by law, as a matter of public policy. Disclaimers of implied warranties must be conspicuous at or before the sale—you know, like the signs on the used cars, big letters that read "AS IS, NO WARRANTY." If the disclaimer is inside the box, it isn't conspicuous. The courts reject these disclaimers as invalid.

The publisher cannot make false statements about the product no matter what the disclaimer says. Publishers make statements of fact in their advertising, in the specifications, the manual, and on the software's packaging. If these statements are false, the publisher can be held liable for fraud, negligent misrepresentation, or breach of express warranties.

Many states have additional consumer protection laws. These laws ban, for example, deceptive advertising and unfair trade practices.

If you have been cheated, the law is on your side.

Action Plan
You must make four decisions:

1. **What do you think is the problem?**   Can you describe it clearly enough to communicate with the publisher or the retailer? For help with this question, see Chapter 3, "Preparing to Make the Call."

2. **What do you want?**   What will make you a happy customer? For help with this question, see Chapter 4, "What Should You Ask For?"

3. **Are you going to talk to the retailer first or the publisher?**   For help with this question, see Chapter 1, "Read This First."

4. **Is there any point making another call?**   Maybe not, if you've already made calls and received no help. Read Chapter 7, "Software Quality and the Law," and consider your rights. Then write some follow-up letters or seek help from a consumer protection agency (see Chapter 6). If that doesn't work, consider filing a lawsuit (see Chapters 8 through 10).

Preparing to Make the Call

 Chapter Map
When a program doesn't work, most customers don't want to spend a lot of time trying to figure out what the problem is or how to fix it. We assume that your goal is to do the minimum amount of work needed to get the problem solved.

This chapter is divided into two main sections:

Technical issues.   You may have to gather information that will help you explain the problem to the support technician or that will help you under-stand what the technician or the publisher's support documents tell you. We suggest a strategy that helps you put off gathering information until you need it. In many cases, you will solve the problem long before you get to the last few steps.

Negotiating issues.   When you ask a publisher for support, you have en-tered into a negotiation. What should you ask the publisher to do for you? We consider this question carefully in Chapter 4, "Knowing What to Ask For." In *this* chapter, we itemize what you might want to collect as background information to back up your requests.

How Much Preparation Do You Need?

In this chapter, we suggest that you write down many details. The more you know about the program and your computer, the more easily a support technician can help you, and the better equipped you'll be to recognize an unreasonable brush-off if the publisher tries one.

This chapter lists a lot of issues to consider. Our purpose is to help you structure your thinking and your requests for support. You won't know all of the details. *We don't know all of these details about our own systems.* The list is long because different details are relevant for different problems.

Don't spend a lot of time trying to learn everything. You might not even
need what you don't know. All you need is *some* of the relevant information
for a good technician to be able to help you (by explaining over the phone
what you can do) to find the rest.

A Troubleshooting Strategy

When a program doesn't work, few customers want to spend time trying to figure out what the problem is or how to fix it. Some customers are more patient
and more technically skilled than others. If you're a really good troubleshooter,
you'll be able to handle more problems on your own. And, when you run into a
problem that you can't solve, you'll be better able to explain it to a support
technician in a way that can help him figure out how to help you much more
quickly.

We assume here, however, that you aren't a professional troubleshooter and
that you don't want to become one; we also assume that your goal is to do as
little as you have to do to get the problem solved. In that spirit, we suggest
that you gather your information in a specific order. If, however, you know
more about your system or about the program than we're assuming, you might
want to do your work in a different order.

Here's our basic approach:

1. Start by making a few notes about what happened.

2. Check the README file that came with the product.

3. *Optional:* Check the publisher's Web site right away.

4. *Optional:* Figure out what this problem has cost you.

5. Look for information in your manual and in online help.

6. Make some notes about your computer and the program version.

7. Look for the answer in the publisher's automated support systems.

8. *Optional:* Check out some other sources of information on the Net.

9. Find your program's serial or registration number.

10. Call the publisher.

Now for the details.

1. MAKE NOTES

Good notes help. The solution to the problem often will depend on details that you have forgotten by the time you start asking the technician for help. Without notes to refresh your memory, you will waste a lot of time. As you learn more about the problem, add to your notes.

We don't expect you to maintain a comprehensive set of notes; yours probably won't cover everything that is in this list. We also don't expect you to have all this information at the start. Some problems take a while to solve. Add information as you go. Here are examples of useful things to note:

What were you trying to do when you had the problem?   What happened? Why is that a problem? For example, you might write down that you were trying to print a document named myfile.doc, and the program crashed.

What did you actually do?   You probably won't remember every detail, but if you remember which keys you pressed or the order in which you did things, write that down. Also note anything special you did, such as turning on the printer just before trying to do this or reading the file from a floppy disk instead of the hard disk where you normally store it.

Did you try it again?   If so, what happened the second time?

Do you know whether the program regularly fails this way?   This question is technical. If you don't know the answer, don't worry about it. But, if you notice a pattern, write it down. This information is very useful to a technician. Here are some common patterns to be on the lookout for:

- You've never been able to get this feature to work.

- The program used to work but recently began to fail.

- The program used to work but started failing after you added a new device (such as a new printer) or after you installed a new program.

- The program does what it's supposed to do for the first few minutes or hours that you use it, then starts failing. If you exit the program, reboot the computer, and start again, the program seems to work again.

Did the program give you any error messages?   If so, write down the exact wording. (You don't have to write down a long list of numbers displayed with the message). It's important to be precise about the wording because programmers often write similar messages that mean (to them) very different things.

Were you running any other programs at the same time?   If so, write them down. What were these other programs doing (printing? calculating? writing to the hard disk?) when the program failed? Try shutting down the other programs, rebooting your operating system, starting your program again, and trying to replicate the process exactly. Does it work this time?

Did you have the same problem on a different computer?   Many problems are tied to incompatibility with specific hardware or with a specific program that runs on one computer. If you have a laptop and a desktop computer (or if a friend has the same program on her computer), find out whether the same problem arises on both machines. If so, then the problem is not related to any aspect of your computer's equipment or other software that is different on the two machines.

What have you learned from the documentation or the publisher's Web site?   We'll talk more about this later in the chapter. The point here is to make a note of what you've been instructed to do. Usually, we jot down page numbers from the manual and print out appropriate Web pages to have them handy.

Have you learned anything important from other people or from other publications?   For example, did a computer magazine article you read describe a problem very similar to yours? What did it say about it?

- Write down the title, date, and page number of the magazine article, or print a copy if you read it on the Web. If you eventually have difficulty with the publisher over the problem, this independently written material will be useful.

Whom have you talked to?   When you do call the publisher's technician or the store that sold you the program, *make sure that you write down the following:*

1. The name of the person you are talking to. Ask, "How can I get in touch with you again?" We often ask for (but don't always get) a direct-dial telephone number and extension or an e-mail address.

2. When you talked to the person.

3. What he said the problem might be.

4. What he told you to do.

5. What the tech said he would do.

6. The incident number (or case number) he assigned to your report. This number will help other technicians look up your report when you call back.

Always enter this information into your notes right away. Make notes while you're on the phone or on the same day that you had the conversation.

Example: You Need Some Information

Sometimes, you'll call for support without much background information. Support staff get calls every day from people who haven't done their homework, and they do the best they can to help. It's their job to help people who aren't experts, and you should expect them to work with you, even when you don't have all of the information.

But, realize that they can go only so far. The nightmare customers don't know anything about their machine or their problem, and they are rude about it. Their calls are hard to handle and, usually, ineffective.

For example, a young executive called to complain that his program wasn't printing correctly and wanted to know what the publisher was going to do about it. He proceeded to interrupt every question the technician tried to ask, explaining over and over again how upset he was and how much of his time this was wasting. When he finally calmed down enough to let the technician ask some basic questions, his response was, "How should I know? That's your job. I just want it fixed." The technician suggested that he might like the competitor's program better (*let them deal with him)* and gave him a refund.

Example: The More You Know, the More You Understand

As part of the research for this book, we called several publishers to see how they handled specific types of calls. In one case, we picked a bug published in *BugNet* (www.bugnet.com) that was a serious concern for long-time users of a program which failed when trying to read documents written with an old version of the same program. The current version of the program had been selling for nearly a year. By the time we called, the publisher had probably received plenty of complaints about this bug. Add the *BugNet* publicity, and we were confident that the publisher would know the bug well. Kaner had the program, and confirmed the bug on two different machines before making the call. Here's his report:

> When I called the publisher, I described the problem without mentioning that I'd seen the report in *BugNet* and without going through all of my troubleshooting. I wanted to hear what the publisher would say to a typical customer.

The publisher's technician said that he had never heard of this problem before, then asked briefly about my computer, and said that I had an unusual type of video card (not true) and that the bug was probably my card's problem (not likely). He suggested that I call my video card manufacturer to update my driver (a program that tells the computer how to control the card). Many problems are caused by video cards, so don't automatically assume that someone who suggests this is a liar. But, in this case, the technician didn't offer to help me figure out which version of the driver I had, or whether it was current, who to call, or how to explain the problem to them. He said, "See if upgrading your video driver works and call back if there's still a problem." He didn't give me his direct number, and he didn't offer to call me back if he learned more about this type of problem. He was ready to end the call, leaving me with no useful information. Most customers find it challenging to check and upgrade their video software and, without help, won't make much progress. If you think that you can't call back until you've fixed your hardware problem (which may be no problem at all), then you probably will not call back. Blaming the hardware is an effective way for an overworked support department to get rid of complaining customers. Instead of hanging up, I changed gears, asking whether there was a new version with bug fixes. (Often called *inline updates* or *silent releases* or *patches*, these fix serious bugs rather than add new features.) The technician said there was one and asked if I wanted to buy it. I asked whether I could get it for free, because the new version was just making the program do what I'd paid for in the first place. He said I'd have to pay, so I asked to speak to his manager.

Like the technician, the manager told me that he'd never heard of this problem and that it was probably my video card. I said this couldn't be the problem because I'd had the same failure on my laptop, which used totally different video hardware. The story goes on, but you get the idea. This publisher never did admit there was a problem, nor agree to send me a bug-fix release.

Because the example, "The More You Know the More You Understand," was a research project, we gathered more information than most customers normally would collect. In particular, four pieces of information helped us to conclude that the support staff were misleading us:

- We knew from magazine articles and reviews that this version of the program had a lot of bugs and that the publisher's previously excellent reputation for customer service was slipping. We didn't expect service this bad, but we did know that they probably were getting more calls than they could handle.

- Seeing the bug in *BugNet* reassured us that the publisher probably had heard of this problem.

- We knew the equipment. The desktop's video card was a mainstream brand bought specifically because of its reputation for good compatibility. The technician's effort to portray this card as an unusual piece of equipment with a shaky reputation was so ridiculous that it was almost (but not) funny. The laptop was also a popular, premium-quality machine with a solid reputation.

- Testing the program on different machines with different video hardware would have convinced us that this wasn't a video card problem, even if we hadn't seen the *BugNet* report (which certainly didn't involve video).

For a typical, time-pressed customer, the following should have been sufficient to facilitate good service:

- We knew that the program was failing to read old files created with an old version of the program. We had the files and could send them to the publisher if necessary.

- The manual described this feature and said it would work. No troubleshooting information was provided.

- We knew that this computer was reliable and that it worked well with other programs.

- We had the program registration number, which most publishers ask for before they'll spend time with you.

Example: It Happens to Everyone

Many people are overwhelmed when they try to collect information about a program and their computer. When is enough enough? Do you have to know everything?

Brian Livingston is a recognized expert on Windows who has been working with computers for 29 years and has written several books on Windows, Windows NT, and Windows 95. He writes the column, "Window Manager," for *InfoWorld*. In early 1997, his computer (a Windows 95-based system) started crashing and having mysterious problems. He tried everything that he could think of and finally begged for help in his columns. After several columns and hundreds of responses, he finally solved the problem, which turned out to be a defective piece of equipment, rather than an error in his system software.

One of his statements (Livingston, 1997, p. 36) was very interesting. He wrote, "I've had a heartening response to my admission that Windows blows up on me, too. Instead of being laughed out of the computer press, I received hundreds of sympathetic messages from IS pros and novices alike."

We've had problems, too, on Windows machines and on Macintoshes, which took us days to investigate. It can be embarrassing to give up and admit that you don't know what to try next or which question to ask next. But, it shouldn't be embarrassing, because it happens to all of us.

Gather what information you can. Keep your eyes open—pay attention to how the computer is behaving and misbehaving while you're working with it. And, when you run out of steam as a troubleshooter, don't be embarrassed and don't let anyone make you feel embarrassed. Do the best that you can and then get help if you still need it.

2. CHECK THE README FILE

Imagine yourself working in a software product development group two weeks before the product is scheduled to ship. The manual went to the printer three weeks ago. The online help was finished last week. This morning, a tester found a defect that is significant but not horrible (as far as you can tell). The programming team checked the code and advised you that the underlying mistake is subtle. They *think* they can fix it in time, but there's a real chance they'll break something else in the process of fixing this bug. This risk is genuine, which has led to serious surprise bugs in the field. What would you do?

Many publishers document bugs they discover at the last minute in a file on the disk called README or README.TXT, which typically contains descriptions of known problems and ways to avoid them or to recover from them. If the problem you found is on the list, don't do any further investigation. The publisher knows about it. If you need help with it, call the publisher's support department now. They're expecting your call.

The README also might contain reports that the program has been found incompatible with certain devices. If, for example, your printer is on the list, don't spend any more time trying to make your printer work with the program. It won't. Ask for your refund; they'll be happy (more or less) to accommodate you.

When a publisher learns of a bug after shipping the product, it might not fix the program right away. Instead, it might include a description of the problem in the README file. This file is updated regularly by some publishers.

Some publishers rely less on README files. They put their late-breaking troubleshooting information into "release notes" on disk, on paper, or in a supplement to the user manual.

In sum, many publishers use the README file (or its equivalent) as their first-line technical support service. Take advantage of it.

3. (OPTIONAL) CHECK THE PUBLISHER'S WEB SITE

You can check the publisher's Web site before you do any research. If you have a very common problem, the publisher might have posted a description of it, with a solution, right at the top of its list of *Frequently Asked Questions*. The publisher also might have a fixed version ready for download.

We'll say more about the publishers' Web sites later in this chapter, in the section, "Search the Publisher's Automated Support Systems."

4. (OPTIONAL) FIGURE OUT WHAT THIS PROBLEM COST YOU

If the problem has annoyed you, inconvenienced you, and wasted your time, *but that's all*, then don't think about the costs yet. Just try to get the problem solved.

If, however, the problem has cost you some real money or destroyed data or files that you can't easily replace, then you probably are going to want compensation that goes beyond a bug-fix or a refund. If so, you must take more careful notes, and you'll want to collect more evidence of your expenses and of the publisher's knowledge of the problem. Read Chapter 4, "Knowing What to Ask For," before calling the publisher.

5. LOOK FOR INFORMATION IN THE MANUAL AND ONLINE HELP

If you're like most of us, you probably didn't read your manual from cover to cover when you installed the program, and you probably haven't read all the topics in the online help. When you have a problem, look at the documentation, which can include a manual, an online help system, a quick reference card, a "Read Me First" card, a "Tips and Tricks" page, a videotape, a tutorial, and others. Different programs come with different teaching and reference materials. Furthermore, if you have any other books about the program, check them, too. Most people solve most of their own problems without having to go to the publisher for support.

When going through the documentation, pay attention to three types of information. First, look for a different way to accomplish your task. There are often different ways to achieve the same result with a program. Maybe the publisher has described one that you haven't considered. If so, try it and see what happens.

Second, look for troubleshooting information. Publishers often describe the most common problems that people have with the program and suggest ways to avoid these problems. Look for this type of information in the following places:

- In a section of the manual called "Troubleshooting," "Tips," "Frequently Asked Questions (FAQs)," or the like.

- In the index. Try to find all the pages that reference the task in question and look up each one.

- In a section that describes every error message that the program can generate. This section often appears as an appendix in the manual, as a supplement printed separately from the manual, or as a main topic in online help. Look for discussion of the error message you got (if you got one).

Third, the publisher might have discussed equipment and operating system configuration. For example, if you're having a printing problem, look in the manual and online help for comments about your particular printer. The manual also might include notes on the problems you're likely to experience if you have too little memory or too little room left on your disk.

In each case, jot down in your notes the advice the book or the help system provides and then follow it. If you still have the problem, you'll have to collect some more information and then get help from the publisher. And, don't feel you have wasted time by reading the manual, because you'll now be better able to understand the material posted on the publisher's technical support Web site and the jargon used by the publisher's technician.

6. MAKE NOTES ABOUT YOUR COMPUTER AND THE PROGRAM VERSION

The more you know about your computer, the more easily a technician can help you. And, the better equipped you'll be to recognize an unreasonable brush-off if the publisher tries one. We suggest that you write down several details about your computer, as itemized in the following subsections. We include every device (or component) attached to your computer, such as printers, speakers, mice, and hard drives.

Tip
You won't know everything about every device attached to your computer. Don't worry about this. And, don't spend a lot of time trying to learn these details. After all, you don't yet know whether the information that you don't know will be what the technician needs. If you have some of the relevant information, a good technician will help you (by explaining over the phone what to do) to find the rest.

Useful Information about Every Device

For each type of device, write down four types of information:

Who is the manufacturer of this device?   For example, maybe Hewlett-Packard or Epson manufactured your printer.

What is the model number?   For example, you might have a LaserJet 5P by Hewlett-Packard.

How has the device been installed?   When you first connect your device (such as a printer) to your computer, you tell the computer what the device is and which program the computer should use to run the device. Such a program is called a driver. Some people install a LaserJet 5P with the LaserJet 5P driver. But, for reasons that don't matter here, other people prefer to run the 5P using the LaserJet 5M driver. If you are using a different driver from the most obvious one, that might be relevant to the technician.

What is the version of your driver?   If you bought your printer two years ago, it came with a driver. That driver might have had several defects that have since been corrected by the manufacturer. If you know the version number or original date of the driver you use today, the support technician might recognize it as a problem version and be able to tell you that your problem will go away if you replace your old driver with a new one. You probably can get a free copy of the latest driver by downloading it from your printer manufacturer's Web site, which probably also has instructions on how to install the new driver over the old one. It is more important, however, to know the manufacturer and model number than to know the name and version of the driver. The technician can help you find out the driver information, when he knows the type of device you have.

Useful Information about Specific Devices

Here are the devices that we suggest you keep track of. For each one, try to find out the manufacturer, the model, the driver, and the driver version. Then try to learn the answers to the questions raised for each type of device:

Printer.   Are you printing in color or in black and white? At what resolution? Some problems show up only if you are printing 600 dots per inch, rather than 150 or 300 dots per inch.

Video card.   What video resolution are you using? For example, your screen might show 640 dots across and 480 dots down. This is called VGA resolution. Super VGA (SVGA) is 800 across by 600 down. Extended VGA (XVGA) is 1,024 across by 768 down. Several other values are possible. If you don't know this, the technician can help you. Video resolution is often an issue when the computer is running out of memory or when two devices (such as a printer and a video card) try to share the same area of memory for temporary storage.

Monitor.   How big is yours? 14-inch screen? 17-inch screen? Which video resolutions was it designed to handle?

Hard disk.   Along with manufacturer and model, it will be handy to know whether the drive uses an IDE interface, a SCSI interface, or something else. How much disk space is available on this drive?

More than one hard disk.   If you have more than one hard disk, provide interface details for each. And, which drive letters are they? Is your first hard drive named C? If so, what is your second drive? Is it D or E or some other letter? How much disk space is available on each? Some programs will fail if not enough temporary-use space is available on C, even if the program and its data are both stored on D.

Location of your program.   If you have more than one hard disk, which drive is your program on, and where does the program store its data?

Removable disk.   ZIP drives and writeable CDs are examples of these. If you use one, are you using it to store the program or any of the program's data? Do you ever switch between disks (take out one, put in another) while using the program? Are these IDE or SCSI drives? Do you use an interface card, or do they connect to your parallel port?

Floppy disk.   What is its capacity? 720K? 1.44M? 120M?

CD-ROM or DVD drive.   How fast is it? 2X? 10X? 24X? Can it store data on CDs, or is it purely a CD-reader?

Sound card.   What special capabilities (if any) does this card offer?

Speakers.   Where do you connect them? To the sound card, to the CD-ROM, to the DVD drive, or somewhere else?

Modem.   Modems and fax cards have so many special capabilities that you are well advised to have your modem owner's manual handy if you call for support about a problem that shows up in a program when it tries to work with a modem.

Keyboard.   Certain programs have problems with some of the more feature-ridden keyboard drivers.

Mouse, trackball, trackpoint, touchpad, or other pointing device.
Perhaps you're one of those people who have two or more pointing devices, such as a mouse on the desk and a trackball built into the keyboard. Do you ever experience conflicts between them or between one of them and your modem or printer?

Scanner.   At what resolution do you scan images? Do you scan in color? How many colors? How much memory does the scanner use? How is it connected to your computer; is there a special interface card; or do you plug into the parallel port (or some other port)?

Uninterruptible power supply (UPS).   Yes, this can be a relevant device. Some of the new ones have special software that you can install into your operating system to monitor and control the amount of power left on the UPS battery and the amount being used. When power is low, this software can shut your system down.

Computer processor.   Pentium? 586? PowerPC? How fast does it run? How hot does your computer get when you keep it running for a while? Some problems are triggered by overheating.

Memory.   How much do you have? Do you ever get messages saying that you're running out of memory? When?

Network.   Is your computer connected to a network? What kind? And, what kind of connection (such as a Network Interface Card) do you use?

Other stuff.   If you have any, write it down.

Additional System Information

You might be able to find and easily print out a lot of additional technical information about your devices and their drivers, some of which the publisher's technician might find very useful, even if you don't understand it. If you can easily access such information, have it handy when you call the publisher.

For example, if you're running Windows 95, the easiest way to get configuration information is to right-click on the My Computer icon on your desktop. Then click on Properties, Device Manager, Print; select All Devices and System Summary. Click on OK to get your printout. Keep this handy when you call for support.

Some programs have a technical support selection on their Help menu or in the About box that gives the program's version number.

Information about Other Software Running on Your Computer

The problem program isn't the only program running on your computer. These other programs might affect how your program works (or doesn't). Therefore, it is a good idea to have information about these other programs that run at the same time as your program. Here are a few starter questions whose answers will set you on the road to getting the help you need:

Which operating system are you using, and what is its version number?
When you start your computer, it loads a program called the *operating system*.

The operating system controls when your program can run, what memory it can use, which devices it can use, and how it can use them. Device drivers are connected to the operating system.

Which utility programs are you running?   You might run several utility programs in the background, while you're running your main programs. For example, on a Mac, you might be running a QuickTime extension or an extension that adds features to all the programs' Open and Save As menus. On Windows, you might run a crash-prevention program, such as First Aid. On either machine, you might run a font-management program, such as Adobe Type Manager, or a virus checker, print spooler, or other programs that extend the operating system almost transparently.

What other major programs are you running?   For example, you might have your Internet browser on and connected all the time, even when you're using your word processor or spreadsheet program. You might run a word processor, a presentation program, and a spreadsheet at the same time, copying data between them.

Information about Recent Changes

If your program and your computer were working well yesterday, but there's a problem today, maybe it has nothing to do with the program. Maybe it has to do with a change you made.

It is beyond the scope of this book to tell you how to fix these problems or even how to do a good job of troubleshooting them. But, you can often get a lot of information from hardware manufacturers' Web sites. User group sites also are a good place to search for relevant information. Several excellent books are on the market, too, that might be of use. Some we like are Landau (1997), Minasi (1993, 1996), Mueller (1996), Tidrow (1996), and Townsend (1992).

We can, however, give you some leading questions to ask yourself:

Have you added a new device?   There are many ways in which a new device, such as a new mouse or modem, can interfere with a program or another device that has been working perfectly.

Have you added a new program?   Sometimes, a new program will update system files that other programs use. The update might not be compatible with your other programs. There are several other ways in which a new program can interfere with files, data, or system settings relied on by other programs.

Have you removed a program?   When you (or the uninstaller program that you use) removes a program, you (or it) also might remove a file that other programs use, too. Consequently, these programs won't work.

Have you picked up a virus?   You can get a virus by downloading files from the Net or by reading a disk from a friend or colleague, if that disk has a virus. You can download fully functional evaluation copies of virus checkers from several sites on the Web. We use www.winfiles.com and www.macworld.com.

It's useful to know about these changes when you call for support, because the publisher's technician might be familiar with the effects of the change you that made. If you talk to someone in a well-run group, you might be pleasantly surprised by the level of information that they can access—as long as you provide basic facts to them, which can help guide their search through a large, complex database of troubleshooting information.

Information about the Program

Note the version of the program you are using. If you don't know it, go to the program's Help menu or Apple menu and find and click on a menu item that starts with "About."

It sometimes also will be useful to check your records for when you bought the program or when the version of the program that you are using was created and first sold to the public.

7. SEARCH THE PUBLISHER'S AUTOMATED SUPPORT SYSTEMS

In an effort to control support costs, many publishers create automated support systems, to which access is usually free. A study by the Software Publishers Association (1995) found that every publisher that charged for telephone support also provided at least one free automated alternative, such as a Web site. In many cases, then, you will find more information, faster and cheaper, on these systems than you'll get from a telephone call.[1]

Our first recommendation is that you check the publisher's World Wide Web site. We've had such good results with several of these that we usually do this before making a telephone call. Here are some of the things that you'll often find:

A list of *Frequently Asked Questions* (FAQs).   If you're stumped by something that has stumped a lot of other people, your answer will (or should be) be right here.

---

[1] If you're interested in additional information on automated support services, we recommend Sterne (1996) as a thoughtful discussion. The services and their economics are in flux and under constant examination. You'll see frequent articles in customer support magazines such as *Support Management* (e.g., Flory, 1997). Most of the best information is still being revealed at conferences. Check www.sbforums.com/sbforums.html (especially the Support Services Expo) and www.asponline.com (Association of Support Professionals) for pointers to the main technical support conferences.

A list of every error message.   This list has notes on what you probably did to cause the message to appear and suggestions about how to avoid getting this message in the future.

A list of all known bugs.   This list has suggestions on how to avoid getting bitten by them.

Updates to the program or to device drivers.   These files probably contain fixes to specific bugs, rather than new features. You usually can download these for free.

More documentation.   This might include additional troubleshooting information, examples of how to use the program, technical specifications, or interactive tutorials.

Links to other companies' Web sites.   If you are having a problem with your printer, the publisher might have a link to the latest version of your printer driver at your printer manufacturer's site.

The technical support knowledge base.   This might be the same database that the publisher's in-house staff use to answer your questions. When you provide information about the problem, the knowledge base will give you a list of troubleshooting suggestions or documents (with links to them) that might be relevant to the problem you're describing.

Diagnostic programs.   These programs enable you to check your computer or your system software, as well as virus-checking programs and other utilities that can help you troubleshoot the problem. These programs are usually available for download for free. They are often evaluation copies of a program that another publisher sells. You are permitted to use this copy for free for a few (maybe 30) days. After that, the program turns itself off unless you register (and pay for) it with that program's publisher.

Great Web sites are hard to create and even more difficult to maintain, so some publishers do a better job with other types of automated or electronic support. Here are other services that might be available:

Fax-back.   You telephone the publisher, step through menus in the voice mail system, and finally select a topic on which you want information. Then the publisher faxes you the appropriate document. Or, when you first call, the publisher faxes you a numbered list of available documents. When you call back, you enter the number(s) of the document(s) that you want faxed back.

E-mail.   You send an electronic mail message to the publisher's support staff and hope that you receive an answer. We say "hope" because a study described at a software support conference in 1996 claimed that 81 percent of publishers weren't answering e-mailed questions within two weeks. Publishers have been getting much better at this, and some are great at it. But, if you don't get an answer within a few days, try something else.

Online discussion groups.   You'll find publishers' discussion groups on CompuServe, America Online, Internet news (USENET), and a few other sites. Some are hosted by the publisher (whose staff regularly respond to users' comments), and others are run independently. The quality of these discussions is extremely variable, but when a group is working well, you'll be able to compare notes with other customers who have experience with the types of problems you're having.

Caution

When you post a message to a public discussion group, it is automatically scanned by programs designed to collect Internet mailing addresses. Your address will be sold to spammers (people who will send you junk e-mail).

Publishers' *bulletin board system* (BBS).   Some publishers host a discussion group on their own BBS. This was more popular before the public had easy access to the Internet.

These services are supposed to save you—and the publisher—time and effort. But, if you find the electronic support to be poor-quality or insufficient, don't waste time on it. Pick up the phone and insist on talking to a real person. If the technical support line doesn't tell you how to reach humans, try pressing 0 instead of one of the numbered options. If that doesn't work, try the phone number (often an 800 number) for the publisher's sales department. We can almost guarantee that you will be able to reach a live salesperson. When you do, explain— calmly and politely, but firmly—that their automated systems are not helping you and that you need to talk to a support technician *now*. Most salespeople will transfer you. If the one you're talking to won't, ask to speak to his manager.

Example: A Device Upgrade

Recently, we tried to upgrade a device (something like a modem or a printer or a sound card). The upgrade involved software that we could download off the Web. We checked the device maker's Web site, which gave us instructions on how to upgrade if we'd bought the device between certain dates. Unfortunately, we didn't have the receipt handy, which we needed to prove date of purchase. No instructions were given for people who had bought the device outside of those dates.

We sent an e-mail message to technical support, explaining our problem and asking how much the upgrade would cost. We got an automated response that listed a bunch of documents that we could request. Our options were to send another message asking for one of these documents or to send a message with a different header to have a human read the message.

We chose to send a message requesting a document on upgrading. What we received repeated what we'd seen on the Web site. It contained no additional useful information.

Our next step was to send a message with the please-read-this header, which got a response saying that we should call the support center. So, we called, and got a list of documents we could listen to or have faxed to us. We listened to the message and requested the fax. The two together led us to understand that the manufacturer hadn't yet figured out how it would sell the upgrade to customers who hadn't bought the device in the stated time period.

We wanted to talk to a technician but never did figure out how to get to one through the phone system. We gave up and stopped buying this manufacturer's devices.

Most publishers do a lot better than this.

Example: A Virus Inoculated

One of us bought a computer for his daughter. One of the devices worked for a few days, but when she tried to use it again a few days later, it didn't work. Having no idea what the problem could be, or what further troubleshooting would make sense, she called for support.

We expected her to be asked a series of questions and then told to call back with answers that could help the technician troubleshoot the problem. Instead, the manufacturer's technician recognized the problem quickly and said that he thought it probably was caused by a virus. He sent her to his company's Web site and told her how to download a virus checker that they supplied to customers for free. He gave her his name and phone number and said she should call him back if the virus checker didn't work.

The Web site was well organized, so the virus checker was easy to find, and the instructions for downloading and using the program were clear. She downloaded it, ran it, and found a virus. After killing the virus, the computer worked again.

---

8. (OPTIONAL) LOOK FOR OTHER SOURCES OF INFORMATION ON THE WEB

If you search the Web for information about the publisher of the program you bought or about the program itself, you'll probably find related Web pages or newsgroups that are not affiliated with the publisher. For example, you can find the following:

- Bug reporting and discussion Web sites, such as www.bugnet.com, www.winfiles.com/bugs, and www.annoyances.org
- Copies of magazine and newspaper articles about the product or company
- Discussions and troubleshooting tips at user group sites
- Troubleshooting discussions published or hosted by consultants, students, and others on their Web sites
- Compatibility information published by hardware (computers and peripheral devices) manufacturers
- USENET discussion groups about the product in question
- A lot of totally irrelevant stuff

These are sometimes great sources of information.

9. LOOK FOR YOUR SERIAL NUMBER OR REGISTRATION NUMBER

Many publishers will require you to give them the program's serial or registration number when you call for support. Look for a serial number printed on the box, on the first disk, or on a sticker on the manual. You also might see it in the About box that tells you the program's version number. (Click on About under the Help menu or the Apple menu.)

The publisher might provide a separate registration number or ask you to use the registration number instead of a serial number when you call for support. This, too, might be on the box, on the disk, in the manual, in the software, on your copy of the program's user registration form, on the license agreement, or in some other handout that reads, "Use this number when you call for support."

If you've paid for support for the software (say you paid for a year of support when you bought the program), you also might need a support contract number.

Finally, if you bought the program on a CD, you might need what's called a *key code* to install the software. If so, you also might need it to reinstall the software (something the publisher's Web site or technician might tell you to do or that you'll do if you ruin your configuration trying to fix the program on your own.) This key code is often on the jewelcase (the packaging) the CD came in, or in the tiny manual that came bundled in that case. Whichever number or numbers you find, write the information in your notes, so that you'll have it handy in case you need it.

10. CALL THE PUBLISHER

We delve into this in Chapter 5, "Making the Call."

Background for Negotiating

Two types of reasons exist for looking for information about a defective product: You might want technical information that will help you solve problems; or you might want information that will help you improve your bargaining position with the publisher. This section addresses the bargaining-related research.

Because chapters 4 and 5 also address negotiating issues, let's clarify the focus of the three chapters:

- This section of this chapter prompts you to ask questions *about the product* and about *the publisher's knowledge* of the product's defects. The facts you collect here help you demonstrate that the publisher (and the product) are at fault.

- Chapter 4 focuses more on *what happened to you* and *what the product has cost you,* which guides you in deciding what you should ask for in compensation.

- Chapter 5 focuses on *applying what you've learned* about the product and on the conduct of the publisher's staff on the telephone.

IS THE PRODUCT AT FAULT, OR DO YOU JUST NOT LIKE IT?

We answer this question by dividing the issue into four possible situations:

The product was misrepresented to you.   In this case, you have a much stronger position, and it is entirely reasonable for you to stand on your rights.

The product is defective; it doesn't work.   Unless the defect cost you a lot, you might be satisfied with a bug-fix or a workaround. You are certainly entitled to a refund. If the defect is obvious, and it has cost you significantly, you have reason to demand compensation beyond a refund.

You don't understand how the product works.   Many calls for product support—*most* of the calls for *some* products—belong in this category. If you call for help before reading the manual and online help, then essentially you're asking the publisher's support staff for a favor. Publishers justify charging people for support because it is so expensive to answer these questions. Nevertheless, if the product is so badly designed and documented that you have real problems understanding how to use it, then it's entirely fair to ask for a refund.

You don't like how the product works.   It is reasonable to return a product simply because you don't like it. Imagine receiving for a birthday present a green and purple striped shirt with yellow polka dots. Probably, you wouldn't think it unreasonable to take it back to the store and say, "Sorry, I don't like it." Some software retailers say that software is different because you bring it back to them *after* opening the box and using the program. But, with software, that's the only way to discover that it has those (virtual) yellow dots. However, even though it is *reasonable* to return a product (of any kind) that you don't like, you might not be *legally entitled* to a refund unless you ask for one within a few days after your purchase. And, if a software seller honestly described a badly designed product before you bought it, you probably aren't legally entitled to a refund at all. But, don't let that stop you from complaining. If you can explain why you don't want to keep the program, many publishers will give you a refund weeks or even months after your purchase. Many stores will give you a store credit, even if they won't give you a refund.

> ***Note***
> *Many calls to support are suggestions rather than complaints about defects. Wise publishers welcome these suggestions because this input is extremely informative (Barlow & Moller, 1996; Van Bennekom, 1994). But, some companies will charge you $3 a minute to listen to your call; in essence, expecting you to pay to help them. Don't even think about spending this money. If you are willing to give suggestions to a company like this, send a letter or an e-mail.*

MISREPRESENTATION

A statement of fact about a product made to you by its publisher or other seller is an *express warranty* that the product will conform to the statement. If the product doesn't work as described, it is in breach of the warranty, and you are entitled to a fixed version of the program, or a partial or full refund, and possibly some additional money. In some states, it makes a difference whether you learned of this statement before or after you bought the product, though this distinction is gradually fading. We write more about this in Chapter 7, "Software Quality and the Law."

A false statement by the publisher is a *misrepresentation,* even if it is an honest mistake. If the publisher (or other seller) knowingly included a false statement as a way to make it more likely that you would buy the program, or less likely that you'd send the program back, then the statement is considered fraudulent. The law doesn't look kindly on fraud, and you can recover significant damages when you are defrauded.

We discuss the legal issues in Chapter 7. For now, think of a *statement of fact* as something that can be proved true or false. Many of the statements in manuals, online help, advertising, and on packaging are statements of fact and can be treated as warranties.

Here are places to find evidence of misrepresentation:

Documents created or published by the publisher.   These documents include advertisements, the box copy, the manual, online help, fax-back memos, and support and marketing materials available on the publisher's Web site.

Sample output.   In advertisements, on the box, and in the manual—don't just look at the words. Look for examples and step-by-step instructions.

Statements made during sales presentations by the publisher's staff. Verbal misrepresentations are warranties, too. You'll find it useful to have witnesses who also heard these statements. (Send a friend or colleague to a sales presentation to learn whether the salespeople still make the same claims.)

Publisher's comparisons.   Comparative claims which say that competitor X's product can't do something, but that the product you bought can, are often inaccurate, in our experience. You can often find a way to make Competitor X do the comparison task. If so, then you might make an interesting point that, not only is it false that X can't do the job, but that X actually does it better or more easily.

Reviews in printed publications.   Many people treat these as unbiased, independent descriptions of programs, and some of them are. But, other reviews are just repackaged summaries of the publisher's marketing literature. If you believe you were misled by erroneous statements that you read somewhere, look at the publisher's marketing and support documents, often available at the publisher's Web site. If the publisher is making these claims, and the publication has reprinted them, then you have a good argument that you were misled by claims made by the publisher.

False statements made by the reseller, whether orally or in catalogs and print ads.   If the statements were made orally to you by a salesperson, it will help if you have a witness (such as a friend who went shopping with you). If you don't have a witness, then it might be your word against the salesperson's. But, don't give up. You also can use similar statements in a catalog or ads to support your claim that the salesperson said what you claim. Or, you can get a witness after the fact by sending a friend to ask the same questions you asked. If the salesperson gives her the same answers, you're set. Hold the reseller accountable for the misrepresentations made by the reseller. Ask for the same damages from the reseller that you'd expect from the publisher. If the reseller misled you, its statement may have been based on literature from the publisher. Look for ads, fax-backs, box copy, application notes, and so on. Sometimes a reseller's sales staff will be very willing to show you this type of material.

When you talk to the publisher's support technician, be ready to quote every incorrect statement of fact. Be calm, but be firm. Technicians are used to having this material quoted back to them, and they don't enjoy it. It embarrasses them. But, they understand that you should be able to believe what the company has told you.

Misrepresentation of Compatibility

Let's say the product doesn't work with your printer (or modem or whatever), and you are unhappy about this. This common problem only sometimes involves misrepresentation by the publisher or by the reseller. To gather evidence of misrepresentation of compatibility, here are some additional places to look:

On the box, in the manual, and in advertisements for statements that the program will work with your printer. The statement might be very specific (a claim that it works with "DeskJet model 340 printers"); it might refer to a class of devices that obviously includes yours ("all DeskJet printers"); it might refer to a broad class of devices that includes yours ("all Windows-compatible printers"). From a legal point of view, your argument is weaker if the publisher said something vague like "works with inkjet printers." However, even in that case, the publisher's support technician might be sympathetic to your request for a refund (but not to a demand for additional money).

For sample output on the box or in advertisements. It should illustrate the quality as it is supposed to appear from your printer, unless the sample is identified as coming from something else.

If the publisher claims that its product is compatible with your printer, the quality of output from your printer should be reasonable. If you have a high-resolution printer, the product should support at least the same mode that most other products provide (which might not be your printer's best mode), not just the lowest-common-denominator compatibility with some inferior machine. In this case, your legal argument will depend on the specific statements made by the publisher; but when talking to the support technician, appeal to his common sense and sense of fairness, which often go beyond the minimum standards prescribed by law.

Software Defects

It's difficult to come up with a legal definition of the phrase "software defect" (or "bug," which means the same thing). Software testing staff are likely to classify program behavior as defective if it does not conform to the reasonable expectations of the customer, or if it interferes with the customer's ability to complete a normal task. This is a reasonable definition for a research and development group, but it won't necessarily work as a legal standard.

In Chapter 7, "Software Quality and the Law," we describe the case of *Family Drug Store of New Iberia, Inc. v. Gulf States Computer Services, Inc.* (1982) which highlights the problems in defining "defective." In that case, the publisher sold a product that was awkward to use, but its salesperson accurately demonstrated the program. After using it for a short time, the customer asked for a refund and was refused. He sued. The court ruled (and we agree) that the program was not legally defective because it worked in the way that the publisher described it.

We think that the legal definition of a defect should depend on the relationship between the buyer and the seller. The rules for a retail buyer—who had no say in the design of the program and who has never seen the program's technical specification—should differ from those that apply to a buyer who wrote the product specifications and had the program specially developed by the seller (Kaner, 1997a). We're not sure how the courts and the new software laws (if and when they are passed) will finally sort this out.

From a practical point of view, we think that most publishers of mass market software (stuff you can buy in a store) will find the following ideas reasonable. We also believe that fair standards would be a bit tougher on publishers than our suggestions here. If you're knowledgeable about software, or if you are a particularly good negotiator, then don't be limited by our suggestions.

Obvious Defects

You have a very strong argument for calling a software product defective if it:

- Doesn't do something that the publisher's advertisements, manual, or product packaging said that it would

- Doesn't work the way the publisher said it would

- Crashes

- Erases, loses, or introduces errors into your data

- Makes calculation errors

- Prints reports with errors

- Gives unarguably bad advice (if it is an advice-giving program)

- Provides information that was erroneous at the time the program was published (if it is an information-giving program)

- Causes any type of damage to your equipment or any type of physical injury to you

- Misbehaves in some other way that no reasonable publisher would intend

In any of these cases, write down what the program did or did not do. Be specific. Write down page numbers from the manual, if the program doesn't do what the manual says. Keep the bad printouts. Save copies of the bad files and write down what you did, and how you know that the program (not you) made the errors. If you won't have all that information, write down what you do know and save it. If you continue to work with the program, begin to pay attention to other details the next time you have a problem. Write them down.

Incompatibility

If the publisher said the program would work with your printer (sound card, scanner, whatever), and it doesn't, you have an obvious defect. But, if the publisher's claims were unclear, here are some guidelines:

- The product is unsatisfactory if it doesn't work with your computer and the devices connected to it. Ask for a refund right away.

- A program probably won't be considered defective if it was obviously written before your printer was developed, or if the publisher said that the program wouldn't work with your printer, or if you're one of only six people in the world who owns a printer like this.

- The problem with your device might have nothing to do with the program. Some hardware manufacturers (including well-known ones) are surprisingly inept at writing drivers, the small programs that tell the computer how to work with the hardware. You might need an updated driver, not a fix to your program.

- If your printer is a popular model, it works with all of your other programs, and the program is current, it's fair to expect the program to work with it.

Check the popularity of your device by looking in magazines or by asking about it at computer or software stores. Many stores subscribe to a magazine called *Computer Reseller News*, which lists the best-selling printers, modems, and other devices. You also can find information like this on the Internet. (Go to several magazines' Web sites.)

Hard to Use or Badly Documented

Even if the program doesn't obviously make mistakes, it may still be worthless. If you knew how the program worked when you bought it, and it works just like you thought it would, it cannot be called defective even if it is outrageously hard to use.

A program is not necessarily defective just because you don't like it. People have strongly differing opinions about design. Many design limitations are left in a program because the development team thinks they are appropriate.

That said, some program designs are obviously unreasonable. For example, no program should have traps that lead the typical person into making frequent mistakes and wasting a lot of time. Furthermore, many other classic design mistakes would not be made by a reasonably careful and skilled development team. Lawsuits have been won because a software product was too hard to use (for example, *Louisiana AFL-CIO v. Lanier Business Products,* 1986), but the law on this is not well developed.

If you can't use the program because its documentation is worthless (not full of errors, but poorly written or containing few useful details), then the product is defective. Be aware that publishers may be surprised if you say that you want to return the product because its documentation is so bad.

If the program's design seems outrageously bad to you, then you should certainly insist on a refund. As with all complaint issues, it will help to have specific examples in your notes so that you can give them to the technician:

- If you claim the manual is bad, point to terms/information missing from the index. Point to sections of the book that no normal human could understand. Point to errors in the book; write down page numbers.

- If the program is bad, write down examples of the types of mistakes that you make. How often do you make them? What is it about the program that makes these mistakes likely? If the program is wasting your time, describe how complicated some of the tasks are. If the program works inconsistently (you have to do similar things in different ways, which is confusing), write down the inconsistencies. If the error messages are insulting or information-less, write them down. Make your complaint specific.

Action Plan
If the program's faults haven't cost you a lot and you'd be happy with a bug-fix or a refund, you can skip Chapter 4, "What Should You Ask For," and contact the publisher now. But, we suggest that you read Chapter 5, "Making the Call," before doing so.

If you do call the publisher and aren't satisfied with the result, we suggest that you go back to Chapter 4 and then read Chapter 5 before calling again.

Knowing What to Ask For

Chapter Map
This Is Our Most Important Chapter
When you call or write a publisher to complain, you are entering into a negotiation. If you didn't pay a lot for the program, and the program hasn't caused you much harm or loss, then the negotiation should be easy. (It might not be, but it should be.)

If the program is defective, and its failure cost you a fair bit of time or money, then negotiating with the publisher will be more challenging. Several publishers train their customer service staff to believe that you have, at most, a right to a refund or a bug fix if the program is defective. If the publisher wants to discourage refunds and has no fix for the bug you're complaining about, you might be treated shabbily. In either case, you should think through what you want and what you think would be fair.

This chapter will help you decide what is fair to ask of the publisher and how to explain your position to the publisher's staff. We operate from the belief that in most business negotiations, if you have solid information and a reasonable argument, and if you can keep emotions under control, then you can make a lot of progress.

Overview

This chapter walks you through a seven-step process of analysis to help you decide what to ask for when a product is defective. The steps are detailed but not complicated. The examples and lists of expenses and losses will help you avoid underestimating actual losses from a defective product.

In any negotiation, it helps to have the continuing advice from a friend or colleague. If you expect a hard time, or if you've already called the publisher and you got a hard time, this is a good chapter to work through with a friend.

Further Reading

We highly recommend James Freund's book, *Smart Negotiating* (Freund, 1992).

We also recommend *Getting to Yes* (Fisher, Ury, and Patton, 1991). This is a solid, classic work, and you will find it especially helpful if

- You are an important customer, and the publisher will want to keep your business, or

- The publisher's staff seem cooperative, but you're finding it hard to reach an agreement or to understand each other's point of view.

Imagine you bought a program to back up your hard disk. When you used it, the program erased your disk instead of backing it up. Oops. You lost hundreds of important documents and had to spend days reloading and reconfiguring your programs and operating system.

When you complained, the publisher said, "We guarantee your satisfaction. Here is a complete refund, $100."

Hmmm. Complete refund. Would you be satisfied? We wouldn't, if that happened to us.

Tip
When you call or write the publisher about problems with the program, you are not just complaining. You are negotiating.

When you complain to a publisher, ask for a result that will leave you satisfied. What does that mean? Well, you probably want the following:

1. A genuine solution to the problem, like a refund, a bug fix, or advice from the publisher on how to use the program more effectively. More extreme cases might call for something extra, like paying a technician to reload and reconfigure all your software.

2. To come out of this negotiation feeling reasonably good (or, at least, not steaming mad) about the process and the result.

3. To spend as little time complaining and negotiating as possible.

Customers are encouraged too often to play the role of helpless victims, begging for table scraps. That's not our approach. We think you have a perfectly good negotiating position, because you spent good money on an unsatisfactory program. You have rights, and you have some power to hurt the publisher. Bargain from your strength.

When you call as a dissatisfied customer, many (most, we suspect) software publishers realize that they are negotiating with you. Most publishers' customer service managers have the authority to be flexible in negotiating with you. The manager will be limited by a budget, but there are many different things that he can do for you within that budget. If he believes it's necessary to go beyond the budget to treat you fairly, he can take your case to more senior management, to the publisher's lawyer, to the marketing department, or (for a bug fix) to the product development department. Of course, if the manager won't do this for you, you can always contact these people yourself.

What should you ask for during your negotiations? This chapter presents seven questions to help you develop and explain your answer. These are our questions:

1. **Is the product at fault, or do you just not like it?**   If the program is defective, or if you were misled about its capabilities or compatibility, you have a strong argument for recovering everything the program has cost you. On the other hand, if the program is merely unsatisfactory, you should probably ask only for a refund.

   For most of this chapter, we assume the product is at fault.

2. **Are you in a simple situation?**   You are in a simple situation if the program was inexpensive and didn't cause much damage. You should be able to deal with the publisher quickly, without having to bother with the rest of this chapter.

3. **What has the product really cost you?**   The actual cost of a defective program can be much higher than the price of the program itself. To determine this amount, list everything that the program has cost you, including nonmonetary losses like lost time.

4. **What would it take to satisfy you?**   What would the publisher have to do to make you feel better? Think about this, without worrying (yet) about whether you're being reasonable.

5. **What do you think is fair and reasonable?**   If you are unreasonable, you probably will be treated as an unreasonable person. You might get nothing. How do you decide if what you want to ask for is fair?

6. **What will the publisher consider reasonable?**   You don't have to agree with the publisher, but understanding its position will help you negotiate.

7. **How can you make the publisher understand and sympathize with your position?**   You probably want more than the publisher wants to give you. Half the challenge in many negotiations is getting the other person to

see the world through your eyes or to otherwise understand that your requests are not unreasonable, even if they might be unusual.

1. IS THE PRODUCT AT FAULT, OR DO YOU JUST NOT LIKE IT?

We raised this question in Chapter 3, "Preparing to Make the Call," and suggested ways to decide whether the product is at fault. Here, our question is, what should you do about it?

We regard a program as defective if it fails to provide the benefits promised by the publisher or if it imposes unnecessary costs on you when you try to use it for its intended purpose. For example, software errors make the product defective if they cause you to waste your time or lose your work or other data. Also, the program is defective if it doesn't live up to the claims made in the manual or the advertisements.

Many publishers will argue that a program is not defective if it is merely awkwardly designed or hard to use. Courts will probably agree with them. However, you can argue that a program is defective if it doesn't live up to a publisher's *specific* promises about the program's performance or ease of use. For example, imagine a program that is advertised to make you twice as efficient at balancing your checkbook. But, the program is so badly designed that it slows you down. You have not received the promised benefit (time savings), so that program is defective.

If you think that the program's design is unacceptable, treat this as a defect. Feel free to complain about it, to ask for a refund, and to write bad magazine reviews about the product. But, don't expect to win a court case if your only gripe about the program is that you just don't like it.

What Are Your Rights When the Product Is Not Defective?

If you simply don't like the program, you don't have a right to much support unless it came with a *satisfaction guarantee*, a *warranty*, or a *service contract*. Let's define those terms:

Satisfaction guaranteed.   You have a right to a refund if you don't like the guaranteed product.[1] The right may be limited to 30 or 60 days, but if so, the advertisement or the package must say so clearly. You don't have the right to recover additional money, such as shipping costs, unless the company has granted you that right.

---

[1]Code of Federal Regulations, Title 16, Volume 1, Section 239.3 (1998).

Warranty and service contract.   Printed warranties often provide some technical support to help you with defects, answer questions, or to suggest better ways to use the product. A *service contract* gives you these rights for a longer period than the original warranty. In either case, if you're having trouble with the program, call for help. You might get an updated program or good advice. Demand a refund if they don't deliver adequate support.

Don't be afraid to ask for advice or an upgrade if the program is unpleasant to use. If the program is weakly featured or poorly designed, you still have negotiating leverage:

- If the publisher deals with your complaints, it keeps you as a customer, probably increasing your long-term loyalty.
- If the publisher fails to satisfy you, you can retaliate by complaining. You can always publish your comments on the Internet, in magazines, or in other media.

But do understand that if the product is not legally defective, and yet the company spends significant effort or money to help you, it is giving you more than the minimum that the law would require.

> **Note**
> *For the rest of this chapter, we will assume that the product is at fault.*

2. ARE YOU IN A SIMPLE SITUATION?

If the program's defects haven't yet cost you much time or money, you don't have to spend time figuring out how much you have lost. Your decision is whether to return the product or keep it. In either case, contact the publisher and make your requests. If you state your position clearly, there's a good chance that the publisher will take care of you.

> **Note**
> *If the problem was misrepresentation, we urge you to file a complaint with the Federal Trade Commission and with the Attorney General of the publisher's home state. This is for enforcement purposes, not necessarily to solve your particular problem. If enough people complain, agencies will realize the problem is widespread and will prosecute the publisher. Prosecution is an excellent deterrent to fraud. We provide a sample complaint letter in Chapter 6, "Consumer Protection Agencies."*

Returning the Program

If you want to return the program, we suggest that you ask the publisher for the following:

- A full refund of the price of the program.

- A refund for the extended service contract for the program, if you bought one from the publisher.

- A refund for any training that you bought from the publisher. Getting this refund should be easy if you've paid but haven't yet taken the training. If you have taken the training, you could use the argument that you deserve a refund anyway because the training is worthless, since the program is worthless.

- Reimbursement for your incidental expenses, such as the cost of your phone calls to the publisher, charges from the publisher for the calls you made to report the program's bugs, the shipping cost of returning the program to the publisher, and the like. We discuss incidental expenses in more detail shortly, in the section, "What Has This Product Really Cost You?"

Keeping the Program

If you want to keep the program, we suggest that you ask the publisher for the following:

A free upgrade to a "fixed" version of the program.   If such a release isn't available yet, ask, at a minimum, for a free upgrade to the next major version of the program.

A work-around.   That is, help from the publisher's technicians on how to do what you are trying to do, without running into this bug.

Extension of your warranty.   Some publishers give you 30 days of free technical support, starting from your first phone call. If this is your first call, and you are calling about a defect, ask the technician to reset the clock so that you'll get 30 days support after your next call.

Toll-free technical support.   This support should be offered for the next 90 days, 6 months, or a year.

Direct access to technical support.   If the publisher leaves you on hold for long times, ask for a direct-dial number, so you can skip the hold queue. If the publisher's staff are unevenly trained, you ask for the name and direct number of a senior staff member.

Incidental expenses.   Consider asking for reimbursement for your incidental expenses, such as the cost of your phone calls to the publisher and the money the publisher charged you for the calls you made to report the program's bugs. But, be fair: You might choose not to ask for these if the publisher grants you extended technical support.

The Program Doesn't Work with Your Equipment

If the only problem is that the program doesn't work with your equipment, the software publisher might not be able to help you. We talk about this problem in more detail in Chapter 5, "Making the Call," in the section "Calling About an Incompatible Device," but for our discussion here, consider asking for the following:

A driver.   For your printer, video card (and so on), or a patch (bug fix sent to you at no charge) to the program that will make the program work correctly with your equipment

A refund.   If the driver or patch didn't solve the problem. If you have good reason to expect the program to work with your equipment, and it doesn't, treat this just like a refund for defective software. You can expect the program to work with your equipment if the publisher's printed material (advertising, box copy, specifications in the manual, and so on) tells you that the program will work with your device. This includes statements about classes of devices. For example, if the box says, "Works with all LaserJet-compatible printers," and you have a LaserJet 6, your machine is covered. If the publisher says, "Works with all Windows-compatible printers," and your printer works with your other Windows programs (but not this one), you're covered.

Ask for:

- The refund (for the program, extended tech support, and possibly training).

- Reimbursement for incidental expenses, including the cost of all those other phone calls you made at the suggestion of the software publisher's technicians.

- A refund if you choose not to update your system with a new (and unknown) driver. In this case, the publisher is not at fault. The publisher offered you a reasonable way to fix the problem, and you chose not to pursue it. Your request for a refund in this situation is similar to the request you would make if you just didn't like the program. That said, we think that a customer-sensitive publisher will give you a refund, but realize that it doesn't have to, and you are not legally entitled to additional compensation, such as reimbursement for incidental expenses.

Example: Microsoft Office Fix

One of us bought a copy of Microsoft Office a few years ago. Here was his experience with Support:

Like all software, Office had some bugs. I was largely satisfied with the product, but a few of its bugs were quite annoying.

A year after I bought the program, I heard that a new bug-fix upgrade version had been released. A bug-fix upgrade has no (or few) new features. These upgrades are sometimes sold but for less than the cost of a major new version. After using the program for a year, I was well outside of any warranty period. In my opinion, I had no legally enforceable right to a new version, free support, additional damages, or anything else. But, I wanted the upgrade to fix those bugs. Because I knew what I wanted, and because I knew that I was willing to pay a reasonable amount for it, I didn't spend any additional time trying to get information about the bugs or troubleshooting my hardware. I just wrote down my product license number and called their Technical Support department.

I told the technician that I had Office; I gave her my license number; and I said that I'd heard there was a maintenance release. I said that I had some bugs, and I really wanted the release. Then I asked, "How much is it?"

She wanted more information about the bugs. I said some relatively vague stuff: one program had crashed a few times, and there had been other problems. I said, "Look, I'm basically happy with the program, but it has screwed up badly a few times and there have been a lot of more minor problems. I'd feel a lot better with an update. If the price is fair, I'm willing to pay for it. What can you do for me?" Because I knew exactly what I wanted, we didn't have to waste any time trying to troubleshoot my problem. Furthermore, because I had offered to pay, the technician knew that I wasn't trying to get something for nothing.

She then offered to ship me the upgrade—about 25 floppy disks—for the cost of shipping and handling, $9.95. I said, "Yes, here's my credit card. Thank you very much." The whole call took about five minutes, and I got exactly what I wanted and paid about $15–30 less than I expected.

If you know what you want, and you treat the technician in a fair and respectful way, she might well try to give you more than the bare minimum that you are entitled to by law (or by the usual policies of the publisher). The benefit to the publisher is that good service builds your loyalty as a regular, satisfied customer.

3. WHAT HAS THE PRODUCT REALLY COST YOU?

The program's price might be only a tiny portion of the amount that you lose because of the program's defects. Think of all the time and money you wasted trying to get the program to work or trying to recover data that the program lost or corrupted. Add in the consequences if, for example, the program causes you to under-report your taxable income or underestimate your expenses when you bid on a contract, or ruins your child's Christmas.

In this section, we want you to make a list of all the losses and expenses caused by the program. We can't list all of the possibilities (we don't know them all). Instead, we give you some categories and examples to stimulate your thinking.

You probably can't get repayment for all these expenses from the publisher. That's not the point of this section. Here, we just want to help you figure out what this program has really cost you.

> **Note**
> *We list many types of expenses. You probably suffered only a few of these. Don't expect to find an example of each and don't list more expenses than you actually suffered.*

Money Spent on the Program

Along with paying the purchase price of the program, you might have spent other money to obtain the program or to use it. Here are some of the common expenses:

- Purchase price of the program, including the sales tax.

- Shipping and handling charges you paid to get the program by mail.

- Cost of a contract for extended service and support from the publisher.

- Cost of additional training from the publisher. This training might include an optional video or a course offered live, via the Internet, or by mail.

- Cost of support or training from someone other than the publisher.

- Cost of books or magazines that you bought to help you figure out how to use the program.

- Cost of equipment or additional software you purchased to upgrade your computer to work with the program. This means equipment and software that you would not have otherwise bought and that you don't need if you give back the program. Don't include equipment or software that you would have bought anyway or that you find useful for other purposes.

Purchases Based on a Technician's Advice

Sometimes people call a publisher to report a problem and are told to buy another product to get full use of the program. If this happened to you, and you bought what the publisher's technician suggested, you should list this money separately from the other money you spent on the program. The difference is that this is money that you spent at the publisher's suggestion.

As we said previously, don't include equipment or software that you would have bought anyway or that you now find valuable for other purposes. If you're not sure whether to include it, ask this: If you give back the program, do you want to get rid of the other equipment? Do you want to make the publisher buy the equipment from you for the price you paid for it? If so, include the equipment in your list.

Here are some common types of equipment:

- New mouse, new printer, new cartridge (memory, programs, typefaces) for your printer, new monitor, additional hard disk, more memory, new serial port or serial communications card, or even a new motherboard or whole new computer.

- New version of the operating system.

- New device driver (printer driver, mouse driver, etc.).

- Books or courses to help you figure out how to use the program.

Incidental Expenses

The legal definition of incidental damages appears in Section 2-715 (1) of the Uniform Commercial Code:

> *Incidental damages resulting from seller's breach include expenses reasonably incurred in inspection, receipt, transportation and care and custody of goods rightfully rejected, any commercially reasonable charges, expenses or commissions in connection with effecting cover and any other reasonable expense incident to the delay or other breach.*

In other words, these are the out-of-pocket expenses that result from having to deal with something that is defective. They are not the losses caused by the program's particular defects. (Those are consequential losses.) Here are some examples of incidental expenses:

- Shipping and handling costs of sending the program back.

- Cost of phone calls to the publisher asking for help.

- Money the publisher charged for the calls you made to report the program's bugs. (Some publishers charge as much as $150 per "incident" or up to $5 per minute. $35 per incident or $1.50 to $3 per minute are more common charges for consumer software. Charges by the minute can add up.)

- Cost of your phone calls to the manufacturers of your computer and peripherals, asking for updated drivers or for information about what might be wrong with your program.

- Cost of on-line charges, connecting to the Net or to the publisher's bulletin board to try to find out whether the problems you're having are due to the program and what to do about them.

- Cost of diagnostic software, if you must run extended diagnostics to prove to the publisher's technical staff that this is the program's problem and not your computer's.

- Cost of a technical consultant that you hired to evaluate whether the program was at fault, your equipment was at fault, or your understanding or use of the program was at fault. This doesn't include time the technician spends training you to use the program, just time spent evaluating the defectiveness of the program.

- Mileage racked up shopping for a replacement program. Some people live 100 miles away from the nearest software store. If you had to drive a long way just to take the program back and get a replacement, list that expense here.

- Cost of parking your car when you drove back to the store to return the product.

- Cost of this book, if you bought it to figure out how to deal with the publisher after getting a run-around.

- Any special expenses associated with finding a replacement for this program.

Consequential Losses

The definition of consequential damages appears in Section 2-715 (2) of the Uniform Commercial Code:

Consequential damages resulting from the seller's breach include:

(a) any loss resulting from general or particular requirements and needs of which the seller at the time of contracting had reason to know and which could not reasonably be prevented by cover or otherwise; and

(b) injury to person or property proximately resulting from any breach of warranty.

In other words, it includes any losses caused by the failure of the program. In court, you would have to prove that your loss was foreseeable (the seller had reason to know that this type of loss was possible). We will ignore the foreseeability issue here. List all of your consequential losses. Whether or not the law will allow you to recover them in a lawsuit is a different issue. When you write the publisher, you'll want to list all the losses, to help the publisher understand just how seriously you've been damaged by this defective program.

Here are some examples of consequential losses:

Lost data.   There are two importantly different classes of loss.

- *The program lost its own data.*   The program erased or corrupted data that you used the program to enter or collect.

- *The program lost other data.*   The program erased or corrupted data that you bought separately from this program or that you collected or entered using a different program. An extreme example is the program that corrupts your hard disk, trashing many files from other programs. Another example is the database program that imports data from another program's files but unexpectedly writes back to those original files and corrupts them. This is property damage (see Kaner, Falk, and Nguyen, 1993, Chapter 14). You have a particularly strong argument for reimbursement in this situation, because your lawsuit (if you ever brought one) would probably be for negligent destruction of property as well as for breach of contract.

Lost wages.   You lost several days' work or were fired or suspended because of errors, delays, or lost sales caused by this program's bugs.

Lost income or lost profits.   This is a common claim in breach of contract suits. Sometimes courts award this claim; often they don't. The more certain it is that you would have earned the money, and the more precisely you can quantify the amount of money you lost, the more likely a court (and, therefore, the more likely the publisher's lawyer) will be to award you consequential damages for lost income or lost profit. Here is a framework that might help you characterize your losses:

- *Interfered with preparations.*   For example, the program failure prevented you from finishing a business proposal, from conducting research, or from preparing to make a sales call. As a result, you lost the possibility of this sale.

- *Prevented delivery of a proposal.*   For example, you finished writing a sales proposal, but your defective fax software prevented you from delivering it. Or, a crisis caused by the program kept you at the computer and made you miss a sales call. As a result, you lost the sale.

- *Prevented you from meeting a commitment.*   You promised to get a task done by a certain time, but the program's bugs stopped you from finishing. You might have lost work or have been forced to attend to the consequences of the bug and, therefore, been unavoidably distracted from doing the promised work. As a result, you lost some or all of the income from the sale.

- *Prevented you from delivering completed work.*   You promised to do some work by a specified time, and you completed your task. The program's error prevented you from delivering the work on time. Perhaps the fax or modem software failed, or the program erased your work. As a result, you lost some or all of the income from this work or suffered some other negative consequences.

- *Cost you hourly-rated earnings.*   For example, the bug cost you time that you would otherwise have been paid for and you were not able to make up that time later. Or, suppose that you rent access to your computer to others, and the bug tied up your computer, costing you rental income.

- *Cost you business that depends on the availability of your computer.*   For example, suppose that people dial into your computer and make purchases. You know from your business records that you normally would have made $5,000 during the period that your computer was down.

Reimbursement for liability to a third party.   Someone sues you for something that was caused by the program's defect. For example, a bug in the program blocked you from meeting a contracted-for commitment, and so you were sued, and you lost. Or, the bug caused you to give someone bad advice, and he sued you. You want to recover what you paid to the victim, plus your attorney's fees for defending the suit, plus any court costs and other reasonable costs associated with the lawsuit.

Lost goodwill.   The program's failures caused you to turn in your work late, to turn in substandard work, or to breach a contract. As a result, your professional reputation suffered.

Compensation for the effects of bad advice or information that you received from the program.   Here are some examples:

- *Bugs in your tax-preparation software caused you to under-report income or miscalculate your tax liability.* As a result, you paid tax penalties or fines or had to pay someone to help you defend yourself in a tax audit.

- *You bought a program that promised to provide professional-quality legal services.* Its promotional materials said that you could fire your lawyer and use the software instead. You used it to create a contract, a will, or a lease, but what it created was inadequate. As a result, you faced legal fees, court costs, and lost money on the contract.

- *A mapping program promised to provide directions to business travelers.* It promised safe routes through all major cities. Unfortunately, the program used old maps and steered you through a neighborhood that was safe 20 years ago but is now very dangerous at night. Your car was hijacked, and you were beaten up when you drove through this neighborhood.

Attorney fees and legal expenses.   It costs money to talk to an attorney about a program's defects, and it costs more money to sue the publisher.

Consulting and other recovery expenses.   Examples:

- You hired a consultant to analyze the program and develop workarounds for you.

- You hired a technician to recover your data or restore your hard disk.

- You hired a data-entry clerk to reenter all your data.

Personal injuries or property damage.   We've already mentioned that it is property damage if the program erases your hard disk or data that is unrelated to the program. In addition, some programs can damage devices (such as monitors, printers, and video cards). Consumer software isn't likely to injure you, but if it does result in harm to you, in any way, take thorough notes about what happened and list every expense associated with the injury.

Other miscellaneous expenses.   Examples:

- *Cost of renting another computer* while your machine was being fixed or diagnosed.

- *Cost of connect time wasted* because the program corrupted data transmissions.

- *Interest:* Whether the publisher owes you a $100 refund or $1,000,000 in damages, if it delays paying you, you are entitled to interest. For amounts that are readily and uncontroversially calculated (such as the amount that would be due if there was a full refund), you can ask for prejudgment interest. This is calculated from the moment it came due (for example, from the first time you demanded a refund). For amounts that weren't finally determined until trial or the signing of a settlement agreement, ask for postjudgment interest.

Wasted Time

A court probably won't order the publisher to pay you for the time that you wasted dealing with the defective program. But, it is still valuable to know the amount of time involved and what you spent it on. Use this information during your negotiation with the publisher, to help the publisher understand how much the program has really cost you. You can also use this time record as an indication, for the publisher and the court, of how hard you tried to get the program to work.

Here are some of the ways that you might lose time with a defective program:

- Time you spend trying to troubleshoot the computer and the program.

- Time you spend on the phone with the publisher's staff, consultants, or other people.

- Time you spend writing letters to the publisher and reading responses.

- Time you spend online with the publisher's support staff, or reading the troubleshooting messages on the publisher's bulletin board, or reading discussions of problems like yours on newsgroups or mailing lists, or searching the Net for sites that can provide you with support.

- Time you spend reading books or magazines to try to figure out the problem.

- Time you spend explaining the problem to your boss, your clients, or other people who didn't get work from you on time because of the program's bugs.

- Time you spend reentering or recovering data.

- Time you spend downloading and applying patches (sometimes called "service packs") that didn't help.

- Time you spend reloading the software onto the hard disk.

- Time deliberately wasted by the publisher's technicians when they give you a run-around. For example:

    - The technician knew that your problem is due to a bug in the product but told you that the problem was with your hardware.

    - The technician demanded configuration information about your computer, even when he knew that your problem is generic, not dependent on configuration details. You had to hang up and then call back with (completely irrelevant) model numbers, ROM addresses, ROM dates, and other hard-to-find technical data.

- The technician wouldn't look up your name in a registration data-base but instead demanded a letter with your manual title page or that you call back from home with your registration information.

- The technician told you to read the fine manual, even though he knew that the issue at hand is not well explained there.

- The technician blamed you for the program's failure, because you hadn't followed the instructions in the addendum sheet to the README file that corrected the manual supplement's corrections to the manual. That page told you that you shouldn't do what you did. So (he says) why are you calling to complain?

- The technician denied that the publisher had ever advertised that the program could do X (even though you have the ad in hand).

- The technician told you that you were trying to use the program in an unreasonable way, even though the manual described ex-actly the task that you were trying to do, and you were trying to follow its instructions.

- The technicians required you to call back every few months to find out whether an upgrade had been published. They wouldn't take your name and put it on a follow-up list.

Aggravation and Other Personal Costs

Sometimes, the most compelling costs of a bad program are the personal ones. These can be persuasive. If you explain them, the publisher will understand why you're upset. Here are some examples:

- You bought your daughter the program as her Christmas present. It didn't work. She thought that the program's misbehavior was her fault, and she cried. You spent more than half of Christmas Day trying to reconfigure her computer but never got it to work.

- You called the publisher for support and were handled incompetently. You're upset because the staff wasted a lot of your time without coming close to solving your problem.

- You were making an important presentation when your slideshow program crashed. Your presentation failed, but more importantly, you were humiliated.

- The program has failed several times. Workarounds or bug-fix versions from the publisher have failed, too. You no longer trust the program, and you are very frustrated.

Other aggravation costs are more dangerous because they are more likely to lead you into a fight with the publisher's staff. Be aware of your feelings, because they can get in the way of your reaching a satisfactory agreement with the publisher. Here are some examples:

- You called the publisher for support and were handled rudely and without integrity. The technician lied to you, cursed at you, hung up on you, or did something else that left you furious with the company.
- The program is so full of bugs, and the manual is so bad, that you are furious with the publisher for doing such an unprofessional job.
- Your boss insisted that you use this program instead of another one that you think is much, much better. You are angry with the publisher and your boss for sticking you with this worthless program.

Finally, here are examples of complaints that will strike the publisher as having come from Mars:

- You spent so much time trying to troubleshoot the program that you had to hire a temporary housekeeper to take over your normal housecleaning chores.
- You were so tied up with asking yourself how you were going to cope with the program's bugs that you lost concentration while driving and had a car accident.
- You want the publisher to pay for all your stress medication, because the program's failures stressed you out.
- You were so stressed out that you had to go to Hawaii for a week to recover.

Example: A Database Program

Imagine buying a sophisticated database program and finding out that you can't make it do what you want. What do you expect from the publisher? A refund? Tips? How about having the publisher create your database application for you? Here's how one customer got just that from one of us when we were serving as managers for software publishers:

The database had originally been designed to appeal to sophisticated customers who understood database design and development and who appreciated high-powered tools. Customers could use this database management system to create applications that would save and report on lots of data-applications to do accounting, inventory management, or to run a video store. For reasons that we can't explain here, the publisher decided to sell this product to a mass-market audience. These customers might use a database to run a very small business, set up records for a school library, or schedule their little league. Not surprisingly, few of these mass-market customers were hotshot database application developers. Some of them found this program very difficult to use.

If a customer couldn't make the program work, we'd sometimes offer them a refund—it was too expensive to support people who didn't understand how to design a database. But, one customer said he didn't want a refund. He wanted more support. He wanted to get this program working. We weren't enthusiastic about this, because he had already taken a lot of our time, much more than any business would want to spend to support a product sold at this price. Normally, we would have said, "Take the refund or don't, but leave us alone."

This customer protested in a very effective way. He explained to us how much work he had put into learning and working with the database, how many times he had reassured his boss that he could eventually get the database working, and how much trouble he'd have starting over with another product. We understood why a refund wouldn't help him.

Still, we couldn't afford to spend more hours on the phone, teaching him how to use the program. We offered a different result. If he could tell us what he was trying to do and send us his work so far, we would finish his program and send him back a working application. He agreed; we did it; and we all lived happily ever after (he never called us again).

We only did this for a handful of people. Each of them was courteous enough that we could work with them, and they were so clear in explaining what this program had cost them that we understood why they needed extra help.

4. WHAT WOULD IT TAKE TO SATISFY YOU?

Up to this point, we've looked at what the program has cost you. What have you lost? For the rest of this chapter, we focus on what the publisher can (and should) do to make it better. Publishers have many ways to help you when you have problems with their products. Giving you money is only one approach. You can help a publisher to be creative and to give you much better service, by thinking carefully about the different types of things that the publisher can do to deal with your problem.

In this section, we ask: What would the publisher have to do to make you feel better about having purchased the program? What does the publisher have to do to make you feel that you've been treated fairly? Think about what that would take, without worrying (yet) about whether you're being reasonable.

> **Note**
> *Take care of yourself. If the advertising was misleading, the program was obviously defective, and the customer service staff and management were rude, then you might be so fed up that you wouldn't be satisfied unless the publisher's president and customer service manager were sent to jail. In this case, realize that this publisher will never satisfy you, no matter how extensively you negotiate. If this is how you feel, then think about taking yourself out of the negotiations by filing a complaint with a consumer protection agency or offering to join a class action lawsuit. Or, if you haven't lost that much, you might just drop it. The aggravation might cost you more than it is worth.*

Here are examples of the types of remedies that you might want from the publisher. We'll consider the reasonability of these in the next section.

Incidental Expenses

You might want reimbursement for all out-of-pocket expenses that were directly caused by the defectiveness of the program. (See the definition of incidental expenses earlier in this chapter.)

Consequential Losses

You might want reimbursement for all consequential losses that were caused by the program. However, customers often want or expect more than the publisher would consider reasonable. (See the definition of consequential losses earlier in this chapter.)

Nonmonetary Remedies

Let's be creative. Rather than think about what the publisher would have to pay you to make up for your expenses, consider what the publisher could do for you. It is probably much easier for the publisher's customer service manager to give you some of her staff's time, some merchandise, or an extended service contract, than it is to get approval to give you money. Here are just a few of the possibilities. All of these are real—we know of cases in which publishers have done each of these things for customers:

- Help you get the program working:
    - The publisher's technician sends you instructions (by fax, mail, or e-mail) on how to fix or work around the problem.
    - The technician gives you step-by-step instructions over the phone, for fixing your configuration or the program or working

around the problem, staying with you for as long as necessary (even if it takes an hour or more).

- Two hours of consulting with the lead programmer, or the lead writer, or with someone else on the publisher's staff who has expert knowledge of the program.

- Upgrade or replace the program:

  - *Free (or discounted) upgrade to a bug-fix release or the next version of the product.* If there isn't a release available now, ask the technician to take your name and address, so that the publisher can send you an update when it's ready. You also want a letter that says you're entitled to the upgrade, so that there's no room for confusion a year from now, when the upgrade is published.

  - *Extended support, to go along with the free upgrade.* There's no point accepting a "free upgrade" if it doesn't work. Ask for 30 days, 3 months, or even a year of toll-free technical support.

  - *Free upgrade from the "Junior" version (typically $40–$100) to the "Pro" or full-featured ($100–$500) version of the same program.* Publishers who sell Junior and Pro versions of the same product want to sell you the Junior now and then upsell you the Pro version later. But, the publisher isn't allowed to cheat. If the ads promise that the Junior version has a certain feature that's important to you, but this feature only works properly in the Pro version, ask for an upgrade to the Pro version.

- Upgrade and give a token of appreciation or apology:

  - *Free upgrade that includes items from the publisher's product line.* For example, suppose that the publisher sells a suite of products which includes a word processor, spreadsheet, and presentation package. If you bought the word processor, and it was defective, maybe the publisher can make you happy by giving you a copy of the presentation program. This is inexpensive for the publisher, but might be very valuable to you.

  - *Free bug-fix plus a souvenir T-shirt or another program from the publisher's line of products.* Perhaps you bought a defective computer game. The publisher might be willing to fix your game and give you another one, to make up for your hassle and loss of enjoyment of the game. Similarly, a publisher who sold you the game through its catalog might be willing to give you something else out of the catalog.

  - *Why would you be happy with a souvenir?* Well, suppose you bought a computer game for your child for Christmas, and it didn't work. He is very disappointed. And, suppose the publisher is reputed to make "cool" games. Your child might be delighted to wear a T-shirt from that publisher to school. If you explain your child's disappointment to the publisher's technician in a way that captures her sympathy, then it might be easy to convince the technician to send your child a corporate souvenir that will make him feel happy about your gift and about the company that made it. Unfortunately, not all companies have souvenirs to give out, so this option might not be available to the technician.

- *Provide additional information or documentation on the product.* (Some of this material will be more important for you if you are a corporate purchaser, trying to support several users of the same product.)

- *Supplementary documentation.* This might include an updated version of the manual or a more complete manual that the publisher sells for an additional fee. The publisher might even be willing to send you a third-party manual (one written and sold by someone unconnected with the publisher) that has material particularly suited to your needs.

- *Technical support materials.* The publisher might sell a technical resource guide or provide a compilation of support notes to major customers or third-party support organizations. Or, the publisher might be willing to send you its collection of faxback materials (answer sheets that it will fax to customers) or how-to booklets that explain how to use the program more fully. Some publishers also sell (and so can give you) subscriptions to product newsletters that provide support information.

- *Diagnostic software, such as utilities that check your computer's configuration or validate the integrity of the program's database.* Publishers often develop this type of software for in-house use. There is no guarantee that it will be bug-free or easy to use, but it might be very useful.

- *Help you deal with the consequences of the program's defect.*

- *Do the task that you bought the program to do.* Suppose that you bought a desktop publishing program to create a newsletter, but can't, because of bugs. The publisher might fix the bugs, then create the newsletter's first issue for you, and then give you a template for creating later issues. Similarly, if you bought a database to create a sales tracking system but can't get the program to do what you want, the publisher might fix the bugs and then create and send you a custom-programmed tracking system.

- *Reenter your data.* If the program corrupted your data, the publisher might agree to have its staff reenter the data from your printout.

- *Pay a third party to fix your problem.* For example, the publisher might pay a third-party technician to recover data from your crashed hard disk.

- *Buy your computer, or your video card, printer, printer cable, or other peripheral device.* This is not as odd as it sounds. If the publisher is trying to develop programs that are compatible with as wide a range of machines as possible, then your equipment might be a useful addition to the publisher's test lab. If so, the publisher might offer to buy it. Alternatively, if the publisher's technical staff told you to buy certain equipment to become compatible with their product, and they were wrong (especially if they knew better), maybe they should buy your equipment if you have bought it and don't want it.

- *Send you a replacement modem, video card, or printer.* If the publisher also sells hardware, it might have a relatively inexpensive source of equipment that it knows is compatible with its program. The publisher isn't likely to send you a new modem if you bought a $25 program, but what if the publisher advertised that its $1,500 program was compatible with your modem? It might be cheaper for the publisher to change your configuration than to fix the program.

- *Send you a coupon for a significant discount on a replacement modem, video card, printer, or other device, to replace the device that is incompatible with the program.*

- *Write a letter of apology to your boss.* If you missed a deadline because the program erased your work, ask for a letter explaining that it wasn't your fault.

Example: Getting Satisfaction

Don't get too attached to a specific outcome that you think that you want. The support technician might be able to suggest something else that serves you even better.

One customer bought a computer game from a company where we worked. The game had levels, and the higher the level, the harder the game. If you "died" (lost the game), you had to start over and go through level after level until you got back to where you had been. The customer called, demanding hints on getting to a very high level. He had played for 30 hours solid and was afraid to go to sleep because he didn't want to have to start over. He needed to get to the end now. We told him that we couldn't give him this information, so he told us, using very colorful language, that if we didn't tell him how to finish the game, he'd throw his computer out the window!

Instead, we told him how to save the game, so that he could come back tomorrow and pick up where he left off. He said OK, slammed the phone, and (we hope) saved the game and went to sleep.

Retribution or Prosecution

If you are angry enough about the false advertisements, the obviously low quality of the program, and the rude support, then some money and a solution to your technical problems might not be enough. Of course, the publisher might not be willing to negotiate these things with you.

This is the last time (in this chapter) that we'll consider retribution or prosecution. Instead of just listing the possibilities, we provide some suggestions on how to achieve the results that you want.

> ## *Warning*
> *When you seek retribution or prosecution, your goal is to affect someone's career or their business relationships. Be careful how you do it, or you could wind up on the wrong end of a lawsuit. Adopt a reasonable, factual, patient tone in your letter. Don't scream, don't threaten, and don't demand (or even suggest) that anyone be fired. Stick to the facts. Say what your problem was and how you were treated. Say what dates you called and whom you talked to. Say what you were told and what was incorrect about the information you were given. If you're claiming that false statements were made over the phone, think about how to prove that those statements were made. You could have a friend call to complain about the same problem (and hear the same lies). Or, look for the lie on the publisher's Web site. Include copies of documents (such as letters or ads) if you have them. Don't exaggerate or embellish anything. Everyone will ignore your complaint (or someone will sue you) if they think that you are pursuing a personal grudge or if you are unreasonable or crazy. Let the facts of your complaint speak for themselves.*

Get an executive fired.   Good luck. You might achieve this indirectly, perhaps as a result of your convincing a law-enforcement agency to prosecute the company. Otherwise, you're going to need special circumstances to arrange this.

Get the marketing manager disciplined.   What is the most effective way to point out the carelessness or dishonesty of the person who wrote the false advertising copy or the false statement on the program's packaging? Try writing a complaint letter to the publisher's president or chief executive officer. Complain about the false advertising, not about the person who wrote it. (The publisher knows who wrote it.) Include a photocopy of the ad or package and explain in your letter exactly what is false. Send a copy to the head office of the store that sold you the program. Send a copy to the *Federal Trade Commission* (FTC) and to the Attorney General of the publisher's home state. In this case, tell the publisher about the agencies who received the complaint. We suggest elsewhere not to tell the publisher that you have complained to the

FTC. But here, your primary goal is to cause an uproar at the publisher's office. That purpose is served if someone at the publisher's office says in a meeting, "This is so bad, these people even complained to the FTC about this!" (See the sample letters in Chapter 6, "Consumer Protection Agencies," and the addresses of the consumer protection agencies at www.badsoftware.com). You may not learn what kind of trouble your letter caused, but it probably won't be ignored.

Get the lead programmer fired.   Don't waste your time. The technical staff are shielded from public complaints. If the program's bugs were that unacceptable to the publisher's staff, the programmer has already been fired.

Get the customer service manager disciplined.   Send a letter to the publisher's president or chief executive officer. If the customer service staff lied to you, send copies of your letter to the enforcement agencies (Federal Trade Commission, Attorney General, see Chapter 6). If they merely treated you badly, send copies of your letter to your local consumer mediation agency or the Better Business Bureau (see Chapter 6). Also send a copy of your letter to the president or buyer of the store where you bought the program.

Get the publisher to reconsider its relationship with a third-party support company.   It is possible that the terrible, rude, inaccurate technical support you experienced was actually coming from a third-party support group under contract to the publisher. Some third-party support groups are superb; others are less good. A group who treats customers rudely is not serving the publisher's best interests. Write a complaint letter to the publisher's president or chief executive officer.

5. WHAT DO *YOU* THINK IS FAIR AND REASONABLE?

If you want to be treated fairly, you have to be fair. You might get nothing if you are unreasonable. In this section, we address the question, "How do I decide what is reasonable?" Your conclusions might be different from the publisher's. Here are some of the factors to consider when evaluating your own position. We discuss the publisher's viewpoint in the next section.

Is the Program Defective?

If you're not sure whether the program is defective, reread the first sections of this chapter and, perhaps, Chapter 7, "Software Quality and the Law." If you're still puzzled, ask your friends for advice.

- If the program is not defective, why do you think you are entitled to anything? You might have some good reasons. For example:
  - The publisher made an unconditional satisfaction guarantee.
  - You purchased a service contract, for the promise that the pub-

lisher's staff would help you get past any difficulties posed by the product's design.

- If the product is not defective, you should think carefully before asking for anything beyond a refund. You might be entitled to more, but you should be able to clearly explain why.

- If the program *is* defective, then it is reasonable to assert your rights. You should certainly feel reasonable in asking the company to reimburse you for out-of-pocket expenses that were directly caused by the failure of the program. Larger consequential damages are more difficult to deal with.

Were You Partially at Fault?

If you suffered a significant loss, ask yourself whether it was partially your fault. For example, if you knew that the program sometimes corrupted files, and you kept using it, isn't it partially your fault that the program wiped out your most valuable records? Shouldn't you have stopped using the program instead of taking this risk?

Don't lose your perspective if you are partially at fault. If the program wiped out your hard disk, it's still the program's bug. Don't be intimidated by someone who makes you feel stupid (even if you did do something foolish).

However, if the loss was partially your fault, maybe you should split the loss with the publisher. You might not volunteer to do this at the start of your discussions, but you should expect and intend to settle on some middle ground.

What Is the Basis of Your Expectations?

The Service Contract

If you bought a contract for extra service or support, read your contract. You are entitled to whatever the contract promised.

If you suffered losses because the publisher failed to give you the support that it promised in the contract, quote the contract and explain the connection between the publisher's breach and your loss.

We want to point out one service-related scam. Some service providers sell different grades of service contracts. You can buy something like Level 1, Level 2, Level 3, or Level 4 service. The following definitions will illustrate the situation. (These are not based on any one company's terms and policies.)

Level 1.   This is the least expensive. Perhaps you are guaranteed that when you call with a problem and leave a message, a technician will call back within 48 hours and find a solution to your problem within two weeks.

Level 2.   You will reach a technician directly when you call. If you have to wait, you'll be on hold for not longer than five minutes. The technician normally will solve your problem within 24 hours. If this is not possible, a more senior technician will call you within 36 hours. Your problem will be solved within a week at least 90 percent of the time.

Level 3.   You will reach a technician directly when you call. If the technician can't solve your problem at once, then you will be immediately transferred to a more senior technician. If necessary, you will be transferred to a specialist or to one of the product development staff. Your problem will be resolved within 72 hours, 90 percent of the time.

Level 4.   You will reach the senior technician immediately and get even faster, better service.

If you buy Level 4 service, you might get Level 4 service. But, some service providers set their staffing levels on the assumption that you won't complain too loudly if you get something between Level 2 and Level 3. And, that's what you get, until you complain. (They may escalate your service level for a few months and then slowly bring it back down.) Similarly, Level 3 customers get Level 2 service, Level 2 customers get Level 1 service, and Level 1 customers get busy signals and heartburn.

If you've paid for premium service, keep notes on how well the company actually performs. If it has made a practice of underperforming, be ready to make this point clearly and in detail. Talk with some of the company's other customers, too. Maybe, you'll find out that the company is making a practice of cheating all of its customers.

If the program is defective and the consequences of its failure (such as erased data) would have been prevented if the service provider had lived up to the service contract, then it is reasonable to insist on reimbursement for the loss.

If you are being cheated on service, then you shouldn't have any illusions about the way this company will treat you during negotiations. Be polite (be very polite) but be firm. And, realize that you're probably going to have to take your case to a lawyer or to a law-enforcement agency.

Publisher's Advertising

A publisher that promises more should be held accountable for more. We aren't necessarily talking about legally enforceable promises. Some companies make statements that are just vague enough to be worthless in court but that are clearly intended to make you think that this publisher provides exceptional reliability or service.

High reliability.   If the publisher promised high reliability, and you believed it when you bought the product, then you aren't being unreasonable in demanding repayment for losses that resulted from bugs in the program.

Rigorous testing.   If the publisher advertises that the program has a seal of approval or has been subjected to extra-rigorous testing by an independent test lab, then you aren't being unreasonable in interpreting this as a promise of extra-high reliability.

"We stand behind it."   If the publisher promised to "stand behind" its product, you aren't being unreasonable in expecting the publisher to take responsibility for problems caused by the product.

"Satisfaction guaranteed."   If the publisher says "Satisfaction guaranteed," then you should read the fine print on the packaging or the advertisement. Normally "Satisfaction guaranteed" is a promise of a refund if you don't like the product. Unless the publisher says more than this, it is not a promise of additional help beyond a refund.

Exceptional support.   If the publisher enticed you to buy the program with claims of exceptional support, then you have every right to expect the publisher to give you good support, such as bug fixes, workarounds, supplementary documentation, and so on.

Quality versus quantity.   If the publisher's promises focus on the product's huge number of features, the publisher may be telling you that you are buying lots of buggy features: quantity, not quality. Your expectations for service and reliability should be lower.

Market Segment and Price

Suppose that you bought a word processing program. Programs like this are available in many different market segments. For example, in the $10.00 bargain-basement category, you shouldn't expect much support or sympathy from the publisher. You still have the right to get everything the publisher promised, but you will probably expect better reliability and support from a $5,000 program with a $1,000 per-year service contract.

But, don't be afraid to remind the publisher that $10 isn't a garbageware price to some people (including you, perhaps); it's just what they can afford. You have a right to everything the publisher promised, no matter how much the company charged for the product.

Industry or Type of Application

Base your reasonable expectations about the quality of the product on what it is supposed to do. For example:

- Telephone systems are so reliable in North America that you might have the same expectations about voice-messaging software.

- You should expect extremely high accuracy in a program designed to provide airplane pilots with maps and approach instructions for airfields.

- You should expect special attention to safety in a program designed to control your home's electrical systems.

- You should expect a disk backup program to safeguard the data on your disk (as opposed to corrupting your data while you're backing up the drive).

If the program fails in a way that violates your core expectations, you have a particularly strong argument for holding the publisher responsible for the consequences.

How You've Been Treated

If you've been treated shabbily so far, don't expect the publisher to negotiate with you in good faith in the future. But, if you've been courteous and reasonable so far, and if you continue to be, then the more unreasonably the publisher acts, the more reasonable it is for you to demand compensation.

Example: Expecting Excellent Service

If a company markets itself as an organization that provides great service, you should ask for great service.

A catalog company sold software and hardware, such as modems, printers, and mice. It wasn't the cheapest vendor on the market. This company competed on the basis of the quality of its customer service and its careful selection of products.

The hardware this company sold came with drivers, small programs that make the customer's computer work with the new hardware. Sometimes, the drivers were out of date or were incompatible with the customer's other programs or equipment. A lot of troubleshooting could be involved when setting up the hardware so that it didn't interfere with the customer's other equipment.

When customers had hardware problems, they either called the catalog company for a no-questions-asked refund, or they called the manufacturer for support. Customers who weren't served well by the manufacturer called the catalog company. The catalog staff worked hard to support these products. Sometimes, they'd spend an hour or two on the phone helping a customer configure a device. Or, they would call the manufacturer and ask for (or demand) a copy of the latest version of the driver, which the catalog company would send to customers for free. The staff insisted that manufacturers create new versions of some drivers. They told some manufacturers to improve their support center or the manufacturer's product would be dropped (as several products were) from the catalog.

The level of service the catalog company provided is beyond normal retailer or discount catalog service. But, if you are paying full retail price (or close to it) for software and hardware, the company should be doing something to earn the extra markup. In this case, the company provided better service. Perceptive customers asked for superior service, received more care, and got what they were paying for.

6. WHAT WILL THE PUBLISHER CONSIDER REASONABLE?

You don't have to agree with the publisher, but it will help you negotiate if you have insight into the publisher's analysis. Here are a few basic points to keep in mind:

Products versus money.   The customer service manager has more negotiating flexibility when you are bargaining for services or copies of the publisher's own products than when you are demanding money.

Lawsuits.   Threatening a lawsuit will probably take the negotiation out of the customer service manager's hands. This might work for you or against you. (See Chapter 7, "Software Quality and the Law," for additional discussion.)

Consumer protection law.   The customer service staff is probably clueless about consumer protection law. Even though the shrink-wrap warranty disclaimer that came with the product is probably invalid (see Chapter 7), the staff probably believes that it is enforceable and that anything that they do for you is a favor for which you should be grateful. You may have to develop a strategy for educating the customer service manager. (See Chapter 5, "Making the Call," for additional discussion.)

Few cases prosecuted.   As of June, 1998, law enforcement and consumer protection agencies have taken action against only a few software-related companies. Thus, few publishers' staffs have learned the hard way that the company is accountable for the claims it makes about its product and that post-sale misrepresentation by the customer service staff is as unlawful as pre-sale misrepresentation (See Chapter 7).

Publishers of mass-market software are used to requests for bug-fixes, upgrades, and refunds. The sharper ones have done their share of creative problem-solving. However, they are sensitive to freeloaders, people who won't take care of their own problems, and people who want them to take the blame for some other publisher's defects. Requests for reimbursement for incidental expenses are a bit unusual, but if you can back them up with receipts and clear and reasonable explanations, you'll often convince the publisher's customer service manager. Demands for reimbursement for consequential losses are more common, but these demands often come from people who are too angry to state their cases effectively. Some customer service managers take requests involving consequential losses seriously; they listen very carefully; and they try to come up with a solution that feels fair. Other customer service managers won't entertain a request involving consequential losses unless you are too powerful or too persistent to ignore. Most customer service managers are unwilling to give you anything that makes them feel that you are making a profit from your bad experience with their product.

The Publisher's Self Image

Companies have different beliefs about how they should treat their customers. What is reasonable to one company sounds ridiculous to another. Some companies take it as their personal responsibility to make sure that you are a satisfied customer. Others say that it's up to you to take care of yourself. Many companies don't expect to see you again. They don't care if you're satisfied. They just want to keep your money.

Company philosophy doesn't necessarily match market segment. Over your years of shopping, you've probably discovered high-service companies that sell budget products and some real jerks selling premium products. It's the same for software as it is for all the other types of products.

If you are dealing with a company that wants to satisfy you, explain your losses to them clearly. (Consider doing this in a letter, not over the phone. A long catalog of losses over the phone will make the listener impatient and defensive.)

- Explain the problem and why you consider it a defect of the program.
- Explain how that problem led to whatever consequences you are complaining about.
- Describe any troubles that you've had with the publisher's customer service technicians.

If you are asking for something unusual, a high-service company will make a real effort to listen to you, to understand the problem, and to evaluate what would be fair and reasonable. Keep your tone friendly and reasonable. This company wants to be your friend—don't blow it.

The Publisher's Image of You

When you talk to the publisher's customer service staff, they evaluate you. This evaluation may not be systematic, but they form an opinion about how reasonable you are and how seriously to take you. They commonly consider the following:

Do you have a genuine problem?   People do call with complaints that would have been solved if they had only read the manual. Other customers blame their own mistakes on the program. As noted in Chapter 2, "Introduction," publishers estimate that as few as 15-to-50 percent of customer calls are related to genuine defects.

We're not claiming for one second that most people who call don't have a legitimate problem. Publishers' statistics are biased because they come from the publisher's staff. Callers discounted by publishers would tell a different story. But, you must be ready to face the perception and expectation of the publisher's staff that your problem is not legitimate.

Does the publisher know of the problem?   The publisher's staff will take your claim more seriously if they have already discovered this problem and determined that it is in fact a bug in the code or an error (or lie) in the advertisements. Similarly, they will be more likely to believe your claim of bad consequences (such as an erased hard disk) if they have found the same error in the lab or if several people have already called with the same problem.

However, some executives instruct customer service staff to mislead complaining customers under such circumstances. They are afraid of exposing the publisher to litigation, bad publicity, or an excessive number of claims.

How much harm did the program cause?   The publisher will probably be more concerned and should be more apologetic, if the program causes serious problems. You also can expect the publisher to be less concerned if the program is merely annoying or inconvenient.

Customers sometimes exaggerate when they complain about products. Exaggerating claims complicates the process because then the technician has to figure out how much harm the program really caused. Related questions include:

Are you exaggerating?   Don't.

What can you prove?   Receipts, letters from witnesses, and the notes in your notebook are useful. We mentioned the notebook in Chapter 1, "Read This First," and Chapter 3, "Preparing to Make the Call," and we'll spend more time on it later in this chapter. Describe your problems with the program as you have them (same day). Write down the details of your conversations with the publisher's customer service staff, while you are on the phone. Put the date on every entry. Write down other information as you learn it.

Can you evoke public sympathy?   Newspapers love to print "dead puppy stories"—easy-to-understand stories that involve an innocent victim. If Grandma lost her savings because of a security defect in a program, or a bug erased your church's membership records, and the publisher wouldn't help, you might be able to get press coverage.

Did the publisher's program cause this harm?   The publisher won't want to take responsibility if your problem was actually caused by bugs in your printer manufacturer's printer drivers or in some other program.

Did you follow the publisher's directions?   Your complaint is very compelling if you were following the publisher's instructions exactly (for example, following the manual or the tutorial) when the program did something bad (such as erasing your hard disk or losing your data).

What is your history with the company?   Are you a long-standing customer? Have you bought many of the company's products? Should you be thought of as a valued customer?

What is your track record when calling for support?   Many publishers keep computerized records on calls for support. When you call with a complaint, the technician might summarize your call, under your name. Do you have a history of being unreasonable? Of being right? Do you call often or rarely?

Do you seem to be a freeloader?   Some people buy the product once and then expect free upgrades forever, plus many other favors or forms of compensation.

With some products, so-called freeloaders may be perfectly justified. If you paid for a product that has never worked, why shouldn't you expect the publisher to be willing to keep trying to fix it until it does work, without charging you an extra nickel?

In other cases, however, a caller will seem to be less angry or upset by a bug and more interested in getting a free upgrade or a refund (after long and full use of the program) or some other special deal. Consider the following questions:

How much use have you made of the product?   If you haven't had any significant benefit from the program (just bugs), the publisher will be more sympathetic than if you've been using it without incident for a year or two. Even if you are only requesting a refund, the publisher's staff will be skeptical if you've gained significant benefits from the program.

Are you courteous and likable?   Many of the most successful negotiators make a point of always being courteous and friendly. If the publisher's staff *want* to help you, they're more likely to help you. We're not telling you to act like a wimp. You can be courteous and firm; you can be friendly while insisting on your rights; you can correct someone's misstatements without calling them a liar.

Are you too trusting?   If you will believe whatever the publisher's technical staff tell you, some technicians will feel free to tell you a quick story and send you on your way. The more trusting you seem to be, the more likely you are to be sent back and forth between 2, 3, or 16 companies, all blaming each other for your problems. The more trusting you seem to be, the less likely any one of these companies will be to take you seriously when you say that a problem is due to their bug. They'll decide that you're blaming them only because some other publisher told you to blame them.

What is your level of technical sophistication and your understanding of your hardware?   Customer service staff are frustrated by people who don't understand computers and who don't know the components of their own machines. The less savvy you sound, the less credible your complaint. And, the easier you are to brush off, if you have a legitimate complaint that they don't want to deal with. On the other hand, if you make a point of sounding like a know-it-all, you risk stirring up resentment and competition rather than trust.

How persistent are you?   Many people with legitimate problems call once and then give up on getting support from the publisher. They don't have the time or the emotional stamina to put up with the skepticism, impatience, arrogance, and casual dishonesty[2] of many customer service staff. If the technician thinks you won't do business with the company again even if you are satisfied with the product, she might not try very hard to make sure that you are satisfied with the results of your call.

If you have a legitimate complaint, you should be persistent. However, some people with unreasonable complaints are incredibly persistent. The publisher has a policy for dealing with unreasonable people who make a nuisance of themselves. Some publishers pay them to get rid of them. Other publishers treat them rudely or find some other way to discourage them. If you're being treated rudely, it might be that the publisher's staff have misunderstood your situation. If so, take a step back during the phone call, apologize for your tone of voice, and then re-explain your problem in a way that the technician will (you hope) understand better.

How much power do you appear to have?   Power becomes the issue in many complaints. We talk about power, in terms of leverage, in the next section. In terms of the publisher's evaluation of you and your credibility, the question is whether you have the power to follow through on any warnings you've made.

Most people who threaten lawsuits will never follow through, so publishers may not take you seriously if you say you'll sue. If you want to begin a lawsuit, do it credibly by sending a *letter of demand*. (See Chapter 10, "Small Claims Court.") Don't say you'll sue—keep your options open. The demand letter is your first formal step in the process of setting up a lawsuit. The publisher will see you are already showing resolve to move forward and some ability to do so. Actions do speak louder than words.

Similarly, most people who threaten to report the publisher to the Attorney General don't follow through. Don't make threats like this. (They can sound like extortion.) Instead, send a letter to the authorities and let them send a copy to the publisher. Then, the publisher won't have any doubt that you're serious.

If you (or your company) buys the publisher's product in bulk, mention this when the technician gives you a run-around. Similarly, let her know if you

---

[2]What do we mean by "casual dishonesty?" If someone feels free to tell you untrue things ("we've never heard of that problem before") and they think that it is just a normal way to do business, they are being *casually dishonest*. These people may not lie about everything, but they seem perfectly comfortable in telling specific lies.

write columns for a local computer users' newsletter. If you have influence, and you aren't being treated fairly, let her know you have influence. She may reconsider her approach.

If the program is defective, and your receipts and notes are in good order, you have considerable power. You have a good case for a lawsuit, a complaint to a consumer protection agency, or for a complaint column in a major magazine. If you appear to understand this, but you aren't rude or pushy about it, the publisher's staff (primarily, the customer service manager) will understand the strength of your position.

Example: Getting a Refund Plus the Product

One request that is unusual but not rare is for the publisher to issue a refund and let the customer keep the product.

The customer explains that the product didn't serve the purpose he bought it for, but he's spent so much time learning the product that he'd hate to give it back. He might find some other use for it.

This request might seem reasonable or unreasonable to the support technician. If the customer has run into genuine defects in the product, and if he has tried very hard to get the program working, then he might have a point. After all, he will have to buy something else to get the job done that he bought this program to do; it is the program's fault; and he has spent a lot of time.

On the other hand, if the customer hasn't spent much time, or if there are ways to work around the problems with this program, the support technician is going to think that the customer is asking for his software for free and will say no.

Example: Subsidizing an Equipment Upgrade

What if the publisher misleads you about the equipment you need? For example, publishers usually tell you how much memory you need in order to run a program. What is the fair result if you bought the program only to discover that the memory you have isn't enough to run the program, even though the publisher said it is.

For a short time, one publisher put a low number on its box. Several dissatisfied customers called and led the support staff to realize that the product only sort of worked with low memory. You didn't get to use all of the features. The publisher put stickers on new boxes to fix the mislabeling. But, it was too late for boxes in the stores or for those that customers had already bought. When they called to complain, the publisher gave refunds whenever they were requested.

One of the first customers to complain wasted a lot of time explaining the symptoms and describing his computer configuration to the support technicians, who didn't yet understand the problem. Once they realized the problem, the customer said that he wanted to keep the program and get it to work, but he didn't think it was fair that he had to buy extra memory. So, he said to the technician, "What can you do for me?" (If you're not sure what you can get away with, this is an excellent way to phrase your question.) The technician (actually the support manager) said that he wasn't willing to pay for the new memory, but he was willing to pay for the cost of installing the memory in the computer (about $50). The customer agreed.

---

7. HOW DO YOU MAKE THE PUBLISHER UNDERSTAND YOUR POSITION?

How can you make the publisher understand your side and agree with your understanding of what is fair and reasonable?

Having worked through the preceding sections, you've probably discovered that a defective program can cost its purchasers a fair bit of time, money, and aggravation. If you could recover everything the program really cost you, it would be a lot more than you paid for the program.

On the other hand, the publisher's starting point is that you are entitled to a refund, at best. Some publishers value customer relations particularly highly, and their starting point is a bit more generous. And, most publishers will listen to you if they think that you are credible and that you have a legitimate problem. But, even so, without some persuasion from you, they will probably conclude that you are entitled to less than you think is fair.

How do you move the publisher toward a fairer conclusion? We have four main suggestions:

- Show that your position is reasonable.
- Show that you are a credible and reasonable person.
- Back up claims with facts.
- Use leverage if you have it and need it.

These suggestions build on the work you've done so far in this chapter, so we'll refer back to sections at appropriate times.

Show That Your Position Is Reasonable

Earlier in this chapter, you listed all your losses and expenses, including the emotional ones. Now, you can write a letter that lists the ones that you think are important.

List the problems that will win you the most sympathy first. (For example, tell them if your young child cried, or you lost your job, or you were injured.) Be warm, polite, and sad. Be nice. Make the publisher's staff feel bad.

For every expense that you claim, provide a receipt (send a photocopy, keep the original) and a clear, precise explanation of how the money was spent, why the money was spent, and how the program's error brought about the need for you to spend this money.

Chapter 7, "Software Quality and the Law," provides basic background material on the law. You can quote this to help educate the publisher's staff that your requests are entirely reasonable and fully in accord with your reasonable expectations under the law. Be conscious of how you are using the law. We're writing here about quoting the law to explain and to teach, rather than as a threat of legal action.

Show You Are Credible

If the publisher's staff decide that you are trustworthy, and a nice person who had a bad break with their product, they will want to help you.

Even if the staff don't like you, if they have the sense that you are honest in your statements, that you don't exaggerate, that you don't take a position without having thought about it and without having justification for it, and that you never make an empty threat, they will respect you. Respect will take you a long way toward a favorable settlement.

We've noted ways to enhance or lose the publisher's trust throughout this chapter.

Back Up Claims with Facts

Information is a major source of power during negotiations. The more you have at stake, the more time you should be willing to spend to gather useful information. Here are some sources and types of information that aren't too difficult to gather.

Your Own Experience with the Product

This information is essential and it is easy to record. Keep a log of your problems with the program, your expenses in dealing with the program, losses caused by the program, and every conversation you've had with the publisher's staff. Put all of this in a log book—any kind of notebook will do.

If you haven't been keeping notes so far, and you've missed the chance to write down many important things, don't worry. Get a notebook now, write down what you remember, leave some room to fill in further details as you remember them, and then start keeping records now. You want to create contemporaneous records. This means that you must write things into your book while they are happening or as soon as possible after they happen. Try very hard to write things down on the same day as they happened. Your contemporaneous notes can be valuable evidence in court.

Diagnostic Information about the Program's Failure

We talked about diagnostic notes in Chapter 3, "Preparing to Make the Call." The more detail that you can muster, the better. The larger the amount of money that is involved, the more detailed your notes should be.

However, don't forget our Chapter 3 suggestion that you should not spend a huge amount of time investigating the problem before making your *first* call to the publisher. It's very possible that the publisher's staff already have heard of the problem, will recognize the problem when you describe it, and have an upgrade or workaround ready for you. Any troubleshooting beyond the minimum that the publisher needs to recognize your problem might be a complete waste of your time. Therefore, plan to call the publisher soon after you have the problem and to add further diagnostic information to your notes after the first call only if you need to.

You should try to write down anything you know about what causes the program to fail. What were you doing when the program failed? Can you make the program fail again? What do you have to do to achieve this? If the program isn't crashing or failing in some other very obvious way, then describe the program's misbehavior as clearly as you can and explain why you consider it unsatisfactory.

You should also write down information about your own computer. Describe your components (monitor, video card, memory, and so on). List the other programs you use. Do you have similar problems with them? Don't just record your problems here. If your experience with some programs is error-free, say so in your notes.

Error Reports from Other People

There are many sources of information about a publisher's bugs. When the publisher says, "Gee, we've never heard of that one," you can check whether the bug is so well known that it has been published.

Yes, some publishers will deny knowledge of widely reported bugs. As part of our research for the book, we deliberately complained to a few publishers' customer service staff about known bugs. These bugs had been published in BugNet or were repeat offenders on the publisher's customer complaint bulletin board. Some publishers flatly denied having ever heard of these known bugs. Here are some tips on finding out about and dealing with known bugs:

Complaints.   If you find the reports, you can check whether other people have been suffering the same consequences as you. If so, your demand for reimbursement for these consequences is reinforced—especially if the publisher was being warned about these consequences before you bought the product. Look for the dates on all complaints.

BugNet.   If you run Windows, check out *BugNet* at www.bugnet.com and at support.bugnet.com. These sites offer a remarkable amount of bug-related information.

Bug report columns.   Several of the computer user magazines have a bug report column or publish bug-reporting letters to the editor. You can search their Web sites.

Publisher's support forums.   Check the publisher's technical support forum on CompuServe, or America Online, or on the publisher's Web site or look for a (USENET/Internet) newsgroup or for an e-mail discussion group that focuses on the publisher's products.

> ## Note
> *The publisher's Web site probably includes bug-fixes and documentation, including tips written by the publisher's staff. The site may include selected or edited notes from customers. The online forum (or a USENET newsgroup dedicated to your product or publisher) will probably also include discussion among customers that is not edited or censored by the publisher. Don't believe everything you read on these forums—some people don't know what they're talking about, and others are making exaggerated or false claims because they are angry with, or in competition with, the publisher.*

The manual.   Check the manual that came with the program. It might list some Internet addresses or give you the phone number of a private customer service bulletin board run by the publisher.

Search engines.   Search the Net using AltaVista, or Yahoo, or some other search program. Look for articles about this publisher or about this program. There are some remarkably thoughtful papers that are posted on some peoples' Web sites.

Other dissatisfied customers.   If enough of you are angry enough about the same bugs, you might have a basis for a class-action lawsuit. As you find error reports from other people, note who filed the report. Write down their address (street address or e-mail address).

Bad publicity.   If your negotiations with the publisher progress slowly, you might start posting notices on relevant newsgroups, bulletin boards, Web sites, and so on, describing your problem and asking whether anyone else is experiencing similar problems. Ask them to post their problem as a response to your message but also to send you an electronic mail message directly. (Note that this gets you information and applies pressure to the publisher at the same time; you are telling the publisher to settle this dispute or risk even more bad publicity.)

Set up a Web page.   One particularly effective tactic can be to create a Web page and get it indexed with as many search engines as possible. For an example, look at users.aol.com/cclass450/index.htm (complaints about Compaq) or at www.geocities.com/SoHo/2439/win2.htm (complaints about Packard Bell).

> ### Warning
> *Describe the bug accurately. Don't exaggerate, don't lie, and be willing to correct your announcement if the publisher alerts you to factual errors. If what you say is true, you can't be successfully sued in the United States for defamation (libel). In the United States, you're probably safe from a successful defamation suit even if what you say is mistaken, if you have taken pains to check your facts, you believe what you are saying, and you are willing to publish a correction as soon as the publisher demonstrates error in a statement you made. But, be very careful about saying nasty things about non-American companies on an international forum like the Internet. Non-American laws can be risky for protesters, especially those who get their facts wrong.*

Bug-related information from the publisher.   Read the publisher's newsletter (if there is one). Check the manuals, especially in sections marked *Troubleshooting*. Look for an addendum or supplement to the manual. (Printed later than the manual, they often list bugs.) Ask if there has been an addendum written since you purchased the product. What does the publisher tell you about the bug? Take notes. Has the publisher been warning people about potential consequences of the bug? Are the warnings consistent with problems you've been having?

Information about the publisher itself.   It's useful to know who you are dealing. Here are a few examples of the things you can learn:

- *Does the publisher pride itself on the quality of its customer service?*

- *Does the publisher have a history of settling lawsuits early?*

- *Will the publisher not be bringing out any new versions of your product?* You will find it useful to know about product discontinuation if the customer service group has been promising that your bug will be fixed "in the next version."

- *Is the publisher vulnerable?* For example, you might discover that the publisher is trying to sell itself or is preparing to make a public stock offering. Or, the publisher might be under investigation by the government for some other reason (such as antitrust violations). Or, the publisher might be the subject of intense media attention—perhaps it is entering a new market with a hot new product. Circumstances like these put publishers under unusual pressure to settle lawsuits and control other problems that could lead to bad publicity. The fact that the publisher is vulnerable doesn't mean that you should sue. But, it does mean that you have more leverage to negotiate, because if you did bring a lawsuit, it would hurt the publisher more than usual. Knowledge of a weakness might or might not affect your negotiating style or your final decisions about what to do. However, the knowledge can help you immensely if the publisher is being unreasonable.

- *Has the publisher's staff been drastically reduced by layoffs or a merger?* In this case, if you're being treated badly by the customer service staff, it is probably because they are unhappy, overworked, and worried. Maybe, you should try to be more likable; or more persistent; or more inquisitive—a demoralized customer service technician might be more willing to share unflattering facts about the product with you.

You can find information about the company in magazines and newspapers. Online, you can search for company information from various news services including the *San Jose Mercury News*, the *New York Times*, and so on. If enough money is at stake, it might be worth subscribing to CompuServe or ZDNet (Ziff-Davis) for access to additional, focused information on the company. On the Internet, you can find materials filed by the publisher with the Securities and Exchange Commission, and you also might find sources of archived product reviews, investor-advice newsletters, and so on. Finally, anywhere that you looked for public bug reports is a probable source of gossip or hard news about the company itself.

The Law. If you know the law, and you know your rights, you'll be less vulnerable to claims by the publisher's staff that you have no rights or accusations that you are being entirely unreasonable. If you're being reasonable and asking only for things that you're entitled to under the law, you can use your knowledge to educate the publisher's staff. Do this well, and you can use this knowledge to build your credibility, your apparent reasonableness, and your apparent power.

Use Leverage If You Have It and Need It

At first glance, the publisher has all the power in your negotiations. The publisher has your money, which it doesn't want to return to you. All you seem to have is a product, which the publisher doesn't want back. The publisher has more information than you, more money to fight lawsuits, and probably more credibility with the press and with consumer protection agencies (this depends on the publisher, of course).

Along with asking the publisher to buy back a product it doesn't want, you want reimbursement for expenses or losses, and the publisher doesn't want to pay you. If the publisher says, "No," and you go away, the publisher wins, and you lose. Therefore, you must be the persistent one. The publisher can usually afford to calmly wait and see if you go away.

In many cases, you will talk the publisher into treating you fairly by explaining the problem, proving your losses and expenses, and giving the publisher's staff whatever other information they need. But, if the publisher says, "No," you want to be in a position to say, "Excuse me, but I don't think you want to say that."

As a customer, you have many potential sources of power over the publisher. Here are a few of your power sources.

Buying Power and Scope of Purchasing Influence

Some companies think about customers in terms of the amount they spend per year, or over a 10-year or lifetime period. A complaint is an opportunity for the company to increase your loyalty or to lose your business forever.

If the publisher's customer service staff decide they are willing to lose your business forever by leaving you dissatisfied, they might be underestimating your purchasing power. When your employer is about to buy new software or new equipment, are you consulted about what products to buy? How many purchases do you influence per year?

Maybe (if it's true) you should tell the publisher that you were involved in (or approved, or made) the purchase of 57 copies of their program last year. (Be prepared to provide some details, such as the name of your company and the reason you were involved.) There's a lot of power in a statement that you used to be happy with the publisher's software, but now that they've changed their service policies, you'll have to recommend against doing further business with them.

Be careful about how you say this. The technician that you're talking to doesn't make much money and doesn't necessarily have much buying/negotiating power when she has a problem. If you describe your situation in an arrogant way, she will think that you're a jerk, demanding special treatment just because of your wealth or your company. Be gentle. Be very polite. Be friendly. But be clear.

Warranty or Written Service Contract

Your warranty spells out your rights. If you bought an additional contract for extended service or support, it gives you additional rights. You probably have more rights under warranty law than you see described on the warranty forms themselves (see Chapter 7, "Software Quality and the Law"), so don't automatically take the warranty's word about any apparent restrictions on your rights.

If you are asking for something that you are entitled to under the written terms of the warranty, at some point you should read those sentences in the warranty to the person you're talking to. Or, read them to the person's boss. Most people don't read their warranty, and they have no idea what their rights are. The publisher can push around these people much more easily.

If the publisher refuses to honor your rights under the written warranty, you can make the publisher regret it. For example, you can complain to a consumer protection agency, or you can file a lawsuit, perhaps under the Magnuson-Moss Act, which lets your lawyer collect her fees from the publisher rather than from you (see Chapter 7, "Software Quality and the Law," and Chapter 9, "Lawyers").

The Publisher's Staff's Time

It costs the publisher money when the publisher's staff talk to you. The amount that it costs the publisher per minute varies, but if you take into account the phone line, the overhead, computer expenses, and the technician's salary, the cost to the publisher probably runs about $3 per minute. The publisher is losing some money even when you're on hold. Therefore, the more persistent you are (if you demand more detailed answers, call back to follow up or to explain that the last "solution" to your problem still didn't work), the more expensive you are. At some point, it is cheaper to give you a refund than to keep dealing with you.

Retail Shops

Consider the publisher's relationship with your retailer. When you write your letter of complaint to the publisher, send a copy to the head office of the retailer that you bought the product from. WalMart, for example, takes customer complaints very seriously and might stop doing business with the publisher if the publisher doesn't treat you reasonably. These letters also give retailers an argument to pay less for the publisher's products: "Dear Publisher: You're a pain for our customers to deal with. We have to read their angry letters and spend time calming them down. Please give us an extra 5 percent discount or else."

The publisher has an incentive to settle with you before the retailer starts getting actively interested in your fight.

Customer Service Morale

How is the customer service group's relationship with management? Your leverage here is in your ability to get the customer service group in trouble with senior management. Usually, the customer service staff care more about customer relations than senior management. But, sometimes they get demoralized and start doing things that would horrify management. And, third-party support companies sometimes misinterpret the support policies of the company that they contract with and do things that would horrify their customer (the publisher). A letter to the publisher's president or *chief executive officer* (CEO) can result in a simple, quick memo to the customer service manager that says, "Fix this now."

Additional Steps

Send copies of letters.   If you ever get to the point that you are writing a letter to a consumer protection agency that is going to mediate your dispute with the publisher, make sure to send a copy to the publisher's president or CEO. (You can probably find out who this is from the publisher's Web site or by asking its support staff.)

Publicity in the traditional press.   Several computer magazines are interested in customer complaints about software companies. Some other newspapers or television shows are willing to publicize consumer complaints. Send them your complaint, and the publicity will probably help you settle it.

Publicity on the Net.   If you subscribe to an online service, you can post your complaints directly on relevant forums, bulletin boards, newsgroups, mailing lists, and so on. Ask for help. If the publisher has denied hearing about your problem or insists that it's restricted to your wierd computer configuration, say so and then ask whether anyone else has been having this problem. You can make the publisher's staff very uncomfortable very quickly.

Be careful when you publish complaints.   Don't commit defamation (such as libel); you don't want to get sued. Stick to the facts. Don't exaggerate. Don't say nasty personal things about any individual person. Don't call any person a liar (you're not calling someone a liar if you say that they said something that didn't accord with the facts. A "liar" is someone who deliberately misstates the facts.) Don't draw unsupportable conclusions about peoples' motives. Don't suggest that anyone should be fired. Don't make any threats. Don't call anyone a criminal until and unless they've been convicted of a crime. Don't use the word "fraud" unless you can prove fraud in court. Stick to the facts.

Consumer protection and law-enforcement agencies.   We discuss these agencies in Chapter 6. The more complaints that are filed by different people against the publisher, the more concerned the agencies get, and the more likely it is that the publisher will be formally investigated and prosecuted if it is engaging in unfair or deceptive trade practices.

Never *threaten* to write a letter to an agency.   The threat probably won't be taken seriously, and if it is, it might be interpreted as extortion. Just write the letter and send a copy to the publisher.

Lawsuit.   Start reading at Chapter 7, "Software Quality and the Law." If all else fails, you might have to face the publisher in court.

- *No publisher wants to face a lawsuit.* They hate them. Lawsuits are expensive, distracting, and sources of terrible publicity. And, the publisher can lose lots of money at the end of the suit.

- *You can lose money, too.* Lawsuits will eat your time faster than a Ninja Turtle eats pizza. Even if you're in the right, if the publisher's staff decide to play hardball with you, you're going to get a whole new type of attention (which might or might not be attention that you like) from the publisher's law firm.

- *Don't even think about filing a lawsuit if you're not clearly in the right.*

Example: A Wise Customer

Here's another example of the way in which wise customers use information effectively and fairly to get an unusual level of consideration from the publisher.

Some copy protection schemes are very sensitive to slightly misaligned floppy disk drives. If your drive is out of alignment, you might not be able to install the software onto your computer.

When customers called to complain that they couldn't install one particular program that was unusually sensitive to misaligned drives, we would ask a few questions and then usually tell the customer to get his drive aligned. One customer said he was sure that this wasn't the problem. We said that it probably was. The next time we heard from him, he sent a letter reminding us of our conversation and telling us that he'd gotten the drive aligned, but the program still wouldn't install. He sent the program back, along with a repair shop's bill for aligning the drive. His letter helped us realize that this was our bad judgment, so we paid both the bill and the refund. Without the well-thought-out letter and the receipt, we would have paid only the refund.

ONE FINAL NOTE

You probably aren't going to get everything that you ask for, no matter how well justified your requests. Don't publicize your willingness to compromise at the start of your discussion with the publisher (if you need advice on negotiating tactics, read Freund, 1992), but understand in your heart that you will probably compromise. Don't back yourself into a corner. Don't beat yourself up for getting less than you initially demanded.

And, realize that you have now thought through your situation more thoroughly than 99 percent of the publisher's other customers. Relax a bit and let yourself enjoy the ride. They are not fully prepared for the likes of you.

Action Plan
What are you doing here? Get back to this chapter's second section and make a list of all the things this program has cost you. It's a pain, but it's worth it. Come back when you're done.

Welcome back.

If you know what you want, and you haven't yet called the publisher for the first time, it's almost time to make the call. Read Chapter 5, "Making The Call."

If you are confused about what to ask for, talk with a friend who has good judgment. An objective second opinion is valuable in any type of negotiation.

If you need additional advice on tactics, read Chapter 5. Consider reading James Freund's book, *Smart Negotiating*.

If you have called the publisher and haven't gotten good results, read Chapter 7, "Software Quality and the Law," and reevaluate the strength of your case. Then decide whether to :

- Reconsider your position. The publisher isn't always wrong. Talk carefully with a friend. Be honest with yourself before wasting lots of time or money.

- Communicate with the publisher again (phone or letter). Ask yourself what you want to accomplish, what new information you'll provide, and whether to contact the person you last talked to or someone more senior in the company.

- Start gathering information about the publisher to prepare for further action.

- Start making waves by making public inquiries or by giving the publisher some bad publicity. Don't libel the publisher.

- Write a consumer protection complaint.

- Consider your legal options more carefully. Don't file a lawsuit until you have to and never threaten legal action.

Whatever you do, have patience and cultivate your sense of humor. You will be a better negotiator and a happier person if you let yourself relax as you go through this dispute. You will probably surprise the publisher's staff with your preparation and style, even if you stumble a bit. Many of these staff are not used to articulate, determined, persistent consumers. Don't misinterpret panic as intentional rudeness. And, don't expect snap decisions, especially if you are asking for significant compensation. And, have fun.

Chapter 5
Making the Call

Chapter Map
This chapter helps you make your call for technical support. The chapter starts with a list of our best twelve tips for making the call. After that, we give some perspective and suggestions for dealing with specific issues that you might encounter. Here are the sections:

Making the Call: Twelve Tips for Success

Stories from the Front Lines: Good Service and Bad

Collecting Useful Information for the Call

Talking Effectively with the Technician

Call Management and Call Avoidance

Calling about an Incompatible Device

Avoiding Costly or Time-Consuming Solutions

Preserving Your Warranty Rights

Deciding if the Publisher Is Dealing with You in Good Faith

Recommended Readings

Tourniare and Farrell (1997), Khandpur and Laub (1997), and Winson (1991) are readable guides to doing and managing software technical support from authors who have solid, real-world experience at it. We also recommended a few books on negotiation at the start of Chapter 4, "Knowing What to Ask For"—they're just as applicable here.

Making the Call: Twelve Tips for Success

This chapter discusses the telephone call for technical support in detail. Some people are intimidated by detail, and so avoid it at all costs. Countless boxes of non-working software decorate our bookshelves because it is too difficult to sort out the details of the phone call. Don't get flummoxed thinking about how to explain the problem to the technician on the other end of the line. "I'll call about it someday" usually means, "Let's face it; I just bought a very expensive dust collector."

Look, the point of making the call is to get help—so you can use the software *now.* If you don't have time to map every detail, don't spend much time on preparation. In most cases, the more you know about the software, the more you'll learn. But, if you wait until you've become an expert before you call, the call might be pointless by the time you call.

To get you started, we list our twelve favorite tips for making the call. This list might be everything you need. If so, skip the rest of this chapter and make the call.

Exhibit 5.1: Twelve Tips for Success

1. When you make the call, be at your computer and have the program running (if it will).

2. If the software came with a serial number or a registration number (on the disk or on the registration card), have it handy.

3. Have as much as you can conveniently collect of the program's name and version number, your computer's name, type, operating system, video card type, modem type, and all those other configuration details that we talked about in Chapter 3, "Preparing to Make the Call."

4. Have a description of the problem ready. (Spend a few minutes figuring out how to describe what the program is doing wrong or what the program is stopping you from doing.)

5. Think about your intended outcome from this call. What will it take to satisfy you?

6. At the start of the call, ask the technician to identify himself. Get his name, a direct-dial phone number so that you can call him back in case the call is interrupted, and his e-mail address so that you call follow up later without having to make another call.

7. Make detailed notes during the call.

8. Be courteous, accurate, and firm.

9. If the technician asks you to do something that you aren't comfortable with (such as making significant changes to the operating system before you've backed up all of your data), don't do it. Ask if there's some other way. Hang up, back up your system, and call back. Use your common sense and take care of yourself before following drastic instructions.

10. If you aren't getting the help you need from the technician, ask for someone else (like his supervisor).

11. If you finish the call without resolving the problem, have the technician repeat back to you (or repeat back to him) what you're supposed to do and what he's supposed to do. Be clear about the next steps.

12. If you promised to investigate something and then discover that you don't know how (for example, how do you find the version of your video card driver?), call back. The technician can often explain what you have to do.

Stories from the Front Lines: Good Service and Bad

We've all heard funny computer customer service stories. Have you heard the one about the woman who called to complain that her computer's cup holder was malfunctioning? She was using the CD-ROM drive as a cup holder. And, what about the man who called to complain that his floppy disk didn't work? It turned out that he'd cut open the floppy disk because he thought the protective shell was just a wrapper and had placed the bare disk media in the drive. There are plenty of stories about customers who don't know enough about computers to realize their actions are ridiculous.

But, even if you know exactly what you're doing, your experiences with customer service groups won't always be good ones. The situation isn't as black and white as "good companies" and "bad companies." Even in the worst companies, most people who work in a customer service department want to help people; that's why they chose customer service jobs. Every company has inspired good stories and bad stories, although some companies are, on average, much better than others.

At its best, a support group is staffed by well-trained people who average four to six hours on the phone per day, spending the rest of the time on training, research (such as looking in detail at customer problems or examining new equipment), and on solving unanswered customer questions. These groups create *knowledge bases*—databases that contain detailed troubleshooting information about the programs supported by the group. Every support technician has access to the knowledge base and can look up information by entering the details that you provide. For you, they can do wonders (if they choose to).

At its worst, a support group is staffed by underpaid, lightly trained, over-worked, data-deprived people who are virtually chained to the phones. Their companies provide no career paths and little ongoing training. These people answer the phone all day, every day and have no time to do research or to share information. Different people have significantly different knowledge of the programs they support and their problems.

In many cases (good companies and bad), the individual customer service tech-nician is genuinely effective and efficient. In some, service is spectacular. For example, one of us bought a home computer from a company, that won't get his business again, and was rescued by a *different* company's support staff. The story follows.

Example: Service Above and Beyond

Not long after I bought it, my computer started misbehaving. I got fre-quent error messages and lockups. I exhausted the tips and tricks that I knew, without much success. Finally, when I was working on a critical project due the next day, the computer just wouldn't operate without locking up. Desperate, I had to call for support.

I called the computer maker several times, waited on hold forever, but got no help. Finally, a technician who called himself "senior" told me to use the diagnostic software that came with the computer and if that didn't work, to call Microsoft.

Microsoft's usual position is that if you get the operating system with a new computer, it's the computer company's responsibility to give you sup-port. (This position is based on its agreement with the computer com-pany, which determines the price the computer company pays for this software.) Microsoft's staff initially said I might not be entitled to support from them, but when I described some of the calls that I made to the com-puter company, the technician took pity on me. He started by setting my expectations well. He explained that the problem might not be with the operating system but that he'd work with me to find out. He stayed on the phone with me for nearly three hours. Over that time, the system gradu-ally got better.

I thanked him and told him I probably could handle the problem from there. He gave me his name and explained that he'd entered enough data into his computer during the call that anyone else in his group could help me if I had to call back. Then we ended the call. I had to work all night, but I finished my project on time.

To my amazement and delight, the technician called back the next day, on his day off, to see whether my system was still working. I told him that it was working perfectly.

No one can *expect* this level of service, but sometimes we get it.

In other cases, the technician is well intentioned but not as effective. The typical software publisher gives a new tech about a week's worth of training (Software Publishers Association, 1995). If you get someone new in a company that doesn't do a good job of mentoring its junior staff, he's going to fumble, make bad guesses, and waste some of your time. If you realize that this is what's happening to you, be pleasant about it. But, feel free to ask if someone with more experience is available.

Sometimes, you'll get excellent service that doesn't solve your problem the first time. If the problem is complex, and several possible causes exist for it, then it might take a while before you and the technician figure it out. In the meantime, the technician will make incorrect guesses and waste some of your time. Please understand that this process is normal. Diagnosis isn't an exact science; it involves a process of elimination.

Example: A Bent Pin

A customer bought a product that included an interface card. The product gave an error code that usually indicates that the card isn't seated properly. The technician told the customer to turn off his computer, unplug it, open it up, and reseat the card. This was probably a challenging task for the customer, but he did it. Unfortunately, the problem didn't go away.

The customer called back, and the technician suggested some other things to try. They didn't work either. Eventually, the technician had the customer describe the physical appearance of the card in detail. It turned out that there was a bent pin on one of the chips on the card.

This process wasted a fair bit of this customer's time, but we still think that it was good service. The technician had a list of possible problems that could generate this error, but hearing a list of 30 possible things to try would waste most customers' time and confuse most of them. The technician went through the most likely problems first and gauged how many alternatives the customer could understand at each step. This is efficient service, even though it sometimes doesn't yield the right answer right away.

And, sometimes you'll get bad, dishonest service. We've had it plenty of times. (Why do you think we wrote this book?)

Example: Bad Software, Bad Support

The program I bought had several problems. I wrote letters to the publisher, and later I wrote another letter specifically addressed to the president of the company, and no one responded. One of many problems was that the program didn't work correctly with my printer. I called the publisher. Its technicians claimed that they'd never heard of the problem.

Later, they announced a new version and sent customers a brochure, offering an upgrade for about $100. I called to ask whether this new version fixed the printer bugs. The technician said that it did. We talked more about these bugs, and eventually I learned that my name was on a list of people who would be sent free upgrades. No one had told me this. Instead of sending me the new version or a letter telling me I was entitled to it, the company had first sent me a brochure asking for money for the upgrade. Instead of making me happy about getting a free upgrade, their approach led me to suspect them of playing a game, to see who would *pay* to upgrade before sending free upgrades to qualified customers.

Eventually, I received the free upgrade and tried it. The upgrade had the same bugs. The program also printed reports differently. The report that I liked best (it showed my weekly appointments very concisely) had been replaced with something that was prettier but much less functional. I called and asked how to print the old report. They said that I didn't need it. When I asked about my printer, they said *again* that they'd never heard of my problems before.

These people wanted money from me for fixing the bugs, and then when I pointed out the fixes didn't work, they went back to denying having ever heard of the problems in the first place!

I checked their *bulletin board system* (BBS) and saw that someone had complained about the same problems that I had. The technician had posted a response "We've never heard of this problem before. Maybe it's something odd about your computer." So, I posted a response. I said that I'd reported the problem a long time ago and that I had talked with the customer service staff about it twice recently. My symptoms were the same as the other customer's, so I didn't understand how they could say that they'd never heard of this problem before.

I checked the BBS a few days later. Other old postings were still there, but the printer bug postings (the customer's, the technician's, and mine) had been deleted.

I called the customer support line again and got them to admit that they had heard of the problem. They now said that there was no fix for it. They also said that it wasn't an important bug because it affected only one printer (my model), which not many of their customers had—a bad response in five ways:

1. They'd sent me a disk to fix this bug. It was important enough for them to send me a free upgrade, so how can they say it's unimportant now?

2. My printer was one of the best-selling printers of all time.

3. The problems occurred on other printers, too. (How do we know? We work with companies that have compatibility test labs. We can check these claims.)

4. Tagging a bug as unimportant is no excuse, it's just a way to intimidate a customer.

5. A fix for the printer problem was actually available. The technician just didn't know about it.

I called the support BBS again to see whether anyone else had posted a complaint about this printer. No one had complained (or none of the complaints had survived), but a patch was available for downloading (it had apparently been there for a while). I downloaded the patch (there were other bugs that needed fixing, too). To my surprise, the patched version fixed the printer problems.

Why did I stick with this program? For the same reason that many people and many companies stick with a bad program for longer than they should. I put lots and lots and lots of data into the program before I decided the problems weren't going to go away. It can be very time consuming to move your data to a replacement program. When I finally did switch, I lost a great deal of data.

 Example: Indifferent Support

A small publisher was bought by a larger publisher. The larger publisher's executives talked about support as an expense center that needed to be reduced. The staff expected layoffs soon (and for good reason). The executives didn't talk about making customers happy. Instead, they suggested it would be a good thing for customers to wait on hold for a long time because people who were making frivolous calls and wasting the company's money would quit calling. The technicians were totally demoralized. They played computer games while they talked on the phone. They didn't follow up on problems (why bother?), and they didn't share information. If you were a lucky caller, you got an answer that solved your problem. Otherwise, you got the wrong answer or a runaround.

Sometimes, when you have trouble getting effective help, the problem is that you aren't providing enough information or listening carefully enough. Sometimes, the technician is trying to explain the right thing but isn't doing a good job of communicating. Sometimes, the technician is making an honest effort at solving a tough problem. And sometimes, you're dealing with jerks. Part of your task as a caller is to listen to the person at the other end. Are you dealing with a helper or not?

We'll start by assuming that you're dealing with someone who wants to help you, as most technicians do. We'll consider questions of integrity later.

Useful Information for the Call

The first part of your call for support takes place before you pick up the phone. Your first step is preparation. Your call will go much more smoothly and be much more likely to end in a positive result if you take a few minutes to gather materials before you pick up the phone. Chapter 3, "Preparing to Make the Call," helps you gather needed information. Chapter 4, "Knowing What to Ask For," helps you figure out what you want from the publisher. Here is some information that is useful to have on hand:

Identification.   The technician will probably want to know your product's serial number or registration number. Some companies don't require this. Others won't talk with you until you give it to them. If you can't make the call when you're at your computer, you'll probably need to bring the identification and the product information with you. You can usually find it in the About dialog, which you reach from the Help menu.

Product information.   Includes the name of the program, the version number, or anything else that would specifically identify it.

System information.   The kind of computer you have, your operating system and version, and as much other information as you can conveniently gather. You might not have to provide much of this information—if you're calling about a known bug, for example, the technician will often be able to help you just from your description and the program's version number.

A description of the problem.   There are two very different issues here. First, what isn't working? Second, what are you trying to achieve, that this problem stops you from achieving? When the technician knows what you're trying to accomplish, he can help you by providing alternative approaches even if he can't fix the underlying problem. (These solutions are called *workarounds.*) In other cases, the technician might suggest a different approach that is more efficient for your task than your initial strategy.

An understanding of what you want to achieve in this phone call.   You might be satisfied with information about the program or tips on what to do next. Of course you want the problem solved in one call, but unless the technician recognizes it right away and has a solution for you instantly, you will resolve this problem in a series of steps. The steps might or might not all take place within one phone call.

An understanding of what it will take to satisfy you.   For example, you might just want information, or you might want a bug fix or a refund. You might want additional money to reimburse you for losses caused by the program's misbehavior. The more you want, the more carefully you should prepare your request.

Receipts and amounts.   If you're asking for reimbursement for specific expenses and have receipts, be ready to state the exact amounts. In the best case, you'll offer to fax the receipts to the technician immediately, and he'll agree to submit a check request for you as soon as he receives the receipts. If you don't have the bills yet (such as the phone bill), make an estimate and be ready to tell the technician that it is an estimate and when you'll get the final bill.

Talking Effectively with the Technician

Here are a few more preparatory tips:

Make the call at your computer.   Have the program running (if possible). If the problem usually occurs when other programs are running, then have them open now too.

Bring your coach.   If you have a friend who coaches you on technical stuff (or who does it for you), have her present to hear the advice you're being given.

Decide what data you are willing to send the technician.   Sometimes, a technician will ask you to send him a copy of a data file that is associated with the problem. This may help him reproduce or analyze the problem. However, your files might be confidential. If they are, don't agree to send them to the publisher. If these files are confidential from your job, don't send them without your employer's permission.

Call when you have the time.   Getting help may take a while, especially because you're likely to be left on hold for 15 minutes or more. You can probably improve your waiting time by calling during nonpeak hours. Don't expect to get fast service first thing Monday morning or at the start or end of lunch hour. Also, if you have a speakerphone, use it. While on hold, you can do other things.

TIPS FOR THE START OF THE CALL

Now that you've dialed the phone, waited on hold forever, and have finally gotten to a human, here are some tips for the start of the call:

Get contact information. Ask the technician for his name. Ask for his direct-dial number in case the phone call is cut off. You won't always get it, but it's worth asking.

Make notes in your log book. Once you realize that you have a significant problem with the program, you should keep a log. We discussed logs in Chapter 3, but we'll make the point here again. In your log, describe your problems with the program as you have them (same day). Write down the details of your conversations with the publisher's customer service staff, while you are on the phone. Write down other information as you learn it.

Communicate your time constraint. After you get past the hold time, typical calls last 4 to 8 minutes (depending on a wide range of circumstances). However, some calls go on for hours. If you have a time constraint, tell the technician and let him structure the call around your time needs. Be prepared to call back later for further instruction.

Don't lose focus by the time wasted on hold. You were put on hold for over an hour. You finally get to talk to a human. What should you talk about? It's common for people to spend half of the call complaining about the long hold time. We don't blame them. But, they aren't helping themselves. First, these people often lose their focus when they start by complaining about something that has nothing to do with the program. They often hang up without ever getting the problem solved. Second, they burn off their anger on something irrelevant to the problem they called about. When they calm down, they're not as demanding in their negotiations to get the problem solved. Third, the technician has heard this all before. He probably agrees that the hold time is outrageous. It's not his fault. Don't waste your time this way.

Complain more effectively about excessive hold times. Feel free to mention the problem to the technician and make it clear that you think the hold time was unreasonable. But, don't push it, yet. Instead, get to the point of the call and get the problem solved (if you and the technician can solve it.) After you've finished with the technician, don't hang up. Ask whether you can speak to the technician's supervisor. Tell him (if this is true) that the service he provided you was very good. And, tell him that the reason that you want to talk to someone more senior is to complain about the long hold times. Ask him to transfer you to the most senior person available. Give that person a piece of your mind. This gets attention, especially if you've gotten a good result, because you're no longer anxious about the result, you're just protesting about the process.

DESCRIBING THE PURPOSE OF YOUR CALL

Early in the call, you're going to describe the purpose of your call (a problem, or a question, or a request.) When you describe a problem, consider these suggestions:

Describe the main problem itself.   What you did, what you saw, what happened, and why you think it's a problem.

Provide troubleshooting information (if you have any) next.   For example, let the technician know that the problem happened when the power went out, or that it happened after you installed a virus protection program or changed printers, or that you were on line, sending or receiving data. Chapter 3 provides many other troubleshooting suggestions.

Fess up if you've been messing around.   Sometimes, people play with the options on their program or operating system files, or they erase files or do something that messes up the program. Then, when they call for help, they're too embarrassed to admit that they did this. This happens a lot. The technician might even ask some pointed questions, and the caller denies (out of embarrassment) having been doing what she actually was doing. This is not an effective way to get help. If you made a mess, help the technician help you clean it up.

It's sometimes OK to call for advice.   Suppose that you bought a program specially designed to help you write term papers. Many people who bought this program will call for support on how to write term papers rather than how to use the program. Many people who buy home accounting programs will call with basic questions about accounting. People who buy high-end graphics programs call about how to work with commercial printers. Within limits, these questions are normal, but you should understand that if you're not paying the publisher for this call, you're asking for a favor. Companies vary a lot in the amount of free consulting they're willing to give you. And, please, if you're calling for advice and not for reporting a problem, tell the technician early in the call.

Make sure you communicated.   If you suspect that you have not succeeded in communicating the purpose of your call, ask the technician to say back to you what he thinks that you said. ("I'm sorry, but I'm not sure that I explained this clearly. Can you say back to me what you think I've described as my problem?")

COMMUNICATING MORE EFFECTIVELY DURING THE CALL

Here are some suggestions for communicating more effectively during the call:

Be patient with the technician and listen carefully to what he's saying.

Ask questions, including dumb ones.   Don't be afraid of sounding stupid. If the technician uses jargon, don't hesitate to tell him that you don't understand what he's saying.

Make notes and sometimes read them back to the technician.   If you're not sure that you've fully understood a set of instructions or if you want to confirm an agreement, tell the technician that you'd like to make sure that you've gotten his points clear.

Be clear about the outcome you want, **but don't be attached to it.**   Be flexible.

Stay focused on the call at hand.   Don't use other programs or try to get other work on the screen done and don't read your e-mail (this is surprisingly common) while the technician is trying to help you solve this problem over the phone.

Remember that the technician cannot see your screen.   Some technicians will work along with you, so that their screen matches your screen. Others close their eyes and visualize your screen (they might not be able to match your system, so they walk through it in their head).

Follow the technician's instructions exactly.   Follow the instructions word for word, when he tells you things to do at your computer. Wait for the next instruction. Anticipating what the technician will tell you and going somewhere that you think he's taking you will slow down the call and cause communication errors and misdiagnoses—very frustrating for the technician and for the customer.

Speak up when you think there's a mismatch.   At times, when the technician is taking you through a series of steps, one of them won't seem right to you. Perhaps, the technician is telling you to select a menu item that is worded slightly differently on your screen, or is referring to an option that isn't obvious on your screen, or isn't telling you to try something that does seem obvious on your screen. Stop the technician and say what you see. This might clear up a misunderstanding and avoid needless confusion.

Don't risk your data.   If the technician asks you to do something risky, feel free to say, "Stop. I don't have this backed up. Can I do that right now?"

Don't assume that a message on your screen (such as an error message) is not important.   Tell the technician about anything unusual that you see on your screen.

Tell the technician exactly what the message on your screen says. Don't paraphrase or summarize. Read the message word for word. The programmers often have 10 different almost identical error messages. You must tell the technician which error message appears.

Refocus the technician if the call doesn't seem to be focused on your desired outcome.   Your technician might go off on a tangent and optimize your machine but lose his focus on your prime issue. If the call doesn't seem especially focused, remind him of why you called, or he might do great stuff for you but not solve your problem.

Ask the technician what he thinks is the problem.   You don't have to just follow the technician's instructions step by step. If you're confused, or if you think the technician might be confused, ask what type of problem this sounds like to him. This question might help to focus him, and it will help you decide whether the requests he's making of you are reasonable. Eventually, you might discover that you have to solve the problem yourself. Understanding the technician's thinking might help you do your own reading and research, and it might help you ask friends or other technicians for help.

Don't be afraid to be firm.   Fair is fair. You're calling about their bug, and your time is worth something. If the publisher has fixed the bug, but the technician wants you to pay for the upgrade, don't feel awkward or embarrassed about asking for a free copy or a price reduction.

HANDLING THE END OF THE CALL

Here are some suggestions that you might find useful toward the end of the call:

Be willing to compromise.   Technicians are outstanding at finding loopholes in company policy, but you have to be willing to work with them. For example, the technician may not be able to give you a free upgrade. Rather than demanding something that you know you can't have, ask if there is anything that the technician can do for you. If the technician doesn't get the message, ask him if he can give you any "special consideration." This question diplomatically opens the door to let him make you an offer. Perhaps he can tell you how to get an extended warranty so that you won't have to pay for the next version (if this one is buggy). Or, perhaps he can get you unlimited phone support for this version. If he doesn't offer something, make suggestions like these yourself. The technician might either accept one or suggest something else that he can do for you. Ask for value.

Don't let the technician brush you off.   If the call has gone on for a while, the technician might say, "I'm sorry, I'd like to help you further, but I've got other calls to handle." This is a polite way to say, "I don't want to talk to you any more." This comment is appropriate if you're in the chit-chat phase at the end of the call, after the technician has solved your problem. But, it isn't appropriate if you haven't been helped. This comment is a form of bullying used most often by inexperienced technicians and technicians who aren't customer focused. Don't meekly accept it and hang up. Politely, but firmly, restate the problem and ask the technician to help you solve it or to transfer you to someone who can.

Don't hang up unless you understood what you were told.   Many people are too embarrassed to admit that they don't understand. So, they just give up or they call back and hope to get someone else. Don't be embarrassed. Don't be afraid to say, "I don't understand what you said. Can you say that or explain it in some other way?"

Are you satisfied with the result?   If not, wait for a few seconds before agreeing to hang up. Say that you're not satisfied and ask whether there's anything else that the technician can suggest to help you. If not, perhaps you'll ask the technician to transfer the call, or perhaps you'll ask for the name and address of the marketing manager or the president of the company so that you can send a letter. Set yourself up so that it is easy to take the next step.

Escalate the call.   The most effective way to get better help if you're not being helped is to ask to speak to someone else. You might first ask for a more senior technician. Or, ask whether some other technician in the department might know more about this problem. Or, you can ask to speak to the supervisor or the manager. If the next person doesn't help you, ask for his boss. If she doesn't help you, ask for her boss. Keep going up the chain until you reach someone who is willing to help.

Before hanging up, ask the technician whether he is closing the incident.   (An incident can be any problem that you call about. Some publishers count incidents or charge for support by the incident, because it might take several calls to resolve (close) a single incident.) If you're not satisfied with the outcome at this point, tell the technician that you are not authorizing him to close the incident. This step may make your next call smoother.

If the problem hasn't been fully solved during the call, finish the call by making sure you understand where you are.   Ask yourself the following questions. If you're not sure of the answer, ask the technician. ("Can you remind me again, what am I supposed to do next?") Even if you are sure, there's value in repeating your understanding back to the technician so that both of you share it.

- What is your agreement with the technician?
- Do you know what you're supposed to do?
- Do you know why you're supposed to do this?
- What are your next steps?
- What are the technician's next steps?
- Who is supposed to call whom next, and when?
- Do you know how to contact the technician?
- Does the technician know how to reach you?
- What incident number (or case number) has been assigned to your call?

CALLING BACK FOR MORE SUPPORT

Finally, here are some pointers on calling back for additional support.

Leave a reminder.   If you're waiting for the technician to call back or to send you something, it's not inappropriate to call and remind her. For example, it's appropriate to call (or e-mail) and leave a message that says, "Sandy, this is David Pels. My incident number is 2347. I'm looking forward to our scheduled call at 4 o'clock this afternoon." This is a courteous reminder to get her to prepare for the call.

Hold the technician accountable.   If she hasn't done something that she promised to do, call and ask when it will be done. Many companies are slow about keeping their promises. Many of the calls they receive are callbacks asking when a promised task will be done. Callbacks are tracked as wasted call time in many companies. Callback tracking encourages technicians to solve the problem the first time or to turn around promised tasks more quickly.

Expect to identify yourself all over again.   Technicians talk to up to 100 people per day. Although very personable, the technician that you talked with during your first call probably won't remember you when you call back. If you're lucky, the technician that you first talk to will record many of the details of your discussion in a computer record that the next technician will be able to access. Don't count on it.

Identify yourself clearly in messages.   Don't leave a message like, "Hi Steve, this is John. I found the problem; give me a call." You are the 47th John that Steve has talked to over the last three weeks. Leave your phone number, your call incident or call tracking number, and other relevant information.

Check your e-mail address.   When you send e-mail to someone from an in-house mail system, make sure that you include your return address as part of your message. The "reply-to" header in your e-mail message might be corrupted by your local mail program, by your firewall forwarder, or by some other part of your system, making it impossible for technicians to respond. If you write from a corporate e-mail system—especially a system that sits behind a firewall—and you don't get a response, don't assume that you're being ignored. Send the message again, making sure that a working return address appears at the start of your message.

Use the return receipt option with your e-mails.   If your e-mail program supports this feature, it will let you know whether the publisher received the message and approximately when it was read. Many reasons exist for why you might not get the return receipt. For example, the publisher's program might not support return receipts. On the other hand, the failure could be caused by an incorrect return address in your e-mail header.

UNDERSTANDING THE TECHNICIAN

If you can see the customer service call from the technician's point of view, you will be able to avoid common mistakes.

How Technicians Gauge You

Along with listening to your problems, the publisher's staff make judgments about your credibility. We discussed this in Chapter 4, in the section "How the Publisher Perceives Your Credibility and Your Claim." If you haven't read that section yet, it's worth reading now.

Ways to Avoid Irritating the Technician

Many of the people who call for support are unhappy, and they don't treat technicians well. Good technicians are used to this, and they roll with it. It's part of the job. But, like everyone else, they have good days and bad. There are ways to make them think twice about helping you. Here are a few pointers:

Don't waste the technician's time.   It is important to take the time you need. Don't rush yourself and don't feel guilty if your problem is complex and takes some time. But, be cautious about wasting the technician's time. For example

- *If you haven't yet made an effort to deal with the problem (you're calling early in the hope that the publisher already knows and understands the problem, will recognize your description, and can give you a fast answer), then be willing to agree to hang up and do a little more troubleshooting on your own.* Ask the technician what questions he'd like you to be able to answer when you call back. If some questions are too technical for you, say so and ask him how to find the answers.

- *If you haven't read the relevant sections of the manual, don't insist on having the technician explain everything to you.* Ask where to find the information and volunteer to read it and call back. (Ask for the technician's direct-dial phone number.) On the other hand, if you have tried to read the manual, and it is unreadable or wrong, say so. Calmly. Give an example or two, to show that you really have tried to find a relevant section or understand the material that you did find, but you couldn't. The typical technician will appreciate your effort and sympathize with your confusion.

- *Avoid giving irrelevant details.* For example, it probably doesn't matter what Aunt Mabel was cooking for breakfast when your computer game crashed. On the other hand, don't leave out potentially important details. Making this distinction isn't easy for some people (or for some technicians.) So say what you believe is relevant, give details, but listen for indications that the technician is getting impatient.

- *In the phone call, don't list all of the expenses this program's bugs have cost you.* It takes too long. And, it makes the technician defensive and irritable. Mail, e-mail, or fax them. The things you send will also have value as evidence later.

- *Don't recite every way that the company has mistreated you in the past.* Sometimes it will be useful or important to walk the technician through the history of your problem. But, ask yourself how necessary this is and how much detail is worth going into. Also consider sending a list in fax, letter, or e-mail, that you and the technician can then discuss during the phone call.

Don't be a jerk.

- Don't use foul or abusive language.

- Don't be rude.

- Don't call the technician an idiot.

- Don't make ethnic or sexist remarks.

- Avoid making jokes at the technician's or the publisher's expense.

- Try not to sound greedy. Don't act like you've won the lottery because you've found a bug, and now you're calling for a monetary reward, or free software—you won't get far.

Think before you insist that you're a genius and an expert. Customer service groups get so many calls from people who claim to be computer experts. Some are genuine experts (in COBOL). Others are knowledgeable, but not as knowledgeable as they think. And, still others are fully knowledgeable but the tone they convey to the technician is that he is either a liar or a fool. Even if you mind your tone, you should understand that some technicians are intimidated when they lose control of the call. There's nothing wrong with communicating that you have some knowledge and experience, but be constructive in the way that you do it.

Don't make it impossible to satisfy you. If the publisher's staff concludes your patronage is lost forever, they will want to hang up and make you go away.

- *Don't call the technician a liar (especially if he is one).* Say things like, "I don't understand. Didn't you just say X?" or "But, the manual says X." But don't say, "You liar! You told me X, and now you're telling me Y."

- *Don't make impossible demands (someone should be fired, or the publisher should pay you exorbitant amounts of money).* Gallagher (1995) describes how skilled technicians deal with unreasonable requests, but you cannot expect that all technicians have developed this level of knowledge and control over their work.

- *Starting on a positive note will help if you're going to lay out a long list of re-*

lated complaints. Start off with, "I'd really like to keep doing business with you. Isn't there some way that we can solve this problem?"

Use honey, not vinegar.   If you're really upset, consider having a charming friend call on your behalf. This strategy can backfire if your friend knows nothing of the problem. Consider showing her the problem and giving her access to your computer when she makes the call.

What Do They Do When You Scream?

Technicians are human. They feel bad the first 2,413 times someone screams at them. After that, they become a little calloused. If you start screaming, you're fair game.

Some technicians will take your anger and unhappiness seriously and try to help you. (Gallagher, 1995, describes the normal techniques that support staff use for handling angry customers.)

Other technicians will decide that you are an abusive jerk and that you deserve all the bugs you get. If the customer service technician hangs up on you (a big no-no in most customer service groups), you are being told that you have crossed the line. Think about that possibility before you call back. The more likely reaction if they decide you're a jerk, will not be to hang up, but to make you the butt of after-hours jokes instead. Will they help fix your problem? Maybe, but only if they have to.

Some technicians will conclude that you are acting (as many people are), that you aren't really upset, you're just using a pretense of anger as a negotiating tactic. If so, you won't be taken seriously because you're using an unacceptably rude tactic.

Some technicians start playing computer games. They weather the storm by tuning you out.

Some technicians transfer you to their "manager," who might be the department secretary or some other powerless victim who has been volunteered to pretend to be manager while listening to the screamers.

On a slow day, the person you're screaming at might put the phone on mute and then broadcast your screams over the speakerphone. If your language is particularly colorful, some people will find you very funny.

If the organization tapes your calls (they'll probably tell you if they do), they will keep the recording where you scream. If you ever take the complaint further, the tape is evidence of how unreasonable a person you are.

Why Do They Hang Up?

Hanging up on a customer is highly discouraged in most customer service departments. The technician is supposed to end the call courteously, at a reasonable stopping point. Anything else is a failure. A technician who slams down the phone will probably get a visit from his supervisor.

Despite the consequences, technicians sometimes hang up on callers. If one hangs up on you, the technician is probably telling you, as forcefully as he can, that you have been so unreasonable (in his view) and so inappropriate that you have crossed the line. You might not have done anything wrong. But, we urge you to think carefully about your conduct on the phone.

Here are possible reasons a technician would hang up:

Abuse.   The customer's behavior was abusive, involving foul language, sexual suggestions, or racial or gender-based insults.

Bragging.   The customer was a self-proclaimed expert about the product. The technician concluded the caller was showing off rather than trying to solve a real problem. Scenario: After 10 minutes listening to the customer boast about his knowledge, the technician asks "OK, how can I help you today?" but is hit with more monologue. His response? <Click>

He doesn't want to lie to you.   The customer asks questions that the technician knows the answer to, but he can't tell the truth, and he refuses to lie. So what does he do when he thinks he's being pinned down? <Click>

Here are a few more reasons technicians hang up that have nothing to do with inappropriate customer behavior:

Job stress.   Some publishers put technicians under tremendous performance stress. The technician is required to keep the average call very short, often too short. Some consultants make a business of telling executives that their customer service cost problems are best solved by putting technicians on strict time budgets. There are positive ways to teach staff how to reduce their call times, but some publishers simply issue repeated management directives to reduce times significantly, without careful training or realistic goal setting. One consultant, when asked how to convince a customer-focused group of technicians to speed up, advised managers that when they noticed that a technician had been on the phone with the same customer for too long, they should walk to the technician's desk and disconnect the call. Another variation: Question from technician, "But how do you hang up on someone who still needs help?" Management answer, "Press the Call Release button." Staff who don't quit the publisher at this point are often demoralized and may act out (such as by being unhelpful, or hanging up).

"No Refunds Allowed." Say the product is seriously defective, but the technician has been ordered to talk people out of their demands for refunds. Suppose the technician says (falsely) that "We're working on a fix for that problem," and you say, "When will it be ready?" You remind the technician that you've heard promises of a fix several times, and you now want details. <Click> Or, suppose that the technician says that he's never heard of this problem before, and you start quoting *PC Week* and *PC World* reports and letters sent by other customers. You demand a refund or at least an explanation. <Click> Or, suppose that the technician admits that there's a problem and starts explaining a workaround (that he knows won't work or is impossibly complex); you press for details, because you don't see how the solution can work. He gets embarrassed. <Click>

Two of the *most common* reasons for disconnected calls:

Lost connection. The technician didn't hang up at all. Your phone hung up (lost cellular connection, or a bug in your company's PBX software, or something else. Stuff happens.)

Phone glitch. The technician's phone has a bug. He didn't mean to hang up. It just happened. If it happens to you, call back. If you don't think there was any discourtesy intended, ask to speak to the same technician. (Always get their name and phone number at the start of the call.) Be friendly. He'll be apologetic, and you'll be in a slightly better bargaining position because the technician knows that you were treated discourteously by the system.

Call Management and Call Avoidance

Publishers spend a fortune on technical support. Many of them track their success in handling calls in several ways, and they train and reward their staff according to their measurements. Those measurements might or might not encourage the technician to do his best to serve you.

First, the measurements. Most customer service departments use *an automated call distributor* (ACD), a system used to direct incoming calls to people who are the most appropriate or most available at the time. (Tourniare and Farrell, 1997, describe these well.) Software associated with the ACD often provides statistics on the average length of each call, how long the average caller waited on hold, how many callers hung up while they were on hold (call abandonment rate), and other aspects of support group telephone handling efficiency (Help Desk Institute, 1997). Other publishers get this data from their telephone service provider. These statistics make it easy to see the average number of calls handled by each technician and the average length of time that each technician spends per call. These numbers don't reflect the content of the call (how many problems were solved per caller, how happy the caller was at the end of the call, and how often the same person called back with follow-up questions).

Additionally, many publishers use call tracking systems (databases) to keep track of problems that people call about. Your call might go into the tracking system as an individual entry. The technician might note on your record that he is to call you back next week with certain information. He might also note the problems you've called about. The system (or a related system) might also contain data organized by problem type, with descriptions of common problems and suggestions on how to help customers deal with these problems.

The call tracking system might provide the publisher with more extensive time-related information. For example, the technician might code each call in ways that let publishers compute total costs per bug, for several bugs that are generating lots of calls. The technician might also be able to record that a series of calls all apply to the same incident or to several different incidents.

Many publishers have decided to reduce their load through a call avoidance strategy. Call avoidance is really a widely used short-hand for "call cost avoidance." This is a strategy for reducing the amount of time that you spend on the phone talking with live humans. At its best, this approach is about managing call flow into the most economical model. The idea is to serve you well, but at the lowest cost (see Tourniaire & Farrell, 1997, especially section 7.1.2). At its worst, which is common, the idea is to get rid of your call at the lowest cost.

Call avoidance is not every company's philosophy, but it is an increasingly common one. Alternative philosophies value customer satisfaction over call cost, and they are optimized differently.

Call avoidance involves four major factors:

Prevention.   The publisher eliminates your need to call by improving the product or the accuracy of the advertising.

Diversion.   The publisher convinces you to check another source for support such as its Web site, fax back, voice message tree, knowledge base, etc.

Minimization.   The publisher finds a way to reduce call times: the amount of time that you're on the phone talking to a human. For example, some publishers have a series of standard answers to common questions. If you ask one of these questions, the technician might fax or e-mail you the answer (or might point you to the answer in the manual.) This can communicate the information (if the material is well written) without spending your time or the technician's while the technician speaks and you write. A less helpful approach: management simply demands that technicians reduce their average call time no matter what.

Evasion.   The simplest evasive tactic is to leave the technical support contact information out of the manual. We suggest that in this case, you should find the publisher's direct sales number (often an 800 number) and call for support on that line. Either you'll get the support toll free, or you'll get the right number. The next evasive tactic is to leave you on hold forever. Publishers know that people will hang up if they're left on hold long enough. Some publishers adopt a policy of not helping all the people who call for help, only the ones who will sit through a long hold period. Some publishers set their average hold times so long that they expect 90 percent of callers to hang up and go away.

Against this background of a strategy for call cost reduction, you should understand that the customer service technician that you talk with is probably under significant personal pressure to handle calls and close incidents quickly. Many publishers measure call times (how long each call lasts). If a technician's average time per call is too long (often measured against a team average), he might have to answer to a supervisor. If he can keep the call time averages really short, he might get a raise or a bonus.

Example: Total Call Time per Customer

At Company X, there was a technician whose call times were half as long as everyone else's. All the managers were singing his praises—look what's possible. We were skeptical, and so we looked deeper. We found that this technician had one of the highest percentages of customer callbacks, meaning that the problem wasn't solved the first time through. If you looked at the total time per customer (or time per incident as some people call it), his times were worse. Another technician had longer than average call times, but he had the lowest return call rate. There are several factors that measure the efficiency of a technician. Good companies look at more than just call time. Bad companies often don't look past call time.

The strategy of leaving people on hold forever also puts technicians under intense time pressure. Many companies have a display that shows the technician how many customers are waiting, how long the longest person has waited, and what the average wait time is. If the technician feels that you're wasting his time, he might also feel that you're cheating other customers who are waiting in line.

Against the background of these pressures, the human who is talking with you will adopt tactics to keep your call short. Some tactics are designed to help you more quickly. Some are designed to bully you off the phone more quickly—whether you have been helped or not.

Long hold times and time pressures are part of the landscape when you call for support. They are management issues, and you should complain to the publisher's management, not the technician. Complaining to the technician will hurt his call times and (if you drag on long enough) make him hate you. On the other hand, the way he handles time pressure is a measure of the human with whom you are talking. If you are being badly served, the time pressure is a cause but not an excuse. Assert your reasonable expectation that you will get help when you call for help. You've waited long enough to speak to a human about your problem. When you finally reach a person, he should be a helper.

Calling about an Incompatible Device

Compatibility-related problems are the most challenging customer service issues. It typically takes (the estimates vary across studies) 3 to 18 times as long to resolve a multivendor problem as a problem that can be pinned to a specific piece of software or hardware (Oxton, 1997; Schreiber, 1997). We discuss this issue in terms of incompatible equipment, but the same issues and strategies apply when your program doesn't work with another program.

If the only problem with the program is that it doesn't work with your equipment, then understand that the software publisher might not be able to help you.

Compatibility issues drive software publishers crazy. There are too many different models of printers, mice, video cards, sound cards, etc. The publisher can't test its program with all of them. Many devices come with drivers (control programs) that have bugs. If a publisher's program fails to work with a device because of a bug in a printer driver, should the publisher rewrite the program, or should the printer manufacturer fix the driver? Another problem is that hardware manufacturers advertise their machines as compatible with others. For example, a printer manufacturer might claim that its printer is LaserJet 5p compatible even though its printer is really only *almost* compatible. If a program works perfectly with the original machine but fails to work with this "compatible" machine, who should do the re-engineering—the software publisher or the company who made the printer? Many software publishers feel that some hardware makers lie to their customers and blame problems with their equipment on the customer's software.

Complicating matters further, many problems aren't just two-way. For example, we've seen failures that involve a specific program, printer, printer driver, video card, and video driver. These problems are difficult for anyone (software publisher or hardware manufacturer) to catch.

Even the best and most responsible software publishers will have problems with incompatible equipment and software. They can be genuinely surprised by the problems you're having despite extensive testing. They can be genuinely puzzled. It might take considerable troubleshooting before they figure out what's wrong. If they don't have your device (your printer and your video card) in house, they might never figure it out.

Unfortunately, not all software publishers are the best and most responsible ones. The publisher you're calling might not have done much compatibility testing, and its customer service group might not have access to records of the testing that was done (if any records were kept). In addition, some publishers blame ordinary software errors on hardware to confuse and intimidate complaining customers.

"IT'S NOT OUR FAULT"

In this confused landscape, here is the toughest question we must answer. What if the technician tells you the problem is in your hardware or other system software? This could mean so many different things. Here is our best shot at troubleshooting:

A popular device.   If the program fails with a device that is a popular model of a popular brand or that the publisher said was compatible with the program, we recommend you look first to the software publisher (rather than the device manufacturer) for help. Why? The publisher probably tested with this device, and certainly should have tested with it, before releasing the product. The publisher might understand the special problems between the program and the device and know whether or not there is an easy solution.

- *Don't accept a brush-off.* If the technician says that you need a new driver from the device manufacturer but can't give you this driver directly, then ask where you can find this driver. For example, you want the driver publisher's mailing address, support phone number, or navigation instructions to its Internet address.

- *Get reassurance that it works.* Ask the publisher's technician whether she has tried this driver herself. If not, have other technicians tried it? Do they know that it will solve the problem? If not, what should you do, and what will they do for you, if the driver doesn't solve the problem?

Fix didn't work.   If a new driver or a software patch doesn't solve the problem, then we suggest that you renew your request for a refund for the software.

A specialized device.   If the program fails with a device that is very specialized, very old, or not very common for some other reason, then you can try asking the publisher for help, but you might only get help from the manufacturer of your device. Call the manufacturer first to ask for an updated device driver and any additional printed information (fact sheets, application notes, etc.) that might help you solve the problem.

A cheap device.   If the program fails with a device that is very cheap or that is known to have compatibility problems with many programs, you might not be able to get help from the publisher or the device manufacturer. Be prepared to hear frustration in the voices of the publisher's technicians. Some device manufacturers sell amazingly bad stuff and then blame their problems on other peoples' software. Publishers see these companies as parasites and may eventually give up on even trying to test or support their equipment. After a few hundred calls about problems that the publisher can't hope to fix, from people who've been pointed at the publisher by the device manufacturer, the publishers technicians get very frustrated.

Questionable track record.   If you don't know about the device's popularity and track record, call the software publisher first.

Try older drivers.   For example, if you have a LaserJet 5p printer and the program doesn't work with it, try a driver for the 4p, or even for the 2p. The newer driver might have an advanced feature that doesn't quite work with the program.

Avoiding Costly or Time-Consuming Solutions

What if the technician recommends drastic action, like reformatting your hard drive or buying new equipment?

Example: Similar Problems

Some programs have two similar problems. One requires a simple change to an operating system variable. To work around the other, you must buy more memory. The technician might tell you to spend $500 on memory when you don't need it. This kind of blunder—forgetting to ask enough questions to figure out the real problem—happens all the time. Some publishers manage this problem by writing "Answer Books" for their technicians or by putting comparable diagnostic information on-line. The Answer Books describe the known problems, and explain what information the technician should ask for when helping a customer with different types of problems. Some companies don't bother developing diagnostic procedures. They train their staff briefly, often using temps who will leave in frustration long before they become expert with the program, and then throw them to the wolves (read: customers).

Example: Reload Everything

It's easier for the technician to diagnose your system's problems if you're running a clean version of Windows. By reloading Windows, you get rid of possible corruption of the Registry and various other problems that might underlie the problem that you're having with your application. Even if this doesn't solve your problems, it simplifies the technician's troubleshooting tasks. Of course, it will take you time to reload Windows and get your other applications working with it again. In some cases, reloading an application will cost you all of the data that you've created or captured while using the application so far.

Some technicians are cautious about asking you to reformat your disk, to reload Windows, to reinstall your application, or to do any task that will take you a significant amount of work or time. The cautious ones don't ask for this type of work unless they don't have a better alternative. Less cautious technicians will make this type of request much more quickly. In their eyes, spending an hour (or more) of your time in order to save them a minute or two is a fair trade.

Use your good judgment before following the technician's suggestions. Don't hesitate to ask why you're being asked to do something and to ask whether a less drastic alternative is possible. Ask whether you're likely to lose data and whether the technician can recommend anything that will make data loss less likely. And, seriously consider backing up your system, your application, or your data before following the technician's instructions.

Finally, be sure to log the recommendations, your questions, and the technician's answers in your notebook. If you waste time and money at the request of the technician, and if it turns out that the underlying problem was a significant defect in the software itself, then you might decide to talk next with the technician's manager, and to ask for some extra consideration from the publisher (see Chapter 4, "Knowing What to Ask for").

Preserving Your Warranty Rights

Even if the program is seriously defective, the seller can sometimes wiggle away without paying you a nickel, even after it made and broke a warranty. To protect your legal options, you should do the following:

1. Give the publisher early notice of the problem. Write a short letter or make a phone call (make notes of the date, time, and content of the call) and describe the problem. From the warranty law viewpoint, the sooner you do this, the better.

2. Allow the publisher the opportunity to cure the problem. Ask whether the publisher wants to send you a bug fix version, and how long it will take to get you a fully tested bug fix. (If they fix the program in a hurry, and give it to you without much testing, they can give you worse bugs than the original version.)

3. In your letter, point out some of the ways that this bug is costing you time, money, lost business, etc. Remember that you might sue over this problem and ask for damages (money). Don't give the publisher a chance to pretend to be surprised at the expense and inconvenience the program cost you.

4. In all of your communications, especially the written ones, be reasonable and sound reasonable. That doesn't mean wimpy—if you have aggravation to express, say that you're aggravated and say why. But, keep your tone of voice level. No swearing. No personal insults. No exaggerations. Make the letter sound as though you're a person who can be dealt with.

5. Be conscious of time. If you have a warranty that is limited to 90 days, you have to prove that the failure occurred, and that you demanded corrective action, within those 90 days. You don't have to bring the lawsuit within 90 days, but you can't sue under this warranty for problems that showed up later.

THEY SAY YOU HAVE NO WARRANTY

When you back them into the corner, a disappointing number of technicians will tell you that you have no right to a working product because it came with no warranty. To prove this, they'll cite the shrink-wrap warranty disclaimer. This is the thing that you found inside the box that said the product is sold "AS IS." The technician is probably ignorant about consumer protection law. Even though the shrink-wrap warranty disclaimer that came with the product is probably invalid (see Chapter 7, "Software Quality and the Law"), the technician probably believes that it is enforceable and that anything that he does for you is a favor for which you should be grateful. You may have to develop a strategy for educating the customer service manager.

We want to draw an important distinction right away:

Time-limited written waranty.   If you got a written warranty, that gave you at least 90 days of promise that the software will work substantially in accordance with the manual and the advertising, and if you are calling more than 90 days after purchasing the product, then you are calling outside of a warranty period that we think most states will recognize as legitimate. You probably don't have any remaining warranty rights unless you have a support contract (in which case, your warranty probably extends through the life of the support contract).

Negotiating after a warranty has expired.   You're not without bargaining strength if the warranty has expired. You can still protest (or sue) about fraudulent misrepresentation of the capabilities of the product, and you still have the power to post complaints about the product on the Internet, to write letters, etc. If the program is indeed defective, you can still write complaints to consumer protection agencies. But, you probably don't have a warranty-based right to repair, replacement, or refund.

No written warranty.   In the more common case, the publisher has simply pronounced that you have no warranty rights; the product was sold "AS IS." As we explain in Chapter 7, in the section "Warranty Disclaimers in Software Packages," this statement is usually baloney.

- *Don't get mad at the technician.* It's rare that technicians say "no warranty" if they know better. You are merely dealing with someone who is ignorant. If the technician tells you, "Look, you know that you have no warranties when you buy software," then you want to explain to the technician:

- *I'm sorry, but you're mistaken.* I know that you put a disclaimer in the package that said that the software was sold *AS IS*, without warranties, but these disclaimers are routinely struck down by the courts. The courts have made it clear that the Uniform Commercial Code requires a conspicuous statement that there is no implied warranty. They say that the customer has to be able to see the disclaimer before the sale. The Uniform Commercial Code also says that express warranties—any statement of fact that your company has made about the product—cannot be disclaimed.

From here, listen to the technician. If he tries to be cooperative, great. If not, cut him off and say that you'd like to speak to his manager. You might decide, when speaking to the manager, to protest that the technician is telling people incorrect things about the law. You know how you negotiate. Some people will say this indignantly; others will be very calm and patient. The calm and patient ones, who sound like they know what they're talking about, are a lot scarier to support managers. Emotional protesters are taken less seriously because they probably won't do much once they calm down. Indignant, ignorant-sounding screamers risk being put on the speakerphone for general amusement.

Deciding If the Publisher Is Dealing with You in Good Faith

Sometimes, the publisher's technician will give you a difficult time when you complain. Does that mean that he's deliberately treating you badly, or dishonestly?

A well-trained technician knows how to greet you, how to listen to you, and how to make you feel welcome while he gets the information from you. (Anderson, 1992, is an example of the type of training material in common use.) But, the technician might not be able to give you the result that you want. It takes a lot of skill to say *no* with grace, in a way that invites customers to keep giving the publisher their business (Leland & Bailey, 1995). You might not be so lucky.

The technician with whom you speak (and the technician's manager and her manager) might genuinely want to help you but might not be very personable. If the technician is rude, does that mean that the publisher he represents is dishonest?

Sometimes, you'll get bad service or bad advice. The question to consider at this point is whether the publisher is dealing with you honestly.

It's not always easy to tell whether a publisher is acting in bad faith. Deciding that an honest publisher (or technician) is lying won't serve you well.

Publishers have a genuine, strong incentive to take care of you. It costs five to ten times as much to replace you as a customer as it does, on average, to do what it takes to keep you. (Brown, 1996b and Whiteley, 1991 offer a readily available discussion of this point.) Khandpur and Laub (1997) cite data from Reichfeld and Sasser (1990) which shows that a 5 percent reduction in customer defections from a software company resulted in a 35 percent increase in profits.

Until and unless the publisher's staff decide that you're not going to do business with them again, they should be willing to make some effort to keep your business. Therefore, you should not automatically assume when you get inferior support that you are facing a problem of corporate policy.

Here are cases where honest technicians give bad information or seem to waste your time:

Bad information from other customers.   Technicians learn a lot about a program's misbehavior from complaining customers. Sometimes, customers are their only source of information (for example, about incompatibility with equipment that the publisher doesn't have.) After a few similar phone calls, a technician might identify a specific problem, try a few suggestions, and mistakenly conclude that he knows a workaround. The next time a customer calls with this problem, the technician might mistakenly say, "Oh yes, we've heard of that problem. Here is what you have to do to work around it."

The problem is not well understood.   The technician may have heard of something like the problem you're calling with, but the call might be rare enough that the technician hasn't yet gotten enough data to replicate or validate it. In that case, he may ask you to run several tests to help him understand the problem more thoroughly.

Two versions of one model.   You call to complain about the program's incompatibility with your printer, the Brand X Model 2001. You describe the symptoms. The technician says, "We tested our program on the Brand X Model 2001, and it works perfectly. Maybe you should look for some other problem with your system." The problem is that the printer manufacturer made two different versions of the Model 2001. You have one version; the publisher has the other one.

Bad records.   Some publishers keep poor records of calls and use many temporary or lightly trained technicians. Sometimes, when the technician says about a known bug, "Gosh, I've never heard of that problem before," he's being truthful, if incompetent.

Mistaken identity.   Finally, sometimes the problem that you're reporting sounds like one that is more common. As we noted near the start of the chapter, diagnosing problems isn't an exact science. The technician's first suggestions might be entirely reasonable but wrong.

Customers also get suspicious when a technician asks them to do work outside of the telephone call, such as reinstalling Windows or getting a driver from someone else. These requests make us suspicious when we call for support. Many requested tasks make sense without the involvement to the technician. However, some technicians assign these tasks in order to get rid of the caller, not in order to help.

The core difference between legitimate call cost avoidance and counterfeit help is that the honest technician is trying to solve your problem quickly; whereas the counterfeiter is merely trying to get you off the phone quickly. If they can get you off the phone once, especially if they convince you to agree to do some kind of research or some other difficult task before calling back, then you probably won't call back. You'll have been successfully serviced (if not served). Ask yourself the following questions:

Is the publisher denying that the problem you are reporting exists?
For example, some technicians have said, "We tested that feature thoroughly, and it works." Sometimes, they know what they're talking about. But, customer service technicians often have no idea how much testing was done on any particular area of the program. If you can reproduce the problem (if you know what steps to take to make the program fail), ask the technician to follow along with you step by step and see what results he gets. When you (and, we hope, he) see the failure on your screen, what does the technician do and say? Does he apologize for his error? Does he take on the responsibility of investigating this and getting back to you?

Is the publisher blaming you for the problem?   Sometimes, you'll have problems that are your own fault. For example, if you use a Delete command to erase a file, and you can't find that file on your disk later, please don't blame the operating system. But, other mistakes are caused by the program. Worst case: you do something exactly as described in the manual, but it doesn't work. They say you're making a user error. In general, badly designed programs can't handle normal input, or they can't deal with common mistakes. If you keep using the program, are you likely to have the same problem again? If so, whether the problem is your "user error" or not, a program that can't cope with this problem is unsatisfactory. What options does the technician offer you to help you deal with this?

Is the publisher blaming you for inability to explain or work through the problem?   Telling you that you don't know what you're talking about is a powerful way of intimidating and embarrassing you. What should you think when the technician tells you that you aren't using the program correctly? He says that you just don't know enough about computers or that you're not reading the manual. He asks you to please try to do some better reading and call back if you still can't handle your own problems. How legitimate is this?

Unfortunately, technicians are often legitimately frustrated by people who demand hours of personal coaching and who will not make a reasonable effort to learn the basics of the program—or of how to use their computer before calling for help. Listen carefully if a frustrated technician says this to you; it might be true that you are being unreasonable or that the program requires more technical background than you have (we suggest that you ask for a refund). But, it might not be true. You might be doing as much as the publisher can reasonably expect of you. Did you try to find the information in the manual, in help, and in the other information the publisher provided? Did you try to do some troubleshooting on your own?

Are you being promised an upgrade in the future?   Sometimes, the publisher is developing a new version that will fix the problem that you're complaining about. And, sometimes people just say this to get you off the phone. Ask when it will be available. Ask the technician whether your name is on a list of people who will automatically receive the update, and if not, how you will find out that the update is available and what you will have to do to get it?

Are they wasting your time in this call?   For example, the technician might demand full registration information even though you have already sent yours in or given this to them before. The technician demands your receipt or the front page of your manual as proof of purchase, even though you bought the program directly from the publisher. Or, you have to explain the problem several times to several people. No one seems to be taking notes. Or, the technician insists on full configuration information from you before you describe the problem in detail. You have to hang up, open up your computer, and dig to find out the information, just to get the technician to listen to you describe a problem that might well turn out to be completely configuration independent. Are they making you jump through hoops or working with you with respect?

If the publisher asks you to call another vendor for information, why hasn't the publisher gotten this information itself?   Well, suppose that you report an incompatibility between the program and your Brand X 9000 printer. Three other people in the world have this printer. When you call for help, most publishers won't know the Brand X, won't want to know the Brand X, and won't spend much time helping you figure out how to work with a Brand X. On the other hand, if you have a bestseller, lots of people have probably called the publisher by the time you call. Normally, a publisher's support staff will do their own research for frequent calls, so when you talk to them, they probably know something. What aren't they telling you?

If the publisher asks you to call another vendor for support, why can't this publisher support you itself?   We raised this issue before, in the discussion of "Calling About an Incompatible Device." If the technician tells you to get an upgrade or a driver from someone else, ask whether the technician knows where to get it, whether it will work, and what you should do if it doesn't. Do they know whether this call will be worth your time?

If the publisher asks you to spend money to upgrade your hardware or software, ask: "Why do I need to do this?"   Is the technician sure? Did the publisher's box or documentation say that this program was compatible with your hardware or software? Did it say that you'd need these updated versions or the more-capable equipment? Does the technician know whether this will solve your problem? How? What is the chance that you will spend this money and still have the problem?

Did the publisher reassure you that an upgrade would fix the problem, but the upgrade didn't work?   Explain that to the technician (and to his manager, and maybe to his manager's manager.) Now that you've spent this money at their request, what are they willing to do in order to make it easy and cheap for you to get this problem solved?

Are you confident that there really is a problem with your hardware?   There might not be. The problem might be common across many different configurations, despite what the technician is (mistakenly or dishonestly) telling you. If you can, do some work with the program on a friend's machine. (For example, if you've been told to upgrade your video card, try to find a friend who has a very different video card, or an upgraded one.) See whether you run into the same problem. If you do, then the problem probably doesn't have anything to do with your hardware.

Are they saying untrue things?   Sometimes, you realize that you're being lied to. For example, the publisher says, "We've never heard of that," to different people about the same bug. Another of our favorites is looking at an advertisement that features a specific capability of the program while the technician denies that the publisher ever advertised any such thing.

If you decide that the publisher is acting in bad faith, consider bringing your complaint more quickly to a consumer protection agency or a lawyer. Be sure to take thorough notes of your conversations in preparation for a more formal dispute. And, of course, you should think carefully about dealing with the company ever again.

Action Plan
* Make the call to the publisher's support center.

* How did it go? If you resolved the issue, congratulations. You can close the book now. But, we recommend that you read Chapter 11, "Safe Shopping," so that you won't have as much of a hassle next time and the Appendix, "A New Threat to Customers' Rights: Proposed Revisions to the Uniform Commercial Code (Article 2B)," to help you preserve your legal rights for the future.

* What if the publisher didn't help you? Well, there's an old saying that the best way to accomplish your goals is to speak softly and carry a big stick. You've done your soft speaking. The next few chapters will supply you with sticks.

Chapter 6
Consumer Protection Agencies

 Chapter Map
Many organizations in the United States are willing to help consumers resolve disputes with businesses. Some of these organizations are private; others are part of a city, county, state, or the Federal government. This chapter describes the roles of these different organizations and guides you in contacting them.

During the research for this book, we did an extensive survey of consumer protection agencies. Our Web site, www.badsoftware.com, provides links to several of these agencies and suggestions on the best ways to file complaints with them. Visiting badsoftware.com is free. We hope that you drop by and that you find it useful.

Overview
The chapter is divided into the following sections:

- Why Complain to a Consumer Protection Agency?

- How Mediation Works

- What to Include in Your letter

- Who Should You Complain To?

    - Sample Letter to a Law-Enforcement Agency

    - Sample Letter to a Mediation Agency

- Disadvantages of Filing Your Complaint with a Consumer Protection Agency

- A Final Note to the Agencies

Contacts

Consumer Resource Handbook. Consumer Information Center, Pueblo, CO 81009. This is the best handbook there is, and it's free. Addresses for most consumer protection agencies and lots of tips. www.pueblo.gsa.gov.

Federal Trade Commission (FTC). Look in your telephone directory under "U.S. Government, Federal Trade Commission." If it does not appear, call the Federal Information Center at 800–688–9889 or contact Correspondence Branch, Federal Trade Commission, Washington, DC 20580 (written complaints only). www.ftc.gov.

National Fraud Information Center. For complaints about telecommunications fraud and Internet-based fraud. 800-876-7060. www.fraud.org.

National Association of Attorneys General. State attorneys general (AGs). Their Web page provides consumer protection information and contact information to the law-enforcement and mediation agencies run by the AGs. www.naag.gov.

United States Postal Inspection Service. Postal Inspectors are located in 30 Divisions. You can send the complaint to the Central Support Group or get the local Division's address at your post office. United States Postal Inspection Service, Central Support Group, 433 West Van Buren, Rm. 712, Chicago, IL 60607-5401, 800-654-8896. www.usps.gov/postofc/welcome.htm.

Call For Action. 2400 Idaho Ave., NW, #101, Washington, DC 20016, 202-537-0585. FAX 202-244-4881. www.callforaction.org.

Better Business Bureau (BBB). The address of the nearest BBB is probably in your phone book. Here is the national office: Council of Better Business Bureaus, Inc., 4200 Wilson Blvd., Arlington, VA 22203-1804. 703-276-0100. FAX 703-525-8277. www.bbb.org.

Consumer World.   Private Web site with excellent agency contact information and other useful advice and news. Excellent set of electronic links to state and local consumer protection agencies. www.consumerworld.org.

Bad Software.   We provide additional notes on submitting information to consumer protection agencies, along with summaries of state deceptive trade practices law, and an update on current legislation that threatens to change your rights. (See the Appendix, "A New Threat to Customers' Rights: Proposed Revisions to the Uniform Commercial Code (Article 2B)," for more information.) www.badsoftware.com.

Introduction

You will contact a consumer protection agency about your complaints with a publisher, in order to:

1. Get help resolving a dispute.

2. Expose the publisher's criminal misconduct and encourage the government to bring criminal charges.

3. Encourage the agency to alert the public to the publisher's misconduct.

We use the term "Consumer Protection Agency" broadly in this chapter to refer to any organization that works to resolve or prevent problems between consumers and businesses. This broad description includes several different types of organizations:

Law enforcement.   For example, the Federal Trade Commission (FTC), most States' Attorney General's Offices, and many District Attorneys' Offices will prosecute companies who show a consistent pattern of unfair or deceptive trade practices.

Government-based mediation.   Many county governments have a Consumer Affairs Department that will mediate disputes between customers and businesses. Some Attorney Generals and District Attorneys also provide this service.

Privately funded agencies.   The Better Business Bureau (BBB) is the best-known private group that mediates disputes between businesses and their customers. Several television stations and newspapers also provide this service.

Consumer advocacy groups.   For example, Consumer's Union publishes the magazine, *Consumer Reports.* If Consumer's Union hears enough serious criticism of a product or publisher, they might publish a warning in the magazine. They might also publicize the company's misbehavior as part of a lobbying or political action effort. Consumer advocacy groups don't mediate individual consumer disputes.

Why Complain to a Consumer Protection Agency?

It's a bit of a hassle to file a complaint with a consumer protection agency. You have to write a letter, photocopy lots of pages, and you may have to explain, explain, explain to someone who doesn't understand the technology. Is it worth it?

Our answer? Seeking help from one or more consumer agencies is usually well worth the effort. Here are a few of the benefits:

They care.   The people who work in these agencies will genuinely want to help you if you persuade them that you have a legitimate complaint and that you are trying to be reasonable. These people are underpaid or unpaid volunteers. They do this work because they believe in it.

Agencies extend your reach.   This is a convenient way to take action against a publisher located far from you. It can be awkward to sue an out-of-state company. You might have to sue the publisher in its own state. In contrast, it is easy to file a complaint by mail with a consumer protection agency in the publisher's home county or state.

Help understanding the process, with little expense.   If the agency assigned a mediator, you have an independent person explaining to you what's going on and helping you to keep a cool head and a smile. This is important for the negotiations and for your overall quality of life.

Your complaint to the agency is probably free. Research on the publisher's background with the agency is free or very inexpensive.

Increase your leverage (bargaining power).   The publisher has a strong incentive to treat you reasonably, once a consumer protection agency takes an interest in your case. No company wants to develop a reputation for being unreasonable, not with the District Attorney or the Attorney General.

A consumer protection agency is unlikely to go away if the publisher tries to brush it off. The mediator will keep calling, writing letters to different people in the company, and making a persistent nuisance of himself until the publisher treats your complaint reasonably, either by reaching an agreement with you or by convincing the mediator that you are being unreasonable.

Communication between you, the publisher, and the agency creates a record. If you do decide to sue the publisher, this record can provide you with useful, credible evidence. If the publisher lied and stonewalled the mediator, your case will be strengthened. And, if the publisher didn't answer the mediator's letters or return the mediator's phone calls, the judge will see that your dispute ended up in court because of the publisher.

You are helping to clean up an industry. This might sound corny, but if we were more likely to report criminal behavior and to publicize unfair and unreasonable behavior, many publishers would become more fair, more reasonable, and less likely to cheat us. In contrast, in the absence of enforcement, even the best companies sometimes slide into misconduct that we should all want to see prevented. Reporting bad practices to law enforcement and consumer advocacy agencies can make a big difference over a period of a few years.

FTC ACTION

The Federal Trade Commission does take action against computer and software companies that engage in unfair or deceptive practices. Here are a few examples of computer-related actions brought by the FTC:

Commodore Business Machines. The FTC fined Commodore Business Machines $250,000 for advertising vaporware—promising people that its machines would be able to emulate a different computer, when that emulation software wasn't available (Commerce Clearing House, 1990).

Apple Computer. The FTC alleged that Apple Computer misrepresented that a Power PC Upgrade Kit was available to consumers at (or not long after) the time they purchased certain "Performa" personal computers when it actually was not available for more than a year and cost almost as much as an entirely new PowerPC computer. See *In the Matter of Apple Computer, Inc.* (1997).

Syncronous Software. The FTC alleged that Syncronous Software made misrepresentations and/or unsubstantiated claims regarding the performance of two computer software programs they manufactured—SoftRAM and SoftRAM95. *In the Matter of Syncronous Software.* (1996).

Internet service providers. The FTC alleged that America Online, Inc. (AOL), Prodigy Services Corporation, and CompuServe, Inc., provided "free trial" offers that resulted in unexpected charges for many consumers. See *In the Matter of America Online, Inc.* (1998), *In the Matter of CompuServe, Inc.* (1998), and *In the Matter of Prodigy Services Corporation* (1998).

Dell Computer. The FTC alleged that Dell Computer violated the FTC's Mail Order Rule when it advertised and sold a "Dell Dimension" computer system bundled with a package of third-party software that was not ready to be shipped. Dell agreed to pay an $800,000 civil penalty. *United States v. Dell Computer Corporation* (1998).

State Attorneys General also bring consumer protection lawsuits. They now share a great deal of information, partially through a law-enforcement data-sharing system set up in conjunction with the FTC. Information sharing helps them act in concert. The National Association of Attorneys General's Web page (www.naag.org) highlights these multistate, joint actions.

How Mediation Works

This section is based partially on requests for information that we sent to several hundred agencies across the country. We received about 200 responses, many of them quite detailed. It's also partially based on Kaner's experience as a part-time volunteer Investigator for the Santa Clara County Department of Consumer Affairs in 1986–1988 and on our experiences as business managers (and the experiences of managers we've interviewed), fielding complaints that have come to us through these agencies. Please understand that each agency follows its own procedures, and no agency follows the exact set of steps we describe.

You will most often use a consumer protection agency as a mediator, to help you resolve a dispute with another business. This method is a much more direct way to solve your problem with a business today than hoping that a law-enforcement agency will prosecute.

The first step is to buy an unsatisfactory product. (Oh, goodie.) Then try unsuccessfully to return it or to collect reimbursement for your losses. Try again. Keep trying until you become convinced that the publisher or retailer is unreasonable and that you need help.

Now write a letter to your county's Consumer Affairs Department. Write a good letter that gives them all the information they need. Exhibit 6.1 lists all the things that you should put into the letter.

Remember to keep a copy of all correspondence that you send to a consumer-protection agency or to the publisher. Even if you hate paperwork, keep copies of these documents.

Exhibit 6.1: Letter to Your Consumer Affairs Department

Tone of the Letter

The publisher will probably receive a copy of this letter. The person reading the complaint probably isn't the one who caused the problem, but he could be very helpful in resolving it. There is little value in making him hate you.

Also, if you end up in court, the judge will probably see your letter.

Be courteous. Keep an even, balanced tone. You don't have to be apologetic or wimpy, but don't sound nasty or unreasonable. Don't say, "he lied." Say, "he said *X*, and it was not correct." Don't say the company should go out of business or that someone on staff should be fired. Never exaggerate or lie in your communications.

Getting Information for the Letter

Everything that we suggest that you include in your letter is discussed in Chapter 3, "Preparing to Make the Call." If you aren't sure how to get the information that we suggest, see Chapter 3.

You might not be able to get some of this information easily. Don't worry about it. Get the best information you can within a reasonable period of time and use that. You can always add more information later if it's needed.

Contact Information

Personal information.   Provide your name, address, home and work phone numbers, and your e-mail address. If they are relevant, provide your account number or purchase order.

Retailer information.   State where you bought the product. Name the store (or catalog) and give the address and phone number. Please provide an 800-number if you know one. If you know names (even first names), name the store manager and the salesperson who sold you the product.

Publisher information.   Name the publisher and list its address and phone number. If you talked to any customer service representatives, give their names and phone numbers. List their e-mail addresses and the addresses of any on-line discussion groups that pay attention to this product. If there's a page in the manual that explains how to contact Technical Support or Customer Service, photocopy that page and include it, too.

Basic Information about the Product

Name the product and its version number.   If you have it, give the product's serial number.

Describe the program briefly.   For example, say that it's a word processor, a fax program, or a program that tracks a video store's tape inventory.

Price and purchase date.   When did you buy it and how much did you pay?

Describe the Problem

Explain the problem. You're going to have to use your own judgment on how much to say. You probably don't need much detail for a refund. You'll need more if you ask for much more than a refund. If you do go into detail, put it at the end of the letter as an appendix or in a separate memo.

What makes the product faulty? You might briefly explain why the problem makes the product unacceptable to you. If the unacceptability is obvious (the program erased your hard disk, or it keeps crashing), don't spend more time on it.

Point out false statements. If the salesperson made promises that weren't kept or incorrect statements, name the salesperson (if possible) and say what was said. Explain why you believe that what was said is not correct.

Include print corroboration. If magazine articles say the same things as the publisher or the salesperson said, include a photocopy of an article or two, to show that you're not just misunderstanding the message.

Negotiations to Date

Summarize publisher contacts. If you've entered into negotiations with the publisher, summarize what has happened in your letter to the agency. Include a copy of all of your letters to the publisher or to the store that sold the product to you and a copy of all of their letters to you. If you talked to them by phone (or in person), you might provide notes that summarize the conversations. Name the people who you talked to.

Mention letters sent to agencies. If you filed a complaint with another agency, such as the BBB or a consumer affairs department, and if they have taken action on your behalf, then describe the results of their negotiations in your letter. If there has been correspondence between the publisher and the other agency, include these materials in your letter.

Documentation

Include photocopies of your receipts and your evidence that the program has a problem. *Never* send your original documents. *Send copies.*

Include copies of the following, if applicable:

- Receipt(s) for purchase of the product.
- Sales contract or agreement.

- Warranty.
  - If the only thing that you have that looks like a warranty is a disclaimer you found inside the box, which says you have no warranty, express or implied, then read Chapter 7, "Software Quality and the Law." This disclaimer is probably invalid. If so, we suggest that you ignore the disclaimer. Don't mention it and don't include it in your letter. If the publisher talks about it, send the agency a copy of the section, "Warranty Disclaimers in Software Packages," from Chapter 7.
- Incorrect advertisements. Explain what is incorrect.
- Incorrect box copy.
  - If there are errors on the box that the program came in, photocopy that part of the box and include it. Explain what is incorrect.
- Errors in the manual.
  - If your complaint is based on errors in the manual, include photocopies of the cover page of the manual and the pages with the errors.
- Your notes.
  - Include any notes you made at the time of sale, which show what the salesperson promised you. Include copies of any memos you sent to the business, or received from it, which confirm your understanding of the promises or the workings of the program.

Explain What You Want

See Chapter 4, "Knowing What to Ask For," for a discussion of what you should ask for from the publisher. If you've lost money because of defects in the publisher's product, ask for reimbursement for what you've lost.

Extra money.   If you want more than a refund, explain why you're entitled to the extra money. Enclose photocopies of every receipt. Explain why each expense or loss that you list is reasonable and how it was caused by the defect in the program.

Help.   If you want help (technical support or a bug fix) rather than a refund, and you are complaining because of inadequate or ineffective support, then tell the publisher what help you need.

Time constraints.   State any special facts that limit how long you can wait for resolution of the problem.

The Agency Receives Your Letter

When the agency receives your letter, one of the staff opens it, stamps it with today's date, and might enter it into a log of complaints received against a particular business. The letter is then assigned to a staff member (who we'll call the mediator) as an open case.

The mediator photocopies your letter and puts a standard cover letter on the front that says, "We are the X County Consumer Affairs Department, and we just received this complaint. Please read it and respond." The mediator then sends the letter to the business you complained about. If you complained about a store and a publisher, the mediator will send a copy to each.

MEDIATOR'S LOCATION

The mediator also considers the address of the business that you complained about. If you live in Piscataway, New Jersey, for example, and you complain against a publisher in San Mateo, California, then a mediator working for the Middlesex County (New Jersey) Department of Consumer Affairs might also copy the letter and send it to the San Mateo County District Attorney's Consumer Fraud and Environmental Protection Unit or to the California Department of Justice.

If the mediator doesn't think that he can be effective with the distant business, he might forward the complaint to the California agency and close the Piscataway file on your case.

Alternatively, the New Jersey-based mediator might keep the case but write to California to alert them to the problem and to ask whether they have any helpful information.

The mediator might send the letter to the second agency right away or wait to see the publisher's response. All consumer agencies are overworked and understaffed. Many of them have a policy against sending anything to another agency until they are certain that a real problem exists, which is hard enough to resolve that it is worth spending the time of the second agency's staff.

THE BUSINESS RESPONDS

Most businesses respond quickly, especially if they are in the same state as the agency sending the letter. The business might respond directly to you, by phone or by letter. Or, it might respond only to the mediator.

It's common for the business to pay up immediately, whether it considers itself right or wrong, just to get the county off of its back.

It's also common for the business to make a counter-offer. Perhaps, they want to give you only a 50-percent refund because you've been using the product for a year. Or, perhaps they'll give you the full refund but no reimbursement for your incidental expenses.

What if the business responds that your conduct to this point has been outrageous and that it will give you nothing, because you deserve nothing? The mediator will consider a negative response very carefully. Is your claim honest? (A claim often has ulterior motives). The county doesn't want to help cheating consumers any more than it wants to help cheating businesses.

The business may ignore the mediator's letter. Not wise. If the business doesn't cooperate with the county, the mediator could forward the business' file to a prosecutor for investigation. Further, you'll probably end up in court. You can call the mediator as a witness. The mediator could testify that the county tried to help solve your mutual problem informally, but the business wasn't even willing to talk. Refusal to negotiate reduces the business' credibility and goodwill with the judge.

> ### *Caution*
> *Filing a complaint with a consumer protection agency sometimes gives you a lot of leverage, but only a fool would send weak or unfair complaints to the County Government or the District Attorney or the State's Attorney General.*

Whatever the publisher's response, the mediator will probably do the following:

- Photocopy the response and send you a copy.
- Telephone both you and the publisher to determine the nature the problem from both sides.
- Offer you advice or an opinion. He could say that you don't have much of a claim and advise you to drop it, or he might suggest taking the publisher to small claims court.
- Offer advice to the publisher, trying to help you and the publisher reach an agreement.

Eventually, you will reach an agreement with the publisher, give up, or take the next step (e.g., go to court). In most cases, the consumer and the business reach an agreement.

NO RESPONSE FROM THE BUSINESS

Some businesses are foolish enough to not respond to a consumer protection agency or to respond arrogantly. In the short run, the business saves time and doesn't have to deal with you. But, it hurts the business and its reputation directly and indirectly. For example, the Better Business Bureau flags companies that don't respond to customer complaints. When customers call BBB to check on the reputation of a potential seller, nonresponsiveness is pointed out. Here are examples taken from Kaner's pre-lawyerly days as a part-time volunteer mediator/investigator for Santa Clara County's Department of Consumer Affairs. The cases are confidential, so we have to hide many of the details.

Example: A Pattern of Refusals to Respond

A California-based mail-order company was treating its customers badly. We got several complaints, which ended up consolidating at my desk. I called them repeatedly, but no one who had any authority was willing to talk with me. In terms of solving the customers' problems, we got nowhere.

The bills showed an interesting pattern, however. The company apparently didn't always charge sales tax, even though several sales were to Californians (so they were subject to sales tax). I made a friendly phone call, one government agency to another, to our state tax collectors and explained the situation. They were delighted to receive the tip (of course), and you can imagine the results for yourself. The customers' complaints never were resolved by our agency, and the company probably never realized what caught the tax collectors' interest. But, they got to experience the old rule: what goes around, comes around.

Example: Deceptive Ads Come to an End

This case demonstrates arrogance instead of failure to respond.

A company ran misleading advertisements. Essentially, a customer (who might be located anywhere) could pay some money to become eligible for a free or inexpensive upgrade of certain services. The problem was that the upgrades were almost never available. The company's ads claimed that the services were available in a lot of cities (they were). However, the ads forgot to mention that the upgrades for these services were only available in two cities.

We wrote our usual letter of inquiry, a neutral document that forwarded a copy of the customer's complaint and asked for a response. The response that came back was from the company's lawyers. Fancy stationary. Lots of big words. And a bottom-line message, terse and barely polite, that the ads contained no false statements; therefore, they were legal, and therefore, we should go jump in the lake.

Well, what can a bunch of overworked, underpaid (or unpaid) nonlawyers do in response to a letter like that? Obviously nothing. So, we sent the file and a cover letter to the California Attorney General's (AG's) office, basically whimpering that these big kids were beating us up.

The AG's response (personally signed by the AG) came back quickly. He sent us a copy of the letter that went to the company. He complimented the big company on the size and learning of its legal staff, expressed his envy that such companies could afford the top legal talent in the country, and that sometimes, government agencies had to go to distinguished groups of lawyers like these in the hopes of getting some free advice. In this case, for example, he hoped that the company would do him a favor. Would it please share with him the extensive legal research that the company must have done when it received our letter and determined that its conduct was not forbidden under the following statutes? He then listed laws that ban deceptive practices, almost certainly including the advertisements that this company was publishing.

Funny thing—those ads stopped appearing in newspapers in California that very day.

Consumer protection agencies that do mediation (instead of enforcement) don't have a lot of power, but they have a lot more power than some people think. Wise companies respond to their friendly offers to help a company and its customer straighten out a deal that has gone sour.

By the way, if you can spare some time to do volunteer work, your local consumer protection agency probably needs your help. The agency probably has a tiny paid staff that trains and supervises a larger group of volunteers. They stay busy. For example, Connecticut's Department of Consumer Protection recently reported that, in one year, it handled 119,549 consumer phone calls and processed 9,297 written complaints. The City of New York's Department of Consumer Affairs reported that it handles about 132,000 inquiries and about 6,500 formal complaints per year. Agencies like these cost their governments almost nothing and recover millions of dollars for American consumers every year.

For the address of your local agency, check the *Consumer Resource Handbook* (Consumer Information Center, Pueblo, CO 81009, www.pueblo.gsa.gov) or *Consumer World* (www.consumerworld.org) or call your local District Attorney's office for a referral.

Who Should You Complain To?

There are hundreds of different consumer protection agencies in the United States. You don't want to send your complaint to all of them. Different agencies have different objectives and will provide you, and the country, with very different services.

> **Tip**
> If you believe that the seller's behavior was illegal or unethical, then report that behavior to a law-enforcement agency. Additionally, seek help from a government mediation service or from a private service such as the Better Business Bureau. The enforcement agency will eventually target illegal conduct and stop it. The mediator will help you settle your complaint with the seller.

> **Warning**
> You might eventually decide that you have no choice but to sue a company. You have a limited time in which to sue. For example, you might have to sue within a year of buying a product on the basis of misrepresentations by a company, or lose your right to sue. Contacting a consumer protection agency doesn't change your deadline.

LAW-ENFORCEMENT AGENCIES

File a complaint with a law enforcement agency if you believe that the publisher (or other business) is engaging in illegal conduct. Unfair and deceptive trade practices, including false advertising and bad faith refusal to honor a warranty, are illegal. For more information, you can check our Web site, www.badsoftware.com, for a table that summarizes unfair and deceptive practices statutes.

Agencies whose primary concern is law enforcement will probably not bring charges against a company based on one complaint by one consumer. These agencies are looking for a pattern of illegal conduct.

The primary value of informing a law-enforcement agency of your problem with a publisher is that it alerts the agency to a pattern of misbehavior. If several people complain against this publisher, the agency is likely to investigate. If this publisher's conduct is illegal, your complaint is putting the publisher on the road to trouble. Several companies have gotten into trouble. You can see lists of current enforcement actions at the Federal Trade Commission's Web site, www.ftc.gov.

Even though a law-enforcement agency will probably not actively mediate your complaint, the agency may send the publisher a copy of your letter and ask the publisher to send it a copy of any response that it sends to you. The following simple letter is very persuasive. The publisher is likely to send you your money, along with a letter like the following one:

Dear Customer,

We're so sorry you misunderstood us. We value our good relationship with our customers. Your complaint was very helpful to us in identifying ways in which we can serve customers better. We have carefully reviewed our product and our advertising, and it is our conclusion that neither of them is defective. However, we value detailed feedback from people like you so much that we have decided to recognize your efforts. Please accept this check as a token of our appreciation and an indication of our wish that you will stay on as our valued customer.

Of course, what they really mean in this letter is:

Dear Law-Enforcement Agency,

In response to your letter, we just want you to know that we're a bunch of really nice people who always take care of our customers. Too bad about this complaint, but you can see that we've taken care of it. So, there's no need for you to spend any time thinking about whether to investigate us. You won't find a thing. Trust us.

Before you send a letter to a law-enforcement agency, you should send a letter of complaint to the publisher (or to the business that sold you the program, if they're the people who misled you). Note that it can lessen the degree to which your complaint is taken seriously if you send a complaint to the law-enforcement agency without having ever complained about the problem to the publisher. It's OK to send an agency a copy of your complaint letter on the same day that you mail the letter to the publisher.

Exhibit 6.2: Sample Letter to a Law-Enforcement Agency

{Your address}
{Date}

Federal Trade Commission
6th & Pennsylvania Avenue, NW
Washington, D.C. 20580

re: Brand X Mail
     Brand X Corp., 123 X Lane, Anytown, USA 12345 408-555-5555

I purchased the Brand X Electronic Mail Program, Version 6.02c, on July 15, 1998. I bought it directly from Brand X and paid $248.22.

According to Brand X's advertisement in the June 15 issue of {name of magazine}, version 6.02c had been upgraded to provide support for BinHex encoding. This feature allows the program to read more documents that come attached to electronic mail messages than it did before. I bought the program specifically to take advantage of this feature.

Unfortunately, I have been unable to get this aspect of the program to work.

On July 24, 1998, I called Brand X for help. They don't have a toll-free line, so I called long distance. They put me on hold and left me hanging on for 28 minutes. Finally, I spoke to Joe X, who said he was a technical support representative. He said that this feature worked perfectly, so there must be something wrong with my computer. No one else was having this problem, he said.

On July 25, I logged onto CompuServe and looked at the messages that were being posted about Brand X mail. There were 57 complaints that BinHex wasn't working, dating back to May 1, 1998. On May 15, 1998, a person who signed his posting as Joe X said that he worked for Brand X as a technical support representative. He acknowledged that there was a problem, but people should be patient while Brand X fixes it. There was no follow-up announcement of a fix.

On July 26, I called Brand X again and, after waiting on hold for 20 minutes, spoke with Joe X. He said, yes, he had posted that message on CompuServe, but the problem affected only a few weird computers, like mine. I asked him why he hadn't told me this last time we talked, and he started shouting at me. Then he hung up.

Along with the $248.22, this program has now cost me $22.00 in telephone charges and 14 hours of my time.

I believe that this is a widespread problem. If you log onto CompuServe and then type {instructions}, you will find at least 57 other people in my situation. I've printed a few of these messages and enclosed them with this letter. There are probably many, many other dissatisfied customers who are not posting their complaints on CompuServe.

I hope that you will investigate Brand X's advertising practices and their policy of truthfulness in communicating with customers who call for post-sale support.

I would also appreciate any help you can give me in recovering my expenses. This would include a refund of the purchase price, $248.22, plus $22 in telephone and CompuServe time, for a total of $260.22.

Yours truly,

Enclosures
Receipt for the purchase of the program
Copy of the advertisement
Copy of other complaints by other customers

Notes on the Letter to a Law-Enforcement Agency

This letter lists several misrepresentations by the publisher's staff. The misrepresentations work together to suggest to the reader a pattern of dishonest conduct. The letter also points out that many people have been affected. And, it suggests a place that the reader can go to find additional complaints and evidence. All are good points to make to a law-enforcement agency. The more dishonest the conduct, and the more people who have been cheated, the more likely they are to prosecute.

The ad and the dated purchase receipt might be useful as evidence. You can send your phone bill and your CompuServe bill now, too, or you could send them later, if the agency actually does try to help you recover your money.

Should You Tell the Publisher?

You are not required to tell the publisher that you have filed a complaint with a law-enforcement agency, and we don't recommend it. Here's our reasoning:

Loses good will.   First, a publisher will do certain things for you in an effort to keep your goodwill or to prevent you from filing a formal complaint against it. At the point that you tell the publisher that you have already reported it to a law-enforcement agency, you're telling it that there is no goodwill to salvage and no remaining opportunity to keep this away from the authorities.

Brings in publisher's lawyers.   If you tell the publisher that you are reporting it to the authorities, the company will probably hand your complaint to its lawyers. The lawyers might decide to give you what you want. If not, you are now dealing with professional negotiators who see you as someone who has threatened their company. Ouch.

Costs credibility.   If you send a letter to a law-enforcement agency, it might or might not contact the publisher. The agency might just put your letter on file and follow up only after more letters like yours come in. For example, suppose that you tell the publisher that you've sent copies of your letter to the *Federal Trade Commission* (FTC), but the publisher never hears anything from the FTC. The publisher might conclude either that you're bluffing or that the FTC doesn't think that the publisher has done anything bad. In either case, your credibility suffers.

Agency action creates credibility.   If you say nothing and then the publisher does get a letter from the FTC, it will come as a surprise. The letter will boost the publisher's sense of how serious and how persistent you're likely to be, at the same time as it forces the publisher to recognize that you have some leverage. There's a good chance that the publisher will send your case to its lawyer, but at least now, the lawyer knows that you really are pursuing your complaint actively, and the FTC is paying attention. You are not just bluffing.

In sum, the only time that you want the publisher to learn that you have reported it to the authorities is when that discovery is more likely to work more to your advantage than to your disadvantage. That happens when the authorities contact the publisher and say, "We have a complaint against you" but not when you say, "I'm going to tell on you," or "I have told."

But, is this nondisclosure fair? Of course it's fair. You'll only report the publisher to the authorities if you believe it's engaging in criminal misconduct. Would you tell a car thief that you had just reported her to the police? Probably not. How is a publisher that engages in criminal misconduct any different from a car thief? Why should you give the publisher a warning that you wouldn't give to any other criminal?

If you do decide to tell the publisher that you are reporting it to a law-enforcement agency, be careful of how you do it. You don't want to use this for bargaining power. In most jurisdictions, it is a crime (extortion, blackmail, that kind of crime) to say, "If you give me a thousand dollars for my damages, I won't report you to the police." Similarly, it would be a no-no to say, "I have reported you to the police, but if you resolve this now, I can call them off."

Which Law-Enforcement Agency?

Federal Trade Commission.   If the publisher's products are sold in more than one state, including sales over the Internet, then it is reasonable to file a complaint with the FTC. For information on the FTC's work on Internet-based fraud, see U.S. Federal Trade Commission (1998). Federal Trade Commission, 6th & Pennsylvania Ave., NW, Washington, D.C. 20580, 202-326-2222, 202-326-2502 TDD, www.ftc.org.

United States Postal Inspection Service.   If you bought a product by mail or were enticed to buy a product by an advertisement that was mailed to you, you can also contact the United States Postal Inspection Service. Postal Inspectors are located in 30 Divisions. You can send the complaint to the Central Support Group or get the local Division's address at your post office. United States Postal Inspection Service, Central Support Group, 433 West Van Buren, Rm. 712, Chicago, IL 60607-5401, 800-654-8896.

National Fraud Information Center.   If you were the victim of telemarketing-based or Internet-based fraud, contact the *National Fraud Information Center* (NFIC). They coordinate with law-enforcement agencies around the world, which can be essential for dealing with Internet-based fraud. They recommend that you call them or that (second best) you file an online incident report. National Fraud Information Center, P.O. Box 65868, Washington, DC 20035, 1-800-876-7060, www.fraud.org.

State's Attorney General.   At the state level, you will probably file a complaint with your state's Attorney General (AG). If the publisher is based in another state, complain to that state's AG, too. You probably can find your state AG's office in the phone book. Or, check the *Consumer Resource Handbook* (Consumer Information Center, Pueblo, CO 81009, www.pueblo.gsa.gov) or the Web page of the National Association of Attorneys General, www.naag.gov.

District Attorney.   In some states, the best office to contact is the District Attorney in the publisher's city or county.

Other agencies.   For other law-enforcement agencies in your city, county, or state and in the publisher's, check the *Consumer Resource Handbook* (Consumer Information Center, Pueblo, CO 81009, www.pueblo.gsa.gov), the links from the National Fraud Information Center (www.nfic.gov) and from *Consumer World* (www.consumerworld.org).

If you complain to only one agency, we suggest that you make it the FTC or the Attorney General of the publisher's state. If you believe that you were the victim of telemarketing or Internet fraud, contact the NFIC.

Government-Based Mediation

You can seek mediation whether you think the publisher's conduct is criminal or not. The agency that conducts the mediation is not enforcing the law. The agency is just helping you and the publisher communicate better.

Many county governments have a Consumer Affairs Department that will mediate disputes between customers and businesses. Some Attorney Generals and District Attorneys also provide this service. If the mediator realizes that the publisher is engaging in a pattern of unlawful conduct, he may refer the case to a law-enforcement unit for criminal investigation and prosecution.

 Exhibit 6.3: Sample Letter to Mediation Agency

{Your address}
{Date}

{Address of Consumer Affairs Agency, Better Business Bureau, or other Agency}

re: Brand X Mail

Brand X Corp.
123 X Lane
Anytown, USA 12345
408-555-5555

I purchased the Brand X Electronic Mail Program, Version 6.02c, on July 15, 1996. I bought it directly from Brand X and paid $248.22.

According to Brand X's advertisement in the June 15 issue of {name of magazine}, version 6.02c had been upgraded to provide support for BinHex encoding. This feature allows the program to read more documents that come attached to electronic mail messages than it did before. I bought the program specifically to take advantage of this feature.

Unfortunately, I have been unable to get this aspect of the program to work. I am writing to ask for your help in obtaining a refund of the purchase price, $248.22, plus reimbursement of $46 for telephone bills and CompuServe time, for a total of $294.22.

On July 24, 1996, I called Brand X for help. They don't have a toll-free line, so I called long distance. They put me on hold and left me hanging on for 28 minutes. Finally, I spoke to Joe X, who said he was a technical support representative. He said that this feature worked perfectly, so there must be something wrong with my computer. No one else was having this problem, he said.

On July 25, I logged onto CompuServe and looked at the messages that were being posted about Brand X mail. There were 57 complaints that BinHex wasn't working, dating back to May 1, 1996. On May 15, 1996, a person who signed his posting as Joe X said that he worked for Brand X as a technical support representative. He acknowledged that there was a problem, but people should be patient while Brand X fixes it. There was no follow-up announcement of a fix.

On July 26, I called Brand X again and, after waiting on hold for 20 minutes, spoke with Joe X. He said, yes, he had posted that message on CompuServe, but the problem affected only a few weird computers, like mine. I asked him why he hadn't told me this last time we talked, and he started shouting at me. Then he hung up.

These two telephone calls cost $42. The research on CompuServe cost $6. I wasted 14 hours of my time trying to get this program working, many of them after Joe X told me that BinHex was working.

Thank you for your help.

Yours truly,

Enclosures
Receipt for the purchase of the program
Copy of the telephone bill
Copy or printout of the compuserve bill
Copy of the advertisement

Notes on the Mediation Agency Letter

Notice that in this letter, you aren't asking for law-enforcement action or for any investigation. Just for help collecting your money.

Many consumer protection agencies recommend that you file your complaint with a mediation unit based in the county or state of the publisher, rather than in your state.

Some government-based mediation or enforcement agencies will let you check their files for their complaint history with the publisher. These files are worth checking before you buy something from the publisher, but they are also valuable after the sale, when you file a complaint. If the publisher has a bad complaint-handling record, you should consider complaining to an enforcement agency because it has more clout. In your letter to the agency, describe the publisher's bad record with local dispute-resolution agencies. You should also consider the possibility of a lawsuit. It can take you months of run around before you realize that a publisher isn't negotiating with you in good faith—if a publisher's bad track record helps you realize earlier who you're dealing with, these records have saved you time.

Privately Funded Agencies

Some states provide no consumer mediation and little or no criminal enforcement of the laws against deceptive or unfair trade practices. To file a complaint against one of their publishers, you have to complain to a privately funded, nongovernmental agency or to the Federal Trade Commission.

The Better Business Bureau (BBB) is the best-known private group that mediates disputes between businesses and their customers. As publishers' customer support and quality-control managers, we've had to deal with more complaints handled by the BBB than by any other consumer complaint mediator. When the BBB is effective, it is *very* effective.

The Better Business Bureau will probably also give you information about its complaint history with the publisher. This information is useful before buying the software and after buying it (to help you when you have a complaint, to figure out whether you're dealing with a responsible company.) If the publisher has settled every complaint against it or has dealt reasonably with every complaint, you'll get a favorable report from the BBB. If the BBB feels that the publisher has acted unreasonably, you'll get an unfavorable report.

However, be aware that the BBB is funded by businesses, not by consumers. It is not always on your side. Further, the BBB is actually a collection of local BBB's whose effectiveness varies. Some local BBB's might not serve you well (Marable, 1995). We think that it is worth contacting your local BBB, but keep your options open. And, if you are dealing with fraud, file a complaint with NFIC or the FTC as well.

The address of the nearest BBB is probably in your phone book. Here is the national office: Better Business Bureau, Council of Better Business Bureaus, Inc., 4200 Wilson Blvd., Arlington, VA 22203-1804, 703-276-0100, 703-525-8277 FAX, www.bbb.org.

Several television stations and newspapers also provide a complaint resolution service—contact Call for the address of a news organization near you that offers this service. Call For Action, 2400 Idaho Ave., NW, #101, Washington, DC 20016, 202-537-0585, 202-244-4881 FAX.

Consumer Advocacy Groups

Consumer advocacy groups do not mediate or arbitrate consumer complaints. They are privately funded and have no law-enforcement power. But, they have influence. They might engage in any of the following activities:

- Publish magazines (such as Consumer Reports) that rate products or alert people to abusive behavior by some product sellers.

- Testify before government agencies or before the legislature.

- Lobby for improved consumer protection laws.

- Write and publicize voter initiatives that strengthen consumer protection laws.

- Publish books or reports or consumer advice guides on the state of consumer abuse within specific industries.

When you file a complaint with a consumer advocacy agency, you may get no apparent response. They probably do not send it to the publisher. They do not mediate the complaint. They read it and then stick it in a file. Maybe a year later, they'll pull out your letter, any other letters or research materials in the file, and start planning some specific research or actions to deal with this publisher or this part of the industry.

The value of filing complaints with these agencies is that the complaints do educate them. They will act more effectively on our behalf if they understand the dynamics and content of the software industry. They will act more quickly if they realize that there is a widespread problem.

More Tips: Mediation Agencies

Keep originals.   Always send copies of your documents. Keep the original copies of your receipts and other documents in a safe place.

Phone first.   Many agencies prefer that you call first, so that they can screen the complaint. They can try to tell you over the phone whether your issue is something that they think they can help you with.

Complaint history.   Some Agencies will let you look at the complaint history of a business. Several of them have asked us to stress to you that these histories do not *necessarily* reflect the underlying reliability or unreliability of the business. Some terrible businesses make a point of resolving their complaints quickly, and some ethical businesses have refused to compromise with customers they considered unreasonable, even after those customers went to the county or state with a complaint.

BBB.   The Better Business Bureau also provides complaint histories for businesses. These are probably based on different data, because few people complain to both a government agency and to the Better Business Bureau about the same problem. Therefore, this is useful additional information.

No guarantee of help.   There is never a guarantee that any agency will actively pursue your case, even if your complaint is well justified. They might be too busy. They might be intimidated by computers. They might lose your letter. Some people send the same complaint to several agencies. Do this if you are complaining about fraud or deceptive trade practices—complain to a mediation agency to get your dispute resolved and complain to the Federal Trade Commission to help the government collect evidence of a pattern of dishonest practice. If you send your complaint to more than one organization, we recommend that you do not indicate on the letter that it is a copy of a complaint that you've sent to someone else. Consumer protection agencies are so overworked that they're likely to file and forget anything that appears to be filed with someone else.

Disadvantages of Filing Your Complaint with a Consumer Protection Agency

There *are* a few disadvantages to filing a complaint with a consumer protection agency, especially if you rely on it as your sole negotiator with, and sole source of pressure on, the publisher. Here are some of the problems:

Restricted to consumers. The agency's charter might be restricted to consumers only. If you are a small business, the agency might not help you at all, or it might do you the favor of providing some help, but it might not fight as hard for you as it would for an individual.

The bias in favor of consumers might be based on a restrictive version of the State's Unfair and Deceptive Trade Practices Act, which limits its protections to consumers. Or, it might be based on some other funding bias that reflects the idea that businesses can afford their own lawyers. Consumer protection agencies might base most of their enforcement on this Act. Their volunteer staff might be ignorant of some other relevant statutes, such as the Uniform Commercial Code, which also protect businesses.

Unfamiliar with computers. The volunteer might not understand computer technology well enough to play a constructive role in the mediation. If the volunteer doesn't understand the consequences of your bug, he won't understand why you are asking for so much money or why you are so upset.

Refund only. The agency might know how to seek a refund for you but might be less willing to help you collect incidental or consequential damages (see Chapters 4, "Knowing What to Ask For," and Chapter 7, "Software Quality and the Law," for discussions of damages). The agency might feel that if you want these extra payments, you should pay your own lawyer. If you've lost or spent a significant amount of money because of a defect in the program, you should try to recover more than just a refund. It's not as if you're trying to make a profit here. You're just trying to recover from a problem that you did not cause and did not want. If the staff of the agency don't understand this, they can put pressure on you to settle for much less than you've lost, without quite realizing what they're doing.

Statute of limitations.   The agency does not guarantee a solution. They may spend a long time mediating your case with the publisher, without success. The delay may put you up against a statute of limitations. (A statute of limitations is a law that says if you haven't sued by now, it's too late.)

Prosecution without payment.   A law-enforcement agency might bring criminal charges against the publisher, but that probably won't yield recovery of your losses and expenses. Prosecution punishes the publisher for its misdeeds and probably prevents future misdeeds, but it doesn't necessarily convince or force the publisher to pay you what you are entitled.

Who's side?   This agency is not necessarily your advocate. A government-based agency is neutral (as it should be). A private agency, such as the Better Business Bureau or a trade association, may identify with the business rather than with you (perhaps because they don't understand your problem well enough).

Grudges.   Especially if you complain to a law-enforcement agency, the publisher may hold a big grudge. Good luck getting enthusiastic future service. (On the other hand, why do you want to keep doing business with a crook?)

A Final Note to the Agencies

Some consumer protection and enforcement agencies have little experience with software. Several of their staff are just learning about software now and can still be talked into blaming themselves, rather than the software, when some bug destroys their work. These staff can be intimidated when they talk to a software publisher on a consumer's behalf.

To these agencies, we can only say that we know how hard this transition is for you. Everyone who has become competent with computers has had to go through a tough technological learning curve. Our recommendation is this: Next time you call the publisher's technician, listen with the same ears that you use when you talk to a car dealer's service manager about a consumer complaint about bad warranty repairs. The words are different, but the structure and style of the arguments are often similar.

Action Plan

If your complaint is reasonable, if you sent in the proper receipts, and if you aren't asking for much more than a refund, then a mediation agency will probably be able to help you.

If a few weeks go by without progress being made by the agency, start thinking seriously about taking this forward yourself:

- Read Chapter 7, "Software Quality and the Law." Once you understand more about the law, you might change your demands or the way you explain your demands.

- After reading Chapter 7, consider sending another complaint letter to a different agency. For example, if you already complained to your county's Consumer Affairs Department, this time complain to the Better Business Bureau or the Attorney General of the publisher's home state.

- If your demands are too complex for a mediation agency, you should change your demands, or take your case to Small Claims Court (see Chapter 10, "Small Claims Court"), or hire a lawyer (see Chapter 9, "Lawyers").

Chapter 7

Software Quality and the Law

Chapter Map
You're probably reading this chapter because you've tried the simpler things that we suggested in the earlier chapters, and they didn't work. So, now it's time to learn about your rights. We explore six different areas of the law. They are warranties, warranty disclaimers, remedies, misrepresentation, unfair or deceptive practices, and personal injury or property damage. (We provide a short introductory description of each of these in this chapter.)

How to Read this Chapter
This chapter was challenging to write because we're writing for readers who have very different levels of understanding of the law. Our goals are:

- To provide you (the consumer) with a reasonable sense of your rights. As you gain a better understanding of the law, you'll be better equipped to call (or write) the publisher again and *demand* that it treat you fairly.

- To provide more depth of understanding and additional pointers to reference material. We're trying to help you make an argument in Small Claims Court if you have to. We also want to give you enough background that you'll find it easier to understand and manage your attorney, if you hire one.

These goals require different levels of detail. You don't need a lot of detail to get a sense of your rights, and you certainly shouldn't have to read lawyers' textbooks. But, if negotiations start breaking down and you start moving toward court, you should learn the language, the definitions of legal terms like "warranty" and "fraud" and the main arguments that you can use in court. This knowledge is power—not just in the courtroom but also in your negotiations with the publisher's customer service manager, long before you ever get to court.

We've discussed each legal area in layers (like an onion). Our goal is to help you get a basic understanding of each area, while making it easy for you to skip past technical material that you don't need. Here are our layers:

Overview. This is the outermost layer. The discussion is broad and gives you a brief description and a basic understanding of the area. You should understand enough, from reading this section, to know whether it is relevant to your problem with your publisher. If so, read the "Analysis." If not, skip to the next legal area.

Analysis. Here is the basic explanation of the legal arguments. This probably gives you as much detail as you need to understand your rights and to talk with the publisher about them.

Footnotes. This is the inner layer of the onion. It's strong stuff, and you might only be able to deal with it a little bit at a time. These footnotes provide additional arguments and references to key statutes and court decisions. We provide many footnotes, but we don't footnote everything that we say. Our goal is utilitarian, not academic. If we think that something might help you in an argument, we point you to it. If it provides scholarly background, without seeming to us to be immediately useful, then we skip it. Please don't let these notes distract you; you can understand the key points in this chapter without reading any footnotes.

If you do end up in Small Claims Court, the representative of the publisher will probably not be a lawyer, because most Small Claims Courts don't welcome lawyers. The executive, or manager, or paralegal facing you will probably have been coached on the law, but she is probably not an expert in the law. You have a fighting chance, if you prepare carefully.

The material in our footnotes is not always interesting (definitions, quotes from statutes, results of court cases, Zzzzzz, ZZzzzz). Some of the wording is awkward (this stuff was written by lawyers and politicians). Some of the arguments revolve around fine distinctions. Adding to the confusion, there is Federal law that applies all over the country (such as the Magnuson-Moss Act), and there is State law (most of the law of contracts and misrepresentation). State law differs from state to state. An argument that is strong in Virginia might be irrelevant in New York. We can't take you through the maze of variations, but we do try to point you to reference books or articles that map laws across states.

The first time you read this chapter, skip most of the footnotes. If you go to court, read the chapter (and footnotes) with a friend and have him ask you questions. Tell your friend the definitions of the terms and make your arguments to him. This is work, but if you're going to all the trouble of taking the publisher to Small Claims Court, you may as well prepare well enough to win.

Caution

Computer-related law is a new area. There have been few precedent-setting lawsuits against software publishers;[1] the law will evolve significantly over the next 10 years. Some points made in this chapter will be obvious in a few years; others will become flat wrong. Also, contracts and misrepresentation are complex legal areas. We've worked hard to describe this material accurately within the larger context of the law, but we know that many important cases will be decided on the basis of factual details and legal issues that we haven't considered in this chapter. The wise reader will treat this material as a starting point for further research or for discussion with a lawyer.

Finally, there is a significant effort underway to rewrite the Uniform Commercial Code. If it is ever passed, it will virtually eliminate software publishers' liability to their customers. This is a serious effort, with bills currently scheduled to start appearing in state legislatures in the Fall of 1999. We discuss this issue at the end of the book, in the appendix, and then point you to our Web site for more current information.

For Further Research

You might need to do additional research if you go to Small Claims Court, or if you hire a lawyer and want to keep up with her. Several excellent books summarize the state of a specific area of the law. Finding and reading sections of these books is often easier than reading and understanding all of the court cases. Here are a few books that summarize this chapter's areas of discussion. Most of these are professional reference books, for lawyers, that are updated every year. They are expensive—$100 to $300 each—so you probably won't want to buy them yourself. You can find them in many law libraries. Non-lawyers can sometimes use private schools' law libraries and can usually use state-owned law school libraries and county law libraries.

---

[1] *People do file suits against software publishers.* But, the vast majority of lawsuits are settled before trial, so there is no published legal opinion to use as precedent. Even when there is a trial, if no one appeals the result, the result usually goes unpublished.

Statutes.   The United States Code is available on the Net at law .house.gov/usc.htm and at www.law.cornell.edu/uscode. The Code of Federal Regulations is available at www.access.gpo.gov/nara/cfr/index .html. The Uniform Commercial Code is at www.law.cornell.edu/ucc/2/ overview.html, and the proposed software revisions to the UCC (Article 2B) are at www.law.upenn.edu/library/ulc/ulc.htm. For updated links, check our website, www.badsoftware.com.

Computer law.   Bernacchi, Frank, and Statland (1995); Hancock, Ed. (1993a, 1993b, 1995); Kutten (1987); Raysman and Brown (1984); Nimmer (1997). All of these have strengths and weaknesses, but if you can use only one, we strongly recommend Kutten.

Contract and warranty law.   Calamari and Perrillo (1987) is a general reference book relied on by law students. Clark and Smith (1984), White and Summers (1995), and Sheldon and Carter (1997) are professional texts.

Consumer protection.   Sheldon and Carter (1997b) is another treasure from the National Consumer Law Center. Keup (1993) reprints many States' statutes. A table comparing consumer protection statutes in different states is available at www.badsoftware.com.

Remedies.   Dobbs (1993) is invaluable. Sheldon and Carter (1997a, 1997b) are also very practical.

Libel. If you're going to speak up and criticize loudly, please read something about libel law. Better that you should read about it in a book than in court papers. *The Associated Press Stylebook and Libel Manual* (Goldstein,1994) is a popular and inexpensive source.

This chapter looks at your rights under the law. Because the discussion here is an analysis of the law, we talk about lawsuits quite a bit. After all, that's ultimately how you enforce the law, if you have to go that far.

However, the point of this chapter is not litigation. We *are* trying to help you sue, *if you must*. But, our hope is that you'll be able to use this chapter to prevent a lawsuit. We want to help you find out whether you have a legal basis for demanding whatever you're demanding from the publisher. If you do have that legal basis, you may want to explain that basis to the publisher's staff.

Customer service managers and staff in software companies are surprisingly ignorant of consumer protection laws. It just isn't an area that software companies train their staff in. So be patient if you speak to a technician or supervisor who doesn't know the law. Be a teacher, not a screamer. You might even photo-copy a page or two from this chapter and send it with a letter of yours to the publisher.

Be warned: when you threaten a publisher with a lawsuit, you trigger a differ-ent analysis at the publisher's office. Without this threat, you probably negoti-ate with the customer service staff. But, after you make a credible threat of a lawsuit, the customer service manager probably will consult the publisher's lawyer. This might speed up or slow down negotiations. You might be bought off quickly, or the lawyers might stonewall. You won't know until you do make the threat. It's wise to negotiate first without pushing the law at the company and see what they do. Point out what they did wrong, what it cost you, what you want, and so on. If you don't get anywhere, then *mention* and *explain* the law without threatening to sue. If that fails, *then* beat them over the head with the law.

We focus on six areas of the law in this chapter. These areas are the ones that we think are most likely to be in dispute between you and the publisher, and the ones that will be most useful for you to explain to the publisher. We cover one area in each section of the chapter. Here's what they are:

Warranties.   Publishers and retailers make some remarkable statements about the capabilities of products. After you buy the product and start using it, you discover that these statements were false or exaggerated. When you com-plain, you get a runaround. You're told that it was just those marketing people, or salespeople, doing their thing. You know you can't believe them. Fortunately, the law sees it differently. Many of these statements are, by law, *express warranties*. If they aren't true, the publisher (or seller) has *breached* its warranties, and you can take a variety of legal actions.

Warranty disclaimers in software packages.   Some publishers will argue that they have no legal responsibility to provide you with a product that works because they have disclaimed all warranties and sold the product "as is." However, these disclaimers are packaged inside the product so that you won't see them until you take the product away and open it. These "shrink-wrapped" disclaimers have been tested in court; they are invalid. And therefore, these publishers have not successfully dodged their responsibilities to you. (By the way, when we say "shrink-wrapped," we are including the "click-wrap" license that you first see when you're installing the software.[2])

Remedies.   Suppose that the publisher admits that its product is defective and that it *did* erase your hard disk. The publisher says, "We guarantee your

---

[2] "Shrink-wrap" is jargon from the days when a software product was sold inside a shrink-wrapped (plastic-wrapped) box. A license agreement that contained a warranty disclaimer was hidden inside the box. "Click-wrap" has nothing to do with a "wrap." It just means that you have to click something that says OK while you install the software. The license is on the screen when you click. Publishers' lawyers claim that opening the package or clicking OK means that you have voluntarily agreed to a complex contract.

satisfaction. Here is a complete refund. $100." Do you have to settle for that—even if it cost you $2,000 to hire a technician to recover your data and restore everything to your hard disk? Many publishers will say so (they'd rather give you $100 than $2,000), but you might be entitled to $2,100 in this case—plus, the cost of your phone calls, and your postage. And, you might be entitled to some other costs, too. Your disagreement with a publisher about how much it must pay you or what it must do to fix the problem is a disagreement governed by the law of remedies.

Misrepresentation. If a publisher's false statements caused you to buy a product, then you have been a victim of a misrepresentation. If the publisher convinced you to buy the product by deliberately lying to you, it has committed fraud. Also, if the publisher's customer service technicians delay or prevent you from returning a product by lying to you, that's fraud, too. Fraud is much more serious than breach of warranty, with much more serious consequences for the publisher.

There are also less serious forms of misrepresentation, based on false statements that are made negligently or innocently. Several states allow you to bring a lawsuit for such misrepresentations even if the product came with no warranty (because the warranty was fully disclaimed) or after the warranty has expired. These laws also allow you to collect damages that might not be available under the warranty.

Unfair and deceptive practices. This is a third way to hold a publisher accountable for its false or misleading statements. You can't recover as much money as you could by proving fraud, but you can prove that a publisher has engaged in an unfair or deceptive trade practice much more easily.

See the pattern? If the publisher makes a false statement to you, and you (correctly) complain that the program doesn't work as described, the publisher can't just dismiss you. The law gives you a one-two-three punch (warranty/ misrepresentation / deceptive trade practice) for dealing with situations like this.

Personal injury and property damage. We'll deal with this topic *here*[3] (in the footnote) because it will be a rare issue for consumer software. If the program injures you or damages your property, the publisher is probably in deep trouble. For *this* type of problem, go see a lawyer.

---

[3]Some bugs have caused disasters. (Some interesting books on the topic are Leveson (1995), Peterson (1995), and Wiener (1993). If the program injures you or causes something that it is controlling to injure you, then you have very broad rights as an injured consumer.

You also have broad rights when dealing with a program that does property damage. How can a consumer-level program do property damage? Here are three ways:

The program might damage your equipment. For example, by burning out your monitor, blowing out your speakers, or damaging an interface card. This is obvious property damage.

Before we go into the details of these issues, here are a few notes on the structure of the American legal system.

The United States is governed by a Constitution. No law can contradict any part of the Constitution. The Constitution gives the Federal government certain powers and the States certain powers. The Federal Congress and the State legislatures have overlapping powers to pass laws governing commercial transactions (buying selling, banking, and so on). When a Federal law directly contradicts a State law, the Federal law wins (this is called *preemption*.)

Each state can pass its own laws. The laws differ from state to state. As long as they don't contradict a Federal law, it is OK under the Constitution for laws to provide Michigan citizens with rights that differ from those available to Wisconsin citizens. Since 1902 (Uniform Sales Act, which evolved into Article 2 of the Uniform Commercial Code), the states have tried to develop commercial rules that are similar or identical from state to state. The Uniform Commercial Code itself is the law of almost all states because they have each introduced it in their legislatures, voted on it, sometimes slightly amended it, and then passed it.

Lawsuits can be brought in State courts or in Federal courts. Many Federal commercial laws can be the subject of trials in State courts. And, under the right circumstances, a suit that involves only State law (such as the Uniform Commercial Code) can still end up in a Federal court.

Courts in two states might differently interpret the same words in the Uniform Commercial Code (or any other law). After all, any law is evaluated by a judge in the context of the rest of the state's laws—those other laws differ a lot from state to state. When two state's judicial (court) interpretations of the same law differ, the application of that law will differ—it may as well be written in different words—between those states.

The program might damage your data.   For example, by erasing data collected by other programs; it might erase your hard drive or corrupt data files that you expected it to read, but not write to. This is another example of property damage. (See Kaner's discussion of this issue in Kaner, Falk, and Nguyen, 1993, pp. 318–324).

The program might damage its own data.   For example, by erasing or corrupting its own data files. This includes messing up data that you enter while using the program. The courts probably would not class this as property damage, and you would treat this as a breach of contract. See Kaner, Falk, and Nguyen, 1993, pp. 323–328).

If the program causes personal injury or property damage, you can sue for negligence, recover all incidental and consequential expenses, and possibly collect punitive damages if the publisher's conduct in releasing the program or keeping it on the market was sufficiently outrageous.

You will, of course, have to prove that the injury or damage was caused by this program. If you can do that, we think that you're in a strong bargaining position with the publisher. In your negotiations, don't be shy about demanding repayment for your consequential losses. If the publisher won't work with you, talk to a lawyer.

With these notes in mind, we hope you won't be dizzied by our illustrations that sometimes involve a Federal court, sometimes a State court, and sometimes a law that is interpreted one way in Virginia and a different way in New York. Despite these variations, there are strong themes and trends.

> ### *Caution:*
> *Here are some points that you should keep in mind throughout this chapter.*
>
> *First, exercise some care when you publish complaints on the Internet or in a magazine. Stick to the facts. Don't set yourself up for a lawsuit for defamation (libel or slander—publishing false statements about someone). Don't make personal insults or personal comments about other people. Don't call people liars. Don't misquote people. Never exaggerate. Don't say that a specific person should be fired. Don't talk about conspiracies or about the intentions of people who work for the publisher unless you have evidence. Don't state broad conclusions about the product that you can't support with facts. Only say what you can prove and be prepared to prove what you say. You can make a powerful statement if you start by saying "I'm unhappy with Brand X's product Y, and here's what happened to make me that way," followed by a list of factual statements.*
>
> *Second, never make threats. For example, it is not (oh, so very definitely not) OK to call the publisher up and say, "Pay me $50,000, or I'll post this bug on the Internet." Don't threaten to sue. Don't threaten to write a newspaper article. Don't threaten to go to the District Attorney. Threats can be taken as extortion. Here are some excerpts from Section 223.4 of the Model Penal Code:*
>
> > A person is guilty of theft by extortion if he purposely obtains property of another by threatening to . . . (2) accuse anyone of a criminal offense; or (3) expose any secret tending to subject any person to hatred, contempt, or ridicule, or to impair his credit or business repute; or . . . (6) testify or provide information or withhold testimony or information with respect to another's legal claim or defense.
>
> *You can post the bug; you can tell the publisher that you're going to post the bug; you can complain to the District Attorney about the bug; but don't make a threat like, "Pay me or else I'll post the bug."*

Warranties

Software publishers make many specific, factual claims about their products. For example, they make these claims in advertisements, on the product's box, and in the manual. If you buy the product, and it doesn't live up to these claims, what can you do about it?

OVERVIEW: WARRANTIES

The typical *warranty* is a legally enforceable statement of fact or promise by the seller (publisher or retailer) about the product. For example, a statement might be "Works with all Windows-compatible printers." A promise might be "We will fix any errors that you discover within the first 90 days after purchasing this product and send you the upgraded version at no charge." If the product doesn't live up to the statement, or if the warrantor doesn't keep the promise, then the warranty is *breached*. On discovery of the breach of warranty, you would be entitled to one or more remedies, such as money (*damages*) or a version of the program that works.

We discuss remedies for breach of warranty in the section, "Remedies."

Warranties come in many flavors. The two we consider in this book are *express* and *implied* warranties:

Express warranties.   These warranties are statements of fact or promises from the seller to you, the buyer. (To a lawyer, a factual statement is a statement that you can prove true or false.) Some sellers will argue that some of their statements of fact should not be treated as warranties. We'll consider those arguments soon, in the "Analysis."

In our experience, customers hold publishers accountable for every factual statement about the program, whether the publisher's lawyer would agree in court that the statement was a warranty or not. It doesn't matter when or where a publisher says something false about the capabilities of the program. If customers see the statement, they expect it to be true. If it's false, they express indignation, surprise, and anger to the publishers' staff. Further, it is our experience that customer support managers take this kind of complaint very seriously. Finally, some publishers' lawyers have told us privately that they expect their companies' factual, written statements to be taken as warranties.

As a practical matter, then, we recommend that when you complain about the product, on the phone or in court, you should treat every statement of fact and every promise made by the publisher as an express warranty. This includes statements and promises:

- In advertisements
- In brochures, spec sheets, sales proposals, fax-back answer sheets
- On the box or packaging
- In the manual or the on-line help system
- In the readme file or other information files on disk
- On the warranty or registration card

- Made during a product demonstration
- Made in direct conversation with its sales or customer service groups.

It is almost impossible to disclaim an express warranty. Additionally, when you can prove a breach of an express warranty, you should consider whether you are also looking at an instance of fraud, negligent misrepresentation, or an unfair or deceptive trade practice.

Implied warranties.   These warranties do not arise from specific promises or statements by the seller. Instead, they reflect expectations about the product that you are entitled to have *as a matter of law*. For example, if you buy food in a restaurant, there is an implied warranty (of merchantability) that the food is safe to eat. If you buy a word processing program, there is an implied warranty (merchantability) that you can do basic text editing tasks (such as deleting a word after you type it), because these are *fundamental* to the concept of a word processor. If the program accidentally erases your hard disk while you use it in a normal way to do normal things, the warranty of merchantability is breached because this error makes the program unfit for ordinary use.

Typically, a breach of the implied warranty of merchantability will be obvious, but remember that the implied warranty is a purely legal creation. Therefore, you might want to speak with an attorney before deciding whether a problem with the program does or does not breach an implied warranty.

One final point to recognize. A program that you consider worthless might not have breached any warranties, express or implied. If the publisher and salesperson described the program honestly, you might not have a *legal* basis for complaint if the program is awkward and hard to use. Exhibit 7.1 provides an example of this type of situation.

Even if you wouldn't win a lawsuit over a bad program, you should still complain and ask for a refund if you hate it. You deserve a good product, and you have negotiating clout. You can still write letters or product reviews for magazines, or post notes on the Internet, that describe just how worthless this program is.

Exhibit 7.1: Satisfaction Isn't Always Guaranteed

In the case of *Family Drug Store of New Iberia, Inc. v. Gulf States Computer Services, Inc.* (1982), the Louisiana Court of Appeal ruled that a buyer had no claim for a refund for a software system that it found "burdensome" because the seller had not misrepresented the product and the product did what it was sold to do without failing or losing data.

Two pharmacies bought a computer program (the Medical Supply System) from Gulf States.

After realizing what they had bought, the pharmacies asked for, and then sued for, a refund. They claimed that

1. All data had to be printed out and could not be viewed on the monitor.

2. The information on the monitor would appear in code.

3. Numerical codes were needed in order to open a new patient file.

4. The system was unable to scroll.

According to the pharmacies, these problems made the system too awkward and time-consuming to use.

The Court also determined that Gulf States had not misrepresented the features or capabilities of the software. When their national sales director demonstrated the software to the pharmacies' representative, a pharmacist who was an experienced computer user, she told the pharmacist about some of these aspects of the system, such as the lack of scrolling.

The court ruled that, if there is no misrepresentation or failure of the program to work as described, a buyer has no legal claim for a refund unless the program is so hard to use that it is essentially useless.

Moral of the story: Even if you hate a program (even if it's a really bad program), you are not legally entitled to a refund (or other damages) if the program does what the publisher said it would do, if the publisher provides the technical support that it promised, and if the program doesn't have any serious bugs that weren't shown to you when (or before) you bought the software.

ANALYSIS: EXPRESS WARRANTIES

A seller can make an express warranty without ever using the word "warranty" or "guarantee." The warranty can be oral; it doesn't have to be written.[4] The seller may not have intended to create a warranty. A statement or promise can create a warranty, whether the seller wants to be bound by it or not. [5] The case of *Daughtrey v. Ashe* (see Exhibit 7.2) illustrates this point.

---

[4] Weng v. Allison (1997) is a typical, recent case. The seller of a used car told the plaintiff that it was "mechanically sound" and had "no problems." Actually, the car needed extensive repairs and was unsafe to drive. The court ruled that the seller's statements were express warranties.

[5] UCC 2-313 (2) "It is not necessary to the creation of an express warranty that the seller use formal words such as 'warrant' or 'guarantee' or that he have a specific intention to make a warranty, but an affirmation merely of the value of the goods or a statement purporting to be merely the seller's opinion or commendation of the goods does not create a warranty."

See *Fundin v. Chicago Pneumatic Tool Co.* (1984) for an example of a case in which the seller inadvertently created an express warranty.

An express warranty by the seller (publisher or retailer) involves four factors:[6]

- A statement of fact
- about the product
- or a promise
- that is part of the basis of the bargain.

Let's consider each factor in turn. The first three are the stuff of misunderstanding. Buyers sometimes read more into what the seller has said than they should. It might be worthwhile to read these points carefully, to see whether you've attached too much importance to some things that the seller has said:

Statement of fact.   Salespeople are so enthusiastic about their products! Talk to one, and you'll quickly discover that the product is *great*; you'll just love it; it's the best one on the market; and so on. Lawyers call these statements by salespeople "puffing."[7] These statements are not warranties.[8] They are just expressions of the salesperson's opinion.[9]

Our rule of thumb is this: if the statement tells you something about the product that is specific enough that you can prove it true or false, then it is a statement of fact.[10]

About the product.   Suppose that you have a printer that can print at a resolution of 300 dots per inch. You buy a graphics program. The graphics publisher's sales literature makes statements about your printer. Are these statements warranties or not?

---

[6] UCC 2-313 (1) "Express warranties by the seller are created as follows:

Any affirmation of fact or promise made by the seller to the buyer which relates to the goods and becomes part of the basis of the bargain creates an express warranty that the goods shall conform to the affirmation or promise.

Any description of the goods which is made part of the basis of the bargain creates an express warranty that the goods shall conform to the description.

Any sample or model which is made part of the basis of the bargain creates an express warranty that the whole of the goods shall conform to the sample or model."

[7] Nonlawyers use a more colorful word.

[8] Most books on contracts and warranties have a good discussion of puffing, explaining the difference between this and warranties, with examples. Sheldon and Carter (1997, Section 3.2.2.7) is particularly informative. So is Dykas (1991).

[9] Sometimes things that sound like opinions or general claims of the goodness of the product are taken by the courts as factual rather than as puffing. For example, the Court in *Eddington v. Dick* (1976) held that the statement that a refrigerator was in "good condition" was a warranty. White and Summers (1995, Section 9–4) conclude that there is so much variation in court decisions about what constitutes puffing that "only a foolish lawyer will be quick to label a seller's statements as puffs or not puffs."

[10] Clark and Smith (1984, Section 4.02) provides an excellent sampler of statements that have been ruled as enforceable express warranties.

- Suppose the literature says that your printer can print 1200 dots per inch. This is a statement of fact because it can be proved true or (in this case) false. But, it is not a warranty because it's about the printer (which the publisher didn't sell to you) not about the program.

- In contrast, suppose that the literature says that the program can *make* your printer print at 1200 dots per inch. This is a warranty because it is a statement about the what the program can do.

Promise.   For example, the publisher might promise to fix any serious bugs that you find or might promise that you will have toll-free telephone access to trained technicians, 24 hours per day. Promises aren't statements about the product, but they are statements that might make you decide to buy one product instead of its competitor.

Basis of the bargain.   This last aspect of the warranty is more complex. The Code repeatedly says that statements, descriptions, or samples must be part of the basis of the bargain to be warranties. But, it doesn't define this phrase.[11]

The most interesting question involves statements on the box, in the manual, and in the online help. These statements are certainly warranties if you see them before the sale. But, are these statements warranties (part of the bargain) if you don't see them until *after* you buy the product? Very few court cases address this directly,[12] but Official Comment 7 to the Code's definition of express warranties (Section 2–313) is helpful. The Comment says:

> *The precise time when words of description or affirmation are made or samples are shown is not material. The sole question is whether the language or samples or models are fairly to be regarded as part of the contract. If language is used after the closing of the deal (as when the buyer when taking delivery asks and receives an additional assurance), the warranty becomes a modification, and need not be supported by consideration if it is otherwise reasonable and in order.*

The case of *Daughtrey v. Ashe* (1992) illustrates this rule. In that case, a jeweler put a description (appraisal) of a diamond in a box. The customer didn't buy the diamond on the basis of that appraisal and didn't even discover it until

---

[11] Official Comment 3 to UCC section 2-313 is as close as we get to a definition. The relevant part says, "In actual practice affirmations of fact made by the seller about the goods during a bargain are regarded as part of the description of those goods; hence no particular reliance on such statements need be shown in order to weave them into the fabric of the agreement. Rather, any fact which is to take such affirmations, once made, out of the agreement requires clear affirmative proof. The issue normally is one of fact."

White and Summers (1990) discuss this Comment well, and in detail.

[12] Clark and Smith (1984, Section 4.03[4]), Sheldon and Carter (1997, Section 3.5), and White and Summers (1995, Section 9–5) provide citations to court cases on post-sale warranties. Sheldon and Carter provide several examples of post-sale statements that were interpreted as warranties. White and Summers (see their footnote 13) provide several counter-examples.

months later. But, the Supreme Court of Virginia treated the appraisal as a warranty, quoting Comment 7. For more details, see Exhibit 7.2.

Different states follow different rules on this issue.[13] A few States' courts require that the buyer at least have been exposed to the document at the time of the sale. Our impression is that in most states, these statements would be taken as warranties. (Kaner, 1995b; Kaner and Pels, 1996; see also Kutten, 1987, Section 10.02[1]).

In the context of computer software, statements of fact on the box and in the documentation *should* be taken as describing the bargain between the buyer and the seller for several reasons:

First it's only fair.   The publisher puts contract terms inside the box, on paper or on disk, knowing that the customer can't see these until after the sale. The publisher expects these terms to be enforceable against the customer, and most of them will be. It seems fair that all those *other* statements that the publisher puts in the box (the documentation) should be legally effective too.

Second, customers rely on the documentation as a description of the product.   (That's what it's there for.) Section 2–313(1)(b) explicitly includes descriptions as express warranties.

Third, the claims in the documentation influence customers' decisions about whether to keep a product.   You usually have some time to decide whether to keep a product. You have an initial acceptance period (the perfect tender period that we discussed in Chapter 1). Many products also provide a satisfaction guarantee that let you return the product within the first month or two.

Finally, the issue just isn't very controversial in the mass-market software community.   The President of the Software Publishers' Association has said that the documentation creates warranties.[14] And, in a survey of the

---

[13] Here are some good surveys of the conflicting interpretations: Adler (1994), Clark and Smith (1984), Dykas (1991), Sheldon and Carter (1997). Kwestel (1992) is an interesting discussion of the issues.

For a statement or promise to have been part of the basis of the bargain, one position would require that your decision to buy the product was partially based on the statement or promise. White and Summers (1995, Section 9–5) develop this argument well for advertising materials (which don't come with the product and which the buyer might never have seen). At the other extreme are cases like *Daughtrey v. Ashe (1992)*. Under this view, it doesn't matter what you knew when you bought the product. What matters is that the seller included the statement or product with the product, so the seller should be bound by it.

[14] The Software Publishers Association (SPA) is the main trade association for publishers of software, representing 1200 member companies. During negotiations over proposed revisions to the Uniform Commercial Code (see our notes in the Appendix on Article 2B), Ralph Nader (1997) wrote an open letter to Bill Gates, protesting that software publishers want to "disclaim all warranties, denying even that the product conforms to claims made on its packaging or in its documentation." The President of the SPA, Ken Wasch (1997), wrote the SPA's official response:

Computer Law Association, 82 percent of the responding members agreed that there should be a nondisclaimable warranty, as a matter of law, that a "software product will operate substantially in accordance with its accompanying user documentation." (Rustad, Martel, and McAuliffe, 1995, p. 4).

From a practical point of view, we're not sure that your time is best spent trying to research the subtle nuances of your State's position on the *basis of the bargain*. We think that you might find it easier, and be more effective, working with the following tactics:

Shame the publisher. After all, you *are* talking about false statements of fact and broken promises. Any competent customer support manager will recognize that readers of newspapers, internet news groups, or magazine reviews won't much care whether the false statements and not-to-be-kept promises were made before or after the sale. They are bad news for the seller in either case.

Show that you had access to these materials. If you flipped through the manual or looked up a few things in the help system before buying the software, you have a strong argument in all States that the manual and help are part of the basis of the bargain.

Show an express warranty that the software will conform to the documentation. Many software products come with warranties that the software's performance will conform, or will substantially conform, to the statements in the user documentation. A court will certainly enforce such a statement, whether or not the customer sees it before the sale. (See, for example, *Microsoft Corp. v. Manning*, 1995.)

Show that you had indirect access to these materials. Before you decided to buy the program you probably talked with a salesperson, read some magazine reviews, talked with friends, read notes on the internet, and so on. Publishers know that writers (*e.g.,* reviewers) check the manual to get their facts straight. So, you got information from the manual even though you didn't

---

"Your assertion that software companies can disclaim all warranties and deny that a product conforms to statement[s] made on packaging or in the user manuals is just plain wrong."

At the next meeting of the Article 2B Drafting Committee, Nader's lawyer, Todd Paglia, asked whether this meant that the SPA considered these statements as warranties. He was assured that this is exactly what was meant. In a later meeting, he introduced a motion to change Article 2B to be very precise on this point (as warranties whether the customer saw them before the sale or after) and the SPA's lawyer said that the SPA did not oppose the motion.

In later meetings of the Article 2B drafting committee, other lawyers representing trade associations and individual software publishers have stated to us that they think that manuals are express warranties.

look through it yourself before the purchase. Therefore, there's no injustice in requiring the publisher to stand behind these statements.[15]

Show post-sale reliance. Show that you acted in the belief that the facts in these statements *were* part of the bargain, that you took some action or made some decision in reliance on the truth of the statements, or that the seller *told you* to rely on the manual's statements.

A final note about express warranties: they are almost impossible to disclaim. The UCC Section 2–316 is very specific about this.[16] A statement that the product is sold "AS IS" or "WITHOUT WARRANTY OF ANY KIND, EXPRESS OR IMPLIED" might succeed in getting rid of the implied warranties, but it has no effect on express warranties.

Exhibit 7.2: A Post-Sale Express Warranty

In 1985, W.H. Daughtrey paid $15,000 for a diamond bracelet for his wife from Sidney Ashe, a jeweler. Ashe put an appraisal form in the box with the bracelet. The appraisal said the diamonds were of *v.v.s. quality* (a high grade). Daughtrey didn't see the appraisal until later, probably not until the box was opened at Christmas.

In 1989, Daughtrey discovered that the diamonds were not of v.v.s. quality. Ashe offered a refund. Daughtrey refused and demanded that the diamonds in the bracelet be replaced with diamonds that were of v.v.s. quality. Ashe refused. Daughtrey sued. He said that the statement that the diamonds were of v.v.s. quality was a description of the goods by the seller. According to the UCC,

> *2-313(b) Any description of the goods which is made part of the basis of the bargain creates an express warranty that the goods shall conform to the description.*

Therefore, Daughtrey said, Ashe created a warranty that the diamonds were of v.v.s. quality, and breached it by selling diamonds of a lower grade. Ashe argued that this claim couldn't have been a warranty because

---

[15] The seller might argue that it can't be held liable for statements made by third parties, such as magazine reviewers. But ,that's not what you're doing here. You're showing that the seller's statements were reaching you, indirectly, before you bought the product. You didn't get them in writing until you opened the box, but they were coming from the seller and were part of the basis of your bargain, anyway. If you expect to make this type of argument, read Sheldon and Carter (1997 section 3.2.3).

[16] UCC section 2–316(1) "Words or conduct relevant to the creation of an express warranty and words or conduct tending to negate or limit warranty shall be construed wherever reasonable as consistent with each other; but . . . negation or limitation is inoperative to the extent that such construction is unreasonable." In other words, an attempted disclaimer of an express warranty doesn't take effect ("inoperative"). Official Comment 4 to section 2–313 is also very quotable if you need to go further on this issue.

he never called it a warranty and Daughtrey didn't read the claim until long after the sale. How could this description be part of the "basis of the bargain"?

Ashe won—in the trial court. But, the Supreme Court of Virginia overruled the trial court. Quoting the Official Comments to the UCC, the Court said (p. 339):

> *The whole purpose of the law of warranty is to determine what it is that the seller has in essence agreed to sell.*

and (p. 339)

> *The precise time when words of description or affirmation are made . . . is not material. The sole question is whether the language is fairly to be regarded as part of the contract.*

The Court concluded that Ashe had agreed to sell v.v.s. quality diamonds, and therefore, that he had breached the sales contract by selling inferior diamonds.

So what does this have to do with computer software?

> A computer program comes with a manual that makes specific descriptive statements about the program, just as the appraisal made a specific descriptive statement about the bracelet. You might not read the manual until after your purchase, just as Daughtrey didn't know about the appraisal until after his purchase. A judge in Virginia (and many other states) would probably treat statements in the manual as warranties.

ANALYSIS: MAGNUSON-MOSS ACT AND WRITTEN WARRANTIES

The Uniform Commercial Code is a major source of warranty law, but there are others. The Magnuson-Moss Warranty Act[17] is also important. This statute applies to all consumer goods. Consumer goods are those that are "normally used for personal, family, or household purposes."[18] This is a very broad definition,

---

[17] United States Code, *Title 15*, Section 2301.

[18] United States Code, *Title 15*, Section 2301(1).

and it almost certainly includes personal computers and most of the types of software that you'd buy in software stores.[19]

Under the Act, the seller is not required to make any warranties, but if it does provide a written warranty (or if it sells you a service contract) then various additional consumer protections come into play.

The Magnuson-Moss concept of a written warranty is narrower than the Uniform Commercial Code's express warranty. In a written warranty, you'd expect to see the seller promising that the program is defect free, or that the program will meet a specified level of performance over a specified period of time, or that the seller will provide a remedy (such as a refund or a bug fix) if the program fails.[20] A simple description of how the program works is not a written warranty—the manual may be an express warranty under the UCC, but it is not a written warranty under the Magnuson-Moss Act.[21]

The Magnuson-Moss Act is probably best known for distinguishing between *full* and *limited* warranties and for thoroughly regulating the content of a full warranty.[22] Software publishers are not likely to intentionally provide full warranties[23] and therefore we will not discuss them.

---

[19]Here is the Federal Trade Commission's interpretation, in the *Code of Federal Regulations, 16*, Section 700.1 (a)

"The Act applies to written warranties on tangible personal property which is normally used for personal, family, or household purposes. This definition includes property which is intended to be attached to or installed in any real property without regard to whether it is so attached or installed. This means that a product is a 'consumer product' if the use of that type of product is not uncommon. The percentage of sales or the use to which a product is put by any individual buyer is not determinative. For example, products such as automobiles and typewriters which are used for both personal and commercial purposes come within the definition of consumer product. Where it is unclear whether a particular product is covered under the definition of consumer product, any ambiguity will be resolved in favor of coverage."

The Software Publishers Association's *Guide to Contracts* (Smedinghoff, 1993, p. 88) considered the applicability of the Magnuson-Moss Act and concluded that "It is reasonable to assume that software purchased for home computer use would be covered by the Act."

[20] United States Code, *Title 15*, Section 2301 (6) "The term *written warranty* means '(a) Any written affirmation of fact or written promise made in connection with the sale of a consumer product by a supplier to a buyer which relates to the nature of the material or workmanship and affirms or promises that such material or workmanship is defect free or will meet a specified level of performance over a specified period of time,' or (b) 'any undertaking in writing in connection with the sale by a supplier of a consumer product to refund, repair, replace, or take other remedial action with respect to such product in the event that such product fails to meet the specifications set forth in the undertaking, which written affirmation, promise, or undertaking becomes part of the basis of the bargain between a supplier and a buyer for purposes other than resale of such product.'"

[21] This point is well made, with examples, by Sheldon and Carter (1997 Section 2.2.5). See also Code of Federal Regulations, *Title 16*, Section 700.3.

[22]United States Code, *Title 15*, Sections 2303-2305.

[23] A publisher who forgets to say 'Limited' in 'Limited Warranty' is going to face a strong argument that it has made a full warranty, even if it didn't intend one. This was a successful negotiating point in a recent class action suit involving computer peripherals, but this line of argument is too legally technical for this book.

A different feature of the Magnuson-Moss Act is important for software customers, but it is often overlooked by lawyers (so if you have a lawyer, draw her attention to this.) The Magnuson-Moss Act says that a seller who provides any written warranty with a consumer product or who sells you a service contract (such as extended technical support) for the product may not disclaim implied warranties.[24] Software publishers often try to disclaim the implied warranty of merchantability, a warranty that the software is reasonably fit for ordinary use. (We discuss warranty disclaimers in the next section.) Publishers' disclaimers will therefore fail if they give any written warranty, probably even the very common warranty that the disks that the program was shipped on are not defective.

Two related lawsuits, *Stuessey v. Microsoft* (1993) and *Microsoft v. Manning* (1995), illustrate the interplay of the Magnuson-Moss Act and the UCC implied warranties. Microsoft warranted that MS-DOS 6.0 would "perform substantially in accordance with the accompanying Product Manuals for a period of 90 days from the date of receipt". (*Manning*, p. 609). One of the features provided with DOS 6.0 and described in the manual was disk compression, DoubleSpace. Unfortunately, because of compression-related problems "about three in 1,000 [people] lost data after using MS-DOS 6.0" (*Manning*, p. 606). In these two suits, customers sued for consequential damages (*Stuessey*) or for a free upgrade to DOS 6.2 (*Manning*). Both suits included a claim for violation of the Magnuson-Moss Act.

We have a copy of the *Microsoft MS-DOS 6 User's Guide* (Microsoft, 1993). DOS 6 was sold in OEM versions, in upgrade versions, and possibly in other ways—we don't know what manual or license terms were supplied in all of these cases. But, in *our* copy (Appendix E, p. 300), there is a disclaimer of implied warranties: "MICROSOFT DISCLAIMS ALL OTHER WARRANTIES, EITHER EXPRESS OR IMPLIED, INCLUDING BUT NOT LIMITED TO IMPLIED WARRANTIES OF MERCHANTABILITY."

Despite Microsoft's disclaimer, both lawsuits included a claim for breach of the implied warranty of merchantability.[25] In a Magnuson-Moss case, this is an appropriate claim, despite the disclaimer, because the Magnuson-Moss Act voids the disclaimer and reinstates the implied warranties.

---

[24] United States Code, *Title 15,* Section 2308(a) says, "No supplier may disclaim or modify (except as provided in subsection (b) of this section) any implied warranty to a consumer with respect to such consumer product if (1) such supplier makes any written warranty to the consumer with respect to such consumer product or (2) at the time of sale, or within 90 days thereafter, such supplier enters into a service contract with the consumer which applies to such consumer product." (Subsection (b) allows only one type of modification—a shortened time limit.)

[25] Referring to the implied warranty claims, the *Manning* court said that "the software was not fit for the ordinary purpose for which software is used." (*Manning,* p. 609).

We'll discuss another important benefit of the Act in Chapter 11, "Safe Shopping." The Act gives you the right to look at a product's warranty before buying it.[26] This is true whether you're shopping in a store or by mail order. As far as we can tell, very few software publishers or retailers comply with these regulations. But, you have every right to insist on seeing the warranty and to help you insist on that right, we've reprinted the regulations in Chapter 11. While you're at it, glance through the product's manual, too.

Warranty Disclaimers in Software Packages

When someone disclaims a warranty, they are saying, "In case there is any doubt, I am *not* giving you this kind of warranty." Not every attempt at disclaiming warranties will work.

OVERVIEW: WARRANTY DISCLAIMERS

The start of the 20th Century was the age of snake oil. Dr. Bye's Combination Oil Cure was the "infallible cure for all forms of cancer." (American Medical Association, 1912, p. 34.) In an unregulated marketplace, companies could (and did) make all sorts of false or exaggerated claims about their products. The Federal Trade Commission was formed in 1914. And, the Uniform Sales Act was first promulgated in 1909. The Uniform Sales Act created an implied warranty (a warranty that comes with a product as a matter of law) that goods sold by merchant sellers "shall be of a merchantable quality." The Uniform Sales Act evolved into UCC Article 2, which says that to be merchantable, a product must be "fit for the ordinary purposes for which such goods are used."[27]

For all or most of your life, it has been a fundamental public policy in the United States that merchandise (especially, but not only consumer goods) should be covered by the implied warranty of merchantability.

To get a sense of how much the implied warranty of merchantability pervades our lives, think about going to the store and buying a new type of laundry detergent. The warranty of merchantability doesn't provide any assurance that the detergent will be good or that it will be better than its competitors—that's what free market competition is for. But you try a new product with confidence that

---

[26] United States Code, *Title 15*, Sections 2302(b) and Code of Federal Regulations, *Title 16*, Section 702.

[27] UCC section 2-314(2).

- It will get your clothes *somewhat* cleaner than they used to be.

- It won't destroy your washable clothes.

The warranty of merchantability creates a foundation, a baseline, a safety net. Below some level of low quality, products may not be sold unless the customer is conspicuously warned before the sale that there is no warranty, that the seller will not stand behind this product, that the goods are sold "AS IS" with no guarantees. This warning is called a "disclaimer." You've seen these disclaimers on used cars—big signs on the window that say, "AS IS—NO WARRANTY." You might have seen one in a clothing store, a sign on a rack of shirts that said "SECONDS—NO RETURNS." We write the disclaimers in capital letters because most disclaimers are written in capital letters to draw your attention. A disclaimer that is not conspicuous doesn't work—the Uniform Commercial Code attaches the warranty to the sale despite the disclaimer.

- This public policy of attaching warranties of merchantability to sales of goods, as a matter of law, is reaffirmed in Federal law by the Magnuson-Moss Act, Section 2308(a), which voids a warranty disclaimer when a consumer product is sold with any written warranty.

- Sheldon and Carter (1997, Section 5.4) describe statutes in 21 states that place restrictions on warranty disclaimers that go beyond the restrictions of Article 2. For example, Connecticut, the District of Columbia, Kansas, Maine, Maryland, Massachusetts, Mississippi, Vermont, and West Virginia simply ban warranty disclaimers in the sale of new consumer goods. (The disclaimer ban is broader than this in six of these states.)

- California's laws are of special interest because so many software publishers are based in Silicon Valley. Under California's Song-Beverly Consumer Warranty Act, "Any waiver by the buyer of consumer goods of the provisions of this chapter, except as expressly provided in this chapter, shall be deemed contrary to public policy and shall be unenforceable and void."[28] The Act voids disclaimers that don't strictly compliance with its requirements.[29] A manufacturer that makes any express warranty with respect to consumer goods may not limit, modify, or disclaim the implied warranties.[30] The buyer must be informed of a warranty disclaimer "prior to the sale" and in writing.[31] If a sale is by mail order, the catalog must show the warranty disclaimer, for each item that is sold with a warranty disclaimer.[32]

---

[28] California Civil Code Section 1790.1.

[29] California Civil Code Section 1792.3.

[30] California Civil Code Section 1793. Note that the Song-Beverly Act defines express warranties more narrowly than the UCC definition. See California Civil Code Section 1791.2.

[31] California Civil Code Section 1792.4(a).

[32] California Civil Code Section 1794(b).

- Microsoft is based in the State of Washington. "Washington disfavors disclaimers and finds them to be ineffectual unless they are explicitly negotiated and set forth with particularity" (*Cox v. Lewiston Grain Growers*, Inc., 1997).

Some software publishers want to sell silicon snake oil. They want to advertise the product of your dreams, but they don't want to take any responsibility if their software doesn't work or has bugs that make it unusable, that waste your time and lose your data.

There are limits on the extent to which publishers can get away with an irresponsible attitude. Disclaimers like the one shown in Exhibit 7.3 look impressive, they use the right legal jargon, and they convince a lot of people that they are legally binding. But, they are bucking a century (or more) of contract law history.

The Warranty Disclaimer in Exhibit 7.3 is based directly on disclaimers commonly used by software publishers. This document claims to limit or eliminate the publisher's responsibility for bugs in the software and for misrepresentations in their advertisements and documentation. In essence, this disclaimer says that satisfaction is *not* guaranteed. Any problem you have with the product is your problem, not the publisher's. Even if the publisher knew about a defect, that defect and the harm it causes are your problems to deal with.

Some publishers don't play quite as harsh a game. Instead, they give an honest limited warranty, lasting perhaps 90 days or a year, that the software will behave substantially in accordance with the advertisements, box copy, and documentation.[33] However, even these publishers usually limit your right to recover your losses to a refund. Even if a known bug (one the publisher knew about when it sold you the product) erased your data, all you get, they say, is a refund. The other losses are yours.

When publishers sell software to the mass market, their disclaimers are usually buried inside the package, on a special insert or a special page in the manual, or in a file on the disk that you see when you install the software.

Hiding the disclaimer inside the box creates an interesting tradeoff for the publisher. On the one hand, the customer doesn't see the disclaimer before he pays money for the product. That's good, because he might not be willing to buy something that the manufacturer refuses to stand behind. On the other

---

[33] It is not unreasonable to expect the software industry to follow basic standards of honest dealing. In 1986, ADAPSO, a major software industry association, published guidelines on *Packaged Microcomputer Software Warranties in the Absence of Negotiated Agreements*. They recommended (1) easily readable product specifications, (2) express warranties that the program will perform as described in the specifications, user manual, and advertisements, (3) warranties that are long enough to allow the discovery of errors, and (4) repair, replace, or refund warranties. Levin (1986, p. 2126).

hand, no matter what the publisher says, a disclaimer that is hidden inside the box is probably not binding on you. Exhibit 7.4 provides an example of a court decision that made exactly this point.

No court in the United States has ever validated a software warranty disclaimer that was hidden inside the box. A few courts have rejected them. And in many other industries, many courts have rejected disclaimers that customers saw only post-sale.

The publishing community is striving mightily to rewrite the Uniform Commercial Code so that disclaimers like Exhibit 7.3 will be enforceable. You can read about that effort in the appendix. But, under current law, you should realize that you have many more rights than the publishers' disclaimers tell you that you have.

Exhibit 7.3: A Typical Warranty Disclaimer

Brand X Software warrants the diskettes on which the programs are furnished to be free from defects in the materials and workmanship under normal use for a period of ninety (90) days from the date of delivery to you as evidenced by your proof of purchase.

The entire liability of Brand X Software, and your exclusive remedy, shall be replacement of any diskette which does not meet the Limited Warranty and which is returned freight prepaid, to Brand X Software. Brand X Software does not warrant that the functions contained in the program will meet your requirements or that the operation of the programs will be uninterrupted or error-free.

THE PROGRAMS CONTAINED IN THIS PACKAGE ARE PROVIDED "AS IS" WITHOUT WARRANTY OF ANY KIND, EITHER EXPRESSED OR IMPLIED, IN-CLUDING, BUT NOT LIMITED TO, THE IMPLIED WARRANTIES OF MER-CHANTABILITY AND FITNESS FOR A PARTICULAR PURPOSE. THE ENTIRE RISK RELATED TO THE QUALITY AND PERFORMANCE OF THE PROGRAMS IS ON YOU. IN THE EVENT THERE IS ANY DEFECT, YOU ASSUME THE EN-TIRE COST OF ALL NECESSARY SERVICING, REPAIR, OR CORRECTION. IN NO EVENT SHALL BRAND X BE LIABLE FOR CONSEQUENTIAL OR INCIDEN-TAL DAMAGES ARISING OUT OF THE USE OF OR INABILITY TO USE THIS PRODUCT, EVEN IF BRAND X HAS BEEN ADVISED OF THE POSSIBILITY OF SUCH DAMAGES. SOME STATES DO NOT ALLOW THE EXCLUSION OF IM-PLIED WARRANTIES, SO THE ABOVE EXCLUSION MAY NOT APPLY TO YOU. THIS WARRANTY GIVES YOU SPECIFIC LEGAL RIGHTS AND YOU MAY HAVE OTHER RIGHTS WHICH VARY FROM STATE TO STATE.

This Agreement constitutes the complete and exclusive statement of the terms of the agreement between you and Brand X Software. It supersedes and replaces any previous written or oral agreements and communications relating to this software. No oral or written information or advice given by Brand X Software, its dealers, distributors, agents or employees will create any warranty or in any way increase the scope of the warranty provided in this agreement, and you may not rely on any such information or advice.

Exhibit 7.4: Warranty Disclaimer Ruled Ineffective

In the case of *Step-Saver Data Systems, Inc. v. Wyse Technology and The Software Link, Inc.* (1991), the United States Court of Appeals for the Third Circuit held that a disclaimer of all express and implied warranties, printed on the outside of the box, was not binding on a mail order customer.

Step-Saver repeatedly bought Multilink Advanced, an allegedly MS-DOS compatible operating system, from The Software Link (TSL). On each box was a disclaimer: the software was sold AS IS, without warranty; TSL disclaimed all express and implied warranties; and a purchaser who didn't agree to this disclaimer should return the product, unopened, to TSL for a refund.

Step-Saver sued TSL, claiming that Multilink Advanced was not MS-DOS compatible. TSL argued that Step-Saver had accepted the terms of the warranty disclaimer when it opened each package, and therefore Step-Saver could not sue.

Step-Saver made each purchase by telephone. The Court ruled that the essential terms of the sale (such as price and quantity) were set out during the calls. The warranty disclaimer on the box arrived later. Under Section 2-207 of the Uniform Commercial Code, the disclaimer was merely a proposal by TSL to add a term to the contract. Step-Saver was not required to accept this proposal. Having already bought the product, Step-Saver could open it and use it without agreeing to this new warranty disclaimer. Nor did it matter that Step-Saver placed additional orders after seeing the disclaimer. TSL never insisted that Step-Saver agree to the disclaimer during purchase negotiations (the telephone calls), therefore the disclaimer was not part of any contract.

The Court said:

> TSL has raised a number of public policy arguments focusing on the effect on the software industry of an adverse holding concerning the enforceability of the box-top license. We are not persuaded that requiring software companies to stand behind representations concerning their products will inevitably destroy the software industry.

ANALYSIS: WARRANTY DISCLAIMERS

A *contract* is an agreement between two parties (such as two people, or a person and a company) to do (or refrain from doing) certain things. The heart of any contract is the *agreement*.[34] But, you never agreed to this warranty disclaimer. So how is it part of your contract?

When you bought the product (at a store or by placing an order over the telephone) you agreed with the seller[35] that you would pay some money in return for this product. *That* was the agreement. You probably never talked about a warranty, so you didn't specifically include warranty terms in your agreement.

The typical sale leaves open (undiscussed) some important terms, such as the warranty. The Uniform Commercial Code (UCC) was written to deal with this situation. The UCC supplies its own standard terms in these cases.[36] As a matter of public policy, the UCC says that *any* product comes with a *warranty of merchantability* unless the seller specifically excludes it.[37] This is a modest warranty. It says that the seller promises that the product is "fit for the ordinary purposes for which such goods are used," that it will "pass without objection in the trade under the contract description," and that it conforms "to the promise or affirmations of fact made on the container or label."[38]

A seller can exclude the warranty by including a conspicuous[39] notice of the exclusion in the sales agreement. This notice is called a warranty disclaimer. The

---

[34] Some lawyers have stopped talking about "agreement" as the basis of contract because contracts have so many standard clauses that no one reads, let alone agrees to. But the replacement phrase is the "voluntary assumption of obligations." At a recent meeting of the Uniform Commercial Code Article 2B Drafting Committee (St. Louis, May 1–3, 1998), Geoffrey C. Hazard, Jr., the Chair of the Permanent Editorial Board of the Uniform Commercial Code, made this point and said that the process of presenting nonnegotiable, post-sale notifications of the seller's terms that come with software is far from the notion of a voluntary assumption of obligations and, generally, from traditional notions of contracting.

[35] You might get confused between "seller" and "publisher." We say "publisher" to refer specifically to a publisher of computer software. To talk generally about a business that sells products, we say "seller." Anything we say about sellers applies to publishers. A retailer (the computer software store) is a seller. Unless we point out a difference between them, don't worry *in this chapter* about the difference between the retailer and the publisher.

[36] UCC Section 2-204

[37] UCC Section 2-314(1).

[38] UCC Section 2-314(2). "Goods to be merchantable must be at least such as (a) pass without objection in the trade under the contract description; and (b) in the case of fungible goods, are of fair average quality within the description; and (c) are fit for the ordinary purposes for which such goods are used; and (d) run, within the variations permitted by the agreement, of even kind, quality and quantity within each unit and among all units involved; and (e) are adequately contained, packaged, and labeled as the agreement may require; and (f) conform to the promise or affirmations of fact made on the container or label if any."

[39] UCC Section 1–201(10) "'Conspicuous': A term or clause is conspicuous when it is so written that a reasonable person against whom it is to operate ought to have noticed it. A printed heading in capitals . . . is conspicuous. Language in the body of a form is 'conspicuous' if it is in larger or other contrasting type or color . . ."

UCC Section 2–316 requires that written exclusions be conspicuous.

exclusion clause in Exhibit 7.3 is a conspicuous part of *that page* because it is and set apart from the rest of the text by being in all capital letters. It says clearly that there is no warranty of any kind, including no warranty of merchantability.

However, this warranty disclaimer couldn't have been conspicuous when you bought the program (unless you have X-ray vision) because it was inside the box. Therefore, the purchase agreement does not include the warranty disclaimer, and therefore, the agreement cannot exclude the warranty of merchantability.[40]

This surprises some people, because the legalese in the disclaimer looks so official and lawyerly. But, try to get past the legalese and think about the situation. By law, the warranty of merchantability comes with the product, unless the seller gives you fair notice that there is no such warranty with this product when (or before) you buy the product. If the seller tells you *later* that there is no warranty, the seller is taking away something that came with the product when you bought it. This is like:

- Selling a house (without saying anything about keeping the doors) and then taking the doors with you. You leave the following note on the wall: "AGREEMENT OF SALE AND PURCHASE: Buyer and Seller agree that this House is sold without doors. Moving into House constitutes acceptance of this Agreement. If Buyer does not accept said Agreement, Buyer must not move into House and must claim a refund for House within 15 (fifteen) days after publication of this notice." Your customer bought the right to move into the House when you made the original sales agreement, just like you bought the right to use the software when you paid for it. You can't use moving into the house—something the buyer already has the right to do—to deprive the buyer of the doors, can you? The warranty is like the doors. It came with the program when you bought it. The publisher can't take it back later.

- Borrowing money from a bank at 10 percent interest and then sending a note with your first payment. "LOAN AGREEMENT MODIFICATION: Lender and Borrower hereby and herewith Agree that the Interest on Loan 4725 is heretofore Reduced to 3% (three percent) per annum, effective immediately. Lender signifies its acceptance of these terms by cashing the enclosed check." Nice try, but do you really think you'd get away with this? You and the bank have made the agreement; the bank has every right to take a pay-

---

[40] *Bowdoin v. Showell Growers, Inc.* (1987, p. 1544) involved a sale of a high pressure spray rig, "The district court concluded that a disclaimer found in the instruction manual that accompanied the spray rig when it was delivered to the purchaser was conspicuous and therefore effective. We disagree. Even assuming that the disclaimer was otherwise conspicuous, it was delivered to the purchaser after the sale. Such a post-sale disclaimer is not effective because it did not form a part of the basis of the bargain between the parties to the sale."

ment that you already owe it without agreeing to new terms in its contract. Similarly, you have the right to use the software after you buy it, so you can use it without agreeing to new warranty terms in your contract.

Exhibit 7.4 summarizes the case of *Step-Saver Data Systems, Inc. v. Wyse Technology and The Software Link, Inc.* (1991). The Court ruled that The Software Link's (TSL's) warranty disclaimer was not valid. This is not an isolated decision.[41] The United States Court of Appeals for the Ninth Circuit (which includes California and Washington) explained this reasoning as follows (*Diamond Fruit Growers, Inc. v. Krack Corp.*, 1986, p. 1444, citations omitted):

> *One of the principles underlying section 2-207 is neutrality. If possible, the section should be interpreted so as to give neither party to a contract an advantage simply because it happened to send the first or in some cases the last form. Section 2-207 accomplishes this result in part by doing away with the common law's "last shot" rule. At common law, the offeree/counter-offeror gets all of its terms simply because it fired the last shot in the exchange of forms. Section 2-207(3) does away with this result by giving neither party the terms it attempted to impose unilaterally on the other. Instead, all of the terms on which the parties' forms do not agree drop out, and the U.C.C. supplies the missing terms.*

---

[41] Here are some representative discussions.

Clark and Smith (1984, pp. 7–18) "The disclaimer may be found in an operator's manual, or in sales literature not sent to the buyer until sometime later, or it may be hidden away in the package that also contains the goods, with no warning on the outside of the package. In all of these cases, it is as though the seller were determined that the buyer should not see the disclaimer until after the fact. Given this seller perversity, it is not surprising that the courts generally nullify such post-contract disclaimers."

Arizona Retail Systems, Inc. v. The Software Link (1993) followed the ruling of Step-Saver and extended the reasoning.

Diamond Fruit Growers, Inc. v. Krack Corp. (1986, p. 1445) "If the seller truly does not want to be bound unless the buyer assents to its terms, it can protect itself by not shipping until it obtains that assent."

Glyptal, Inc. v. Engelhard Corp. (1992, p. 894) "The case law concerning whether warranty disclaimers are material alterations is more uniform. Courts have held consistently that warranty disclaimers materially alter a contract under Section 2–207(2)(b)."

Pawelec v. Digitcom, Inc. (1984, p. 479) involved the sale of a milling machine; "Digitcom also urges that its limitation of warranty and remedy set forth in the operating manual attached to its control unit should be given effect. . . . there was no showing that [the customer] saw the warranty or limitations, which were strapped to the machine in an envelope."

There are dozens of additional cases like these. Sheldon and Carter (1997, Section 5.7) cite many of them. White and Summers (1995, volume 1, Section 12–5) cite plenty of others.

One other myth that we want to dispel here is that the implied warranty of merchantability is in some way a consumer protection statute. None of the cases cited in this footnote involve consumers. Step-Saver wasn't a consumer, it was a reseller. Few of the cases cited by Sheldon and Carter or White and Summers on this matter are consumer cases. The implied warranty of merchantability applies to all sales of goods, including big sales between sophisticated parties.

White and Summers (1995) is widely considered the authoritative treatise on the UCC. In Section 12-5 (pages 639-40), they say:

> *The buyer might be given a disclaimer at the time of the delivery of the goods. That disclaimer may be printed on a label, in an operator's manual, or on an invoice. According to most pre-Code law, '[I]f a bargain with even an implied warranty has once arisen, a subsequent disclaimer of warranty when the goods are delivered will not avail the seller.'[42] The same rule has generally prevailed under the Code.*

We have reviewed the literature extensively. Based on that review, we state that courts uphold post-sale warranty disclaimers rarely and only under special circumstances.[43]

---

[42] White and Summers' quote is from Williston's classic treatise on Contracts (1961, 3rd Ed., Section 993A, p. 610).

[43] Attorneys will find it informative that, as part of our final editorial process, in the summer of 1998, we shepardized *Belcher, Diamond Fruit Growers, Gateway 2000, Sanco, Step-Saver,* and *ProCD.* Over the five years that we researched and wrote this book, we shepardized dozens of other cases. Here are the results of our search for cases that *disagree* with our conclusion.

Belcher v. Versatile Farm Equip. Co. (1983) is sometimes cited as an example of a contrary case, but it illustrates our point (special circumstances) well. Belcher bought a tractor. The owner's manual came with the tractor, and Belcher probably didn't see it until after the sale. The warranty in the manual restricted the buyer's remedy to repair or replacement. The tractor's spindles broke several times. A repair shop authorized by the seller to do warranty repairs did repair the spindle each time until the last time, when Belcher sued rather than seek warranty repairs. The key defense involved a section of the owner's manual that said that unauthorized modifications of the tractor would void the warranty. Among other modifications, Belcher partially filled the tires with water (to add ballast) to an extent that went beyond the seller's authorized limits. According to the evidence presented at trial, this appeared to be the cause of the damage to the spindles. The court stated that Belcher "disregarded the terms of the warranty" (p. 915). Given this conclusion, *Belcher* is not a case about a seller that breached its warranty.

In the case of *Hahn v. Ford Motor Corp.* (1981), the court upheld a limitation of the implied warranty of merchantability (to 12 months, the same length as the express, written warranty) even though it was contained in a Warranty Facts booklet that was in the car's glove compartment and not seen by the customers until after the sale. However, the case had two unusual features. First, the jury was given evidence (testimony of the customer) that, at the time of sale, the customer knew the car had only a twelve-month warranty. Second, the appellate court wrote at length that it might have found the warranty limitation void if it had been given the chance. It cited many cases in support of its statement that "A modification of warranty or limitation of remedy contained in a manufacturers manual received by purchaser subsequent to sale has not been bargained for and thus does not limit recovery for implied or express warranties which arose prior to sale. In essence, the parties have not consented to and are not contractually bound by the modification or limitation." (p. 948) However, the argument made by the customer's lawyer was not that the limitation was void because it wasn't given to the customer until after the sale. Instead, "The specific argument advanced by the Hahns . . . alleges the booklet was inadmissible on evidentiary grounds . . . We are, of course, limited in our scope of review and address only those issues properly raised by the parties." (p. 948) The court then ruled that Ford had been entitled to show the booklet to the jury. If we understand this opinion correctly, the court implied that if the case had been argued and briefed differently, the court might well have ruled differently.

Sanco, Inc. v. Ford Motor Co. (1985) is another case that is sometimes cited as an example of a post-sale warranty disclaimer that was upheld. The purchaser bought 42 heavy trucks from Fairway Ford. The trucks came with a limited written warranty that excluded the implied warranty of merchantability. (This is *not* consumer merchandise, so the Magnuson-Moss Act is not applicable here.) Sanco argued that this warranty disclaimer should be void because it was delivered at the time of sale. However, Fairway Ford's president was also the president and controlling shareholder of Sanco, Inc. In his capacity as president of Fairway Ford, the president of Sanco did know about the disclaimer. The court's ruling that that the disclaimer was enforceable tells us that when the seller is the same person as the buyer, the law doesn't require him to tell himself in writing that there is a warranty disclaimer.

In the case of *Seekings v. Jimmy GMC* (1981), the court enforced a disclaimer of the implied warranty of merchantability (of a mobile home) by the dealer. The customer argued that such a disclaimer was unconscionable under the circumstances, but the court ruled that it was not. First, there was a written, limited warranty from the manufacturer, and several repairs were made under that warranty. Second, the written disclaimer appeared in the purchase order and in the purchase money security agreement, both of which were signed by the customer. The fact that the customer *didn't read them* at the time of sale didn't make them any less binding. Additionally, despite the disclaimer, the Arizona Supreme Court awarded a refund plus consequential and incidental damages to the customers.

In *Tolmie Farms, Inc. v. Stauffer Chemical Company, Inc.* (1992), the court enforced an oral express warranty (for a soil fumigant), but also enforced a disclaimer of implied warranties even though the disclaimer appeared in an acknowledgment form that the customer received after the sale. The court said, "The general rule is that a disclaimer presented after the sale is made is ineffective to exclude a warranty. However, the U.C.C. recognizes that certain circumstances are in themselves sufficient to call the buyer's attention to the fact that no implied warranties are made or that certain implied warranties are excluded. Accordingly, the U.C.C. provides that implied warranties can be effectively disclaimed by a 'course of dealing.' A 'course of dealing' is a 'sequence of previous conduct between the parties' which is fairly to be regarded as establishing a common basis of understanding for interpreting their expressions and other conduct. Hence, where parties engage in repeated sales transactions, a seller's otherwise inconspicuous or untimely disclaimer can become part of the parties' contract." (Citations omitted). Several other cases, such as *Diamond Fruit Growers* and *Step-Saver* have reached the opposite conclusion (holding that a course of dealing wasn't enough to establish that the customer assented to the disclaimer), but the point to note here for your purposes is that the customer made many purchases from the seller, negotiated transactions on credit over a period of years and never objected to the warranty disclaimer. This is a much closer relationship than the purchase of mass-market software under non-negotiable terms.

Waukesha Foundry, Inc. v. Industrial Engineering, Inc. (1996) is similar to *Tolmie Farms* in that the court held that a warranty disclaimer was no longer a material change to a contract if it had appeared in the sellers packing slips and invoices (to the same buyer) over a period of years. This is a 7th Circuit opinion, following the *ProCD* case. In *Waukesha Foundry*, the court adopted a new definition of the word "material." It said, "The district court determine that 'courts in Wisconsin and elsewhere generally consider warranty disclaimers and limitations of remedies to be material alterations.' Although the district court cited to two cases of potentially persuasive authority for this decision . . . we do not share its interpretation of the term 'material.'" Note, though, that this case reflects a long course of dealing between a merchant buyer and a merchant seller. As with *Tolmie Farms*, there is no indication, *in this opinion,* that this decision would spill over to one-shot non-negotiable mass-market transactions.

We have a copy of the defendant's (The Software Link's) appellate brief in the case of *Arizona Retail Systems, Inc. v. The Software Link* (1993). This case involved the same defendant as the *Step-Saver* case, and the issues were similar. The court ultimately ruled that the disclaimer attached to one package (a demo copy that could be upgraded to a full product) was effective because the customer saw it on the packaging before accepting the product. Later (non-demo) copies of the product were all purchased by mail order and the disclaimer was not mentioned or agreed to during the order and acceptance discussions on the phone. The court ruled that these disclaimers were invalid. The brief was *Arizona Retail Systems, Inc. v. The Software Link: Response to Plaintiff's Motion for Partial Summary Judgment and Defendant's Cross-Motion for Partial Summary Judgment,* August, 1992. The brief cited only one case for the proposition that a warranty disclaimer should be enforceable if it is given to the customer at the same time as the product, *McCrimmon v. Tandy* Corp. (1991). But in *McCrimmon*, the customer received the warranty disclaimer at the cash register, at the time of purchase, and so it is not surprising that the Court said it was binding.

We checked Gomulkiewicz and Williamson (1996), a paper defending shrink-wrap software licenses in general. Mr. Gomulkiewicz is a senior corporate attorney at Microsoft Corporation, and an active participant in the UCC Article 2B project that we discuss in the Appendix. Ms. Williamson is an attorney at Preston Gates & Ellis (Seattle office), which often represents Microsoft. Their paper criticizes *Step-Saver* and *Arizona Retail Systems* (and *ProCD*, 1996b, which was overruled by *ProCD,* 1996) but cites no cases in which a post-sale warranty disclaimer was upheld.

Along with the arguments that we've discussed in this section, there are several other ways to defeat an implied warranty disclaimer. Sheldon and Carter (1997) lay out 14 different lines of attack.[44] Each of them is interesting and useful, but one more merits special notice for consumers. If you buy the software from a retailer or other reseller, the publisher's disclaimer might well protect the publisher, but how does it protect the reseller? Think about this when you read in the next section about the two-contract model of the case of *ProCD, Inc. v. Zeidenberg* (1996). There are cases that hold that the publisher's disclaimer does not extend to the reseller. [45] Therefore, if you can't get satis-

We checked the Software Publishers' Association's (1996) *Brief of Amicus Curiae* in the *ProCD* appeal. We also checked the jointly submitted *Brief of Amicus Curiae* of the Information Industry Association, the American Medical Association, and the Association of American Publishers (1996). In the original *ProCD* ruling, the United States District Court ruled that a shrink-wrapped restriction on the use of the software was invalid. These two briefs argued, convincingly to the Circuit Court, that shrink-wrap licenses should be enforced. Neither of them provide examples of enforcement of post-sale (e.g. shrink-wrapped) warranty disclaimers.

We checked all of the cases mentioned by Nimmer (1997) in his sections on warranty disclaimers. Professor Nimmer is the Reporter (lead author) of the proposed UCC Article 2B and is the most prestigious advocate for the enforceability of shrink-wrapped software licenses in the United States. Nimmer (1997) cited cases already mentioned, plus *ProCD* and *Gateway 2000,* which will be discussed in the main text shortly. As to the other disclaimer cases in Nimmer (1997), several involved enforcement of conspicuous disclaimers that appeared in signed contracts. One case enforced a disclaimer that didn't appear conspicuous (not contrasting type, etc.). However, the disclaimer was in a negotiated contract between two sophisticated businesses. The court determined that between these parties, any of the terms would have been seen and therefore they should all be treated as conspicuous (*AMF Inc. v. Computer Automation, Inc.*, 1983). Another case, *Alloy Computer Products, Inc. v. Northern Telecom, Inc.* (1988) was described by Professor Nimmer as follows "disclaimer on acknowledgment form shipped with tape drive units enforceable when buyer did not object." (Nimmer, 1997, Section 6.08[4] footnote 157). However in its *Alloy Computer Products* opinion, the court specifically stated that the decision was based on *Roto-Lith, Ltd. v. F.P. Bartlett & Co.* (1962). The court said, "Plaintiff points out that Roto-Lith has been subjected to academic and judicial criticism, because it reverses the outcome that the plain language of Section 2-207 would lead parties to expect. . . . Nevertheless, *Roto-Lith* continues as binding precedent within this circuit." (*Alloy Computer Products*, p. 14) Recently, the First Circuit Court of Appeals overruled its *Roto-Lith* decision in *Ionics, Inc. v. Elmwood Sensors, Inc.* (1997, p. 189): "Our decision brings this circuit in line with the majority view on the subject and puts to rest a case that has provoked considerable criticism for courts and commentators and alike." (*Ionics*, p. 189). The court placed its Footnote 4 at the end of this sentence, and gave examples of court cases that illustrated the majority view. The first case listed was *Step-Saver* (a 3rd Circuit case.) Given the change in position of the 1st Circuit Court of Appeals, we would expect that if *Alloy Computer Products* were decided after *Ionics*, the result would have been different.

[44] (1) Express warranties can't be disclaimed. (2) Magnuson-Moss Act voids some disclaimers. (3) Several state laws limit or bar disclaimers. (4) The disclaimer has to be worded properly. (5) The publisher's disclaimer doesn't protect the retailer. (6) Post-sale disclaimers are ineffective. (7) The disclaimer must be conspicuous. (8) The consumer may have to actually know about the disclaimer. (9) Any ambiguity in the scope of the disclaimer will be interpreted against the seller. (10) Special circumstances might limit the applicability of the disclaimer. (11) The disclaimer might be unconscionable (grossly unfair). (12) The disclaimer might be voidable due to the seller's bad faith (such as the seller's knowledge of a defect in the product when it sells you the product). (13) The disclaimer might be voidable because of bad faith conduct by the seller. (14) You might still be able to revoke acceptance if the product has a material defect that would have caused you to refuse the product in the first place. Additionally, they note that disclaimers don't extend to fraud, deceptive practices, or defects that cause personal injury or property damage. Finally, the seller can probably not disclaim liability for contract violations (such as defects) that are due to the seller's gross negligence. We'll discuss known defects and gross negligence in the section on Remedies.

[45] For example, *Barazzatto v. Intelligent Systems, Inc.* (1987) (reseller was accountable for an implied warranty of fitness for use, even though the publisher's software contract disclaimed it). Sheldon and Carter (1997, Section 5.6, footnotes 65 and 67 provide many additional non-software examples).]

faction from the publisher, think about recovering your losses from the company that sold you the software.

ANALYSIS: SHRINK-WRAPPED TERMS IN PACKAGED SOFTWARE

Most publishers add a twist—they put the disks inside a sealed envelope and print on the envelope that you must not open the disks unless you agree to the terms of the warranty disclaimer. The envelope is contained inside the shrink-wrapped software package (which is why these are called "shrink-wrapped" disclaimers.) The publishers say that if you do not agree to the terms printed on the envelope, you must return the disks, unopened, within a few days, and you will be given a complete refund. Opening the disks, they say, consummates the purchase and constitutes acceptance of the terms of the disclaimer. Another variation on the same theme is the click-wrap disclaimer. In this case, you see the disclaimer when you install the software. You click OK, or you can't finish installing the software. In that case, you return the software to the seller. This is just like opening the envelope except that you see the license onscreen. This line of argument failed in the *Step-Saver* case. Under that decision, if you buy software, pay for it, and bring it home, then by the time you open the package and read what's on the disk, it's too late for the software publisher to add new terms to the purchase agreement.

Publishers call these shrink-wrap and click-wrap notices, "License Agreements" or "End User License Agreements" because they usually include additional terms, such as limitations on your right to use the product, not just the warranty disclaimer. We'll consider those limitations briefly in the appendix. Our presentation of issues here is done specifically to explain a new trend in interpreting these license "agreements," that threatens to have a major impact on courts' interpretation of warranty disclaimers.

For years, this entire shrink-wrapped approach to contracting was considered suspect and it was unclear whether any court would accept it. Lemley (1995) lists several cases from around the world that declined to enforce shrink-wrapped limitations. At that time, no case in the United States had validated a shrink-wrapped software term.

In the case of *Vault Corp. v. Quaid Software Ltd.,* (1987), the United States District Court rejected a shrink-wrapped term that banned reverse engineering as unlawful. It said that these shrink-wrap contracts were contracts of adhesion. A contract of adhesion is one that has non-negotiable terms and is written by a party (typically a big company) that has overwhelming bargaining power compared to the person being asked to sign it. We face adhesion contracts every day, when we buy insurance, airline tickets, new and used cars, when we rent cars or homes, open bank accounts, sign up for telephone service, and so on. But, almost all of these contracts are regulated. Laws were passed to regulate them because the drafters of adhesion contracts tend to write them just the way they like them, usually taking more rights for themselves than anyone else would think is even minimally fair. (Read Exhibit 7.3 for an example. Read the appendix for a discussion of an influential industry-backed proposal, UCC Article 2B, that makes Exhibit 7.3 seem tame.) This is called "overreaching" and, industry by industry, the American legal system has had to deal with it by regulation (which has been a pain in the neck for everyone). Software contracts aren't (yet) regulated, so the *Vault Corp.* court was willing to consider these contracts suspect.

The United States Court of Appeals for the Fifth Circuit wasn't as uncharitable to shrink-wrapped notices in general, but it still threw out the restriction on reverse engineering and declared that the Louisiana law that authorized the restriction was pre-empted by the Copyright Act of the United States. (Under the Supremacy Clause of the United States Constitution, a state law is pre-empted if it conflicts with a [federal] law of the United States. A pre-empted law is unenforceable.) See *Vault Corp. v. Quaid Software Ltd,* (1988).

We've already discussed *Step-Saver Data Systems, Inc. v. Wyse Technology and The Software Link, Inc.,* (1991) and (mainly in the footnotes) *Arizona Retail Systems, Inc. v. The Software Link* (1993). These threw out warranty disclaimers in software shrink-wrapped notices. Lemley (1995) cites additional cases. In 1996, it was commonplace to see statements like "Courts have generally refused to enforce traditional shrink-wrap licenses." (Moore and Hadden, 1996)

This trend was reinforced in early 1996, in the case of *ProCD, Inc. v. Zeidenberg* (1996b). Zeidenberg bought copies of ProCD's *Select Phone* software, downloaded telephone listings stored on the CD-ROM disks to his computer, and made the listings available to Internet users by placing the data onto an Internet host computer. In the case of *Feist Publications, Inc. v. Rural Telephone Service Co.* (1991), the United States Supreme Court ruled that telephone listings are not copyrightable. Therefore, the key issue was whether Zeidenberg used the ProCD software and data outside of the scope of the shrink-wrapped license "agreement" that came with the product. The court noted that (ProCD, 1996b, p. 654):

> *The terms of the Select Phone(TM) user agreement were not presented to defendants at the time of sale. The sole reference to the user agreement was a disclosure in small print at the bottom of the package, stating that defendants were subject to the terms and conditions of the enclosed license agreement. Defendants did not receive the opportunity to inspect or consider those terms. Mere reference to the terms at the time of initial contract formation does not present buyers an adequate opportunity to decide whether they are acceptable. They must be able to read and consider the terms in their entirety. The potential incorporation of terms can occur only after the purchaser opens the package and has a reasonable opportunity to inspect the user agreement.*

Consistent with the reasoning in *Step-Saver and Arizona Retail Systems*, the court decided in favor of Zeidenberg.

Many of us liked the court's reasoning but thought the result was massively unfair to ProCD (the publisher of Select Phone). The company did a huge amount of work and this decision meant that anyone could take ProCD's data and publish it to the world. How could ProCD stay in business?

There are many, many complexities in the question of intellectual property protection for uncopyrightable material. We aren't even going to begin a discussion of this issue. All we'll say is that, sitting in our armchairs, we thought that the *ProCD* court should have ruled in favor of ProCD on the basis of unfair competition, not breach of some license or violation of the Copyright Act.

The United States Seventh Circuit Court of Appeals adopted a new approach. In effect, the court ruled that there were two contracts in the contract for sale of software (*ProCD*, pp. 1452–53).

- The first contract is between the retailer and the customer. Basically, that gives the customer the right to take the software away, open the box, and attempt to install the software.

- The second contract is between the publisher and the customer. This is the one that gives the customer the right to use the software. The customer learns the details of this contract when he installs the software. If the customer chooses not to accept the publisher's terms, he can return the software to the retailer for a refund (at least, that's what the publisher's license "agreement" says).

- In effect, the contract between the retailer and the customer is an option contract. The customer buys an option to make a contract with the software publisher.

This model of the transaction elegantly (though, we think, erroneously) side-steps the reasoning of the *Step-Saver* and *Arizona Retail Systems* courts.[46]

---

[46] In *ProCD* and in *Gateway 2000*, the court says that UCC 2–207 doesn't apply because there is no battle of the forms. This was fascinating argument (kind of like watching a big tornado is fascinating) in the *ProCD* case because the initial sales agreement was between a reseller and a customer. So where is the "privity" (the contract relationship) between the publisher and the customer? We can play mental acrobatics with this issue for a long time (and have). But the *Gateway 2000* case is more direct. The customer ordered the computer directly from Gateway 2000. There was no reseller. As we understand Article 2, the manufacturer makes an invitation for offers when it advertises. The customer makes an offer when he calls to place the order. The seller accepts the offer when it says "OK" and takes the credit card number. We now have an Article 2 contract, with several Article 2 default terms supplied. It is enforceable, whether it is on paper or not. But the *Gateway* opinion (p. 1150) says that "By keeping the computer beyond 30 days, the Hills accepted Gateway's offer, including the arbitration clause." *What offer?* As in *Step-Saver* and so many other cases, offer and acceptance had come and gone by this point.

In the *ProCD* case, the court used this reasoning to justify a result that we thought was sensible. But, what results are possible under this reasoning? Or, more precisely put, what limits are there? How outrageous an "agreement" can the publisher create this way and still get away with it?

The Seventh Circuit has recently ruled on another mass-market case, *Hill v. Gateway 2000, Inc.* (1997). As you read about this, keep in mind that the subject of the *Gateway 2000* lawsuit was a computer, hard goods, not software. Article 2 governs this transaction now, and it will continue to govern sales like this in the future, even if the special software law (Article 2B) passes. If you have concerns about the results of this lawsuit, understand that the same approach to contracting will be valid for traditional goods, such as stereo equipment or laundry detergent.

According to Hill (*Hill v. Gateway 2000, Inc.,* 1997b), here is what happened:

- Hill saw advertisements for Gateway 2000's Tenth Anniversary System in magazines, and he placed his order for a system based on advertising.

- "Gateway's advertisement specified system components including a 6X EIDE CD-ROM Drive, Altec Lansing Surround Sound Speakers with Subwoofer, and a Matrox MGA 'Millenium' 2MB Graphics Accelerator. Gateway claimed it would furnish a 'new blazing 6X CD-ROM Drive . . . the fastest EIDE CD-ROM *anywhere*' (emphasis in original) and '*the first* speaker system designed to create theater-type surround sound' (emphasis in original). The advertised graphics accelerator is an upgradable video card." (Note: punctuation, italics, etc. are as they appear in *Hill*, 1997b, p. 3. We have changed nothing except double quotes " to single quotes ')

- "Gateway did not supply what it advertised. Plaintiffs' CD-ROM performed like a 4X drive (which is significantly slower than a 6X drive) and would jam while running a number of programs (requiring a complete reset of the computer system, losing any unsaved work in the process). A faster CD-ROM drive was available when Gateway made its claim. The Altec Lansing speakers plaintiffs received did not have 'surround sound,' although they came in the 'surround sound' packaging. The speakers produce static and hiss. After inquiring about this, plaintiffs were informed by Gateway that the 'surround sound' speakers were not available through Gateway, and that it was a 'misprint' in the advertisement. Gateway did not supply a Matrox MGA Millenium 2MB Graphics Accelerator, but substituted another less-expensive component from the same manufacturer that was not upgradable without informing its customers." (*Hill*, 1997b, p. 3–4).

- "It would cost the plaintiffs approximately $1,000 more than they paid (and than Gateway advertised) in order to obtain the actual system advertised by Gateway." (*Hill*, 1997b, p. 4)

- Inside the shipping containers "was a four-page document entitled 'Standard Terms and Conditions.' There was no prior notice of such a document in the advertisement, on the outside of the box, or on the order confirmation that Gateway faxed to plaintiffs." (*Hill,* 1997b, p. 4)

- The standard terms and conditions included an arbitration clause: "Any dispute or controversy arising out of or relating to the Agreement or its interpretation shall be settled exclusively and finally by arbitration. The arbitration shall be conducted in accordance with the Rules of Conciliation and Arbitration of the International Chamber of Commerce. The arbitration shall be conducted in Chicago, Illinois, U.S.A. before a sole arbitrator." (*Hill,* 1997b, p. 4–5)

- "The Standard Terms and Conditions" purport to become effective thirty days after receipt of the computer system without any further action by purchasers; rejection would require that the consumer, at the consumer's expense, repackage the computer system and return it to Gateway. The "Standard Terms and Conditions" do not contemplate a signed agreement to be so bound by the purchaser. The Hills did not acknowledge or sign an agreement to the 'Standard Terms and Conditions.'" (*Hill,* 1997b, p. 5)

- "The rules of the International Chamber of Commerce also require each side to pay an arbitration fee in advance of approximately $2,000—half the list price of the Tenth Anniversary System." (*Hill,* 1997b, p. 5)

- "Gateway began including the 'Standard Terms and Conditions' in shipping containers for the first time in July of 1995. Gateway began taking orders for the Tenth Anniversary System on the last business day of June, 1995, and did not begin shipping the Tenth Anniversary System until August of 1995." (*Hill,* 1997b, p. 5)

We have no way of knowing whether Hill's claims were true or false, but based on the reports in the press and on the Net, there appears to be evidence in support of his claims. According to these, Gateway shipped 10,000 of the 10th Anniversary Systems.[47] Many[48] customers were unhappy. Some of them formed a user group, *The 10th Anniversary Club*, to share information and work collectively with Gateway to resolve problems.[49] They complained about hissing speakers that were less valuable than they expected.[50] They complained about faulty CD-ROM drives (too slow, lock up, or "faulty")[51] and about a "stripped-down" video card.[52] Sengstack (writing for PC World) said the "Matrox MGA Millenium graphics card described in Gateway's ads (which appeared in PC

---

[47] Sengstack (1996).

[48] Foster (1997) reports that the 10th Anniversary Club had "300 vocal members."

[49] The 10th Anniversary Club (1998), Foster (1997).

[50] Sengstack, (1996), The 10th Anniversary Club (1998), Foster (1997).

[51] Sengstack, (1996), DiCarlo (1996), Cringely (1996), The 10th Anniversary Club (1998), Foster (1997).

[52] Sengstack, (1996), The 10th Anniversary Club (1998), Foster (1997).

World and elsewhere) was actually different from the board sold in stores. Unlike the retail version, Gateway's card couldn't be upgraded with hardware . . . and it used a slower RAMDAC chip." Sengstack quoted a Matrox spokesperson who allegedly said that these cards were built to Gateway's specifications. He also claimed that a faster Teac 6X drive was available when Gateway rolled out the 10th Anniversary System.

In its *Gateway 2000* opinion (an "opinion" is a court's official memo explaining its ruling), the court noted that "Hill kept the computer for more than 30 days before complaining about its components and performance." (*Hill,* 1997, p. 1148).[53] The court then decided that "Terms inside Gateway's box stand or fall together. If they constitute the parties' contract because the Hills had an opportunity to return the computer after reading them, then all must be enforced." (*Hill,* 1997, p. 1148). Following its reasoning in *ProCD,* the court ruled that the contract was binding on the customer. Hill lost his day in court and had to go to arbitration.

So what are the limits on terms in these contracts? In the contract described by Hill, a dissatisfied customer will have to travel to Chicago, pay travel expenses, pay lawyers, and pay a $2,000 arbitration fee, all in order to sue for a $1,000 difference in value in a $4,000 system. Compare this to Small Claims Court. No travel expenses for the consumer (just for the manufacturer). No lawyers. And no $2,000 arbitration fee (the filing fee in Small Claims Court is probably less than $100). It looks to us as though it might be rational to take a manufacturer to Small Claims Court under these circumstances but much riskier and more expensive to go to arbitration. But, Small Claims Court is not an option, just this expensive type of arbitration.[54] It seems to us that this arbitration clause was every bit as "material" as a remedy limitation or warranty disclaimer. Under the *Gateway 2000* and *ProCD* decisions, the Seventh Circuit appears to be willing to enforce all of the seller's terms if the customer keeps the merchandise beyond some minimal period (which can probably be much less than a month).

We'll never know whether Gateway 2000 intended or committed consumer fraud, because there will never be a public trial. We do know that Gateway has

---

[53] Here's a reality check—if you had bought a computer with these problems, how long would it have taken you to figure out that the video card was an OEM version or that the 6X CD-ROM drive was slower than its competitors, or that a pair of speakers sold in surround sound packaging didn't have surround sound capability but that other speakers sold in the same or similar packaging did have this capability? Is it reasonable to condition basic customer's rights on early discovery of defects that will be difficult for a reasonable consumer to recognize?

[54] By the way, Hill's complaint included a RICO cause of action, alleging mail and wire fraud. He filed a class action lawsuit. With 10,000 customers allegedly involved, there seems to be a public interest in having public proceedings, open to the press, so that the other customers would hear about it and perhaps participate in (or opt out of) the suit. Arbitration is usually a private dispute resolution system. The Seventh Circuit ruled that a class action lawsuit is not an option for Hill, just arbitration, albeit perhaps class action arbitration.

earned tremendous customer goodwill over the years and we believe that they are a reputable company. But, we are concerned about the *Gateway 2000* opinion because we see it as a road map that can be followed by less ethical companies who want to engage in sharp practices without fear of a public trial.

Is this an isolated decision or a preview of 21st century American contract law? We don't know. The decision will probably be made in connection with the development of an amendment to the Uniform Commercial Code that is specific to software and information contracts. One such amendment, a proposed new Article 2B, has been in the works for over ten years and is coming up for state legislative decisions. It has largely adopted the approach that you see in *Gateway 2000*. We've been active in the Article 2B drafting process for nearly three years, pushing for a compromise that would respect the rights of consumers and small businesses as well as publishers. Unfortunately, in rooms that are typically full of up to a hundred publishers' lobbyists, there hasn't been much interest in compromise. For details, please read the appendix.

Remedies

When you buy a defective program, what should you expect from the publisher?

We explored this in detail in Chapter 4, "What Should You Ask For?", listing many different expenses you might face when you get a defective program. There our question was *pragmatic*—what did it cost you, and what are you willing to settle for? Here, the question is *legal*, what does the publisher *owe* you?

OVERVIEW: REMEDIES

A remedy is "the means by which a right is enforced or the violation of a right is prevented, redressed, or compensated."[55] There are several types of remedies, including (but not only) money.

The remedies available to you are partially determined by the general law of remedies and partially by the specifics of the agreement (if any) that you reached with the publisher. License agreements (valid and invalid ones) typically include clauses that limit the remedies you can claim.

If the program *is* defective and the publisher owes you *anything* as a result of that defect, then you are probably entitled to better treatment than the publisher is offering you, possibly better than you realize yourself.

---

[55] *Long Leaf Lumber, Inc. v. Svolos*, p. 124.

The real cost of a defective program is much higher than the price of the program itself. Think of all the time and money you can waste trying to get the program to work or trying to recover data that the program lost or corrupted. Think of the consequences if the program under-reports your taxable income or underestimates your expenses when you bid on a contract or erases your slides in the middle of a sales presentation or ruin's your child's Christmas. The program's price might only be a tiny portion of the amount that you lose because of the program's defects.

The question of how much you should lose, and how much the publisher should repay you, is very complex. It is caught up in tradeoffs between different important public policies.[56] A lot of money is at stake. As a result, this type of issue goes to court frequently and the decisions often turn on specific details of the case. Here are two competing viewpoints:[57]

Your perspective.   You're not the one who broke this contract. You paid your money, so now you're entitled to a program that works. You shouldn't have to pay extra for an upgrade to make the program work, and you shouldn't have to absorb losses that resulted from the program's errors.

Unless your agreement with the publisher explicitly limits its liability, your perspective is the one dictated by traditional contract law and by the Uniform Commercial Code. Even though you will run into resistance and ridicule when you tell the publisher that you want the bugs fixed plus reimbursement for losses caused by the product's defects, this has been the law for a long, long time.[58]

Publisher's perspective.   No publisher wants to sell a program for $100 per copy and accept a liability risk of $1,000,000 per copy. Publishers must be able to limit their risks to some degree. Otherwise, they'll either go out of business quickly or have to charge much higher prices to cover their risks.

---

[56] Laws exist to reflect and serve public policy. In some cases, the policy is obvious—murder is against public policy, so we make laws that ban it. In other cases, important policies collide. Consider the following:

Publishers should do as much as reasonably possible to ensure that their products have no serious bugs. We want to create laws that encourage publishers to design carefully, document well, test thoroughly, advertise honestly, and treat their customers with respect.

In contrast, business conditions for high technology companies must reasonably be favorable. We want to encourage the growth and survival of ethical high tech businesses. If the risks associated with a product are unknown (but they just involve losing money, not injuring people), then we should allow businesses to find ways to limit their risks (e.g., to limit their exposure to consequential damages). Otherwise, companies will stop creating or selling these types of products in America because they can't afford the risk.

[57] Dobbs (1993, Chapter 12) includes an excellent discussion of different interests protected by the general contract rules. His chapters 1 and 3 provide background discussions that any serious student of remedies should read attentively.

[58] *Hadley v. Baxendale* (1854) is the classic English case that *limited* contract-breakers' liability for consequential damages to the ones that would be foreseeable at the time the contract was made. This is a case in English Common Law, from 1854. The notion of consequential liability is a very traditional one.

The publisher's fear is very real and entirely reasonable. It is impossible to ensure that the program is bug-free (Kaner, 1997f). Therefore, publishers will want to make agreements with customers to limit liability. In effect, publishers want to cut a deal with you that lets you pay less for the product, but that denies you consequential damages, if you ever win a lawsuit. This is a perfectly acceptable agreement in contract law. [59] But, the publisher can't just announce after the fact that it is free from liability; this has to be part of the agreement when you buy the product.

The negotiation that you go through over the remedy for a defective product is a balancing act between your perspective and the publisher's perspective. Both views are reasonable. Don't lose sight of the fact that your view—you should be fully compensated—is completely reasonable and has a long legal history. But, don't expect the publisher to give you everything you want without a fight. Plan to compromise. If you are too stubborn, it will cost you too much time and work to get (if you ever get) everything that you insist that you are entitled to. People who are too stubborn often get nothing.

ANALYSIS: REMEDIES

Inside every purchase is a legally enforceable contract. You give the seller money and in return you receive a product. If the product is defective or doesn't do what the seller said it would do, the seller has broken the contract.

You have a right to receive the product that you paid for, and if the seller doesn't keep its side of the bargain, you're entitled to seek your remedies. The basic rule of contract remedies says that you should be awarded those remedies that are necessary to put you in the same position as you would have been in had the seller kept its side of the bargain.[60]

You are probably entitled to several types of remedies, available under several different statutes.[61] Some of the remedies available are repair, replacement, re-

---

[59] The UCC Section 2–719 doesn't allow publishers to limit liability for personal injuries caused by its consumer goods.

[60] Dobbs (1973) is a well-respected text that is worth quoting in court. He puts it this way, "The traditional goal in awarding damages for breach of contract is to award a sum that will put the non-breaching party in as good a position as he would have been in had the contract been performed. This gives him the benefit of his bargain, that is, the 'profit' he would have made upon performance. This is said to give him his expectancy." (p. 786).

The UCC says "The remedies provided by this Act shall be liberally administered to the end that the aggrieved party may be put in as good a position as if the other party had fully performed but neither consequential or special nor penal damages may be had except as specifically provided in this Act or by other rule of law." (Section 1–106).

[61] Dobbs (1993, Chapters 1 and 12) discusses the range of contract remedies and the considerations for selecting among them at trial.]

fund, partial refund, cost of a replacement product, cost of an upgrade, incidental damages, and consequential damages. Let's look at each of these in turn:

Repair, Replacement, and Refund

First, what are these?

Repair.   The publisher fixes the program and gives you a new version.

Replacement.   The publisher gives you a new copy of the program, perhaps replacing a disk that didn't work or a manual that was ripped.

Refund.   You get your money back.

Have you ever asked the publisher to fix its bugs? It's not easy to fix and adequately retest a program, so publishers might not be willing or able to do this on demand. Recognizing that they can't say, "Yes" to this request, some customer support groups make callers feel foolish or unreasonable for asking for a fixed version of the program. Other companies expect you to pay for upgrades that fix the bugs.

Under the Magnuson-Moss Warranty Act,[62] however, your request for a fixed version of the program is entirely reasonable. The publisher must provide you with it unless that is commercially impracticable, or impossible to do within a reasonable time.

Partial Refund, Cost of a Replacement Product, or Upgrade

What are these?

Partial refund.   You get some of your money back. If you paid $100 for a product that (with its bugs) is only worth $50, you get $50 back.[63]

Cost of a replacement product.   You get enough money to buy a different program, that does everything the publisher promised that the program that you bought would do. This might be more than you paid.[64]

---

[62] United States Code, Title 15, Section 2301(10): "The term "remedy" means whichever of the following actions the warrantor elects: (A) repair, (B) replacement, or (C) refund; except that the warrantor may not elect refund unless (i) the warrantor is unable to provide replacement and repair is not commercially practicable or cannot be timely made, or (ii) the consumer is willing to accept such refund."

[63] *Louisiana AFL-CIO v. Lanier Business Products* (1986) is an interesting example.

[64] Under the Uniform Commercial Code, Section 2–714:. . . "(1) [T]he buyer . . . may recover as damages . . . the loss resulting . . . from the seller's breach as determined in any manner which is reasonable.

"(2) The measure of damages for breach of warranty is the difference . . . between the value of the goods accepted and the value they would have had if they had been as warranted, unless special circumstances show proximate damages of a different amount."

See Clark and Smith (1984, Section 7.04[2]) for discussion of the buyer's ability to purchase substitute goods that differ from the original.

Publisher gives you an upgrade.   The publisher gives you a different program that does everything that the one you bought was supposed to do. This makes sense when the publisher sells another program that actually can do what your program was supposed to do. For example, if you bought the "Light" version of a program, the publisher might give you the full version of the program.[65]

Incidental Damages

Incidental damages (often shortened to *incidentals*) cover your out-of-pocket expenses in dealing with the defective product.[66] This includes, for example, the cost of mailing the program back to the publisher, your mileage in driving to a software store to buy a new program, and the cost of your telephone calls to the publisher. We give examples of these in Chapter 4.

We can't speak for the entire industry, but our sense is that many (perhaps most) technical support managers will authorize reimbursement for documented incidental expenses that were caused by a bug that they consider "genuine." Or, they'll find some way to help you reduce your expenses, such as by giving you their shipper number so that you can mail the product to them on their nickel. No one volunteers these reimbursements—you must ask for them.

You might have trouble getting reimbursement of these expenses from a third-party support organization. It's hard to tell whether you're talking to someone who actually works in the publisher's support group. If you don't make headway over the phone, write a letter to the company's head office.

Consequential Damages

Don't feel awkward if you get confused between incidental and consequential damages. Sitting in legislative drafting meetings for the past few years, we've learned that even commercial lawyers get confused about these. The terms

---

[65] This is another example of allowing the publisher to *cure* a defect. See UCC Section 2–508 and 2–608(1)(a).

[66] The UCC says you can collect incidentals and consequentials in Section 2–714:

(3) In a proper case any incidental and consequential damages under the next section may also be recovered.

The UCC defines incidental damages in Section 2–715:

"(1) Incidental damages resulting from seller's breach include expenses reasonably incurred in inspection, receipt, transportation and care and custody of goods rightfully rejected, any commercially reasonable charges, expenses or commissions in connection with effecting cover and any other reasonable expense incident to the delay or other breach."

For our purposes, "effecting cover" means buying a replacement program that works. We give additional examples of incidental expenses in Chapter 4.

overlap, conceptually and especially, in many slightly differing definitions adopted in different court opinions.[67]

Consequential damages (which are often shortened to consequentials) includes anything the publisher must pay you to compensate you for your *consequential losses.* [68] Any loss that you suffer that is a consequence (result) of the defects in the program is a *consequential loss.* Consequential damages for a defective product include those losses that the seller should have anticipated would be caused by the defect. This is a broad definition, but with broad limits.[69] We gave examples of these in Chapter 4.

The issue of how much the publisher should pay you in consequential damages will probably be the most difficult dispute in your negotiation with the publisher, because the consequentials involve the most money, The publisher's contract will often (attempt to) limit your ability to recover consequential damages. We'll discuss that limitation shortly, but you can sometimes get out of it. We'll start this discussion by assuming that there is no remedy limitation.

Here's an illustration of the basic definition. Suppose you buy a $100 communications program to exchange contract drafts with an important customer. The program crashes and destroys your disk files, and as a result, you lose the $1,000,000 deal. The lost disk files and the lost $1,000,000 deal are both consequential losses.

- The lost disk files are a good example of the kind of consequential damage that you should be compensated for. The destroyed files are a natural and direct result of the program's failure, and everybody knows that bugs can trash disk files. The publisher should pay to recreate the files (e.g., to re-enter the data).

[67] As usual, Dobbs (1993, Section 12.16(4)) provides an interesting insight that we haven't seen anywhere else: "The UCC also created a category of damages which it calls incidental damages. 'Incidental damages' appears to be a subset of what the common law would call consequential damages. . . . The idea seems to be that incidental damages . . . are always within the parties' contemplation [in the sense meant by the court in *Hadley v. Baxendale*]. By making incidental damages recoverable without proof that the defendant had reason to know they might be incurred, the Code takes a short cut to reach the same result that would normally be reached at common law." Based on the Code's very brief definitions and Official Comments, the courts and professors have had to use their own judgment in classifying damages as consequential or incidental. The result, not surprisingly, has been variable.

[68] The Code defines consequentials in Section 2–715:

(2) "Consequential damages resulting from the seller's breach include: (a) any loss resulting from general or particular requirements and needs of which the seller at the time of contracting had reason to know and which could not reasonably be prevented by cover or otherwise; and (b) injury to person or property proximately resulting from any breach of warranty.

[69] Dobbs (1993, Section 12.4(3)) is a good discussion of the problem of forseeability (what the seller "had reason to know") in consequential damages. Also, see White & Summers (1995, Section 10–4(c)).

- If the crash occurred during a communication session, the waste of the phone call would also be a natural result of the program's bug. a consequential loss, and reimbursement should be non-controversial.

- But the $1,000,000 deal is a particular requirement. The publisher might know that you might lose a data file. But not a $1,000,000 data file. You might not be able to hold the publisher to a risk of this magnitude unless you make sure that the publisher understands your requirements when you buy the program.[70]

We discussed several examples of consequential losses in Chapter 4.

As a general rule, you must be able to estimate your damages with reasonable certainty. Claims for lost profits and lost goodwill fail when it's too hard to prove how much was lost.[71] You are also unlikely to recover the value of your own time.

The next problem that you'll run into in negotiations is that even if the publisher did breach the contract, you cannot recover damages for losses that you could have reduced or prevented with reasonable efforts.[72] When do you have to make these efforts, and what is reasonable?

Here's an example to clarify the issues. Suppose that you bought a program with a bug that erases your disk. You didn't back up your floppy disk or your hard disk. You used the program and lost everything on a floppy disk that you were using. You paid a typist $1,000 to re-enter all the data on that disk. You still didn't back up your hard disk. You continued to use the program and it wiped out your hard disk. To recreate everything on this disk will cost $100,000. Where should we draw the line?

Let's start with the floppy disk. The $1,000 is an easily foreseeable cost arising from the bug and will be recoverable as a consequential loss unless we decide that reasonable precautions would have prevented it.

We have colleagues who would argue that you should have backed up your floppy disk, and therefore it's your own fault that you had to re-enter all the data. They would award you nothing. Our understanding of the law is that you *should* receive the $1,000. You don't have a duty to take steps to minimize the

---

[70] So, when you buy the product, put the publisher on notice of your intended use: "Dear publisher: I need a communications program to set up multi-million dollar deals. The program must be ultra-reliable or I'll lose a fortune. I hear that your Brand X Com program fits the bill. Here's my $100. If Brand X Com fits my needs, please send it right away so I can start making those deals."

Clark and Smith (1984, Section 6.03[1]) discuss the rules that apply when sellers know the special needs of their customers.

[71] See White & Summers (1995, Section 10–4)

[72] Mitigation of damages (minimizing the damages you suffer from a breach) is discussed by White and Summers (1995, Section 10–4(f)) and Dobbs (1993, Section 3.9).

losses from a breach of contract until you have some hint that there is a breach of contract.[73] Therefore you don't have a duty (to the publisher) to back up your data until you realize that the publisher's program might erase your data.[74]

What about the $100,000 for the contents of the hard disk?   You were put on notice that the program might erase the hard drive when it trashed the floppy. At this point, a reasonable person would back up every disk in sight before continuing to use the program.[75] Therefore, you would probably not receive these damages.[76]

What if you called Customer Service?   One last twist. Suppose that you called the publisher after the program erased your floppy, and the technician explained that this could not have been the result of a bug in their program. You believed her, and therefore, you didn't take any additional precautions and so you lost your hard drive. In this case, the publisher has just bought itself a $100,000 lawsuit.[77]

---

[73] Hancock (1993b, p. 4.018) states the rule as we understand it, "*When a party has breached* a contract, the nonbreaching party must take reasonable steps to minimize the amount of damages it will suffer as a result of the breach. If the nonbreaching party does not do this, it may be barred from recovering those damages which it could have prevented."

The italics are ours—they highlight the point that the nonbreaching party has to take preventative steps once it is aware of a breach, not before.]

[74] We haven't done an *exhaustive* search of the court cases but we have taken a reasonable look. So far, we have not found a court or a textbook that says that the buyer must take preventative steps before finding indications of a breach, just in case the seller breaches the contract. White and Summers (1995, Section 10–4(f)) cite an interesting case, *Bevard v. Howat Concrete Co.* (1970) as an example. The buyer bought concrete and his preliminary tests indicated that it *might* be too weak. However, it was impossible to be sure whether the concrete was too weak for 28 days after pouring. The buyer used the concrete, the concrete was too weak, and the buyer sued. The seller said that the buyer should have avoided the loss by not building until he knew for sure whether the concrete was defective. The court ruled otherwise, saying that the buyer wasn't required to take that action (delay construction) to prevent a *potential* loss which might be caused by a potential defect.

[75] Of course, we're assuming that you realized, or at least suspected, that it was a bug in *this* program that caused the failure of the floppy. We can imagine circumstances under which a reasonable person would have thought that the floppy had simply worn out, and therefore wouldn't have any reason to up the hard disk.

[76] Consider the case of *Erdman v. Johnson Bros. Radio & TV Co.*, (1970). Erdman bought a color television and left it plugged in. The set turned itself on and burned the house down. Erdman sued for $62,000, but lost because the set, which had an "instant-on" feature, had turned itself on before and had given off sparks and smoke before. A reasonable customer would have unplugged the television rather than leaving it unattended.

[77] Clark and Smith (1994 supplement, Section 7.07[2]) makes much the same point, saying "a seller may not insist on mitigation when, by its words or deeds, it has led the buyer to believe that it will repair defective goods." They cite *Cates v. Morgan Portable Building Corp.* (1985).

ANALYSIS: LIMITATION OF REMEDIES

The main argument that you're going to run into is the claim that you are not entitled to consequential or incidental damages because the License Agreement/Warranty Disclaimer that came with your product said that you can't have these damages.

The UCC certainly does allow the publisher to reach an agreement with you that limits the remedies available to you.[78] Some states make it much harder to limit these remedies. Not surprisingly, most (maybe all) warranties and warranty disclaimers for consumer software products specify a small group of remedies that are available to you (for example, you might be restricted to repair, replacement or refund), and exclude incidental and consequential damages.

But, it's not quite that simple. You have four critical points to make:

1. **A post-sale remedy limitation may not be binding.**   Many of the cases that we discussed in the section on warranty disclaimers also considered remedy limitations. When they threw out the disclaimer, they also threw out the remedy limitation. The same reasoning applies—telling you after the sale is too late, because changing the remedies is a material change to the contract.[79]

---

[78] Section 2–719 states:

"(1) Subject to the provisions of subsections (2) and (3) of this section . . . (a) the agreement may provide for remedies in addition to or in substitution for those provided in this Article and may limit or alter the measure of damages recoverable under this Article, as by limiting the buyer's remedies to return of the goods and repayment of the price or to repair and replacement of non-conforming goods or parts; and (b) resort to a remedy as provided is optional unless the remedy is expressly agreed to be exclusive, in which case it is the sole remedy.

"(2) Where circumstances cause an exclusive or limited remedy to fail of its essential purpose, remedy may be had as provided in this Act.

"(3) Consequential damages may be limited or excluded unless the limitation or exclusion is unconscionable. Limitation of consequential damages for injury to the person in the case of consumer goods is prima facie unconscionable but limitation of damages where the loss is commercial is not."

[79] *Altronics of Bethlehem, Inc. v. Repco, Inc.* (1992), *Diamond Fruit Growers, Inc. v. Krack Corp.* (1986) and *Step-Saver Data Systems, Inc. v. Wyse Technology and The Software Link, Inc.*, (1991) are illustrative cases. We also note the case of *Waukesha Foundry, Inc. v. Industrial Engineering, Inc.* (1996), a 7th Circuit case decided after *ProCD* and before *Gateway 2000*. The court said that Wisconsin (whose law it interpreted and allegedly applied in *ProCD*) appeared to have a *per se* rule that complete disclaimers of liability are always material. The court then cited a prior decision of its own for the proposition that deletion of consequential damages was material. "[B]ecause the parties contracted with the expectation that the UCC would govern their relationship, a party's consent to the deletion of UCC-provided remedies could not be presumed." (p. 1008). See also Clark & Smith (1984, Section 8.04[1][d]).

We don't think that this issue is as clear-cut as the disclaimer of implied warranties. In some states (but not others), a seller can limit remedies in an inconspicuous part of the contract, whereas the seller must make any warranty disclaimer conspicuous. (See Sheldon and Carter, 1997, Section 9.7.2 and Kutten, 1987, section 10.02[5][a], "[U]nlike a disclaimer of implied warranties, UCC Section 2–719 does not have an explicit requirement that the limitations be conspicuous. Some jurisdictions require it and others do not" [citations omitted].) Additionally, some courts define materiality in a way that says that anything that changes the allocation of risk between the parties is material.

2. **It's not fair.** A second type of argument that you can make is that the remedy the publisher is proposing to you (such as a refund) is unreasonable.[80] For example, if you enter all of your professional data into a contact management program, and the program crashes and corrupts the data file, a refund for $100 doesn't begin to solve your problems. Many customer service groups will try to recover your data, and some will re-enter it by hand if they can't recover it electronically.[81]

Official Comment 1 to Section 2–719 of the Uniform Commercial Code says that[82]

[I]t is the very essence of a sales contract that at least minimum adequate remedies be available. If the parties intend to conclude a contract for sale within this Article they must accept the legal consequences that there be at least a fair quantum of remedy for breach of the obligations or duties outlined in the contract.

3. **It is outrageous when the seller knew about the defect, was grossly negligent, or intentionally breached the contract.** For example, Kutten (1987, Section 10.02[8]) says,

---

Courts treat consumers and sophisticated businesses quite differently (see *Schurtz v. BMW of North America, Inc.*, 1991) and are more likely to award consequentials to consumers. One interesting question is how the court will treat a small, unsophisticated business. If you are a one-dentist office without lots of computer or legal sophistication, you might well qualify for consumer-like treatment in your State. Talk with your lawyer.

[80] ***The argument that available remedies are fundamentally inadequate.*** See Clark and Smith (1984, Section 8.04[3][b]); Sheldon and Carter (1997, Chapter 9).

If there are no available remedies, or if the remedies available are trivial compared to the losses of the person who didn't breach the contract, then the person who breached the contract can be required to pay incidental or consequential damages. The statutory basis for this is the rejection of an "unconscionable" exclusion on consequential damages in UCC Section 2–719(3). Quote Official Comment 1 to Section 2–719 (which we quote in the main text, two paragraphs after this footnote.)

Also, use this—Section 1–106 of the UCC says that,

"The remedies provided by this Act shall be liberally administered to the end that the aggrieved party may be put in as good a position as if the other party had fully performed."

(Note that Section 1–106 also says that you can't collect consequential damages except under the rules of the UCC, so don't be surprised in court if that sentence is quoted back at you. But, we're telling you how to collect consequentials *under the rules*, so that's a non-issue. The point you make with Section 1–106 is that the Code's policy is to have the person who broke the contract fully compensate the person who didn't.)

As Sheldon and Carter (1997 Sections 9.3 and 9.6) point out, this type of argument is especially well made in the consumer case, where you didn't get to negotiate the terms of the warranty.

There are other ways to argue that a contract is unconscionable (see any of the books on warranties in our list at the start of the chapter) but they are more subtle that you might expect.

[81] This is based on our personal knowledge and experience in the industry, and on discussions with *many* other customer service technicians.

[82] Official Comments to the Uniform Commercial Code are not law, but they are highly respected by judges. They are included by the Code's drafters as an aid to interpreting the Code.

Contractual language to the contrary, no disclaimer is effective if the vendor or supplier acted in a manner that was grossly negligent.[83]

He also says (Section 10.02[5][b]),

Most courts will allow a licensor or vendor to use a limitation of remedies as a shield against the buyer's attacks. However, the same courts will not allow the licensor or vendor to use it as a shield if it refuses to abide by the contract.[84]

We've been told repeatedly that selling a product with known defects will nullify a remedy limitation,[85] but our search of the legal literature has been less productive than we expected.[86] One author claims that this is not the rule.[87] This is a powerful argument if you can make it. In your state, you might have to argue that the seller has violated the duty of good faith and

---

[83] Dobbs (1993, Section 12.19[1]) provides a few citations and criticisms regarding willful breach. See also *Colonial Life Insurance Co. of America v. Electronic Data Systems Corp.* (1993) which held that New Hampshire would nullify a remedy limitation in the event of a willful and wanton breach. *Long Island Lighting Co. v. Transamerica Delaval, Inc.* (1986) is also cited for the proposition that breach of contract in bad faith will nullify the remedy limitation.

Regarding gross negligence, the most often-cited computer case is *Orthopedic & Sports Injury Clinic v. Wang* (1991). The clinic bought a computer from Wang Labs and contracted with Wang to maintain it. "While attempting to fix the computer, Wang's employees requested and used the Clinic's last back-up disk and, in the course of their attempted repairs, lost five years of medical and accounting data stored on the disk." (*Orthopedic & Sports Injury Clinic v. Wang*, 1991, p. 221). Oops. The contract limited Wang's liability, but Louisiana's laws allow the victim full recovery (despite the consequential damages limitation in the contract) if the breach of contract involves gross negligence. The Clinic's expert witness said that using the last backup disk with a broken computer was grossly negligent, but he didn't explain specifically how he came to that conclusion. Result: in this case, the court tossed out the gross negligence claim. Five years later, the Fifth Circuit explained that its decision had been based on the weak affidavit of the expert (*First United Financial Corp. v. United States Fidelity & Guarantee Co.* 1996, footnote 8) and that "It is undisputed that general contractual provisions seeking to limit liability for gross fault are invalid and unenforceable." (*Occidental Chemical Corp. v. Elliott Turbomachinery Co.*, 1996, footnote 9.)

[84] For example, see *Hawaiian Telephone Co. v. Microform Data Systems, Inc.* (1987).

[85] Kaner has been proposing for three years to the UCC Article 2B drafting committee that they restrict the availability of consequential damages *except* when the damages are caused by a known but undocumented bug (or one that would have been so obvious during testing that failure to find it is gross negligence). For the exact wording, see Kaner and Paglia (1997). The proposal has been discussed twice in committee. In both cases, publishers' lobbyists said that this is already the law, and said the UCC shouldn't be modified to include such a provision because this would duplicate (or interfere with or something) existing law. We've also been told that this is the general rule by attorneys who we consider more neutral.

[86] While we have found some articles and some cases, and a few brief discussions in treatises, the numbers are small. The rule is well established in the sale of real property (land, buildings, etc.), but it seems not so clearly established in every state for goods. Our search was not exhaustive but it was not modest either.

[87] Professor Nimmer (1997, Section 6.19[1] footnote 300), the Reporter of the UCC Article 2B drafting committee (senior author of 2B), says that remedy limit nullification for wanton and reckless conduct "does not affect contracts involving UCC transactions. See *Metropolitan Life Ins. Co. v. Noble Lowndes Int'l, Inc.* [1993] . . . (concept does not apply to intentional breach of contract, but is limited to tort actions and describes an aggravated form of negligence)."

fair dealing[88] or that the remedy limitation is unconscionable.[89] Courts are wary of both arguments.[90] If you're going to make either one on your own (perhaps in Small Claims Court), we recommend that you seek legal advice.

4. **You're going to scream about this on the Internet.**   You have access to a communications medium that lets you speak directly to thousands of the publisher's customers and prospective customers. If bugs in the product have really caused you big losses, and the publisher's being unreasonable about it, those people will want to know about it.

As we noted at the start of this chapter, you must take care in how you protest on the Net, lest you commit libel or extortion.

There are two other common ways that lawyers use to attack these clauses. If you're interested, read the footnotes.[91, 92, 93]

---

[88] UCC Section 1–203 "Every contract or duty within this code imposes an obligation of good faith in its performance or enforcement." Section 2–103(b) "Good faith" in the case of a merchant means honesty in fact and the observance of reasonable commercial standards of fair dealing in the trade."

[89] UCC Section 2–719 "Consequential damages may be limited or excluded unless the limitation or exclusion is unconscionable."

[90] Kutten (1987, Section 10.02[6] discusses this well. Sheldon and Carter (1997 Sections 9.6, 9.10, and 11.2) provide the consumer-side counter-arguments.

[91] ***The argument that the remedy is not exclusive***.   See Clark and Smith (1984, Section 8.04[1][a]). The UCC requires that the remedy must be "expressly agreed to be exclusive." If the warranty isn't absolutely crystal clear that the remedies that it provides are exclusive, they aren't. So, if the warranty says that you're entitled to new disks or a refund, but doesn't say that these are your only possible remedies, then you are entitled to a new disk or a refund, but you are also entitled to incidental and consequential damages and any other remedies the Code allows.

[92] ***The argument that the exclusive remedies fail of their essential purpose***.   See Clark and Smith (1984, Section 8.04[1][a]); Sheldon and Carter (1997 Section 9.5); Katz (1994). Clark and Smith (1984, Section 8.04[2][a]) say of this argument that "It is hard to find any provision in Article 2 that has been more successfully used by aggrieved buyers in the last 15 years."

The typical case involves a repair or replace warranty. These fail if the seller doesn't make a reasonable effort to make repairs, or if the attempts fail to provide the buyer with an acceptable level of use of the product. (Nimmer 1992, Section 6.18[1]). In computer cases a repair or replacement warranty will fail if the publisher can't fix the bugs within a reasonable time (*Chatlos Systems v. National Cash Register Corp.,* 1980) or if the design is fundamentally incompatible with the warranted performance (making repairs impossible) (*Consolidated Data Terminals v. Applied Digital Systems*, 1983) or if the seller never delivers the product (*Hawaiian Telephone Co. v. Microform Data Systems, Inc.*, 1987).

If the limited remedies fail, are you entitled to consequential damages even if there is a separate clause that explicitly excludes consequential damages? Maybe. The courts are split. For discussion of the split, see Kutten, Section Clark and Smith (1984, Section 8.04[2][b]) and make sure to read both the main volume and the supplement. White and Summers (1995, Section 12–10) and Nimmer (1997 Section 6.19) argue that the clause excluding consequential damages should stand on its own and survive.

Sheldon and Carter (1997 Section 9.5.3) argue that consequential damages should now be available, especially in consumer contracts. This argument is well explained in *Schurtz v. BMW of North America, Inc.* (1991).

[93] Sheldon and Carter (1997) list 10 approaches for defeating a limitation of damages clause. We've covered most of these in this section, but they provide more depth and many more case citations.

If Article 2B passes the state legislatures, or if the *Gateway 2000* and *ProCD* cases spread to other courts, then customers won't often be able to sue for breach of contract (bye, bye implied warranties) and even if you can sue, you typically won't be able to collect any remedies beyond a refund, and you'll probably have to travel to a court far, far away (this is called a forum selection clause), which will probably cost you more than you can get back from the refund.

Under those rules, you will almost have to make your claim under a different legal theory. The remedy limits apply only to contract disputes (including warranty claims). Therefore, the typical lawsuit involving defective software should not just claim a breach of warranty. If you can prove it, you should also sue for fraud, misrepresentation, deceptive or unfair trade practices, malpractice, and anything else you can allege without failing the blush test.[94] Often, the defendant can be held liable under several different theories.

The rest of this chapter explores the other main theories.

Misrepresentation

When the publisher tells you something about the product that is not true, you can probably make a strong argument that the publisher has made a warranty and breached it. Unfortunately, you might not recover anything in the breach of warranty claim, and you probably won't recover all of your damages.

The story is different if you can prove *misrepresentation*. Many factors that shield the publisher in a warranty suit become irrelevant. You have a much better chance of collecting a refund, plus full consequential and incidental damages, plus (under the right circumstances) punitive damages.

A statement can be both, a misrepresentation and a warranty. Suppose that this morning, a salesperson showed you a word processor and told you (knowing that he wasn't telling the truth) that this program will print text in different colors on your color inkjet printer. He committed a misrepresentation this morning. But, if you don't buy the program until next week, his statement won't become a breach of an express warranty until next week. The misrepresentation is a false statement that helps to convince you to take (or refrain from) some action. A warranty is a promise that, when you enter into the contract for goods, those goods will conform to the statement that the seller has just made.

---

[94] A legal argument passes the *blush test* if a lawyer of average intelligence and integrity can make the argument in front of a judge without blushing.

If you've been lied to—and we believe that there is an *outrageous* amount of fraud in this industry—you should not be shy about holding the publisher fully accountable.

OVERVIEW: MISREPRESENTATION

Software publishers have many opportunities to tell you false things. For example, they speak to you in advertisements, brochures, specification sheets, sales proposals, fax-back answer sheets, face-to-face demonstrations, telephone calls, on the product's box or packaging, in the manual or the on-line help system, in the README file or other information files on disk, and on the warranty or registration card.

Not every false statement is a misrepresentation. For example, suppose that a salesperson tells you a joke that includes false (he thinks funny) claims about the capabilities of a program. You misunderstand him and buy the program, believing he was recommending it. Is he liable to you for misrepresentation? No. He was joking, not lying.[95]

Also, there are different degrees of misrepresentation. The publisher might have made an honest mistake, it might have been careless, or it might have lied deliberately. Misrepresentations that are deliberate are called *fraud*.

Fraudulent conduct is so widespread in the software industry that many publishers, retailers, and customers just don't take it seriously any more. But it is very serious. Lying to customers is outrageous misconduct. And, the government (State or federal) can bring criminal charges against a publisher that makes a practice of defrauding its customers. If you are a lied-to customer, you do not (not, *not*, *not*) have to put up with it.[96]

If you believe that you have been defrauded, talk with a lawyer. If you have in fact been defrauded, a good lawyer can help you recover more of your consequential losses than you would probably recover in Small Claims Court on your own (plus, perhaps, punitive damages). And your State's statutes on Unfair and

---

[95] However, if a reasonable person in your situation would have thought he was not joking, and if you actually believed him and based your purchase decision at least partially on his statement, then he has just given you an express warranty that the program behaves according to his claims.

[96] A word of caution. The law of defamation (libel, slander) makes it risky to say publicly that someone is engaging in criminal activity (like fraud). You might decide to publicize a publisher's misbehavior, perhaps by writing letter to magazines and posting notices to the Internet. Sometimes, this will be an excellent thing to do (good tactic, and a valuable service to the community), but do it with care. In particular, stick closely to the facts. Under American law (but not under all other countries' laws) true statements are not libelous, no matter how much you embarrass the publisher with them. See Keeton *et al.* (1984). But, be prepared to prove that your statements are true. For example, if the publisher makes false statements in writing, you can reprint them, say that they're false, and give the evidence that proves that the statements are false. But don't use the F-word ("fraud") in public unless you can also prove the publisher's knowledge of falsity and intent to mislead.

Deceptive Practices may well allow you to collect your attorney's fees from the publisher.[97]

ANALYSIS: MISREPRESENTATION[98]

We start this analysis by looking at the difference between the law of contracts and the law of misrepresentation. Any time you complain (or sue) over misrepresentation, you will probably also be complaining about breach of contract. So it is well worth seeing how these areas of law fit together. At one level, things look the same—the publisher provides incorrect information about the product. You buy it, and you're disappointed. Beyond that level, the worlds are very different:

The law of contracts (which includes the law of warranties) is about promises that were made but not kept.   These are business disputes. The judge doesn't automatically look for good guys and bad guys in contract suits. There are usually two sides to the arguments. Circumstances might have changed, or the risks or costs might have been too much more than one side expected, or the people who made the contract might have discovered that they just don't work well together.

Your conduct is important in a contract dispute. Even if the other person breached the contract, you might have contributed to the breakdown. The judge[99] will ask questions like, "Did you report the problem promptly?" "Did you give the publisher a chance to fix the problem?" and "What damages does the contract call for if one of you breaches it?"

In deciding how much money to award if you win a breach-of-contract lawsuit, the judge's goal will be to carry out the agreement underlying the contract. For example, if the contract remedy for a breach is a refund, with no consequential damages, the judge will give you a refund, and no consequential damages.

The law of misrepresentation is about statements that were false when they were made.[100] Lies, damned lies, reckless lies, negligent lies, little white lies, and (in some States) simple mistakes. The maker of these misrepresentations is at fault, and you are an innocent victim.

---

[97] See our next section, on *Unfair and Deceptive Trade Practices*. And Chapter 9, "Lawyers." And, of course, ask your lawyer if this applies to your State.

[98] We recommend the following discussions of the law of misrepresentation: Keeton *et al.* (1984, Ch. 18) is a thorough, classic discussion. *Restatement (Second) of Torts* (1965, Chapter 22) is an authoritative summary of the law. Sheldon and Carter (1997, Section 11.3) provides a strong, customer-focused presentation of the issues. All of the computer law treatises have sections on misrepresentation.

[99] In Small Claims Courts, the judge asks many questions. In more formal courts, your lawyer or the other lawyer would ask these questions.

[100] See *Centon Electronics, Inc. v. Bonar* (1993). A broken promise (such as a breach of contract is not fraudulent) unless the promissor didn't intend to keep the promise when he made it.

Your conduct is much less of an issue in a misrepresentation suit because the statements were false when they were made. The focus is on the statements themselves, on what the publisher knew when it made the statements, and why it made them.

In deciding how much money to award you, the judge's main goal will be to see that you are fully paid back for your losses. Contract clauses that limit damages that might be available to you don't come into play, because misrepresentations fall outside of the scope of the contract.[101] You can recover incidental damages and consequential damages, and you may also be able to recover punitive damages[102] and attorneys fees.

Analysis: What Do You Have to Prove

To prove misrepresentation, you must prove[103] that the publisher made a statement of fact,[104] that the statement was false,[105] that the statement was material,[106] that you relied[107] justifiably [108] on the false statement, that the publisher intended that you would rely on the statement[109] and that you suffered some loss as a result.[110] You will also have to support the claims that you make about the publisher's intent in making the misrepresentation.[111] In many states, you must prove misrepresentation by clear and convincing evidence-weak cases will lose.[112]

---

[101] This division between the law of contracts and the law of torts is fundamental in American civil law. On the contract side, Calamari and Perrillo (1987, Sections 9–13 to 9–24) is a good discussion. On the torts side, Keeton *et al.* (1984, Chapter 18) is the classic discussion. The Uniform Commercial Code Section 2–721 says, Remedies for material misrepresentation or fraud include all remedies available under this Article for non-fraudulent breach. Neither rescission or a claim for rescission of the contract for sale nor rejection or return of the goods shall bar or be deemed inconsistent with a claim for damages or other remedy.

This allows the refund, plus incidental damages, plus foreseeable consequential damages, as a matter of contract law. State laws provide additional remedies beyond this.

[102] Punitive damages are awarded to punish the defendant, rather than to compensate the victim. They are available, in most States, when the victim can show that the defendant's conduct was oppressive and outrageous, or *fraudulent*. Dobbs (1993) provides an excellent discussion of punitive damages.

[103] This list is derived from Keeton *et al.* (1984, Chapter 18). They analyze each element in detail.

[104] **Statement of fact.**   There is no liability for puffing. See the discussion of *puffing* in this chapter's section on *Express Warranties*. But, see the criticism of this rule, with case citations, in Keeton *et al.* (1984, Section 109).

The statement doesn't have to be about a feature. It might be a claim that the software has been fully tested. For example, see *Accusystems, Inc. v. Honeywell Information Systems* (1984). Or, it might be that the program is fully compatible with another program or piece of hardware or that it has been endorsed by someone, or that work is currently underway on an upgrade.

[105] **Falsity.**   There's a subtlety here. The statement itself need not be false. An ambiguous statement or a half-truth is fraudulent if the speaker is intentionally creating a false impression in your mind. See the *Restatement (Second) of Torts* (1965, Sections 525-530); Keeton *et al.* (1984, Section 106); Sheldon and Carter (1997 Section 11.3.4). For example, in the case of *Glovatorium v. NCR Corporation* (1982), NCR aggressively marketed a system with major problems, without revealing the problems to Glovatorium. Had Glovatorium known of the problems, it probably wouldn't have bought the system. The Court held that the nondisclosure was fraudulent.

[106] **Materiality.**   The misrepresented fact must be significant enough that a reasonable person might, at least partially, base a decision on it. See Keeton *et al.* (1984, Section 108).

[107] **Reliance.**   You must have actually relied on the statement. That is, on the basis of that statement, you must have taken an action, or refrained from taking an action.

Before we get into the details of reliance, there is one evidentiary issue that confuses people. You don't have to have anything in writing (though that might be convenient) or any other witnesses' statements to prove reliance. This is about your state of mind. You know what you were thinking when you bought the product. You can testify about that. Your testimony is evidence of your reliance.

Reliance will often be your major issue. This is a more severe test than whether the statement is part of the basis of the bargain, under warranty law. See our discussion in the section of this chapter on *Warranties*.

Suppose you don't know that the publisher claims the program can do X until after you buy it. Then you read about X in the manual, try it, and discover that the manual's statement is false. In this case, you did not rely on this misstatement when you bought the product.

On the other hand, if a salesperson promised you that the program could do X, but later denies having made the promise (which you heard and relied on), a description of X in the manual can be presented as evidence that the salesperson probably did make the claim.

Mirken v. Wasserman (1993) provides an extended discussion of the requirement of actual reliance on the false statement. The case also highlights the fact that you don't have to hear the misrepresentation directly from the publisher. If a publisher's misrepresentation comes to your attention indirectly, through a third person, the publisher is still accountable for it. (see p. 575).

In *Westlye v. Look Sports, Inc.* (1993) the plaintiff lost the suit even though the defendant's (alleged) misrepresentations were contained in advertisements in magazines. The plaintiff hadn't read the advertisements before renting the ski equipment. The court concluded that he hadn't relied on the misstatements, even though they were quite public.

[108] **Justified reliance.**   Your reliance must have been reasonable. For example, if you knew when you read it that the statement was false, then you would not have been justified in relying on it. *Foundation Software Laboratories, Inc. v. Digital Equipment Corporation* (1992) is an example of a case lost for lack of justified reliance. The buyer assigned its chief computer technician to do a feasibility study before buying the computer, and the court decided that the buyer relied on the technician's recommendations rather than on misrepresentations made by the seller's salespeople.

In practice, unless you have reason to doubt the specific statement, if the publisher tells you a fact about the program, you can rely on it. We are very experienced with computers and software but we still rely on the representations made by software publishers. We know (because we've published some of them) that less expensive products can have a broad feature set compared to more expensive competitors and that less expensive products are sometimes more reliable than more expensive competitors. The publisher understands its own specifications, and has done its own testing of its features and of its compatibility with other products. We can't begin to evaluate another publisher's product to the extent that that publisher knows it. In our experience, most statements by most mass market software publishers are true. We avoid dealing with people who we think are liars, and we rely (sometimes to our dismay) on the factual statements of the remaining publishers. Even when we do our own brief evaluation of a product, our tests are conducted against a background of factual claims by the publisher that we expect to be true.

There are circumstances under which you can rely on predictions and opinions. See Keeton *et al.* (1984, Section 107–109).

[109] **Intended reliance.**   The publisher must have made the statement *with the intent* that you would rely on it. Jokes, for example, don't qualify.

[110] **Damage.**   You must have suffered some loss or injury as a result of your reliance on the statement. Example: the money you spent on the fraudulently misrepresented program is a loss.

[111] See the next sub-section, *Analysis: Fraudulent and non-fraudulent misrepresentations*

[112] See, for example, *Riley Hill General Contractor, Inc. v. Tandy Corp.* (1987).

Fraud is easy to allege and hard to prove. Even the allegation damages a defendant's reputation. Therefore, the American legal system poses some hurdles for fraud suits. In a lawsuit for fraud, your complaint (the document you file with the court) must be specific about the alleged fraud. That means that you probably have to say who said the false statement, where she said it, what the false statement was, and how you know that it is false. You are allowed to say that you expect to find some of this information in the publisher's records, but you must explain specifically why you believe that.[113]

In a fraud suit, the seller will probably deny that it lied deliberately. These are normally hard-fought lawsuits. The publisher will probably claim that any false statements that it made were accidental misstatements or misunderstandings, or that it believed that the statements were true when it made them.

In a standard lawsuit (as opposed to one in Small Claims Court), your attorney will get copies of the publisher's internal records and will probably hire a software expert to analyze the boxes and boxes of paper. Kaner has served as an expert in three lawsuits and has discussed fraud litigation with other people who have served as experts. This type of analysis is time consuming and expensive. The questions that are constantly asked are, "What did they know? When did they know it? What did they say? When did they say it?"

Most of the fraud cases haven't turned into published lawsuits because they settle before trial. If the experts put together a strong pattern of false conduct, the defending publisher has a strong incentive to put the matter to rest. Otherwise, the publisher will face bad press, a bad record with the courts (no one wants a series of findings of liability for fraud on their record), and the possibility of punitive damages awarded by a jury. On the other hand, if the experts can't show knowledgeable false statements, the fraud suit evaporates. Disputes arise over what statements are actually true, what they mean, what the company actually knew—everything is very, very fact-intensive.

If you are suing in Small Claims Court, your ability to gain access to the publisher's records is probably quite limited. If the misrepresentation is obvious, you might argue in court that it's unbelievable that the publisher didn't know it was lying. And even if it didn't know, it could only not know because it was reckless (*e.g.,* it didn't do any checking of the box for accuracy before shipping it.)

Here's an easy trick for proving that a publisher has made a practice of intentionally misrepresenting its product to its customers. When you discover that the publisher's statement is false, send a letter of complaint—to the president of the company—that clearly describes the error. Give the publisher a few weeks to think about the letter. During this period, talk to the publisher's customer service staff. If you're satisfied with the way that the publisher takes

---

[113] Kutten (1987, Section 10.04[3][a]).

care of you, then don't take any further action. But if the publisher isn't treating you honorably, then go to your friendly software store and ask to be called when they receive their next shipment of this program from the publisher. If the problem hasn't been corrected, have a friend buy the still-defective program to use as evidence.

Similarly, for false advertisements, notify the publisher, then save copies of subsequent ads.

You can also send out requests for information to newsgroups or to individuals who you (somehow) know are users of the product.

In Chapters 3 and 5, we talked about techniques for gathering evidence of the publisher's bad faith, such as checking the Internet for reports to the publisher of defects and for false statements made by the publisher's technical staff. We suggest that you reread those chapters and think through your information-gathering strategy. To prevail in a small fraud suit, you will probably have to rely on this kind of external evidence of false statement rather than on in-house records. (If you get enough external evidence, we suggest that you approach a lawyer with it. Given a strong starting point, you should be able to find a good lawyer who will take this case on contingency.)

The list of requirements to prove fraud is long and filled with technicalities. A fraud suit *can* fail on any one of them, but in practical terms you have a strong argument if the seller made a false statement, you can prove that the statement was false at the time it was made, and you relied on it. In your negotiations with the publisher you should stress the fact that you relied on the publisher's *false statements*. Your letters should be cordial, calm, but firm that your losses were the result of the publisher's *false statements* and therefore you expect reimbursement for the losses you sustained as a result of the publisher's *false statements*. Even if you don't win the fraud suit, you will probably have a case for unfair or deceptive acts or practices. (See our upcoming section, on Unfair and Deceptive Practices.)[114]

Analysis: Fraudulent and Non-fraudulent Misrepresentations

Why did the publisher make the misrepresentations? Was this fraud, sloppiness, or an honest mistake? The answer to this should play a big role in determining how you'll deal with the publisher now and in the future. The answer is also important to the lawsuit, if you file one.

To illustrate the possibilities, suppose that you own a Model 2001 Brand X printer. You read the program's box, which says "Compatible with all Brand X

---

[114] For more information about the structure of the fraud suit—what the court documents look like, how to organize the case, etc., read Raysman and Brown's (1984) Chapter 13, "Litigating Computer Actions."

printers." You bought the program and discovered that the program crashes whenever it tries to print to your printer.[115] Why did the publisher incorrectly claim compatibility with all Brand X's (including the Model 2001) on the box?

Fraud.   The publisher knew that its statement was false but wrote it anyway. It takes a lot of space on a box cover to accurately list the printer models that a program is compatible with,so the publisher decided to save space by ignoring the Model 2001.[116] Such a publisher is liable for fraud in every state and is liable for punitive damages in most states.

Reckless misrepresentation.   The publisher didn't *know* that the statement was false but did know that there was a substantial probability that the statement was false or that it had no idea whether it was speaking truthfully or not. *The publisher had never tested any Brand X printers. Maybe they were compatible with the program, maybe not.* Reckless misrepresentation is treated as equivalent to deliberate fraud in most States.[117]

Negligent misrepresentation.   The publisher didn't know that the statement was false and might very well have believed that the statement was true, but a reasonably cautious person would have discovered the error or wouldn't have spoken without investigating further. *The publisher tested a few Brand X printers but didn't test the Model 2001 and could have easily obtained a Model 2001 for testing.*

---

[115] Note the effect of this simple misrepresentation. Model 2001 owners will buy the program, even though they shouldn't. So this adds sales. Of the purchasers, several will decide that the publisher *must* be telling the truth about compatibility so the problem must be with them or with their printer. Therefore, they won't call the publisher to complain or to ask for a refund. Another group of purchasers (a large one if the program is $100 or less) won't take the time to complain; they just won't use the program. Net result: at least over the short term, the publisher makes a profit from this lie.

[116] Yes, this decision *is* sometimes made in *exactly* this way.

[117] *Computer Systems Engineering, Inc. v. Quantel Corp.* (1984) is an example of a case that makes this point. It held (p. 67-68) that "a misrepresentation made with reckless disregard for its truth or falsity is" fraudulent. In contrast, in North Carolina, to prove fraud you must establish that the defendant knew it was speaking falsely. Recklessness is classed with negligent misrepresentation instead. See *Myers & Chapman, Inc. v. Thomas G. Evans, Inc.* (1988) and the discussion of this and related cases in Byrd (1992).

[118] In a lawsuit for *negligence*, you have to prove that the defendant owed you a legal *duty*, that he *breached* that duty, and that you were harmed *as a result of the breach*.

As an example, think of lawsuits for negligence in auto accidents. Drivers have a *duty* to drive safely. A driver *breaches the duty* if he doesn't drive with the level of care that a normal, reasonably cautious driver would use. Running a stop sign is an example of a breach. If you get into an accident with someone and the accident *was caused by* their running the stop sign, then you have a good negligence lawsuit.

In a negligent misrepresentation case against a software publisher, you must show:

Duty.   You must show that the publisher had a legal duty to you to take reasonable steps to make sure that what it was telling you was true.

Breach.   The publisher make an incorrect statement that it would not have made if it had made a reasonable effort to get its facts straight. (You might *believe* that the publisher lied deliberately, but you might only be able to *prove* that no reasonable person would have gotten these wrong.)

Some states allow recovery for negligent misrepresentations made during a sale of goods. We've found it difficult to determine which states would allow these suits for software purchases. We discuss some complexities in the footnote.[118] In practical terms, if you ever pursue a negligent misrepresentation case in Small Claims Court, we recommend that you stress that:

Causation and Damages. You heard or read the publisher's statement, and because of it, you took some action, you did something or stopped yourself from doing something. As a result, you lost money, gave up a right, wasted time, or suffered some other type of loss.

The most intense discussion of negligent misrepresentation cases has been about "duty." Most people don't owe you this duty.

Publisher (book, newspaper) liability. Newspapers and book publishers aren't under a *legal* duty to you to get their facts straight. *See Barden v. HarperCollins Publishers, Inc.* (1994); *Birmingham v. Fodor's Travel Publications, Inc.* (1992); *Daniel v. Dow Jones & Co.* (1987); *Smith v. Linn* (1989); *Winter v. G.P. Putnam's Sons* (1991); *Yanase v. Automobile Club of Southern California* (1989); and *Hoffman* (1991). The general rule that shields newspapers, called the *Jaillet rule*, says that a newspaper is not liable to its readers for negligent misrepresentation "*in the absence of a contract, fiduciary relationship, or intent to cause injury.*" (*First Equity Corp. of Florida v. Standard & Poor's Corp.*, 1987, p. 117, italics are ours.) If you can show a contractually-based duty or a relationship of special trust, you can make a case against any publisher.

The author of a book may (perhaps) be held liable for negligent misrepresentation even if the courts won't hold the publisher liable. See *Alm v. Van Nostrand Reinhold* (1985). And under personal injury law, a publisher can be held liable if it knows that you will follow its instructions exactly under life-critical circumstances and you are injured (*Saloomey v. Jeppesen & Co.*, 1983).

For additional discussion of publisher liability, see Kaner (1996c)

Professional 3rd Party Liability. *Accountants have a duty* to conduct audits in a professional manner. Suppose that an accountant negligently audits a company and gives it an inappropriately clean bill of health. If you invest in the company and lose money because its finances aren't in order, can you sue the accountant? The most commonly followed rule is that accountants are liable to the people who hired them, and if the accountant knew that its work was being done for the benefit of some specific third party, it can be liable to that third party. But members of the general public can't sue, because the accountants didn't owe a legal duty to them. *Bily v. Arthur Young & Co.* (1992); *Raritan River Steel Co. v. Cherry, Bekaert & Holland* (1988).

Fiduciary liability. If you have a special relationship of trust with someone, such as an attorney or a real estate broker who you are relying on to reveal information to you about property you're about to buy, then you probably can hold them liable for negligent misrepresentation. *See*, for example, *Meighan v. Shore* (1995) (attorney); *Salahutdin v. Valley of California, Inc.* (1994) (real estate broker); *Forbes v. Par Ten Group, Inc.* (1990) (real estate); and *Flamme v. Wolf Insurance Agency* (1991) (insurance agent).

So what does all this mean, if the relationship between you and the misrepresentor is one of buyer and seller of goods? It depends. In *Ritchie Enterprises v. Honeywell Bull, Inc.* (1990), the answer was that the seller is not liable to the buyer for economic damages arising out of the sale of goods. Similar answers come in many other cases between businesses, such as *21st Century Properties Co. v. Carpenter Insulation and Carpeting Co.* (1988), *Black, Johnson & Simmons Insurance Brokerage, Inc. v. IBM* (1982); and *Rio Grande Jewelers Supply, Inc. v. Data General Corp.* (1984).

In a scholarly opinion, the Court in *Ott v. Alfa-Laval Agri, Inc.* (1995) pointed out that knowledgeable business people take on these types of risks as part of doing business. (See its page 1453 discussion of *Sacramento Regional Transit District v. Grumman Flexible*, 1984.) It is important to your case that you are not (or so we assume) a big business that regularly buys computer software. If you are a consumer, or a small business that doesn't have a lot of software knowledge, make this point repeatedly. The *Ott* Court cited several cases to support the argument that California follows a six-factor test in deciding whether the seller owes a duty (to not commit negligent misrepresentation) to the buyer. Existence of a special relationship depends on:

- The extent to which the transaction was intended to affect the plaintiff

- The forseeability of harm to the plaintiff

- You are a consumer or a non-computer small business rather than an expert in the computer field.[119]

- The facts (mis)stated by the publisher were things that you couldn't be expected to know about independently from what the publisher said.

- The inaccuracy of the misrepresentation would have been discovered by the publisher if it had followed even minimally reasonable testing procedures or if it had listened at all to previous customer complaints.

- The facts (mis)stated by the publisher were important in your decision to buy or keep the product.

Exhibit 7.5: Seller Liable for Negligent or Innocent Misrepresentation

In the case of *Burroughs Corporation v. Hall Affiliates* (1982), the Supreme Court of Alabama held Burroughs liable for innocent (or negligent) misrepresentations in the sale of a computer system.

Hall imports artificial flowers, and bought a Burroughs B80-40 computer in 1977 to handle its accounting and inventory functions. The system didn't work and Hall sued claiming that Burroughs' salespeople's' representations about the system were fraudulent. The Court listed 4 claimed misrepresentations:

1. The machine would do inventory and accounting simultaneously.

2. The machine was capable of multiprogramming.

- The degree of certainty that the plaintiff suffered injury

- The closeness of the connection between the defendant's conduct and the injury suffered

- The moral blame attached to the defendant's conduct

- The policy of preventing future harm

These factors are not recognized in every state. North Carolina, for example, specifically rejected them (*Raritan River Steel Co. v. Cherry, Bekaert & Holland*, 1988). However, these will help you structure your argument if you have to argue that the seller had a duty to you.

[119] Courts sometimes say that professional consulting firms, such as lawyers and accountants are sophisticated businesspeople, and then deny them the consumer-like protections that they would give to someone who ran a convenience store. But our experience is that lawyers and accountants are just as clueless about computers as convenience store owners. If you run a small professional office, don't let the judge or the opposing attorney get away with saying that this makes your business "sophisticated" without an argument. (No offense intended to convenience store owners. We know that some of you are computer hotshots, but then again, so are some accountants.)

3. The machine was capable of operating a terminal display unit in a data communications environment.

4. The machine and all of its component parts were new.

The jury found that Burroughs had committed fraud and awarded $500,000. Burroughs challenged the finding to the Supreme Court of Alabama. The Court upheld the verdict, explaining that in Alabama, all that was required for a finding of fraud was:

(**a**) A false representation by the seller.

(**b**) The false representation must concern a material existing fact.

(**c**) The plaintiff must rely upon the false representation.

(**d**) The plaintiff must be damaged as a proximate result.

Intent is not part of the basic definition of fraud in Alabama. What we call innocent or negligent misrepresentation in California is fraud in Alabama.

In Alabama, the proof of intent is still relevant, in order to make a case for punitive damages. The Court reduced the award against Burroughs from $500,000 to $91,870 for compensatory damages. (Compensatory damages normally include incidental and consequential damages.)

Innocent misrepresentation.   The publisher was mistaken, but it was an honest error of a kind that a reasonably cautious person might have made. For example, suppose the printer manufacturer made two different versions of the Model 2001. You have one version, the publisher has the other one, and the one the publisher tested works.[120] Yours doesn't work with the program, so the statement that the program will work with your printer is incorrect.

Several states impose some liability for innocent misrepresentation. Again, there are complexities in determining whether a particular state allow this type

---

[120] This is a real problem for customer service technicians. Several dot matrix printer manufacturers did this. It is currently a major nuisance for some types of video cards—there seem to be dozens of different BIOS versions for the same model of card.

For the lawyers reading this example, yes, OK, we acknowledge that this is *not necessarily* an example of innocent misrepresentation. It would be *negligence* if a reasonably knowledgeable technician in the department should have known that there are several versions of the printer, and that one version doesn't work with the program (sensible customer service groups do track this kind of information). It would be *reckless misrepresentation* if the technician knew a simple question to ask to tell which version of the printer the customer had, but just didn't bother.

of suit between a consumer-level purchaser and a business.[121] In a Small Claims Court case, or in a letter to the publisher, you might find it useful to read and quote one of the cases mentioned in the footnote, if it is a case from your State.

Whether you can find a case in our list that supports your argument or not, you have the strong argument that there is a natural justice in making the publisher pay the bill. You trusted the company and they were in a better position than you to know the facts about their own product. They should reimburse you for losses that directly resulted from your trust in the publisher's word.

Analysis: Post-Sale Misrepresentations

Many misrepresentations are made after the sale. Much of this is not fraudulent: the statements are made innocently or negligently. But too much post-sale misrepresentation is deliberate lying. We described these, and many of the common post-sale lies, in Chapter 5, "Making the Call."

If You Have Been Defrauded

Many people in the industry believe that false statements are not fraudulent if they are made after the sale. They are sadly mistaken. Whether before or after a sale, if someone lies to you with the intent of making you take any action (or refrain from taking an action) and you believe what they say and do what they want you to do, then you have been defrauded, and you can SUE, SUE, SUE.

---

[121] Most of the following cases are from Cumming (1992) and Sheldon & Carter (1997). We have not reviewed all of them, nor have we thoroughly searched for cases in other States. Not all of these cases involve innocent misrepresentation in *consumer transactions for goods*. These are starting points for research.

Alabama. *Burroughs Corporation v. Hall Affiliates, Inc.* (1982); *Mid-State Homes, Inc. v. Startley* (1979); *Resolution Trust Corp. v. Mooney* (1991); *Smith v. Reynolds Metals Co.* (1986).

Alaska: *Bevine v. Ballard* (1982).

Connecticut. *D'Ulisse-Cupo v. Board of Directors* (1987); *Richard v. A. Waldman & Sons, Inc.* (1967).

District of Columbia. *Stein v. Treger* (1950).

Idaho. *Lanning v. Sprague* (1951).

Indiana. *Clarke Auto Co. v. Reynolds* (1949).

Iowa. *Beeck v. Kapalis* (1981) (reviews cases; Iowa may not recognize innocent misrepresentation).

Kansas. *Roome v. Sonora Petroleum Co.* (1922); *Shambaugh v. Lindsay* (1983) (discussing Kansas law).

Massachusetts. *New England Foundation Co. v. Elliot A. Watrous Co.* (1940); *Logan Equip. Corp. v. Simon Aerials, Inc.* (1990); *Zimmerman v, Kent* (1991).

Ritchie Enterprises v. Honeywell Bull, Inc. (1990) is widely cited as an example of this principle. We summarize this case in Exhibit 7.6.

Exhibit 7.6: Seller Liable for Post-Sale Misrepresentation

In the case of *Ritchie Enterprises v. Honeywell Bull, Inc.* (1990), the United States District Court in the District of Kansas ruled that Honeywell could be held liable for fraudulent statements made after the sale.

Honeywell sold a computer and software to Ritchie.

In the lawsuit, Ritchie claimed the following: After taking delivery of the system in 1984, Ritchie discovered several misrepresentations that Honeywell had made about the capabilities of the computer. Ritchie also discovered several bugs. Honeywell provided bug fixes that didn't work. Honeywell made additional misrepresentations while trying to fix the bugs. Eventually Ritchie concluded that the system would not work, and pulled the plug.

- The contract included a disclaimer of all warranties, express and implied. The Court ruled that Honeywell had successfully excluded all statements of fact that Honeywell had made before the contract was signed that weren't included in the express warranty that was made part of the contract.

Michigan.   *Essenburg v. Russell* (1956); *Schwartz v. Electronic Data Systems, Inc.* (1990); *United States Fidelity & Guaranty Co. v. Black* (1981); Mitchell v. Dahlberg (1996).

Minnesota.   *Osborn v. Wills* (1931).

Nebraska.   *Paul v. Cameron* (1934).

New Mexico.   *Archeluta v. Kopp* (1977); *Snell v. Cornehl* (1970); *Wolf & Klar Co. v. Garner* (1984).

New York.   *West Side Federal Savings & Loan Association v. Hirschfeld* (1984).

Pennsylvania.   *Sullivan v. Allegheny Ford Truck Sales* (1980).

Texas.   *Wilson v. Jones* (1932).

Virginia.   *Trust Co. of Norfolk v. Fletcher* (1929).

Washington.   *Pratt v. Thompson* (1925).

West Virginia.   *Lengyel v. Lint* (1981).

Wisconsin.   *Reda v. Sincaban* (1988); *Whipp v. Iverson* (1969).

According to Sheldon and Carter (1997, Section 11.3.3.2), the following states do not allow suits for innocent misrepresentation, or their status is unclear: Arizona, Arkansas, California, Colorado, Delaware, Florida, Georgia, Hawaii, Idaho, Illinois, Iowa, Kentucky, Louisiana, Maine, Maryland, Mississippi, Montana, Nevada, New Hampshire, New York, North Carolina, North Dakota, Ohio, Oklahoma, Oregon, Rhode Island, South Carolina, South Dakota, Tennessee, Utah, Vermont and Wyoming.

- The Court ruled that Ritchie could not sue Honeywell for negligent misrepresentation for the pre-sale claims it made about the computer. These were matters for warranty law.

- The contract included a limitation of remedies that provided only for repair, replacement or partial refund, and barred consequential damages. The Court ruled that even if the limited remedies provided in the contract failed of their essential purpose, Honeywell would still not be responsible for Ritchie's incidental or consequential damages.

Ritchie's only remaining claim was for fraud. Ritchie claimed that it was defrauded by Honeywell after the sale, that Honeywell had concealed problems with the system and the operation of new patches. Honeywell argued that the post-sale representations were "not separately actionable" because Ritchie's injuries were the result of its buying the computer. Ritchie said that Honeywell's post-sale misrepresentations caused Ritchie to extend its acceptance testing period from one month to six, and to delay terminating the contract over the earlier misrepresentations. The Court ruled that this extension and delayed cancellation were sufficient to support an action for post-sale fraud.

If a publisher's lies cause you to delay returning the program and instead to continue testing a product and cooperating with the publisher to get it working, under Ritchie, you have an action for post-sale fraud.

Clement v. Smith (1993) is another interesting example. In this case, an insurance broker allegedly misrepresented the extent of coverage of the Clement's policy. The misrepresentations occurred after the plaintiff bought the insurance, but before Clement needed to file a claim. When he did file the claim, he discovered that the insurance didn't cover his problem. He sued, and won. The Court said (p. 44):

> *Defendants suggest that since the dispute between Clement and Carter concerning the signing of the subordination agreement did not occur until after the issuance of the Scottsdale policy, Smith could not possibly have misrepresented to Clement that litigation arising from such a dispute would be covered. The argument fails, however, because defendants have adopted a far too narrow view of the actionable misrepresentation. . . .*

> *Defendants focus on the period before the policy was purchased on the theory that later misrepresentations cannot be deemed to have caused Clement to have purchased the Scottsdale policy in lieu of another alternative. Later misrepresentations, however, may have deflected Clement from purchasing additional insurance, which was the theory adopted by the trial court. Under this theory, misrepresentation of coverage made at any time before the beginning of the subordination dispute would be relevant.*

Again, then, post-sale and post-contracting statements can be held against the seller as misrepresentations.

Unfair and Deceptive Practices

Proving fraud involves all manner of picky, picky, picky details. Normal humans don't interact well with fraud laws.

The Federal and State Governments have simplified the problem of dealing with certain types of seller dishonesty by writing simplified consumer protection laws that ban unfair and deceptive practices:

- It's easier for you to prove your case (if you have one) under these laws.

- It's easier to get free help (from a consumer protection agency) under these laws, because the laws are often written simply enough for volunteer mediators to learn.

- And most of these laws make it easier to afford a lawyer—If the business is in the wrong, in most States, the business pays your legal fees.

These laws are your friends, and it's worth getting to know them.

Here's a standard abbreviation: UDAP means "Unfair or Deceptive Acts or Practices". A lie is a deceptive act if a seller says it once. It's a deceptive *practice* if the seller uses it on every customer who walks through his doors.

UDAP statutes are usually widely circulated. You might easily get a copy of your State's statutes (or a pamphlet describing them) at your neighborhood public library.

OVERVIEW AND ANALYSIS: UNFAIR AND DECEPTIVE PRACTICES

Most UDAP statutes provide a laundry list of dirty practices. Here's California's, for example:

Some of the Deceptive Practices Banned under California Civil Code Section 1770(a):

(1) Passing off goods or services as those of another.

(2) Misrepresenting the source, sponsorship, approval, or certification of goods or services.

(3) Misrepresenting the affiliation, connection, or association with, or certification by, another.

(4) Using deceptive representations or designations of geographic origin in connection with goods or services.

(5) Representing that goods or services have sponsorship, approval, characteristics, ingredients, uses, benefits, or quantities which they do not have or that a person has a sponsorship, approval, status, affiliation, or connection which he or she does not have.

(6) Representing that goods are original or new if they have deteriorated unreasonably or are altered, reconditioned, reclaimed, used, or second-hand.

(7) Representing that goods or services are of a particular standard, quality, or grade, or that goods are of a particular style or model, if they are of another.

(8) Disparaging the goods, services, or business of another by false or misleading representation of fact.

(9) Advertising goods or services with intent not to sell them as advertised.

(10) Advertising goods or services with intent not to supply reasonably expectable demand, unless the advertisement discloses a limitation of quantity.

(11) Advertising furniture without clearly indicating that it is unassembled if that is the case.

(12) Advertising the price of unassembled furniture without clearly indicating the assembled price of that furniture if the same furniture is available assembled from the seller.

(13) Making false or misleading statements of fact concerning reasons for, existence of, or amounts of price reductions.

(14) Representing that a transaction confers or involves rights, remedies, or obligations which it does not have or involve, or which are prohibited by law.

(15) Representing that a part, replacement, or repair service is needed when it is not.

(16) Representing that the subject of a transaction has been supplied in accordance with a previous representation when it has not.

(17) Representing that the consumer will receive a rebate, discount, or other economic benefit, if the earning of the benefit is contingent on an event to occur subsequent to the consummation of the transaction.

(18) Misrepresenting the authority of a salesperson, representative, or agent to negotiate the final terms of a transaction with a consumer.

(19) Inserting an unconscionable provision in the contract.

Some other statutes are very broadly written.[122] For example, the Federal Trade Commission Act simply says:[123]

> *Unfair methods of competition in or affecting commerce and unfair or deceptive acts or practices in or affecting commerce, are hereby declared unlawful.*

The Federal Trade Commission can bring a lawsuit against a business for unfair or deceptive acts or practices anywhere in the United States. Most (or all) Attorneys-General can bring charges for a UDAP violation in their own State. Consumers can also bring private lawsuits under UDAP statutes in every State but Arkansas and Iowa.[124]

You don't have to prove as much to win one of these suits. For example:

Knowledge.   You probably don't have to prove that the seller knew that false statements were false.[125]

Reliance.   You probably don't have to prove that anyone believed a seller's false statements. The seller isn't allowed to make false statements (except in jest), whether anyone believes them or not.

Materiality.   You probably don't have to prove that the statements played an important role in your having made a decision.

However, you probably don't have a very broad range of remedies (e.g. types of damages) available if you do win the suit. There are a few different possibilities:

Rescission or cover.   You are entitled to a refund or to the value of the product you were told you were going to get.[126]

Statutory damages.   You might be entitled to a statutory minimum amount. If you win the lawsuit, your are entitled to collect the statutory minimum even if your actual losses were much less. This compensates you for the

---

[122] For a thorough discussion of each State's laws, with analysis of many issues in depth, Sheldon and Carter (1997b) is a gold mine. Keup (1993) provides a useful summary of the consumer protection statutes affecting mail order businesses. Holdych (1994) is an exceptionally long (110 page), thoughtful analysis of the underpinnings of these statutes and their possible effects on the market.

[123] United States Code, *Title 15*, Section 45(a)(1).

[124] Sheldon and Carter (1997b, Section 7.2) suggest ways to bring UDAP cases in these States.

[125] The knowledge requirement varies. For example, in Colorado, the statute bans *knowingly* passing off goods, services or property as those of another, and *knowingly* making certain other false representations. (See the discussion in Lee, 1992)

[126] Not every state allows this in these types of cases, but if it makes a difference worth arguing about, ask for it. Here's an example of what we mean by "value of the product." Suppose you buy a word processor for $20, based on advertisements that it is 100% compatible with Word Perfect. (We know of no word processing programs making such claims—this example is purely hypothetical). The program is not compatible with WordPerfect. If you ask for a refund, you'll get $20. If you ask for the value of the product as advertised, you're really demanding a product that is 100 percent compatible with WordPerfect. That's what you bought and paid for. Rather than $20, what you want back is enough money to buy a copy of WordPerfect.

hassle of bringing the lawsuit. Statutory minimums range from $25 to $2000. These change, so contact your local consumer protection agency for current numbers.

Multiplier of your losses.   You might be entitled to a multiplier of your actual damages, such as treble damages. If you are entitled to treble damages, the Court takes the actual damages that you proved, multiplies by three, and awards you that amount.

Incidentals or consequentials.   You might be entitled to incidental expenses or consequential damages.[127] Probably, you'll have to prove a few additional special circumstances to recover these types of damages.

Attorney's fees.   You are usually entitled to reimbursement of your attorney's fees if you win in court.[128] The judge will determine the amount of a fair fee, which might be less than your lawyer requested. An interesting problem arises if you reach a settlement before the case ever gets to court. The statutes don't authorize you to collect attorney fees as part of a settlement agreement, but you will want to do this because otherwise, you might end up having to pay your lawyer yourself.

We haven't said this in a while, so we want to remind you that, even though we are talking entirely in terms of lawsuits here, you will almost never bring one of these lawsuits. You'll almost never bring *any* lawsuit. Unless your negotiations with the publisher have fallen through completely, you shouldn't be reading this with the idea that you're learning how to sue the company. What you are really learning in this chapter is negotiating leverage.

There is power in explaining to a publisher that:

1. An advertisement was misleading in a way that is considered an unfair trade practice (be specific about what practice, and how you know it's banned).

2. In your state, if you have to go to court, you can get three times your actual damages, plus attorney fees.

EXAMPLES OF UNFAIR OR DECEPTIVE PRACTICES CASES

Here are a few examples of private and public lawsuits for (alleged) unfair or deceptive acts or practices. We are being cautious in our wording (saying "al-

---

[127] Sheldon and Carter (1997b, Section 8.3.3) discuss this issue and cite many cases. If you have significant consequential damages, you (or your lawyer) should read this section of Sheldon.

[128] We talk about statutes that shift attorney fees, and how to find lawyers that specialize in using these statutes, in Chapter 9, "Lawyers."

legedly" a lot), because we don't have personal knowledge of the cases and in many cases, the cases settled without a final determination of guilt or liability. Sometimes, innocent companies settle lawsuits just to get them out of the way. We list links to Web sites and trust that you will form your own opinion based on your own research.

The Syncronys SoftRAM95 Cases

Syncronys Softcorp published SoftRAM95. This was allegedly promoted as a software alternative to expanding your computer's memory. For example, in its Complaint, the Federal Trade Commission claimed that Syncronys had claimed that its product would have the effect of doubling your computer's memory, from 4MB to 8MB. (*In the Matter of Syncronys Software,* 1996).

According to the FTC, Syncronys sold approximately 600,000 copies of SoftRAM95. Andrew Schulman, a Senior Editor of O'Reilly and Associates, maintains a web page called SoftRAM95: "False and Misleading." This page is an archive of documents related to the SoftRAM95 case. One of the documents at that page is said to be a press release issued by Syncronys, that reported the results of a customer survey allegedly done by Dataquest, an internationally recognized technology market research and consulting firm. The results reported included these:

- "80 percent of customers surveyed said that SoftRAM 95 performed as expected."
- "82 percent described themselves as being either very satisfied or satisfied with the product."
- "48 percent described SoftRAM95 as being their favorite or one of their favorite utility programs."

The only problem is that, according to the FTC's complaint and several analytical reports reproduced at Schulman's site, SoftRAM95 did little or nothing to increase the amount of available memory on a Windows 95-based computer.

The case illustrates a core problem with high technology products: most people can't tell if they are being cheated.

The Federal Trade Commission took action against Syncronys, but retailers continued to sell the product. Schulman's site provides links to or summarizes of articles identified as being from the San Jose Mercury News and the Computer Reseller News that said that retailers were still selling SoftRAM95 even after Syncronys had allegedly recalled it.

Eventually, to clear this up, Donald Driscoll (an expert in deceptive trade practice litigation, based in Oakland, California) brought a class action suit against several retailers, alleging unfair competition, fraud, and breach of warranty. (For a copy of the Complaint, see Driscoll and Henley, 1996).

The Starcraft Suit

Our understanding is that this is another Donald Driscoll case and that it is in progress. According to (what is claimed to be) a long excerpt of the Complaint, at the gamespot.com Web site (Driscoll, 1998),

> *Blizzard sells to consumers a video game for IBM PC computers known as "Starcraft." That computer game can be played . . . as a multi-player game over the Internet. . . . When Blizzard is played via www.battle.net, computer instructions which Blizzard put in Starcraft without the knowledge or permission of the consumer, can, at Blizzard's in struction, cause data to be uploaded from the consumer's computer to www.battle.net.*

In essence, this is a lawsuit for an alleged violation of the user's privacy.

The Marketing of "Compatible" Products

We've seen one compatibility suit already. The *Step-Saver* lawsuit involved an operating system that was marketed as MS-DOS compatible. It was, according to Step-Saver, not fully compatible, and the result was a lawsuit.

Suppose someone sold product X as compatible with product Y. How incompatible would X have to be with Y before this sale would be a violation of one of these statutorily banned claims:

- Representing that goods or services have sponsorship, approval, characteristics, ingredients, uses, benefits, or quantities that they do not have or that a person has a sponsorship, approval, status, affiliation, or connection that he or she does not have.

- Representing that goods or services are of a particular standard, quality, or grade or that goods are of a particular style or model, if they are of another.

The case of *Princeton Graphics v. NEC Home Electronics* (1990) was an unfair competition-type suit brought by one competitor (Princeton) against another (NEC). Apparently, both sold monitors that were equivalently almost-PS/2-compatible (essentially, VGA-compatible). Princeton did not advertise its monitor as PS/2-compatible. NEC did. The court determined that, even though the NEC Multisync monitor worked with the PS/2, it was necessary to make a manual adjustment to the monitor to assure that the 480-line picture fit on the screen.[129] Because of the need for manual adjustment (each time you switched modes), the court ruled that the Multisync was not fully PS/2-compatible[130] and that NEC was liable.

---

[129] *Princeton Graphics v. NEC* (1990), p. 1263.

[130] *Princeton Graphics v. NEC* (1990), p. 1264.

The recent case of *Creative Labs, Inc. v. Cyrix Corp.* (1997) extends the compatibility analysis further. Creative Labs markets the "Sound Blaster" line of sound cards. According to the court, Cyrix marketed the "XpressAUDIO" component of its Media GX microprocessor as compatible with the Sound Blaster.[131] "Creative Labs tested the Media GX on a Presario 210 computer . . . [with] 200 computer games and discovered that sixteen games, or 8% of the total tested, did not run properly on the Presario 2100. . . . Creative also found that the Presario 2100 did not support two functions supported by Sound Blaster."[132] "Cyrix counters that it did not encounter problems when running six of these games on a properly configured computer. . . . Cyrix's own study indicates a failure rate of approximately 2%."[133] The court concluded that even if the failure rate is closer to 2 percent than 8 percent, this "indicates that some games that function with the Sound Blaster do not function with XpressAUDIO."[134] Based on this, the court found that claims of compatibility between Sound Blaster and XpressAUDIO "would probably mislead consumers who would interpret the claim of Sound Blaster compatibility to mean that any product that functions with Sound Blaster would also function with XpressAUDIO."[135] The court then granted an injunction stopping Cyrix from claiming that the two devices are compatible.

In short, "compatible" means "compatible." Not "kind of, sort of," compatible. Not "take two workarounds and call me in the morning" compatible. Compatible. You don't have to settle for anything less.

Final Notes on UDAP

There are many more UDAP suits involving software. We'll link to some at our website, www.badsoftware.com. The range of misbehavior that they can cover is most impressive; and necessary.

If decisions like *Gateway 2000* and statutes like Article 2B spread, then sellers won't be under much contract-law-based pressure to honor their contracts with you. Sometimes, lawsuits for fraud are good vehicles for dealing with publishers who deliver less than they promise. But fraud suits are tough work. Your best defense over the next decade might well come from UDAP statutes. It will be worth getting to know your State's versions well.

---

[131] *Creative Labs, Inc. v. Cyrix Corp.* (1997), p. 1873

[132] *Creative Labs, Inc. v. Cyrix Corp.* (1997), p. 1873

[133] *Creative Labs, Inc. v. Cyrix Corp.* (1997), p. 1875

[134] *Creative Labs, Inc. v. Cyrix Corp.* (1997), p. 1875

[135] *Creative Labs, Inc. v. Cyrix Corp.* (1997), p. 1875

Action Plan

Regarding Article 2B, we urge you to read the Appendix and check our website, www.badsoftware.com for more information and to write your State's governor and your state legislator to express your concern about Article 2B. Please send us a copy of your letter.

Regarding your dispute with the publisher under current law:

1. Calculate your damages. Work through Chapter 4, "What Should You Ask For?" Figure out how much this program has really cost you and how much you could (if all went well) recover in court.

   - If your losses are in the thousands of dollars, seriously consider talking with a lawyer. See Chapter 9, "Lawyers." Do this right away.

   - If your losses are smaller, ask whether you have the benefit of a fee-shifting statute that will allow you to bill the publisher for your legal fees. See Chapter 9, "Lawyers."

   - If you bought the program recently and your damages aren't huge, why not take a refund? Review this chapter and ask yourself whether you're likely to get much more than a refund. See Chapter 1, "Read This First."

   - If you're willing to settle for a refund, but you can't get one from the publisher, ask for help from a consumer protection agency. See Chapter 6, "Consumer Protection Agencies." And, think about Small Claims Court.

   - If you want more than a refund but it doesn't make sense to work with a lawyer (damages too low and can't shift fees), then you are probably on the road to Small Claims Court. Read Chapters 8 "Overview of a Lawsuit," and 10, "Small Claims Court."

2. You know more about your rights, so you're probably better able to negotiate with the publisher.

   - If you haven't yet been in touch with the publisher, make the call or write the complaint letter now. Focus on your problems with the program. Don't talk about the law. Save that for later. Listen to what the technician and service manager have to say about the law. See the first chapters of this book.

   - If you've been making phone calls, it's time for your first letter. Don't threaten a lawsuit, don't use jargon, but ask for everything you're entitled to. Address it to the Manager of the Customer Service group. (Call the publisher to get his name.) Say that you'll call him in 10 days and make the follow-up call.

- If you've made some phone calls and written some letters, it probably still makes more sense to continue with a letter than another phone call. Be firm. Show some of your knowledge of the law. But don't threaten yet.

- If you've followed up with calls or letters and you get no satisfactory response, write a *demand letter*. See Chapter 10, "Small Claims Court."

Chapter 8
Overview of a Lawsuit

 Chapter Map
If you haven't been able to work out something reasonable with the software publisher, one of your options is a lawsuit. This chapter provides a road map, briefly looking at typical stages of litigation.

Lawsuits are hard work. They are expensive. They are unpleasant. They eat your time. And, despite the baloney you read in the newspaper and see on television, lawsuits are *not* lotteries. Unless the publisher you are suing engaged in practices that are astonishingly outrageous, you are extremely unlikely to receive an award of punitive damages. In a lawsuit for breach of contract, your goal should be to recover your actual losses, plus as much of your legal costs and attorney's fees as possible. Under the right circumstances, consumer protection laws may provide you with some limited additional recovery—up three times your actual losses, plus attorney fees. Plus, you have the satisfaction of having beaten a bad publisher. If you expect more than this out of a lawsuit, you will be disappointed. The odds are good that you won't even get this much, even if you are 100 percent in the right.

There are some nice aspects of lawsuits:

Publishers hate lawsuits. Most publishers hate them as much as you do; even more, probably. They are distracting, angering, unpleasant. They eat the executives' time and rack up fees for the company's lawyers. Win or lose, the publisher probably will come out of this wishing that it had never heard of you. The publisher might even think of changing its policies so that people like you won't be tempted to sue it again.

Negative publicity. Your court documents are public records. Starting with the complaint you file in court, your documents might make the News (or at least some USENET newsgroup). Other people who've been cheated by this publisher will be encouraged to make their own complaints or to file their own lawsuits. Other publishers will consider checking their policies to make sure that someone like you won't be tempted to sue them.

Your case may set a precedent. A precedent is a decision by one court that will be followed by later courts that consider the same legal issue.[1]

---

[1] Your case will set a precedent if an appellate court reviews it, and that court publishes its decision. That *decision* will be the precedent—it will bind all other courts within that appellate court's jurisdiction. In

In short, lawsuits serve a valuable social purpose. They are one of the most important tools available for customers to fight back against rip-offs by dishonest businesses.[2]

Phases in a Lawsuit

Legal disputes don't necessarily lead to lawsuits. There are many other ways to settle a dispute, and (with cooperation of the other side) you can switch methods and settle the suit at any point along the way.

SOMETHING BAD HAPPENS TO YOU

The first event in any legal dispute is that "something bad happens." Usually, that "something bad" must have happened to you. You can't sue because someone else was injured, cheated, or lied to. You sue because you were injured. cheated, or lied to.[3]

---

effect, the court is announcing that if it ever sees another case like this, it will rule the same way, so any judge whose cases can be appealed to this appellate court will rule in accord with the decision. Cases also have a broader, persuasive effect. They will influence lawyers' and judges' thinking about legal issues across the country, not just in the county or state(s) in which they are binding.

[2]After much thought and argument, we have decided not to say much about the "Tort Reform" movement. Our comments are limited to this footnote. We know that you have been bombarded with stories of abusive lawsuits and of nasty, evil plaintiffs' lawyers who work on contingency, and of poor, innocent corporations who are being driven out of business by a rising tide of lawsuits. Yes, some people try to steal from companies by filing phony lawsuits against them (like faking falls in a supermarket). But, these lawsuits don't show that we have a litigious society. It shows that we have white-collar criminals who try to steal this way, just like we have street criminals and white-collar criminals who steal in other ways. But, as to the story that there is a rising tide of litigation, that's just baloney.

Here's an example from California, where we live. The Governor has often talked about the "explosion of lawsuits," so we looked at the 1994 Annual Report to the Governor and the Legislature of the Judicial Council of California (1994) for some actual data (see the report's Table 6). These particular numbers from this 1994 report were quoted widely in political campaigns to prove that there was a lawsuit explosion. It is true that from 1983–84 to 1992–93, civil filings in the California Superior Court rose from 561,916 to 684,070, an increase of 122,154 cases. This jump looks impressive, but everything changes when you look at another category in the Table, "Other Civil Petitions." "Other Civil Petitions" includes the civil lawsuits filed by district attorneys in counties to collect reimbursement for child support payments. It doesn't include suits for fraud, personal injury, consumer protection violation, products liability, malpractice, etc. "Other Civil Petitions" rose by 156,178 cases. Suits for fraud, consumer protection, and so on, actually dropped. This increase was about child support, not about consumer protection or commercial litigation. Lawsuits for fraud, deceptive trade practices, breach of warranty, and otherwise defective products are powerful tools for consumers to use to force dishonest businesses to clean up their act. Dishonest businesses have a powerful incentive to spend a lot of money on advertising and lobbying to blunt these tools, making it harder to bring the suits, harder and more expensive to win them, and less profitable (if profitable at all) for the attorneys who handle them. As we see it, this is the foundation of the "Tort Reform" movement.

[3]There is an exception to this. In some states, a company that engages in a practice of deceptive trade practices can be sued by anyone in the state. California's statute against Unfair Competition (Business and Professions Code section 17500 and onward) is an example of such a law.

PRECOMPLAINT NEGOTIATIONS

If you file a lawsuit, you will include a court document called a *Complaint* that sets out your case and demands your money.

Before you file a Complaint, you'll try to solve your dispute with the publisher in many ways, such as:

- Calling the publisher to ask for help and/or money
- Writing letters to the publisher
- Asking a consumer protection agency for help
- Publicly confronting the publisher with complaints in a letter to a magazine or to a news group on the Internet or on some other online service (such as CompuServe, America OnLine, or the WELL)
- Hiring a lawyer to complain to the publisher and ask for help and/or money

The vast majority of disputes are resolved by negotiation.

THE DEMAND LETTER

Sending a demand letter is one of the final steps before filing the lawsuit. Often, this step is required before you can file a suit in Small Claims Court—you have to be able to prove that you sent a demand letter to the person you're suing before you can file the suit. The demand letter may not be required for other types of litigation, but sending it is often useful.

In the demand letter, you:

- *State your issue.*   Describe your problem and the problems you have had getting fair treatment from the publisher.
- *State your demand.*   What do you want?
- *State that this is a demand letter.*
- *State that you will take further action.*   Unless they resolve this matter by such-and-such a date, you will take further action. But, *don't* specifically threaten to sue. Keep your options open.

We provide an example of a demand letter in Chapter 10, "Small Claims Court."

Many, many people threaten to sue and most of them never do. The letter of demand is often the first credible threat of a lawsuit. When you send the letter by Certified Mail to the publisher's Agent for Service (see Chapter 10), you are announcing that you know something about the process and that you are fed up.

The demand letter is probably going to end up on the desk of the publisher's lawyer. The lawyer will read the letter as a warning that you are not kidding and that the publisher will be sued unless it settles your dispute.

The publisher will probably respond to your letter of demand. If negotiations look promising, keep negotiating. If not, file your lawsuit. You don't have to send a new letter.

You must file a lawsuit within a reasonable time after the event you are suing over. For a breach of contract, you probably have three or four years, but you might have less (maybe just one year). If you file the suit after that, the court will rule that you have blown the *Statute of Limitations* and will throw out your suit. You might have only six months or a year after you bought the product for a suit based on deceptive trade practices.

GROUND RULES OF A LAWSUIT (DUE PROCESS OF LAW)

When you file a lawsuit, you are asking a judge to award you a remedy. Usually, the remedy is money, but you might ask for and receive a different remedy, such as a bug-fixed version of the program. (Lawyers would call this specific performance of the contract—giving you what you negotiated for.)

When you file a lawsuit, you are the *plaintiff*, and the person or company that you are suing is the *defendant*. The plaintiff and the defendant are the two parties in a lawsuit. Under our Constitution, the judge can deprive the defendant of property (such as money) or liberty (such as the work required to provide specific performance) only if certain ground rules have been followed. These rules are collectively called *due process of law*. Here are some of the rules of due process:

There must be a law that says that if a person does a specified bad thing, someone can sue this person for it.   These laws might be defined in statutes, such as the consumer protection statutes, or they might be generally defined in statutes but much more rigorously defined by the courts. A law can be broken into a series of requirements or elements. For example, in the last chapter, we explained that misrepresentation involves the following elements:

- The publisher made a statement of fact.
- The statement was false.
- The statement was material.
- You relied on the false statement.
- Your reliance was justifiable.
- The publisher intended that you rely on this statement.
- You suffered some loss as a result.

To prove a case of misrepresentation, you have to prove every element. If you can't prove them all, you might be able to prove something else (such as deceptive trade practices), but you can't win a misrepresentation case.

The defendant must have a reasonable opportunity to defend itself.
The defendant is entitled to reasonable notice of the filing of the lawsuit and of the claims made in the lawsuit. Additionally, the defendant can't be sued in a state that it has no significant contacts with, because this is fundamentally unfair. In such a case, the defending publisher would have such high expenses (repeated travel of its executives and legal staff, plus research of that state's laws) that it would pay off even groundless lawsuits just to control its total expenses. Therefore, to sue an out-of-state defendant, you must prove that it has enough contact with that state (such as a sales office, or a substantial amount of business) so it shouldn't be surprised that it can be hauled into the state's courts.

Both parties must have appropriate time and opportunity to investigate the facts of the case.   The rules for this investigation, called discovery, vary across different types of lawsuits. Obviously, in a $500 lawsuit, it would be unfair to subject a company to $100,000 in discovery-related expenses.

The decision-making process must be unbiased.   If the trial involves a judge and a jury, the judge listens to the lawyers' arguments and decides what the law is. The jury listens to the witnesses and decides what the facts are. Both parties are entitled to a judge and a jury that are not biased against either party and who won't take an unreasonable (positive or negative) approach to this type of lawsuit.

THE COMPLAINT

The *complaint* is the legal document you file with the court to begin the lawsuit. Different states have different rules for what must be in the complaint.

The complaint states your claim for *relief.* That is, it alleges a set of facts that, taken together, would entitle you to a remedy. Some states require that you explicitly cite the legal rules (statutes and cases), list the elements underlying your claim, and provide facts supporting each element. Other states, and most Federal cases, require only a simple statement of facts without extended legal discussion.

The complaint usually also includes a statement of jurisdiction—explaining why this is the right court in which to bring this case and why it is lawful to bring this defendant before this court.

You arrange to serve the complaint on the defendant, meaning you have someone deliver a copy of the complaint to the defendant in a way that lets you prove that the defendant received it. A defendant who raises your costs by evading your attempts at service is subject to penalties.

CLASS CERTIFICATION HEARING

Rather than filing the lawsuit on your own, it might makes sense to join with several other people who have been cheated in the same way and file together. Joining cases lets you spread legal expenses across a larger group of people, making it more economically plausible to bring a case involving a smaller claim (less money). Additionally, the judge may take the case more seriously when she realizes that many people are involved, not just you.

If there are only a few of you, your cases are joined as separate cases that are tried together. If there are many of you (it could be as few as 12), and if you request it, the judge will treat the group as a *class*. One or a few of you will be selected as *class representatives*. Rather than trying all these individual cases, there is one trial, and it focuses on the details of the case of the class representative(s). This is called a *class action*. Everyone else watches from the sidelines. What is determined in the case of the class representative applies to the other members of the class as well.

When the plaintiffs seek to file a suit as a class, one of the first hearings held is a hearing to determine whether the case should be certified as a class action. Defendants will often argue against certification or to narrow the class certified. They want to keep the class small. If the class is small and the amount of money involved per customer is small, the plaintiffs' lawyers can be easily beaten (whether their clients are right or wrong), because they can be so easily outspent by the defendants' lawyers. The larger the class, the larger the budget available to the plaintiff to pay for the litigation.

Every plaintiff has a right to a fair trial of her claims. In a class action, the judge must protect the rights of the absent class members. The judge will narrow the class or ask for new (or additional) representatives if the details of the claims of the absent class members aren't similar enough to those of the suggested representatives. If the claims of the various class members are too dissimilar from each other, the judge will refuse to certify any class, and all of the cases will have to be tried individually. If the judge determines that the plaintiffs' attorneys aren't working in the best interests of the class as a whole, she may refuse to certify the class or may insist that other attorneys play the lead role in the case.

TEST FOR FAILURE TO STATE A CLAIM

Another hearing that can occur early in the case involves defendant's contention that the plaintiff hasn't brought a valid lawsuit. The defendant argues that, even if all the facts alleged by the plaintiff were true, they still wouldn't add up to a legally sufficient claim.

For example, in a lawsuit for misrepresentation, you have to be able to prove that you relied on a false statement. If you admit that you heard the false claim after you bought the product, then it doesn't matter whether the defendant's claims were false and the defendant wanted you to believe them—you will never be able to prove that your purchase was based on a misrepresentation. Rather than letting you waste everyone's time with this losing case, the defendant will deal with it as early as possible by asking the judge to rule that you can't possibly win this case even if you prove everything that you've promised to prove.

FILE ANSWER TO THE COMPLAINT

If the defendant can't convince the judge to throw out the case, the defendant will file its answer, laying out its own allegations that, if true, refute your case. At this point, the plaintiff and the defendant are arguing about the facts. You say X happened, and the defendant says X didn't or that other facts show that X doesn't mean what you say that it means.

Additionally, the defendant might file counterclaims (suing you, the plaintiff) or third-party claims (for example, a defendant retailer, suing the publisher). And, you might file a response to the defendant's documents. Ultimately, out of this phase, comes a dispute over the facts of the case.

DISCOVERY

The plaintiff (you) and the defendant (the publisher) ask each other for information and documents, and, within limits, you are required to satisfy each other's requests.

The opposing attorneys are supposed to manage this process between themselves, but courts often are brought in to supervise discovery disputes. Here are some examples:

Unfair requests by the plaintiff.   The defense attorney might believe that your attorney is asking for a huge number of documents in order to drive up the costs of defending the suit (it costs a lot to find, copy, and review all these documents) or to go fishing for unrelated embarrassing information in the defendant's files that can be used as a negotiating lever. (Sometimes, the defendant is right.)

Unfair requests by the defense.   Similarly, your attorney may believe the defense attorney is asking for an overwhelming amount of unnecessary, irrelevant, and private information, as a method of harassing or embarrassing you. (Sometimes, this is true.)

Making the case unprofitable.   Your attorney might believe that the defendant is refusing to give up documents in order to force him to go through the repeated expense of going to court. A plaintiff's lawyer who works on contingency gets no additional compensation when he drafts each new court document and makes each court appearance. Some defense lawyers believe that they can reduce the amount of litigation against their client, over the long term, by making cases unprofitable for the plaintiff's lawyers who take the cases.

Hiding records.   When the defense attorney pleads that you are asking for too much information, this might mean that your attorney is in fact wasting everyone's time, or it might mean that he is getting too close to some damaging records. Some defendants turn over damaging records when they are properly requested (as they are required to do), some fight to protect the records, and some defendants (or their lawyers) hide the records or destroy them.

The judge (or a magistrate, commissioner, or master appointed by the judge) might rule that the requesting documents be treated as confidential by both sides. He may rule that the requesting party must pay the cost of sorting and copying the requested documents. The judge might review documents before turning them over to the other side. Or, the judge might just say, enough is enough, no more documents, no more depositions, no more interrogatories, stop it.

Some (most?) small claims courts allow one party to require the other to bring documents to the trial itself but allow no pre-trial discovery. In small cases, the cost of full discovery would exceed the cost of most of the claims. Similarly, a relatively small claim for a few thousand dollars would warrant less discovery than a multi-million dollar class action suit (even if both trials involved the same fraudulent behavior by the publisher).

SUMMARY JUDGMENT MOTION

In the complaint, your lawyer might have laid out several different claims, perhaps suing for fraud, negligent misrepresentation, unfair competition, deceptive trade practices, breach of contract, breach of express warranty, breach of implied warranty, breach of the Magnuson-Moss Act, etc. You might not have had enough evidence to support all of these claims, but you might have expected to find that evidence during discovery.

Discovery has come and gone, and it is now time for pruning. The defendant will challenge some or all of your claims in a summary judgment motion. In other words, the defendant says, claim by claim, that you have no evidence to back up your claims, that they are worthless, and that the judge should throw them, and you, out of court. You show that you have evidence to support each. If the judge decides that no reasonable jury could find that you have enough evidence to support one of your claims, then she will throw it out.

TRIAL

The plaintiff (you) and the defendant (publisher) present their case and the judge/jury decide what "really" happened.

DAMAGES

At the end of the trial, the jury (or judge) determines whether or not the defendant is liable to you. If so, you will probably receive money, rather than a new program or other types of work from the defendant.

We discussed several types of damages in Chapter 4, "Knowing What to Ask For," and Chapter 7, "Software Quality and the Law." In summary, you are most likely to recover compensatory damages. These make good your losses without giving you any profit. These damages include a refund or an amount that gives you the difference between what you paid and the value of what you received. They also include consequential and incidental damages. Unless you are suing for a personal injury, you probably can't claim for pain and suffering.

Under special circumstances, you might also be awarded punitive damages. These damages are awarded to punish the defendant, not to compensate the victim. They are closely scrutinized by the judge and by appellate courts. You must generally prove, by clear and convincing evidence, that the defendant's conduct was fraudulent, oppressive, or outrageous. You probably cannot recover punitive damages for breach of contract or warranty.

POST-TRIAL MOTIONS

The trial isn't over when it's over. If the defendant lost the lawsuit, it can keep on fighting.

The defendant can move (formally ask the court) for a new trial, for a reduction in the amount of damages, or for a judgment that it is not liable to you even though the jury said it was. The defendant might honestly believe it is entitled to one of these judgments, or it could be buying time. In either case, you are now in the post-trial negotiation phase, which can last for years (without you or your lawyer receiving any money) while the case drags through appeals and other motions. You may eventually settle for a pittance simply to end the case.

APPEAL

After finishing with its motion in the trial court, the defendant can file an appeal and have a hearing in an appellate court. This court will not overrule findings of fact unless they are patently wrong. The court might overrule the trial judge's rulings on the law. If it does, it will probably send the case back to the trial court for new proceedings, perhaps a new trial.

The appellate court might also reduce the amount of damages payable to the defendant (especially punitive damages, if any were awarded).

The trial court's rulings are rarely published.[4] Appellate rulings are often published. These become widely read decisions about the meaning and application of the law—that is, precedents.

MEDIATION IS AN ALTERNATIVE TO LITIGATION

Mediation is a structured form of negotiation that is facilitated by a mediator. The mediator is a neutral person who uses a variety of techniques to try to find out what is important to both parties. The mediator might help you and the publisher reach a compromise, or he might help you find a win-win solution, in which both of your needs are met.

The consumer protection agencies often try to mediate your complaint against a publisher.

Mediation is usually much less expensive than a lawsuit, and when it works well, you might get a solution that meets your requirements much better than money.

However, you should realize that there is almost no discovery in a mediation. If the publisher has deliberately defrauded you, you probably won't find this out in mediation. You might never realize what a powerful negotiating position you have. You might never learn that other people (perhaps also in mediation) are receiving much larger settlements than the one that you have settled for. The results of the mediation are usually private, and they set no precedent. Mediation settles the dispute between you and the publisher but serves no broader social purpose.

ARBITRATION IS AN ALTERNATIVE TO LITIGATION

An arbitration is a hearing, presided over by an arbitrator or by a panel of arbitrators. Several organizations train and provide arbitrators. The largest is the American Arbitration Association.

Going to arbitration is sometimes a voluntary process, and other times you are stuck with it. If you agree in a contract that you will arbitrate any dispute, then you probably have to go to arbitration whether you want to or not. There is a lot of disagreement within the legal community over whether it is fair and reasonable to allow mass-market sellers to require their customers (who were

---

[4]Many, but not most, federal trial court rulings are published in the Federal Supplement.

never allowed to negotiate their contracts) to take their disputes to arbitration.

The advantages of arbitration are that it is generally cheaper and faster, especially for small disputes.

Non-binding arbitration allows you to avoid many of the risks of binding arbitration. Non-binding arbitration gives you a decision, but lets you go to court if you can't live with the arbitrator's decision. Non-binding arbitration can often be arranged through the Better Business Bureau.

Here are some of the problems with arbitration.

Limited discovery.   It is easier for a publisher to hide critical documents from you.

No appeal.   If the arbitrator makes a bad decision that doesn't accord with current law, you can't go to an appellate court and get it corrected. In fact, the arbitrator is not required to base her decision on the law. (This is both a blessing and a curse. Sometimes common sense prevails over the law; sometimes something much worse happens.)

Repeat player advantage.   Large companies who use the system often get to know the arbitrators. You have to agree on the arbitrator(s) with the defendant. Knowledgeable defendants will simply disqualify someone who rules against them.

Limited damages.   Punitive damages are almost never awarded, even when they are appropriate. An arbitrator who awards punitive damages will probably not be selected for many future arbitrations. Defendant businesses will veto them as often as possible. Remember that arbitrators aren't paid by the government. They make their money by the case, and they need the goodwill of their prospective customers and the good reference letters from previous customers. If they make decisions that are unpopular with their business customers, they don't get many more cases.

Confidentiality.   The hearing and the results are usually controversial. Unlike a court trial, the press is not welcome. The documents are not public. People who have been cheated in the same ways as you won't learn that the publisher you have pressed a claim against has been successfully attacked. And, they won't learn what tactics worked when the publisher was successfully attacked. The publisher gains experience fighting essentially the same case in arbitration after arbitration, but if the different customers use different lawyers (the typical situation), the lawyers can't share information because of the confidentiality of the arbitration, and so they go into the hearings less well prepared than the publisher. (This is another repeat player advantage, exaggerated by the confidentiality of the proceedings.)

No precedent.   Even if many decisions are issued against many outrageous practices by many software companies (lots of arbitration decisions have gone this way), they set no precedent. No court learns of them. No court in the future has to follow them. The arbitrator's reasoning doesn't educate the thinking of the next judge or the next arbitrator. The arbitration settles the dispute between you and the publisher but serves absolutely no broader social purpose.

You will probably be represented by an attorney in an arbitration. You might have a choice of arbitrating a dispute or not. We recommend that you talk with your attorney about the relative advantages of arbitration for your specific case.

For more information on alternative dispute resolution, we recommend Craig Kubey's excellent book, *You Don't Always Need a Lawyer*. We understand that Kubey (1991) might be getting harder to find. Crowley (1994) is also useful.

Action Plan

If you've gotten this far, you're probably thinking about suing the publisher. Suing might be the right choice, but don't forget those consumer protection agencies that we wrote about in Chapter 6. If you haven't tried them yet, give one a call. Maybe they can help you get this matter settled.

- Read Chapter 9 for tips on hiring a good lawyer.
- Read Chapter 10 for tips on small claims court.

Also, please read the appendix, which describes a proposed new law, Article 2B, to govern sales of software. Now that you've read this far, you probably know a lot more about the law than you used to know. The Appendix, "A New Threat to Customers' Rights: Proposed Revisions to the Uniform Commercial Code (Article 2B)," will give you a sense of how the law will change if this proposed legislation goes through.

Chapter Map
Welcome to Lawyer Land

Just because you are in the right doesn't mean that the publisher will treat you ethically or reasonably. Sometimes, you just have to sue the bums (or to credibly threaten them, with a lawyer).

If you are involved in a legal action, such as an arbitration or a trial, you are walking in the land of lawyers. Being right offers no guarantee that you will win a legal fight. The law, the procedural rules, the traditions of the particular court or hearing agency, this is all the stuff of lawyers.

Lawyers provide legal *services*. Like any other service you can buy, you might or might not get great service. Our goal in this chapter is to help you to be a better consumer of the legal services that you might need.

Overview

In this chapter, we will address the following six questions:

1. Should you hire a lawyer?

If you're headed into a legal action, we think you probably will want to get help from a lawyer.

2. How can you pay for a lawyer?

Lawyers' time is expensive. It is easy to spend more on a case than you can possibly hope to recover. But, you can limit your expenses. One way is to get the software publisher to pay for all of your legal expenses. We will explain some of these opportunities and point out issues in legal fee agreements.

3. Can you limit expenses by doing some of the work?

You may not want or need someone to handle your case from start to finish. You can have a lawyer perform a few specific services and take care of the rest yourself.

4. How do you interview and hire a lawyer?

You want a lawyer who has the skills and resources required to achieve a positive result for you, who you can trust and get along.

5. How can you supervise your lawyer?

Yes, you have to supervise your lawyer. Otherwise, you'll probably pay a lot of money without getting the services you need.

6. How do you fire your lawyer?

Hopefully, you won't have to. But, if you do, there are ways to smooth the transition to a new lawyer and to settle money issues, without much ill will.

Recommended Reading

Several excellent books are available on how to hire and supervise an attorney. Unfortunately, most assume that you are a business or a wealthy person who is developing a relationship with an attorney that might last across several matters. Additionally, several convey a lower opinion of the profession than we have. Despite problems like these, we recommend the following books:

Jay Foonberg (1995) *Finding the Right Lawyer.* This is the American Bar Association's book on the topic, written by someone who teaches lawyers how to keep their clients. The book cuts through a lot of baloney, discusses attorney qualifications, sources for finding lawyers, fee agreements—all in a clear, direct way.

Irwin Cherovsky (1992) *Competent Counsel.* More good thoughts on interviewing and selecting counsel.

Dennis Powers (1994) *Legal Street Smarts: How to Survive in a World of Lawyers.* Excellent discussion of the differences between large and small firms. Excellent discussion of fee agreements. Written more for business readers than for consumers.

Dudley Gray and Arthur Lyons (1996) *How Not to Get Screwed by Your Attorney.* Unfortunately, there are jerks in every profession—including lawyers. But, remember this when you interview the lawyer, if you treat a good one as if she's a jerk, she probably won't like you. She'll probably be less interested in taking your case, and she'll probably charge you more money if she does take it. Get past the attitude of the authors and you'll find some solid advice.

Tanya Starnes (1996) *Mad at Your Lawyer? What to Do When You're Overcharged, Ignored, Betrayed, or a Victim of Malpractice.* The title says it all. Added bonus: tips for what to do if the lawyer for the publisher is acting unethically.

Should You Hire a Lawyer?

A lawyer joke compares lawyers to nuclear missiles. They are horribly expensive to have around, but if one side has them, the other side has to have them too. If either side launches one, the other side will launch, too, resulting in mutual destruction, or at least, in a terrible mess. The survivors come out of it hating each other.

You might prefer to handle your case yourself, without using a lawyer. (But, remember, if you're suing a business, they have a silo of lawyers.) There are several excellent self-help books that can help you handle your own case. We particularly like the Nolo Press books, such as Warner (1997) *Everybody's Guide to Small Claims Court*, Bergman and Berman-Barrett (1998) *Represent Yourself in Court: How to Prepare and Try a Winning Case* and Duncan (1996) *How to Sue for Up to $25,000...and Win! Suing and Defending a Case in Municipal Court without a Lawyer.*

Be careful and rational in your decision to represent yourself. The jokes are funny, but they present an unfair picture that might not help you make the right decision. We believe that a good lawyer can greatly help her clients.

It is always a serious decision to use someone else to speak on your behalf, to represent you in negotiations and in arguments. This is true in your love life, your school life, your business life, and your legal life. It is true whether your representative is a friend, a spouse, a partner, an employee, or a lawyer. There are risks, costs, and benefits of having a representative.

Example: Benefits of Having a Lawyer

A few years ago, Kaner's staff had problems that were resolved much more smoothly because he was a lawyer. This sequence of events illustrates the point that sometimes you just aren't taken seriously until you bring a lawyer into a dispute. Here is Kaner's story.

Sandy (not her real name) was a Production Coordinator. A Production Coordinator (or her staff) takes a writer's words and illustrations and turns them into an attractive, finished book. This process involves designing the book, placing words and illustrations on pages, making arrangements with commercial printers, and many other tasks. Sandy had the excellent taste that the job requires, plus a lot of technical skill and (like many other survivors in this very difficult job) a well-developed nobody-makes-a-sucker-out-of-me type of attitude.

Sandy bought a desktop publishing program to lay out our book. She also bought a few typefaces to use in the book from the same software publisher. Unfortunately, the program didn't work correctly with an important typeface. So she called the software publisher for help.

Sandy got the usual runaround.

The first problem was the long, long, long wait on hold.

When the publisher's technician finally came online, she said that they'd never heard of this problem and suggested that Sandy must be using the product incorrectly. (Sandy is an expert with this program.)

Next, the technician suggested that Sandy use a different typeface. (Not acceptable. Senior management had carefully reviewed and approved Sandy's book design, which relied heavily on this typeface. Changing the design would have been a big hassle.)

Eventually, the technician agreed that there might be a problem but said that the program was working just fine, and the problem was in the typeface. (Hmmmm, sounds like they had encountered the problem before, doesn't it?)

I don't understand why Sandy spent her time on this excuse, because the same company sold us the program and the typeface—to work together. But, Sandy does things her own way, and this time, she created test documents in a competing product to see whether it could handle this supposedly defective typeface. Everything printed perfectly. Evidently, the problem was with the program that couldn't handle the typeface properly, not with the typeface itself.

So Sandy called back yet again (and waited and waited and waited on hold yet again). The technician said, oh yes, they knew the typeface worked with this other program. (Progress—at last they were admitting that they had heard of the problem.) But, *their* program was expecting *their* typeface to provide extra information that the competitor didn't need. They said the typeface was flawed because of this lack of information, so we should use a different typeface.

Enough already. Sandy said, "Fix it or give me a full refund. Management has approved a specific page design, using specific typefaces. If this program couldn't generate those pages, other page layout programs could."

To Sandy's surprise, the technician said no. If she wanted a refund for the typeface, fine. But, not for the program. She said the program worked perfectly, only the font was at fault. And, when Sandy protested further, she told Sandy to read the program's warranty disclaimer. The disclaimer made it perfectly clear that there was no guarantee that this program would work with this typeface or with anything else. The program was sold "As Is." Therefore, she said, Sandy had absolutely no right to a refund.

Steaming mad, Sandy put the technician on hold, told me the story, and put me on the phone. I said,

"Excuse me. I'm a lawyer. I think that you need to talk with someone about this claim of yours that the program has no warranty. I think your lawyer will tell you that you are mistaken. When you advertise two products together, to be used together, they have to work together. Now, what would you like to do?"

An amazing thing happened, now that we had put a lawyer on the phone. The technician apologized. Then she transferred me to someone else. The someone else apologized. She offered to take care of the problem. I said fine, but that I was upset at all the time of Sandy's they had wasted in calls, on hold, and in unnecessary research. She apologized again. Then she offered some free software to make up for all this hassle.

I put Sandy back on the phone from here. I don't know exactly what deal Sandy worked out, but Sandy has smiled about it ever since.

WHY WOULDN'T YOU WANT A LAWYER?

Consider the following problems:

Lawyers are expensive.   You might spend more on the lawyer than you can possibly get back from the publisher—a significant risk with consumer-priced software. However, you may be able to get legal fees paid for, or you could split the fees with a large group of people. We will discuss cost controls later in this chapter.

Lack of technical knowledge.   Your lawyer might not fully understand or appreciate your problem. Clueless lawyers might not negotiate good deals.

Lack of sympathy.   An unsympathetic lawyer might give you bad advice.

Pressure.   Your lawyer might pressure you to accept a bad deal. Maybe she'll simply accept the deal for you and then tell you the result.

Shark.   Your lawyer might be a difficult and unpleasant person to work with.

Burning bridges.   If your lawyer acts too aggressively, the people you're negotiating with will come to hate you. This is OK if you'll never do business with them again. But, if you want to keep the computer or software they sold you, what will happen when you need help in the future?

All of these are genuine, serious problems. We will discuss them in more detail later in this chapter.

WHY WOULD YOU WANT A LAWYER?

"A lawyer who represents himself has a fool for a client." This saying applies just as well to nonlawyers who represent themselves. Even though he is an attorney, Kaner has hired other attorneys to represent him in legal matters. Sometimes, it makes a lot of sense to work this way.

During Negotiation

It's valuable to work with a lawyer during negotiation (while you're still arguing with the software publisher) if:

You find it hard to be firm and demanding.   When the publisher's technician refuses to take care of you.

You don't speak English well enough.   Or, you don't understand the culture well enough to be effective in negotiating.

The publisher is giving you the runaround.   The presence of a lawyer changes the negotiating environment. The fact that you have a lawyer tells the other side that you're serious and that the dispute has just gotten more expensive. At a cost of $100 to $400 per hour for its corporate defense lawyers, the publisher has a real incentive to settle your case quickly.

You aren't sure whether the law supports your case.   Your lawyer can research your legal claim, give you an opinion, and (if it will help you) write a letter to the publisher.

You want help.   If you think that a professional negotiator can achieve a better result than you can, seek help.

At the End of Negotiation

If you've given up on negotiating with this publisher and are about to sue, you might want to work with a lawyer in order to:

Issue a final warning.   Your lawyer can draft a final letter that is clear and legally precise, giving the publisher one last chance to see reason before seeing a lawsuit. When the publisher realizes you are ready to sue and that you have a lawyer to bring the suit, it may reconsider facing you in court.

Weigh your chance of winning.   A lawyer will walk through the legal details of your case and help you determine if your lawsuit is likely to win. The last thing you want to do is spend time and money on a losing lawsuit. Before you sue, ask yourself if it is wiser to drop the matter.

Estimate costs.   A lawyer can help you figure out how much time and work the lawsuit will cost you. Even if you are in the right, you might decide that the lawsuit will cost you far more than money and more grief than it is worth.

Help you figure out how to pay for the lawsuit.   Sometimes, you can force the publisher to pay for your attorney's fees. You want to know if and how you can accomplish this before bringing a suit. It might make the difference between you deciding whether to sue or to stop after doing your best with the consumer protection agencies (see Chapter 6, "Consumer Protection Agencies").

During the Lawsuit

You can take your case to court, from start to finish, on your own. Nolo Press publishes excellent books on this. You can also get recommendations on books specific to your area from your local court's clerk or from your county's Bar Association. The Bar probably offers reduced-rate services for those who qualify. This service operates differently from county to county, but if you call the Bar Association, they can tell you who to talk to, or what other organization to call.

In a Small Claims Court, you will probably have to represent yourself (though in some states, the publisher will be able to send its lawyer to represent it.)

---

[1]In California, Municipal Court is the court that hears cases in which the plaintiff demands less than $25,000. This is the first step up from Small Claims Court. Larger cases go to Superior Court. Different States name their courts differently.

The rules are very informal in a Small Claims Court, but they are much more formal in a Municipal Court[1] trial. To handle a regular court trial (a trial in a court more formal than Small Claims), you have to learn:

- Which Statute of Limitations sets a time limit on when you can file a lawsuit. If you file too late, you lose your claim.

- How to file your case.

- How to state your case, in a *complaint* (the document that says what you're suit is about), in a way that convinces the judge that your suit is not frivolous and should not be thrown out of court.

- How to do discovery (get evidence from the publisher) and how to force the publisher to give you critical evidence that it doesn't want to give up. And, how to resist unreasonable demands for information the publisher might make of you. (For example, what if the publisher demands your mental health records? What legal arguments do you have to put forward in order to say, "No"?)

- Local court rules that might require you to take some steps to negotiate in good faith or impose consequences if you turn down a reasonable offer. (For example, if the jury gives you less than the publisher's best offer, you might have to pay some of the publisher's legal fees.)

- How to research the law of your case. Remember that laws relating to computers are in flux right now. You may have to convince the judge that you are citing the most up-to-date legal cases.

- How to explain the law of your case to a judge.

- How to collect evidence that can be used in court and how to present that evidence in court.

- How to ask questions of witnesses during a trial (and before trial, in depositions) and how to resist the publisher's lawyer's attempts to improperly question witnesses or to interfere with your questioning.

- How to explain the facts of your case to a judge or jury.

- How to explain the money issues to the judge or jury (how much should they give you, and why).

- How to ask for extra money for attorney's fees or for penalties if the publisher's lawyer engages in misconduct that costs you time or money.

This is complex stuff. Neither of us would want to go into a court without a lawyer.

Arbitration proceedings are usually less formal than standard courtrooms but more formal than Small Claims Court. Procedural rules exist for arbitration and for getting evidence and calling witnesses. The more you know, the more you can do. The publisher will send its lawyer and that lawyer will know the rules. You should think carefully before going into an arbitration on your own.

How Can You Pay for a Lawyer?

A fundamental aspect of the lawyer/client relationship is that the lawyer looks out for your interests. The lawyer is required to protect your interests, even if it is inconvenient or costly for her.

Unfortunately, when it comes to attorney's fees, there is a fundamental conflict of interest between your needs and the lawyer's. You want to keep your money. The lawyer wants, and might be entitled to, some of it.

ALWAYS GET A FEE AGREEMENT

When you retain a lawyer, you should understand how she will be paid. Make sure it is spelled out, precisely, in a written fee agreement with the lawyer. You should be given a fee agreement at the start of your work with the lawyer. You should not authorize the lawyer to do work for you until you have read, signed, and returned the agreement. If you find anything puzzling, question-able, or objectionable in the agreement, you should ask the lawyer to explain it. You should feel free to take the agreement home, without signing it, and to have it reviewed by another lawyer. If the lawyer with whom you are talking gives you any hassle about contract review, don't hire that lawyer.

Some lawyers don't like to lay out their policies in written fee agreements—a big mistake. This practice creates too much risk of misunderstanding or of deliberate misrepresentation of the terms under which the lawyer has agreed to represent you. This is no good for you, and it is no good for the honest lawyer. As James F. Towery, a recent President of the California State Bar said during a course on fee arbitration, "Any lawyer who doesn't use a written fee agreement is insane."

Another point to keep in mind when talking with the lawyer about your fee agreement: Do you have to pay for the time that the lawyer spends drafting and explaining the fee agreement?

Don't be afraid to ask the question: "Do I have to pay for this time?"

You can reasonably and courteously argue against paying for time the lawyer spends explaining the fee agreement and drafting modifications. After all, the lawyer isn't representing you at this point, she is representing herself while she sells you a service. If the lawyer's standard fee agreement has strange terms, or if the agreement is so full of legalese that no sane human would want to be able to understand it, it serves the lawyer right if she has to spend time explaining the thing to you. Why should you have to pay for this?

Listen carefully to what the lawyer says. She has a point of view and a policy. If you're getting deep discount rates already, or if the lawyer is giving you a reasonable contract and you're asking for changes that are very unusual, then maybe she has every right to charge for the time she has to spend on the fee agreement. If you are unreasonable, the lawyer might (and should) refuse to take your case.

HOW DO YOU PAY THE LAWYER?

In the United States, the standard rule is that the people on each side of a dispute pay for their own lawyers. This is unfortunate in consumer protection cases because no individual customer has lost much money in the first place. A relatively simple lawsuit can cost $20,000 in lawyer's fees and expenses. Obviously, it would be crazy to spend $20,000 just to recover $100.

Unfortunately, when companies know that no one can afford to fight them, many will be tempted to lie about their products and to refuse to negotiate reasonably with dissatisfied customers.[2] Even if these companies eventually go out of business, they cheat a lot of people in the process, and they are likely to kill honest competitors in the process.[3]

There's little benefit to society in shielding the worst companies from their customers. Therefore, consumer protection advocates strive to make it easier for the government to prosecute cheating companies and for cheated customers to sue them. If one of the key barriers is the cost of the lawsuit, we have to look for ways to make the lawsuit cost less.

Your most promising means to control legal costs are based on *fee-shifting* or on *class action lawsuits*. We'll explain these first, followed by the more traditional approaches to legal fees.

Fee Shifting: The Publisher Pays for Your Lawyer

Several consumer protection statutes will make a company pay your attorney's fees if you win a case against that company for fraud, false advertising, or other unfair or deceptive trade practices. These are called *fee-shifting statutes*.

---

[2]Yes, yes, some companies will always try to do what it takes to make their customers happy. We've worked for some of those companies. We like companies like that. But, in this book, we're talking about all those other companies.

[3]Why do honest competitors go out of business? Think about it. Suppose that Company A is honest, and Company X is not. Company A's products have to work well, but X's products don't, so X can sell them for lower prices. Eventually, people will stop buying from Company X, but if A loses enough business to X, then A will be gone by the time X is gone. Many of the best companies in the software industry have disappeared over the years. We mourn their loss and are not comforted by the fact that their garbageware competitors eventually died (or are now dying) too.

These statutes differ from state to state. We listed some of them at www .badsoftware.com. Several others exist. Ask your lawyer (or the lawyer you are interviewing) what fee-shifting statutes might apply to your case.

Fee-shifting statutes turn the tables on a publisher that refuses to negotiate with its customers. Defense tactics that are designed to stall and to drive the plaintiff's costs through the roof are turned against the defendant in these cases. All the money the plaintiff wastes on lawyers gets charged back to the defendant.

Some lawyers specialize in handling consumer protection cases that are covered by fee-shifting statutes. At the moment, few of these lawyers know much about computer-related law, but they might be your best bet for strong representation.

Class Action: Spreading the Fee across Thousands of Lawsuits

In a class action lawsuit, several hundred or several thousand customers join together in one lawsuit. The trial focuses on what happened to a few specific customers, who represent the class (everyone else). The result of the trial (or the settlement reached before trial) applies to the entire class.

Over the years, procedural requirements for class action suits have gotten much more difficult and expensive. The lawyers who represent the plaintiffs (the customers, called the class members in these suits) in one of these cases might have to spend hundreds of thousands or millions of dollars before trial on advertisements and notification letters and extensive expert testimony. No one will reimburse these expenses if the case is lost. The law firm is thus betting its own money, and lots of it, on the success of the suit.

After they've worked on a case for a long time and spent a fortune on it, the lawyers handling a class action case might come to feel that it's their own case. The result is often an unsatisfactory settlement. We're not going to name cases here, but you've probably heard of a case or two in which the lawyers collected large fees and the plaintiffs got discount coupons to buy more products from the company that cheated them. Such a deal.

Because of the obvious potential for a conflict of interest between the class lawyers and the class members, the judge presiding over the class action suit is required to scrutinize any settlement agreement in a class action lawsuit, to make sure that it is fair to the class. If you are a member of a class, and you see (or receive) a notice of a proposed settlement that seems ridiculous, approach a lawyer of your own and ask her to represent you to protest the settlement. If your objection is sound and easy to explain/understand, you should be able to find a competent lawyer who will agree to look to the class settlement fund, and not to you, for payment for your representation.

Free Services (Pro Bono Representation)

A good deal, if you can get it. Lawyers do a lot of work *pro bono publico* ("for the public good"), but it may be difficult to find a lawyer to take your particular case on a pro bono basis. Your chances are better if your case involves a matter of broad public interest, that would interest the press or that could settle a hotly disputed legal issue. If you think that you have a case that could warrant pro bono interest, call your county's Bar Association and ask for advice on finding lawyers who might work with you. If there is a law school near you, call them, too.

Flat Rate: You Pay a Standard Amount

Flat rate is a common way of setting legal fees for a well-defined task that can be handled in a predictable amount of time. For example (these rates vary widely), it might cost $100 for a simple will, $500 for a simple divorce, or $1,000 for a green card. A lawyer might charge you a flat rate to write a letter or review a complaint, but you're not likely to get full representation at a flat rate in a defective software case. The issues are too complex and too new.

Hourly Billing: You Pay by the Hour

You pay for the lawyer's services by the hour. The lawyer will probably also charge you for the time of her support staff (such as secretary, paralegal, or clerk) at a lower rate. The more time the lawyer spends on your case, the more she makes.

Contingent Fee: You Pay a Percentage If You Win

You pay a percentage of what you receive. You pay only if you win the case or reach a settlement. The percentages vary. Perhaps, you will pay 33 percent if you settle with the publisher before trial and 40 percent (or more) if the case actually goes to trial. If you're trying to collect $100 or $1,000, it won't make sense to a lawyer to agree to a contingent fee. There won't be enough money to pay the lawyer for her work.

Mixed Fee: Alternative Methods

A fee agreement can combine several payment methods. For example, the agreement might say that:

- If a judge awards attorney's fees (makes the publisher pay), then the lawyer will accept the amount specified by the judge.

- If the judge doesn't award fees, the lawyer will accept a fee of 33 percent or an hourly rate of $150 per hour, which ever is greater.

You have to read the mixed fee agreement carefully. Get help if you need it. Figure out the worst case—if everything goes wrong, and you pay the highest possible fee, how much will that be? If the lawyer helps you figure this out, and gives you examples, have her write the examples down and attach them to the fee agreement.

ADDITIONAL ISSUES

Fee agreements have technical, tedious details that normal humans will want to skip over when reading a contract. But, you would be wise to pay attention to them when you review a fee agreement, rather than being surprised by them later.

One issue to pay particular attention to in your fee agreement is its treatment of fee-shifting. Fee-shifting—getting the publisher to pay your legal bills—is your best bet for being able to afford a lawyer. Here are some questions to consider:

- How should your agreement handle situations in which the publisher agrees (during negotiations) to pay your legal fees?

- What if the judge awards you payment of legal fees but less than your attorney is billing you? Will you have to pay your attorney the difference?

- Another issue in your fee agreement involves "costs," such as photocopying. How are these handled in your agreement?

Negotiating (with the Publisher) for Attorney's Fees

Fee-shifting statutes can complicate settlement negotiations. The problem is that the lawyer's fees quickly become larger than the small amount of money that you and the publisher are arguing about.

Judges only award attorney's fees at the end of trials. There is no law that says that your lawyer is entitled to a fee from the publisher if you settle out of court. If the lawyer isn'tvery careful to protect herself in the fee agreement, you can settle the case in a way that costs the lawyer all or almost all of her fees.

The lawyer will protect herself by putting clauses in your fee agreement that can make you responsible for her fees on an hourly basis. Some clauses are OK, and others are dangerous. You must read yours carefully, before you sign the agreement.

Let's illustrate the problem with an example.

Example: A Lawyer's Fees

Suppose that you bought a program for $100. It didn't work. You wanted a refund. The publisher's support line put you on hold forever, and no one answered your letters. Eventually, furious, you went to a lawyer. You signed a fee agreement with the lawyer that included the following provisions:

- The lawyer will seek her fees under a fee-shifting statute that applies directly to your case.

- The lawyer is entitled to one-third of your recovery. This probably isn't worth much, but if a jury awards punitive damages, maybe this will be a big number. Any money that she collects from the publisher, because of fee shifting, will be subtracted from this third of your total award.

Your lawyer haggled and argued and sniffled and spit at the publisher's lawyer; after she spent months (200 lawyer hours) of work, the publisher's lawyer finally made an offer. He would give you $1,000.00 to settle your claim.

Let's see how this works out:

- If you accept this offer, you will get two-thirds of the $1,000, or $667.00. This amount is more than six times what you were originally asking for. It will make you happy. Your lawyer, however, will only get $333.00, about $1.67 per hour.

- If you reject the offer and go to trial, maybe you'll win $300 (some consumer protection statutes give plaintiffs "triple damages" so you collect $300 for a $100 lawsuit). Your lawyer will collect attorney's fees at a rate of $150.00 per hour, earning $30,000 for the 200 hours spent so far plus perhaps $10,000 more for the time spent in trial.

You will do better under the first offer, but your lawyer will do much better at trial.

Can you accept the first offer and then pay the lawyer just $333.00? Yes! This is your lawsuit, not the lawyer's, so you can agree to whatever settlement you want. There is nothing in the fee agreement that says that you have to pay the lawyer more than 33 percent ($333), so that's all that you owe. This type of situation has come up several times; courts side with the client. A lawyer who wants to ensure that she is appropriately paid must put all of her terms in the fee agreement. If she doesn't, she loses.

So how can the lawyer fix the fee agreement?

The simplest way to fix this agreement is the wrong way. In this case, the lawyer just adds a clause saying that she is entitled to $150.00 per hour for her work, which she will try to collect from the publisher. If she works for 200 hours, she is entitled to $30,000. If the publisher doesn't give her this fee, you have to. Obviously, you can't afford this. Your lawyer might explain that she will only ask you for the hourly fee if you try to settle the case early, in a way that freezes her out of any fee recovery. You must get this in writing, or you risk facing a surprisingly big bill.

A better agreement might look more like this:

- If the case goes to trial, the lawyer will accept whatever the court awards as attorney's fees under the fee-shifting statute or a one-third contingent fee, whichever is greater.

- If you settle the case before trial, the attorney is entitled to a fee of $150 per hour for time she has spent on your case.

The attorney is guaranteed $150 per hour if you settle the case before trial. The settlement negotiations change because of this. If the publisher offers $1,000 (after your lawyer spends 200 hours on the case), you have to reject the offer because it won't cover your lawyer's fee. If a fee-shifting statute is applicable, the publisher will change its offer because it knows that it will have to pay your lawyer at some point, and her fee will be even larger by the end of a trial.

Suppose that the publisher's next offer is $25,000. This is still less than the lawyer is entitled to under your fee agreement, but it's a lot closer. Ask your lawyer if she is willing to reduce her fee so that you get $300 (what you would win in court), and she gets the rest. If she says yes, ask her to put this in writing. Now you can accept the offer without having any further responsibility to the lawyer.

Discretionary Awards of Attorney's Fees

Here's another complication with fee-shifting statutes. The statute might state that

- The judge "shall" (which means, "must") award attorney's fees to you if you win your case. If so, then at the end of the trial, the judge will ask your lawyer for detailed billing-related records. The judge will award a fee that he considers reasonable, which might be less than your lawyer has requested.

- The judge "may" (which means, "doesn't have to") award the fees. Even if you have a great case, the judge might refuse to award attorney fees. The refusal to award fees could have more to do with the judge's politics than with the justice of your case or the work of your lawyer.

The publisher has to pay whatever the judge awards. But, what if the judge awards nothing or less than your lawyer has asked for? What does your fee agreement say about this? Do you owe her the difference between her normal fee and the amount awarded by the judge?

Dealing with Costs in Fee Agreements

Most fee agreements say that you will pay for costs on top of the attorney's fees. These costs include fees charged by the court, plus costs of photocopying, expert witnesses, travel expenses, and so on. Some law firms charge for standard office expenses that other firms would not consider charging as costs. Therefore, it is wise to ask for a list of the things that the attorney can charge as costs.

The next task is to determine when costs are calculated. Here's an example that illustrates the problem.

- You are awarded $100,000.

- Costs total $50,000.

- The lawyer is entitled to a 25 percent contingent fee. How do you calculate the fee? There are two ways:

  - Subtract the costs first and then give the lawyer 25 percent of what's left. In this case, the lawyer gets 25 percent of $50,000, or $12,500. You get $37,500.

  - Pay the lawyer first and then subtract costs. The lawyer gets 25 percent of $100,000 ($25,000). You get $75,000, then pay $50,000 in costs, and so you keep only $25,000.

> **Note**
> You may be required to pay for costs even if the lawyer is handling your case on a pro bono basis. In the typical pro bono case, the lawyer will give you her time for free but will expect reimbursement for actual expenses. In every type of agreement, whether services are pro bono, flat fee, contingent, or something else, be clear on what expenses (if any) you will have to pay.

> **Caution**
> You might be required to pay the other side's lawyer. Some contracts specify that in the event of a lawsuit, the losing side will pay the other side's legal fees. If you see a clause like this in your software license, talk with your lawyer about it and ask her to appraise your risks.

Can You Limit Expenses by Doing Some of the Work?

You may not want or may not be able to afford someone to handle every aspect of your case from start to finish. You might be able to save money by doing some or most of the work yourself.

A lawyer provides:

- Knowledge of the law.
- Knowledge of local court procedures and of the individuals (attorneys, judges, clerks) in the local legal community.
- Ability to command respect as your advocate.
- Ability to give you negotiating advice or to handle a negotiation on her own.
- Ability to represent you in court.

You may decide that you don't need some of these services and that you would rather do some of the work yourself, to save money. To make this possible, you have to make a basic decision. Are you representing yourself and asking for some limited legal consulting from the lawyer, or are you retaining a lawyer to represent you? Consider the differences in the following sections.

YOU REPRESENT YOURSELF; THE LAWYER IS A CONSULTANT

We'll talk more about money in the next section ("How You Can Pay for a Lawyer"). Here, we'll just note that in the consulting situation, it is unlikely that you will be able to work out a contingent fee agreement. You will probably pay the lawyer by the hour, whether you win or lose.

The lawyer's responsibility to you will be limited to the specific tasks that you ask her to perform. The lawyer will (or should) want those limits precisely spelled out, in writing. Her concern is that if you do something foolish, that she would never have done, she doesn't want to face a lawsuit for malpractice. Don't take this personally. All professions have a malpractice-lawsuit problem. Many malpractice lawsuits are fully justified, but some are absolutely unfair or just plain crazy. Making the agreements clear is a good way, fair to both sides, to avoid misunderstandings, to make sure that the attorney doesn't do (and charge for) more or less than you requested, and to prevent crazy lawsuits.

Here are examples of the types of services that you might contract for:

Basic legal research.   What laws apply to your case? What are the relevant Statutes of Limitation? What are some of the main recent court cases? We've provided some of that information in this book, but the law is changing rapidly, and some of the rules will have changed by the time you start reading this book.

You can expect your lawyer to have a background in contract law, consumer fraud, and so on, but very few lawyers have expertise in computer law, let alone consumer-related computer law. It will take your lawyer time to do this research. At the end, you should expect an opinion letter or an essay (a *brief*) that explains the current state of the law.

Research guidance.   If you know your way around a law library (or can learn), you might ask the lawyer for advice on what to look for. You might also have the lawyer look over what you found, to tell you whether anything obvious is missing.

Note the difference between the two cases:

*   *In the first case, you retain the lawyer to do a complete legal task (write an opinion letter or a research paper).* As with all legal services, you are entitled to expect the lawyer to do the research competently. If serious problems exist with the legal quality of the work, you are entitled to a partial or complete refund of your fees, and you might be able to recover additional damages if the bad work caused you additional harm (such as causing you to lose the lawsuit).

*   *In the second case, you aren't paying the lawyer to take the time to do the research.* Therefore, when you ask her if you have everything that you need, she won't know what she doesn't know, and so she can't know whether you have found all of the important material. If you do the research, it is your responsibility, not the lawyer's, to do the research well.

A letter.   The lawyer writes a letter to the publisher, on her firm's letterhead, explaining your position and demanding remedies on your behalf.

*   *There are subtleties to this letter.* If you retain a lawyer to represent you, she will probably write demand letters. But, that's not what's happening here. In this case, you have gone to a lawyer and said, "Will you write one letter for me?" Your agreement covers just this one letter. The lawyer has not agreed (and may have refused) to handle the entire case. Consider carefully what you want in this letter. For example, you might not want this letter to threaten a lawsuit. If the company calls your bluff, you'll have to find a lawyer (this one hasn't agreed to do it) to handle your suit.

Review your complaint.   The complaint is the document you file with the court to start the lawsuit. You might want a lawyer to read the complaint and any other document that you will file with the court, before you submit it.

THE LAWYER REPRESENTS YOU;
YOU DO SOME OF THE WORK

You can still save the lawyer some time (and save yourself some money) by doing some of the work yourself, but now your work is done under the lawyer's supervision.

When the lawyer represents you, she is responsible for making sure that the case as a whole is handled competently and thoroughly. You make the final decisions about the results (you have to approve any settlement, for example), but the lawyer will make all or most of the final decisions about tactics (such as, when to temporarily cut off negotiations) and all of the decisions about legal issues (such as, in which court to file the case or what legal arguments to use in briefs and in court).

You have room for negotiation on how the case will be handled, but there is a limit. Any lawyer knows that you can sue her for malpractice and file complaints against her with your State Bar Association if she handles your case incompetently or dishonestly. A good lawyer will be absolutely unwilling to do anything that she considers illegal, unethical, embarrassingly stupid, or otherwise likely to create a risk that some part of the case will not be handled competently (that is, handled as well as one would expect from an average lawyer). There are risks and shortcuts that she, as your representative in this case, will not be willing to take, even if you are.

Few people are trained in legal research, legal procedure, or legal argument. Lawyers are naturally cautious about assigning tasks to clients. What happens if you try very hard, but you still don't do a good job, just because you don't have the training (and can't get it soon enough). Whenever a lawyer assigns a task to a client, she has to ask herself, "What happens if this person screws this up?" If the lawyer rejects a client's work and redoes it, how insulted will the client be?

If you want to work actively on your case, you should say so when you retain the lawyer. Ask her how she feels about that, before you decide whether to retain her. As your case progresses, ask your lawyer whether there's anything she wants you to do.

Here are examples of things you might be able to do:

Gather evidence.   For many types of evidence, you'll be faster and better at this than the lawyer. Here are a few examples:

- You need receipts, notes on your phone calls to the company, and any printouts or screenshots showing the kinds of problems that you've been having.

- You can dig through the manual and all the advertisements to find examples of false claims about the product.

- To prove that many people are having the same problem, check CompuServe's and AOL's support forums, check the news groups on the Internet, look for Web pages that talk about your product, and look on the company's BBS. Look for customer complaints and the company's responses. Look for admissions ("Oh, yes, we know about that already") and look for lies, such as 25 responses by the same person about the same problem, to 25 different customers, that all say "Gee, we've never heard of that one before."

- Look for newspaper reports of problems with this product.

- The lawyer might suggest other tasks. The more you can do (if you can do it well), the less time your lawyer has to spend (saving you money).

Library legal research.   If you know your way around the law library, you could save your lawyer time by digging up and photocopying several court cases. You are helping the lawyer doing the research. The lawyer does most of the thinking, while you do the legwork. The lawyer might give very specific instructions, such as naming the specific cases that she wants you to look up and photocopy.

Other research.   Your lawyer might want to talk to experts about the program. For example, suppose that you buy software that does small-business accounting. Your lawyer might want to talk to an expert on software development or software quality and to an expert on small-business accounting. These experts might be able to help the lawyer (and later, a jury) decide whether the program is truly terrible or just of average mediocrity. Your lawyer might insist (Kaner says, "As the lawyer, I would always insist") on making the final decision about which experts to talk to or use at trial, but if you have computer experience or accounting experience, you might be able to help the lawyer quickly find, check the background of, and screen potential experts.

Office work.   Typing memos, running errands, and photocopying, will not save much of the lawyer's time, but the time of legal secretaries and paralegals is fairly expensive too.

Maybe there are other tasks that you can do. Talk with your lawyer about the possibilities. But, make sure of one thing: if you agree to do a task, do it as well as you can and promptly. If your lawyer can't count on you to finish tasks on time, she won't give you many tasks.

HOW DO YOU INTERVIEW AND HIRE A LAWYER?

Many lawyers will let you meet with them for a free or low-priced initial consultation. You and the lawyer have different objectives during this meeting. You have to decide whether to retain her, and she has to decide whether to accept you as a client.

Here are some suggestions for your initial meeting:

Come prepared.   This first interview is important. It can also be intimidating. You can help yourself get the information you need by writing out a list of questions that you'd like the lawyer to answer. Ask her the questions on your list. Also, come to the meeting with a written summary of your case, if you can. Lay it out historically. When did you buy the software, and where? When did you first use it? When did you find problems? What were they? When did you complain or call for support? What happened? Did you ask for a refund? When? What happened? Bring the program with you. Bring the manuals and any other books or documentation that you have.

Keep originals.   Even though you will bring documents (receipts, letters, and so on), you should not give the lawyer the originals of anything. Give her photocopies. Keep your originals in a safe place.

Ask questions.   You will have to give the lawyer a quick summary of your problem but don't spend all (or even most) of your time talking. You want to learn whether this lawyer has the necessary skills and experience to achieve a good result for you, and you want to know whether you can trust her, understand her, and get along with her. If not, you need a different lawyer.

Ask for clarification.   If the lawyer speaks in legalese, and you don't understand her, ask her to explain what she's saying. If she won't explain, or she makes you feel like a dummy, get a different lawyer.

Ask whether she has handled cases like yours before.   Ask her to describe them. She may describe computer cases or consumer protection cases. Not many lawyers have handled computer-related consumer protection cases, so don't be surprised if this one hasn't either. If she's not an expert, does she admit it? Ask her how she will gain the additional knowledge that she needs. You are entitled to answers to questions like these. If the lawyer doesn't treat your questions with respect during the initial interview, it's not likely to get any better in the future. Find a different lawyer.

Don't confuse caution with ignorance.   Good lawyers often express themselves carefully and cautiously. The current state of computer law is in dispute. At some point, judges will make rulings and tell us what the law really is. Until then, all a lawyer can say is that she predicts that a court would rule this way or that way given the facts of your situation. When the law is in dispute, you cannot find a lawyer who will always be right. What you can find is a lawyer who knows the difference between legal issues that are settled and issues that are still in the air.

Don't be confused or intimidated by appearances.   Some lawyers have to invest a fortune in lavish furniture and prestigious office locations in order to impress corporate clients. That's nice, but remember that they have to make a lot of money from their clients to pay the rent. Lawyers who represent individuals instead of businesses are usually less wealthy. First-rate consumer protection lawyers may work out of offices that seem shabby.

Research her history.   Before you interview a lawyer, call your State Bar Association and ask whether there have been any disciplinary actions taken against the lawyer. Some states make this information very easy to get for free. If other clients have filed complaints about the lawyer, ask her about them. She might not be able to give you details (she is required to protect the secrets of her clients, even clients that have fired her and complained about her), but you can still gain an insight into her attitudes about dealing with difficult clients.

Ask the lawyer for a copy of her standard fee agreement.   Don't sign it until you read it. Seriously think about taking the agreement. You don't have to sign it on the same day that you get the agreement. A fee agreement is a significant legal document that might involve a lot of money. Any decent lawyer will tell you to carefully review legal documents before signing them and that includes the lawyer's fee agreement.

Here are some things to understand about how the lawyer handles this meeting:

She has to decide whether you have a reasonable case.   If you are asking her to handle your case on a contingent-fee basis or under a fee-shifting statute, then you are asking the lawyer to bet her time and money on your case. If you lose, she doesn't get paid.

She has to get a lot of information quickly.   Experienced lawyers often conduct interviews at a very fast pace. Don't be surprised by a series of fast, direct questions. Just make sure that you have time to ask your questions, too. If you're going to be paying the lawyer by the hour, and she offers a half-hour of free consultation, don't let her take the entire time with her questions. Stop her after a few minutes and ask whether she'll extend the time so that you can ask her questions, too.

She has to decide whether she can work with you.   Are you going to exaggerate or mislead her? Are you going to argue with her about every decision?

She will want to know whether you have used other lawyers before. How did you get along with them? If there were problems, she'll want to know why. She's trying to figure out whether the two of you can get along.

She might misunderstand your attitude.   She may think that you know more about the law than you do or that you know less and care less about the legal issues. Don't be offended, just be clear. Ask for explanations if you need them.

Be realistic. If your case doesn't involve much money, there's a fair chance that you'll end up with a new lawyer, or a law student, or someone who is trying to gain experience in this area of the law. Maybe this isn't so terrible. If your case doesn't involve much money, and the publisher is already refusing to cooperate with you, you don'thave a lot to lose. Being able to get along with the lawyer might be much more important than her experience.

Read the fee agreement carefully to make sure that you don't have a lot to lose. Pay particular attention to costs. Costs can mount up, even if the lawyer has agreed not to charge you for her time. For example, some law firms charge 50 cents per page for photocopying. For a small consumer protection case, costs like these are probably not affordable.

How Should You Supervise Your Lawyer?

This is your case, not your lawyer's. You have to supervise her, or you may not get the results you want. Keep the following points in mind.

Settlement offers.   You are entitled to hear every offer the publisher makes to settle the case. Your lawyer can advise you not to accept a bad offer, but the final decision is yours. The lawyer should tell you about every offer—you shouldn't have to call and nag the lawyer for status information.

Communication.   You are entitled to communication from your lawyer. The lawyer must return your phone calls, for example. In some states (like California), the lawyer is required by law to return your calls. In other states, failure to communicate is a breach of the lawyer's code of ethics. Breaches of the code of ethics are serious. You can complain about them to your State Bar Association. We'll have more to say about complaints to the State Bar Association shortly.

Documents.   Ask your lawyer to send you copies of all documents that she prepares in your case (all letters, for example).

Don't nag.   There is no point in nagging your lawyer. Don't call for status reports every day. Things won't change that quickly, and the lawyer will feel that you are wasting her time.

Schedule.   Your case will proceed on a schedule. The lawyer will negotiate with the publisher's lawyer for a while and then file a complaint in court. After that, the publisher and your lawyer will have to file other documents by deadlines that are published by the court. There will also be hearings in court, scheduled by the judge before the trial. And, there will be witness interviews. Ask your lawyer to tell you what the schedule is for these and ask her for progress as each schedule date passes. The schedule will change many times. This is normal.

Estimate.   Ask for an initial estimate of the costs of your case. Ask your lawyer what role you can play in keeping costs down.

Regular statements.   If your fee agreement requires you to pay the lawyer by the hour, ask for a statement every month. The statement should show how long the lawyer worked, each day, and a quick summary of what was done.

There are several excellent books that talk about lawyer-client relations, such as the ones listed at the start of this chapter. However, we have a concern about books like these, including this chapter. It is easy to take away the wrong message. We *are* telling you that you don't have to put up with someone who is rude and arrogant, but we are *not* suggesting that you treat the lawyer rudely or without respect. Be nice. Be firm if you have to, but be nice. This person will represent your interests in some complex negotiations and hearings (perhaps including a trial). Lawyers are used to abuse from other lawyers, and most lawyers do get used to dealing with clients that they don't like, but lawyers are human. They do have feelings. If they feel like you're going to give them attitude every time they talk with you, they're going to want to avoid your case, and they're going to want to avoid you. That makes them harder to supervise and less likely to win.

It is difficult to change lawyers mid-case. Not impossible. But, it can be difficult to find a second good lawyer, who is willing to take a small case. It can be very difficult to find a third lawyer or a fourth lawyer. You should fire a lawyer who is representing you badly, but your goal as the lawyer's supervisor is to keep your lawyer, to make her successful, and not to give her a hard time.

How Do You Fire Your Lawyer?

If the lawyer is rude to you and is mishandling your case, talk with her. If you decide that she is not going to finish your case well, consider firing her.

Before you decide to fire a lawyer, talk to another lawyer about your case. You might be able to get a free interview, or you might have to pay for the lawyer's time. Here are some things to keep in mind:

Your lawyer might be doing a good job.   Even if she seems rude to you, your lawyer might be doing a good job. Many lawyers, especially trial lawyers, eventually develop a hard shell because they are forced to argue with people all day, every day. You should try to focus on your lawyer's performance—what was she supposed to do in your case; is it getting done; and how do the results look?

Be specific.   In your discussion with this new lawyer, don't make a bunch of broad statements like "This lawyer was a real jerk." These statements don't add much information. But, they do begin to convince the second lawyer that you are hard to work with. The second lawyer probably won't take your case if you just broadly complain about the first lawyer. Instead, be specific. What was the lawyer supposed to do? What actually happened? Why are you unhappy?

Complain privately.   Complain to another lawyer, who you meet for this purpose. Don't complain to your friends. If you talk with your friends about your talks with your lawyer, you can lose your right to the privacy of your conversations with your lawyer. This can be very damaging to your case.

Define your purpose.   Decide in advance what you are trying to understand in the interview. Do you need to know whether your lawyer is doing an acceptable job? Do you need advice on how to fire the lawyer and find a new one? Are you looking for this second lawyer to become your new lawyer?

When you fire your lawyer, you have certain rights, and she has certain rights.

Dismissal.   You have a right to fire her. Period. This is your case, not hers.

Files.   You have a right to your file, including all of the documents you gave her. They are your property. In most states, your lawyer cannot keep your documents even if you haven't paid her. She has to give them back. She is entitled to keep them for a reasonable time (maybe a few days) to make photocopies for her files. That's all. If you have a problem with files being returned, call your State Bar Association.

Notes.   You probably have a right to all of her notes, witness interviews, and so on. You certainly have this right if you have already paid the lawyer for her time. In some states, you have the right to get this material even if you haven't yet paid the lawyer. If you have any questions about this, call your State Bar Association.

Payment.   She has a right to be paid for her time, unless you fired her "for cause." She gets paid on the basis of the value of her work to this point and might get paid by the hour. If she did a terrible job and you believe that she deserves nothing, talk with your next lawyer about this. Maybe she will waive (forget about) her fee. Maybe you will have to file a complaint with the Bar Association to make her forget her fee.

Delayed payment.   If your case involves a contingent fee or a fee-shifting statute, then you might not have to pay the fired lawyer anything until and unless you collect money in a settlement or at the end of the trial.

Caution.   If you fired Lawyer #1 simply because you didn't like her, then she does have a right to be paid for her time. When you bring in Lawyer #2, he will be entitled to payment as well. If you fire Lawyer #2 and hire Lawyer #3, then you're going to pay fees to three lawyers. This adds up. In a fee-shifting case, the judge probably won't award extra money just because you've gone through a bunch of lawyers, so this might cost you money out of your own pocket.

The breakdown of a relationship with a lawyer can pose a lot of difficult problems. Call your State Bar Association for help if you have trouble firing a lawyer. In most states, the Bar has plenty of information and power. In California, for example, there is a State Bar Court that can suspend lawyers' licenses, fine them, disbar them, and punish them in other ways. Many lawyers in California fear and dislike the California State Bar's disciplinary staff more than the IRS.[4]

---

[4]California's lawyers recently voted to keep the State Bar in its current form, which includes the harsh disciplinary team. The majority of us, Kaner included, believe strongly that there is great value to the profession in having strong enforcement of professional ethical rules. In response, our Republican Governor (Wilson) has vetoed funding (which we pay as Bar dues) for the State Bar. Our disciplinary system might be badly damaged, but please don't blame the shambles on the state's lawyers. We support a strong system, and we will rebuild it.

When you call the Bar, explain the nature of your dispute (your lawyer isn't returning your calls, won't give you your documents, is demanding too much money, and so on) without going into all the underlying details. Don't reveal private details about your case. Ask what your options are. Ask whether they have any brochures that explain your rights in your state. Ask whether they have complaint forms. Be courteous and clear, and you could get a wealth of information.

You can usually find your State Bar Association's phone number in your local phone book. In case there's a problem, though, we provide a table of contact information at www.badsoftware.com.

Action Plan

At this point, you're in the midst of a legalistic approach to your dispute with the publisher. Think carefully about what you want to achieve, before you spend far too much time and money on a fight that escalates simply because you've started launching lawyers at the opposition.

What do you want?

- A simple settlement of your dispute?

- A more complex, negotiated settlement of a larger claim?

- Legal action against this publisher that will stop it from cheating people ever again?

- A trial, because there's no other way to make progress? (Is the trial worth it?)

Chapter 10 discusses the small claims court trial.

Chapter 11, "Safe Shopping," discusses ways to shop more effectively next time, so that you'll only have to read these legal chapters again for entertainment or to help your friends.

Chapter 10
Small Claims Court

Chapter Map
Overview
If you've decided to sue the publisher, your best option may be to sue in Small Claims Court. This chapter looks briefly at some pros and cons, as well as risks of suing in Small Claims Court, and provides some suggestions specific to software.

Further Reading
Anyone who sues in Small Claims Court should read Ralph Warner's (1997) classic book, *Everybody's Guide To Small Claims Court.* Individual states also publish useful material. For example, California's Department of Consumer Affairs offers *Using the Small Claims Court: A Handbook for Plaintiffs and Defendants* (quite a good book) for free, *Collecting Your Small Claims Judgment* (a 78-page manual) for $7.90, and *The Consumer Law Sourcebook for Small Claims Court Judicial Officers*, a 3-volume set for $65. State publications like these are increasingly available for free download on government agency Web sites.

What Is Small Claims Court?

Small Claims Court handles small civil lawsuits. The largest suit allowable varies from state to state. In your state, it is probably between $1,000 and $15,000. If you want to sue for more than the Small Claims Court maximum, you have to sue in a different type of court. You can sometimes split a larger lawsuit into smaller pieces and bring a separate suit for each, but get advice before trying this. You might destroy your case if you split it improperly.

Small Claims Court is usually run informally. In most states, lawyers aren't allowed to represent either the plaintiff or the defendant. In most (or all) states, the judge will listen to all evidence, even to evidence that would be ruled inadmissible in a more formal court—the judge understands that you're not a lawyer and that you don't know the legal rules of evidence.

Should You Sue in Small Claims Court?

Think first about whether you should sue anywhere. Lawsuits aren't a lot of fun. They are tricky, demanding, and often frustrating. Remember the gypsy curse, "May you be involved in a lawsuit in which you know you are right." You could be much better off settling with the publisher for less than the full amount you believe you're entitled to than to sue for the works.

But, if you are going to sue, and the amount in dispute is less than the maximum amount you can obtain in Small Claims Court, then this court offers benefits and risks.

On the positive side, in many states, plaintiffs win the majority of suits brought to Small Claims Court. Wins are possible without much expense and without a lawyer. The trial is fast, and the waiting period before trial is usually much shorter than the waits for trials in higher courts. The filing fees and other court-related costs are relatively inexpensive (relative to the higher courts).

On the risk side, your rights to discovery are very limited rights in a Small Claims action. (Discovery is the legally supervised gathering of information.) Why do discovery? Because discovery lets you get documents from the publisher that help you prove your case. You can get these in higher courts but not necessarily in Small Claims Court. Further, you have to represent yourself. You have to gather evidence and present your case to the judge. For some people, this is very challenging work.

Consumers' success in Small Claims Court varies across states. Repeat players (like large corporations) can have a big advantage if the court has surprising or highly formalized procedures. Companies also have a huge advantage if they are allowed to send an attorney (as in New York).

Should You Get Help?

Small Claims Court's style is informal, but it is a court of law. You must follow whatever procedural rules the court has established. (Procedural rules specify mechanics of the lawsuit.) The business that you're suing has probably gotten legal advice over this suit, and it may oppose your suit with well-coached legal arguments. Your legal arguments have to make sense, and they have to be persuasive to a judge.

The first people to turn to for help are your friends. (If you don't have any, go make some. They're a lot cheaper than lawyers.) Your friends can read the letters before you send them and the documents that you prepare for the judge. Ask them: Does what I've written make sense? Do I sound reasonable? They can also visit the court with you before your trial to see how it works, and they can compare notes with you. If you're going to make a brief statement to the judge, you can practice in front of them. Get help from your friends.

You might also be able to get free advice from a government agency. Many counties run an advisory service to coach people for Small Claims Court lawsuits. These services are often designed to help you understand the court's procedures, but many advisors are willing to read over your documents and help you organize your case. Call the Small Claims Court in your county and ask them to refer you to an advisory service.

Finally, it might be worth your while to spend an hour or two with a lawyer. The lawyer can review your case with you and suggest things you should read, documents or other evidence you should bring to court, and arguments that might be particularly effective with the judge.

What Is Your Case?

You're not a lawyer, and the judge knows that. You aren't going to have to make precise legal arguments to get the judge to understand the justice of your case. But, the judge will be trying to fit what you say into a legal framework. You can help him a lot by being aware of the main legal issues that the judge will have to consider. Review Chapter 7, "Software Quality and the Law," for some of the legal issues.

The trick in court lies in tying facts to the issues, in a way that the judge can understand. We take a quick look at the breach of contract lawsuit in order to illustrate this.

Example: Breach of Contract Lawsuit

If you sue the publisher because the software is defective, you could argue that the publisher has breached its contract with you and that it has breached an implied warranty.

A case for breach of contract is based on broken promises. The seller or the publisher promised you something about the product, and the product didn't live up to that promise. You find these promises in advertisements, in the manual, on the box, help screens, and in statements that salespeople made to you, face to face. To convince the judge that there has been a breach of contract, you should show the judge the promise and then show him how the promise was broken. What exactly does the program do, or not do, that is wrong?

But, suppose that you buy a program that has a bug that erases your hard disk. You wouldn't expect a product to run wild and erase your hard disk, so you probably didn't raise or discuss this when you bought the program. Nowhere does the manual promise that the program doesn't erase hard disks. The box doesn't say "safe for your hard disk." No salesman ever reassured you that your hard disk could trust this program. You might not be able to point anywhere and say, "Here! This is the promise that was broken." This is why products come with *implied warranties*.

The implied warranty of merchantability is a promise that the Uniform Commercial Code writes into almost every sales contract. It says that this product is reasonably fit for normal use. A program that accidentally erases your hard disk is not fit for normal use and so the law says that the contract has been broken, even though there is no specific promise that you can quote.

To convince the judge that the implied warranty has been breached, you should show the judge the ways in which the program doesn't work. You might present serious individual bugs or you might show that the program is so infested with fleas (little bugs) that it is unusable, even if no individual bug is disastrous. Bring witnesses and letters that explain just how unusable the program is.

The publisher's major defense against an implied warranty argument might be to claim that there is no implied warranty because the publisher successfully disclaimed it. If so, you'll have to provide the judge with evidence that counters this claim. For example, it will strengthen your case if you show that you couldn't see the disclaimer (the publisher's denial that there was any warranty) until after you bought and opened the product. It will also strengthen your case if you can show that your product is a "consumer good" under the Magnuson Moss Warranty Improvement Act. Show that it is not unusual for people to use this product for personal, family, or household use and that you have in fact used it that way yourself. For example, if you bought a project management program to use in your work, don't forget to mention that you also used it to plan one of your parties at home.

How to Write the Demand Letter

A well-written demand letter makes it clear to the publisher (or the retailer) that you have a good case and that you mean business. Many cases are settled shortly after the defendant receives a well-written demand letter.

The most important thing to keep in mind as you write the demand letter is that, even though you've addressed it to the publisher and will deliver it to the publisher, it's really a letter from you to the judge. If you do file a suit in Small Claims Court, the judge will read this letter carefully.

You should achieve five objectives in the demand letter:

1. **Lay out your case in a clear, organized way.**   At the end of reading your letter, a reader should feel that you have a strong argument and that you deserve to get what you're asking for.

2. **State clearly what you are asking for.**   Don't ask for more than you think you can reasonably get.

3. **Show that you are a reasonable person.**   Your tone must be factual and polite. Avoid threats and insults.

4. **Preserve your credibility.**   Everything in the letter must be true. No exaggerations—not even as part of a joke.

5. **Make it clear that this is a *letter of demand*.**   This letter is the last stop before the lawsuit. (Some states require that you send such a letter before filing a small claims suit.) Don't be rude or threatening but be clear about what you expect to get paid.

Exhibit 10.1 illustrates such a letter. You can compare this letter to the sample letters for consumer protection agencies (based on the same hypothetical situation) in Chapter 6, "Consumer Protection Agencies."

Exhibit 10.1: Sample Letter of Demand

{Your Address}
{Date}

Brand X Corp.   Letter Of Demand
123 X Lane
Anytown, USA 12345

I purchased the Brand X Electronic Mail Program, Version 6.02c, on July 15, 1998. I bought it directly from Brand X and paid $248.22. I demand a refund of the purchase price, plus reimbursement of $22 for telephone bills, for a total of $260.22.

According to your advertisement in the June 15 issue of {name of magazine}, version 6.02c had been upgraded to provide support for BinHex encoding. This feature allows the program to read more documents that come attached to electronic mail messages than it did before. I bought the program specifically to take advantage of this feature. Unfortunately, I have been unable to make the BinHex feature work.

On July 24, 1998, I called your company for help. I called long distance. Your staff left me on hold for 28 minutes. Finally, I spoke to a person who called himself Joe X, who said he was a Technical Support Representative.

He said that BinHex worked perfectly, so there must be something wrong with my computer. No one else was having this problem, he said.

On July 25, I logged onto CompuServe and looked at the messages that were being posted about Brand X mail. There were 57 complaints that BinHex wasn't working, dating back to May 1, 1998. In a message dated May 15, 1998, two months before my call, a person who signed his posting as Joe X said that he worked for Brand X as a Technical Support Representative. He acknowledged that there was a problem but said customers should be patient while Brand X fixed it. There was no follow-up announcement of a fix.

On July 26, I called Brand X again and, after waiting on hold for 20 minutes, spoke with Joe X. He said, yes, he had posted that message on CompuServe, but the problem affected only a few weird computers, like mine. I asked him why he hadn't told me this the last time we talked, and he started shouting at me. Then he hung up.

The two telephone calls to Brand X technical support cost $22. I wasted 14 hours trying to get this program working, many of them after Joe X told me that BinHex was working.

Copies of my receipts are enclosed.

All of my expenses would have been avoided if your program had worked or if you had advertised the feature in a way that would have allowed me, and many other customers, to realize that this program would not work correctly on our systems.

I will be glad to return my copy of the software to you—please let me know where to send it when you send my refund.

If you would like to discuss this further, you can reach me at 415-555-5555.

Please respond by {two weeks from now}, or I will take this matter further.

Yours truly

Enclosures

Copy of the receipt for the program.
Copy of the telephone bill
Copy of the advertisement

Warner (1997) provides several other examples of demand letters along with good advice on how to write them.

Warner recommends that you conclude by telling the publisher to respond by a given date or you will sue it in Small Claims Court. Our letter is less specific. We say, please respond by a given date, or we "will take this matter further." This gives you a little more flexibility—it lets you change your mind and do something else (complain to the BBB, for example) instead of filing a lawsuit.

Where Do You Get Evidence?

Chapters 3 and 4 will help you gather evidence for your case.

Chapter 3, "Preparing to Make the Call," explains ways to get information about the program, about what is wrong with the program, about the publisher's discussion and explanation of the problems you're having, and about the rest of the user community's reactions to the program. Chapter 3 focuses on obtaining information you can use to get better support. But, you can use the same approaches to help prove that:

- The program failed to work as promised.

- The program had defects (crashed, for example) or misbehaved in ways that violate reasonable expectations, even though they don't conflict with documentation.

- The publisher knew that the program was defective, or the publisher was on notice (had been told) that the program was defective.

- The publisher's staff denied knowledge that the program was defective even after they had been repeatedly informed of the problem.

- The publisher's staff didn't make a fair effort to help you.

- The publisher made promises to you when you called to complain and didn't keep its promises.

We have a few recommendations that are specific to gathering evidence:

- Whenever you see anything on the Net that might be useful as evidence, print it. Tomorrow, it might be gone.

- If someone complains about the company in a posting on the Net, send them an e-mail and ask for more information. Their sworn statements can carry weight in court.

- Small Claims Court judges will often accept letters as evidence, especially if the letter writer swears, in the letter, that everything in that letter is true. It can be useful to get letters from other people who have had similar problems with this publisher.

- Your sworn testimony is evidence. Your sworn statement that someone said something to you is evidence that they said it.

- Your contemporaneous notes (notes made at the time that the event happened, such as notes made during a technical support call) are usually given more weight as evidence than a simple, unsupported statement.

- If you filed a complaint with a consumer protection agency that attempted to mediate your dispute with the publisher, and if the publisher refused to cooperate, the mediator may be willing to testify in court or write a letter describing her experience with the publisher.

- If you bought the program at a store, the salesperson might be willing to testify on your behalf. Sometimes salespeople learn about serious problems in the software and call the publisher themselves to ask when the next version will be available.

- Make sure to document any blameworthy conduct on the part of the publisher.

Chapter 4, "Knowing What to Ask For," gives you suggestions about how to calculate and explain your losses—all of them. If you can prove that you lost a lot of money because of the program, you might be able to get some of it back. Even if you don't recover all of the money, the judge may be more sympathetic about your case if he realizes that you spent 75 hours of your own time dealing with its defects, spent $1,500 getting help from your local computer guru, and lost a total of $1,000 in other ways. The total losses could convince the judge that for your uses, the program really is unsatisfactory.

Forum Selection Clauses

Several shrink-wrapped software licenses contain a forum selection clause. This clause says that you can sue the publisher only in its home state or in some other place, far, far away. Don't let these clauses discourage you. Consumer protection laws in your state might preserve your right to sue at home, if you bought the software in your own state.

We discussed forum selection clauses at length in the Drafting Committee meetings for Article 2B, the proposed amendment to the Uniform Commercial Code (discussed in the Appendix, "A New Threat to Customers' Rights: Proposed Revisions to the Uniform Commercial Code [Article 2B]). Article 2B will extend the enforceability of forum selection clauses. A claim repeatedly made by attorneys during those meetings has been that, in their state, Small Claims Court judges refuse to enforce forum selection clauses when those clauses would force a consumer to travel to an out-of-state court.

At court, we suggest that you argue that it is unreasonable and unfair to expect you to spend hundreds or thousands of dollars in travel expenses just to collect a few hundred dollars. The publisher is accepting the benefit of your state's laws when it sells products in your state. The publisher sells plenty of products in your state. (The more evidence you have of this, the better.) So, it is fair to require the publisher to defend itself in your state.

If you see a forum selection clause in your license, call your Small Claims Court and ask how to find out whether the clause is enforceable. They might recommend a local consumer protection agency that can advise you, and that agency might know the answer. Consider discussing the clause with an attorney.

Other Preparatory Tips?

Warner (1997) offers several excellent pieces of advice, and we suggest that you read his book to get that advice. Here are a few points that we want to stress.

We strongly recommend that you attend a session or two of Small Claims Court before the day of your trial. Get there early. Watch what happens over the next few hours. If you're not too shy, introduce yourself to the bailiff (the person who says, "Everybody please rise" when the judge comes into the room) and to other courtroom staff. Tell them that you're there to watch because you've never been to Small Claims Court before and you've got a trial coming up soon. Ask them if they have any advice about what to do on the day of the trial. Smile. Be friendly. If they're on duty on the day of your trial, you'll have a friendly face or two in the courtroom.

We also recommend that you make an outline of your case that simply lists your key points. Make a list of your exhibits (your pieces of evidence) as well. Bring two extra copies of the outline, of the evidence list, and of each piece of evidence. At an appropriate time during the trial, you'll give a copy to your opponent and a copy to the judge.

Organize your evidence so that it is easy to find. You can put loose pages inside page protectors and then into a binder.

If you plan to show the judge a specific page of the manual, photocopy that page and put it in your binder. Give the photocopy to the judge and to your opponent but have the original manual handy in case the judge wants to see it.

Finally, get a good sleep the night before the trial.

What If the Publisher Offers to Settle?

If you've filed a Small Claims Court suit, don't dismiss it (don't sign a form that terminates the suit) when the publisher agrees to settle the case. Wait until the publisher has paid you everything that you're owed.

If you make a settlement agreement with the publisher just before the trial (or on the day of the trial), bring it to court and ask the judge to enter a judgment for the agreed amount.

How to Collect Your Judgment?

Even if you win your case, you might not get paid. Some states don't provide simple, efficient procedures for collecting Small Claims Court judgments. Here are some suggestions:

Get advice from the court.   When you win, ask the judge how to collect your judgment. He's probably too busy to give you detailed advice at trial, but he can give you a brochure, recommend a book, or give you a phone number to call. If the judge isn't helpful (not all of them are), ask the court clerk or the bailiff.

File a negative credit report.   If the publisher won't pay you, file a report with a credit reporting agency. Be precise. State that you won a lawsuit against the publisher, that the court ordered a judgment in the amount of $X and that the publisher has not paid despite repeated requests. The last thing that a potential lender wants to discover is that a potential borrower doesn't make court-ordered payments. It makes them nervous. Investors don't like this type of conduct either.

Publish reports on the Internet.   If the publisher won't pay you, complain on the Internet. Stick to the facts and keep the report short and simple. State that you bought a defective product from the publisher, that the publisher didn't take care of you, and that you eventually had to sue. You won the suit. The court ordered the publisher to pay you; you've asked for the money; and the publisher still hasn't given it to you. Don't forget magazine publishers' Web sites. Columnists (such as Ed Foster, at www.infoworld.com) are interested in this type of news because it is factual; the case is proved; and the failure to pay seems utterly irresponsible. It makes a good story.

If you've won your case, the law is most definitely on your side. Don't be discouraged if the legal system isn't always efficient for a small claim. Be creative.

Action Plan
If you haven't read all of the relevant material in Chapter 7, "Software Quality and the Law," read it now. (It's time to read the footnotes.) Talk with your friends about your case. Can you win it?

If you decide to file suit, you have to decide whether to sue in Small Claims Court or in a more formal court. Get a book on Small Claims Court. If an advisory service is available in your county, get advice from the government on how to run your suit. Ask them:

- How often do consumers win their cases in Small Claims Court?

- What is the procedure for filing a case in Small Claims Court?

- If the shrink-wrapped license does contain a forum selection clause, do your state's consumer protection laws protect your right to sue in your own state?

- What is the procedure for compelling witnesses (such as corporate employees) to appear in court?

- What is the procedure for requiring the publisher to produce documents before trial or at trial? What can you request and how can you do it?

- How will the court help you collect a judgment if you win your case?

Most lawsuits settle, and many of these settle on the day of trial. Think about what you're willing to accept as a compromise so that you'll know what you'll settle for when you negotiate with the publisher.

Chapter 11
Safe Shopping

 Chapter Map
Overview
There are ways to improve your chances of getting better software, better support, and—the next time you buy bad software—a much better bargaining position.

This chapter reviews general suggestions for safer shopping and then looks specifically at software purchasing.

Giving advice on software shopping is more complicated than we'd like because the laws are in a state of flux. Our expectation, based on the progress of draft legislation that we've evaluated and/or worked on, is that the laws will keep changing through 2002, maybe even beyond that. We point to trends and traps in the new legislation.

Recommended Readings
Garman (1996) is an excellent college survey text on consumer issues, including safe shopping.

The U.S. government publishes the *Consumer's Resource Handbook*. Get the latest edition at www.pueblo.gsa.gov. This book, and material that you can get for free from many state and county departments of Consumer Affairs or Consumer Protection (see Chapter 6) provide many useful tips and alerts. You can reach many of these other agencies via Consumer World at www.consumerworld.org/pages/agencies.htm. We also recommend the National Consumer Law Center's site, www.consumerlaw.org and the National Fraud Information Center, at www.fraud.org.

At this writing (mid 1998), there are no readable consumer-sensitive books on the laws governing electronic commerce. We suggest that you check our Web site, www.badsoftware.com. This site supplements this book and collects several of our publications on software-related revisions to the Uniform Commercial Code, electronic commerce, and customer rights provided by current law.

Better Luck Next Time

Buying bad software is no fun, and it's even less fun getting bad support.

You can shop more effectively, to improve your chances of getting better software and better support. Also, you can do some things while shopping that will put you in a much better bargaining position if you do buy a turkey masquerading as a software product.

We start with a list of the tips that you will often see in government publications on consumer protection. This is good advice that applies to most types of products. From there, we'll consider several issues that are more specific to computer law.

Good Common Advice

These tips are derived mainly from the *Consumer's Resource Handbook*, Friedman (1998) and several pamphlets published by various local, state, and federal agencies. Some are based on our experience (both of us have retail sales management experience). Some of the sales tactics that we mention are more common to computers, stereos, and appliances than to software, but no one ever said you couldn't teach a new dog (software) old tricks.

Shop with a friend; complain with a friend.   It's often handy to have a witness.

Make the seller aware of your requirements.   You can talk with the salesperson whether you shop in person or by telephone. If you're shopping electronically, ask questions by e-mail before you buy. If you have a specific requirement, tell the salesperson and ask whether the product that you're discussing meets that requirement. If he says, "yes," he's given you an express warranty and/or an implied warranty of fitness for a specific purpose.

Get it in writing.   After they've made the sale, some people will forget or deny what they told you. But, while they're trying to make a sale, it's amazing what some people will sign. For example, while doing research for this book, one of us bought a new printer:

- I was doing a massive amount of printing, dumping thousands of pages of court cases, industry gossip, complaints, test plans, and drafts of this book. I pushed my indestructible LaserJet 2P so hard that it broke down twice. I gave it to my mother and went shopping for an even sturdier replacement.

- At the store, the salesperson described one printer as indestructible. I said, "Yes, yes, it's an HP. But, can I see the warranty and the specs? What is the duty cycle?" (The duty cycle is the number of pages per month that the printer is warranted to be able to handle.) The salesperson said that he didn't have a copy of the warranty, and he was unwilling to open a box to let me see one. As to the duty cycle, he said that LaserJets could handle anything. I told this enthusiastic fellow that I wanted to print up to 20,000–30,000 pages per month and asked him to check with his manager about this.

- The manager wouldn't let me see the warranty or the documentation. He assured me that this number of pages would be no problem. I said, "Fine, I'll tell you what we'll do. I'll buy the printer and a four-year extended warranty if you'll give me your business card and sign on the receipt that the printer can handle this kind of load." He was delighted to do this.

- The actual duty cycle listed in the printer's manual is 10,000 pages, but that's OK. If the printer wears out, I'll just take it back to the store and make a claim against the extended warranty. Maybe the manufacturer would tell me that I've overused the printer, but this store made a stronger claim, and because I got it in writing from one of their managers, they'll be accountable for it.

Walk out or hang up on high-pressure sales tactics.   Salespeople sometimes use high-pressure tactics to push merchandise that won't sell any other way. Don't be pressured to buy anything. Don't fall for the tactic that gets you to agree to a deal one tiny piece at a time, leaving you what feels like no room to back away. You can back away. And, make sure that you can get a refund if it turns out that this product doesn't match your needs.

It is never rude to take your time to decide to make a purchase.   Even if you only give yourself a few minutes, walk out of the store and think before you pay your money in a high-pressure situation. If you like the salesperson you're dealing with, ask the salesperson if he's on commission. Ask for his name so that you can give him credit when (if) you buy the product. After you've left, call a competitor and see whether they can match or beat the price.

More pressure tactics.   If the salesperson hangs around and hangs around while you shop, he's wasting his own time. Don't feel guilty and buy something just because he's spent time with you (unless you asked him to). If prices or other key information about products are kept off the display, making you ask a salesperson for basic information, don't feel that you have to buy something from him because you asked him to spend time with you.

Beware of special deals.   Don't rush into a large purchase because the price is "only good today." Be cautious about unexpected claims that you are special (such as, you are entitled to a special deal because you are the 1,000th customer this year.) And, if the salesperson is really, really friendly, it is probably because the price is really, really high (at least, in comparison to a fair price) or the program is really, really broken. In many companies (storefront and telemarketing), salespeople get "spiffs" (additional commission) for selling hard-to-sell items. For a big enough spiff, we could make anyone feel special.

Beware of price guarantees. The store advertises that they will match any competitor's price on the Brand X Model 100. The only problem is, this is the only company that sells the Model 100. Brand X sells something very similar to the Model 100 to other companies, so you see the Model 99 at one store and the Model 101 at another one. But, you'll never find a Model 100 anywhere at a lower price. Check the reasonableness of the price you're about to pay. Don't rely on the price guarantee.

It's not unreasonable to ask for a different salesperson. If you're not getting answers to your questions, or if you don't trust what you hear, ask to speak to someone else (such as the manager). This works well in person, in the store, and in e-mail. If you don't like the next person, or if you can't speak to someone else, well, you've learned something important about this business. They probably won't be any nicer to you after they've got your money.

When you find a knowledgeable salesperson, cherish him. Few software retailers pay their staff well enough to keep the good ones for long. When you find someone good, treat him well. Customer appreciation is often the biggest payback for competent retail staff who stick around.

Don't sign anything that you don't understand. If you need it, get advice before you sign a lease for a new computer or before you sign a complex license agreement for a $5,000 program that you'll use to run your small business.

Take advantage of sales but compare prices. Don't assume that an item is a bargain just because it is advertised as one.

Beware of a seller who wants to send a courier to pick up your check. This is a common indicator of fraud. This seller is willing to spend a lot of money on a courier to get your money before you see what's being sold.

Look for signs that specify a store's return policy. If the store posts a no-refund policy, then you probably don't have a right to a refund for nondefective merchandise. (However, you probably do have a right to return defective merchandise. See Chapter 1, "Read This First.")

Handle rebates with care. Most people don't claim rebates on products. It's an interesting advertising tactic. You buy the product expecting to claim the rebate but then discover that it's a pain in the neck or that you're missing something that you need. Or, you fill out the form slightly wrong and don't get your money. One of us got a letter (to his post office box) saying that the rebate couldn't be sent to him because he hadn't filled in his mailing address (presumably meaning, street address). It's usually cheaper to deny your request than to send you the money. Read the rebate offer carefully before making the purchase so that you're familiar with special requirements, such as the expiration date (oops, it's too late) or the need for a label that is supposed to be on the box (but often isn't). Don't send the original receipt, send a photocopy. Keep a copy of the form that you send in requesting a rebate and note the date that you mailed it on the form.

Check the seller or the product.   Contact the *Better Business Bureau* (BBB),or the *National Fraud Information Center* (NFIC) (1-800-876-7060), or your county or state consumer protection office for any complaint recorded against the company. Request any consumer information they may have on the product that you're thinking of purchasing. Few of these agencies have much on software companies yet, but they're getting more information every day.

Shopping By Mail

Only deal with reputable companies.   Don't trust the company just because it has a pretty brochure, a slick Web site, or a big ad in a computer magazine. Check up on it. Call the magazine and ask how many years this company has been advertising. Call the BBB or NFIC. Make a small purchase at first. Try larger ones after you've had a good experience.

Use your credit card to pay for the merchandise.   You have the right to dispute your bill if you order merchandise and don't receive it. Your credit card company will help you if you get ripped off by a fly-by-night mail order firm.

Don't pay by check.   By the time you realize that you're having a problem with the product, your check has been cashed. It's easy to put a hold on a credit card payment. It's hard to get your money back once the seller has it, especially from a crooked company.

Get them to mail it to you, using the postal service.   There's a big benefit to the U.S. Mails over courier services (UPS, Fed Ex, etc.). You can go to the postal inspectors for help. Check the Postal Inspection service's Web site for its discussion of mail fraud, www.usps.gov/websites/depart/inspect/ statutes.htm:

> *Mail fraud is a criminal scheme where the postal system is used to obtain money or anything of value from a victim by offering a product, service, or investment opportunity that does not live up to its claims. To obtain a mail fraud conviction, a prosecutor must prove (1) the facts surrounding the offer were intentionally misrepresented and (2) the U.S. Mail was relied on to carry out the scheme.*

If the merchandise doesn't arrive when you expect it, contact the company immediately.   The company is required to deliver merchandise within 30 days (unless you and they agree to some other time) or to notify you if they're going to be late. If they're going to be late, you're entitled to cancel the order. If they're going to be more than 30 days late, then they have to get your permission to fill the order. Timeliness is important here. If the merchant charges your card and then doesn't fill your order for 90 days, it might be too late to dispute the charge with your credit card company. (See the FTC's mail order rules at United States Federal Trade Commission, 1995.)

Look for a 30–90 day satisfaction guarantee. Local superstores often don't provide the support, service, or refund policy that the best mail order houses provide. Many mail order houses offer unconditional money back guarantees. Why buy from anyone who doesn't?

Ask if there are charges if you return the product. Who pays for shipping? Is there a restocking fee? Ask if it makes a difference whether you return the product because (a) you don't like it or (b) you don't agree to the warranty terms or (c) there's a defect.

Be aware of extra charges. Such as delivery fees, service charges, and additional charges for using your credit card. A great price can turn out to be a very high price after you factor in the extra charges.

Don't trust offers that seem unbelievably cheap. You might get pirated copies of the software,or nothing, or outdated versions of the software.

- When a publisher makes an in-line fix (an unpublicized minor upgrade) to the program from Version 2.01 to 2.02, what do you think happens to the 2.01's remaining in the warehouse? The answer varies a lot, partially depending on how serious the problems were in 2.01. If the publisher considers the 2.01's unsalable at regular price, it might dump these in bulk to warehouse stores or discount mail order sellers. These are very attractive for a discount reseller because the products look identical to the most current versions offered at full price.

Always keep a copy of the order form or advertisement. Especially if the advertisement is the order form (the company expects you not to keep a copy).

Check the merchandise immediately when you receive it. Check to be sure that you got what you ordered (no substitutions and no missing components).

Shopping for Software

Here are suggestions that are specific for software. You might use these when shopping in person, by mail, or electronically.

Create a list of your computer's specifications. This list would include the make and model of your computer, video card, sound card, and so on. You can use this list as a little pocket guide when you go shopping or when you order software by phone. The idea is to match your list against the system requirements of the software that you are thinking of buying. In case of doubt, ask a salesperson to check the match between your list and the software. If you don't know your computer's specifications, ask a computer-savvy friend to make a list for you.

Check the packaging for statements about the hardware and software that the program is compatible with.   You are likely to find detailed statements. For example, the Software Publishers Association Software Packaging SIG (1995) advises publishers to specify the operating system and version number, the memory requirements in a way that includes total memory required (including operating system overhead), the video cards and video resolutions supported, the CD-ROM speed requirements, the amount of available space on the hard disk, the audio sound cards supported, and other comparable information (such as printers supported). If your system meets these specifications, the program should work on it. If your system doesn't meet these specs, you'll probably need to upgrade to use this program.

Look for evaluation copies.   Many companies will let you use their software for a short period (perhaps 30 or 90 days) before you pay for it. The software probably automatically disables itself at the end of the trial period. This is a great way to shop. Try the product. If you don't like it, try something else. Don't pay unless you get something worth buying.

Download first, pay later.   At some sites, you pay for the software and then get to download it. If there is a transmission error or if the file is corrupted in some other way, then you have to call the publisher or reseller to ask for a refund or for another copy (and then hope that the reload of the new copy works). At other sites, you download the software first and then pay for a code to unlock it. If there's a transmission error, you try again. You don't pay for the code until you get a good copy downloaded. We think that this is a much more desirable way to buy software.

Check the publisher's Web site.   A good Web site will tell you what is the most recent version of the product (you don't want to buy an outdated one from the store or mail order shop). It will tell you (or you can ask by e-mail) how to tell the version of the product. The site might tell you the product specs, known defects or performance limits, the warranty details and service policy for the product, and how (and when) to reach their support staff.

Check the technical support section on the publisher's Web page.
Several publishers provide support materials at their Web sites, including lists or discussions of known bugs and configuration problems. Can you live with these problems? (If not, don't buy the software.) Can you understand the materials? (If not, don't expect to be able to understand them later.) Are the materials there? (If not, maybe you won't get great support later. Perhaps you should call the publisher and ask them about this.)

E-mail the publisher with a presale technical question before you buy the software.   Tell them that you're thinking about buying the program, but you need to know the answer to this question first. Usually, you'll get an answer quickly. Publishers want to sell their software. If you don't get an answer, or if you get a long-delayed answer, or if you get a runaround, or if you don't understand the answer, then you can make a good guess about how support will be after the sale. The support is probably better before the sale (when the publisher is still looking for your money) than after (when the publisher has already collected it.)

Check electronic sources for information about the publisher and the products. You might like to know, for example, whether a publisher provides good support or how well a specific product performs on a machine like yours. You might find this out by looking at the Web sites of computer magazines (summaries of customer surveys) or by posting a query to a USENET news group, CompuServe forum, or one of the increasingly common Web-based discussion groups. Explain what kind of product you're looking for and ask participants for their opinions. Explain what you want to do with the product and ask them how well they think this product will do the job. In Chapter 4's section, "Gather Information That Backs Up What You Have To Say," we've provided additional suggestions of other useful information to gather about the publisher and the product.

Ask to see the warranty. If a product is often used for personal, family, or household use, it is a consumer product and is covered by the Magnuson-Moss Warranty Improvement Act. You see this Act at work when you buy home appliances or stereo equipment. In most stores, it is very easy to look at the warranty before you buy the product. It should be just as easy for software and for any other consumer product costing more than $15.00. As the Software Publishers Association's contracting guidebook (Smedinghoff, 1993, p. 88) puts it, "It is reasonable to assume that software purchased for home computer use would be covered by the [Magnuson Moss] Act."

Surprisingly, many software sellers (and many computer sellers) are unaware of the Act or have decided to ignore it. We reprint the relevant part of the Code of Federal Regulations at the end of this chapter so that you can photocopy them and bring them to the store. You have a right to see the warranty even if the only way the retailer can do this for you is to open the package and let you inspect it.

By the way, suppose that you ask to see the warranty before the sale, and the retailer refuses. If you then buy the product, get it home and hate it, this gives you another strong basis for demanding a refund.

How long is the warranty period? We've seen warranties as long as a year and as short as a few days. Ask before you buy.

You might still have an implied warranty. Getting a written warranty with the product might give you additional rights. If this is a product that you will sometimes use for personal, family, or household use, then your use of the product is covered by the Magnuson Moss Act.[1] When there's a written war-

---

[1]**Magnuson-Moss Act 2308(a)** No supplier may disclaim or modify (except as provided in subsection (b) of this section) any implied warranty to a consumer with respect to such consumer product if (1) such supplier makes any written warranty to the consumer with respect to such consumer Product, or (2) at the time of sale, or within 90 days thereafter, such supplier enters into a service contract with the consumer which applies to such consumer product.

ranty, the Act overrides the publisher's attempt to disclaim the implied warranties of merchantability and fitness for use.

Consider buying a service contract.   A service contract is like a warranty in that it entitles you to repair or maintenance for a period of time. The difference between them is that warranties are included in the price of the product; you pay separately for a service contract. Look back at the extract we printed from Section 2308(a) of the Magnuson Moss Act. If the Act applies to your product, and if you buy a service contract from the publisher of the software within 90 days of buying the software, then the implied warranties will probably last as long as the service contract.

Ask the publisher about the cost of support.   Some publishers provide telephone support for free for as long as you own the product. Some provide Web and e-mail support for free but charge for phone support. The ones who charge for phone support usually don't charge until 30 days, or 90 days, or a year has passed. Some start the clock running from the day you bought the product. Others don't start the clock until your first call for support. Support calls can be very expensive. Rates of $3 per minute or $30 per call are not unusual. For more technical products, we've seen rates of $90 per incident (the cost of one or several calls required to settle one problem.) Some publishers will waive the charge if you're calling about an actual defect in the product. Others will charge you even if they knew about the defect when they shipped the product. These details are probably not in the publisher's warranty. You might find them on the publisher's Web site, or you might get them from the publisher by e-mail. Get them. It can be valuable to get the rules clear and in writing, in advance. Otherwise, you might believe that a publisher has promised not to bill you when you call about defects, but then it bills you anyway. This is the core allegation of a class action suit filed against Compaq (Johnson v. Compaq, 1997).

Look through the manual before buying the program.   In Chapter 7, "Software Quality and the Law," we noted that in some states, statements of fact in the manual will be considered as express warranties whether you looked at the manual before buying the product or not. In other states, you will have a much stronger argument if you looked at the manual before the sale. You don't have to read everything in the manual. Just flip through it and note a

---

- Under the implied warranty of merchantability, the publisher guarantees that the product is fit for ordinary use and that it conforms to all statements of fact in the documentation and on the packaging. This is what you would normally expect when you buy any product, which is why it is implied into almost every sale as a matter of law.

- Even if the only written warranty that you can find is one that says that the disks are guaranteed non-defective for 90 days, you have a written warranty. From that, you can argue that you are protected against the warranty disclaimer. If you are buying a consumer software product, look for one with a written warranty.

few of the statements being made about the product. You probably won't remember in the future which particular statements you read, but that's OK. Everything in the book will probably be treated as part of the "basis of the bargain."

Look at the online help, if possible, before buying the program.   This suggestion addresses the same issue as our suggestion that you check the manual. Some stores will let you quickly look at the program on a computer at the store. While you're playing with the program, quickly look at the help that comes with it.

Look at books published by the software publisher, before buying the program.   Several publishers authorize special books about their products. They might publish the book through their own press or through a related press, or they might simply allow the author to use a title like, "The Authorized Guide to . . ." or "The Official Guide to. . ." You can make a good argument that all of these are collections of statements of fact made by the publisher/seller to the customer (you), just like the manual.

Read reviews and comparisons in more than one magazine.   Many magazines publish reviews of products. Many of these reviews are little more than slightly edited reprints of the publisher's press releases. Others are obviously biased. When several different magazines are published by the same publisher, they seem to us to have similar biases. Look for product comparisons in different magazines that are published by different companies. Also, realize that many comparative reviews are feature-crazy. Look carefully at the things that the reviewer praises in each program. You might sometimes be better served by a third-ranked product that has fewer features but is more reliable and easier to learn and use. Several of the leading magazines have Web sites. You can often access back issues and recent reviews at these sites.

Confirm with a purchase order.   If you live in the Seventh Circuit (Illinois, Indiana, and Wisconsin) or if you order software from a business in the Seventh circuit, we suggest that you follow up every mail-order purchase with a letter that confirms the order. The United States Court of Appeals for the Seventh Circuit is the court that decided the ProCD and Hill v. Gateway 2000 cases. It said that the Step-Saver decision was inapplicable because that case involved a conflict between the customer's purchase order and the seller's terms in the package. We don't think that this was the right reading of the UCC precedents, but why fight it when you can work around it? The letter should identify itself as a purchase order, give the date, an a confirmation of the price, item ordered, and quantity. Then include a section titled "Standard Terms and Conditions." Include whatever terms that you think are appropriate. Two that come to our minds right away are: "Disputes arising out of or in connection with this purchase may be tried in any court of competent jurisdiction in the

State of <your state here>." And "Seller's warranty of merchantability extends for at least one year from date of delivery of the software."[2]

After You Buy

Inspect the software as soon as you get it. Some people order upgrades but don't install them promptly on their computers. If the upgrade doesn't work, you won't have much basis to complain if you make your complaint months after receiving the software.

Protest quickly if there's a problem.   This is essential in order to preserve your warranty rights.

Keep your warranty, service contracts, extended warranties, and receipts in a safe place.   You will often have to provide a serial number or an extended warranty number to get free support.

Check your contract for any statement about cancellation rights. If there is a cancellation period, make your decision within that period.

If you're unhappy with the product, go back to Chapter 1, "Read This First."

Cautions When Shopping Electronically

Electronic commerce promises new opportunities and poses new challenges for consumers. In comparison to traditional retail and mail-order sales, there are great opportunities, such as:

- It's easier to do comparison shopping.

- Sellers might be able to do business for a lower cost per unit, in which cases prices will gradually drop.

- It's often easier to check a manufacturer's reputation and a product's capabilities.

- It's easier to contact consumer protection agencies.

---

[2] These terms don't necessarily become part of your agreement with the seller. After all, you are giving them to the seller after the sales agreement was made. But, if the court is willing to interpret the seller's post-sale terms as binding on you, these set up a conflict between your post-sale terms and the seller's post-sale terms. The net result should be that the conflicting terms knock each other out, and those aspects of the contract will be filled in by the default rules of the UCC (which supplies an implied warranty of merchantability). Confused? You aren't alone. In law school, this is one of the sets of legal rules that puzzles law students. For details, read White and Summers (1995) Volume 1's discussions of the "Battle of the Forms" and of UCC sections 2–207.

- It's easier for the software publisher to distribute (and let you try out) demo versions of software products.

There are also the usual scams, translated to the Internet. The Federal Trade Commission posts discussions of consumer fraud on the Net at www.ftc.gov. Here's an example that caught our attention:

Federal Trade Commission v. Hare (1998)

> *Online auctions are a new way to sell computers and software. What is to stop a company from conducting the actions and taking your money, without ever delivering the merchandise? The FTC filed a complaint against Craig Hare (Experienced Designed Computers), alleging that Hare conducted online auctions for computer equipment, accepted payment, and failed to deliver the merchandise. At the FTC's request, a federal court issued an injunction in the matter in April, 1998.*

It is easy for a con artist to create a professional-looking, respectable-looking Web site. You think that you're dealing with an established business, but you're just dealing with a facade, a phony front created by a crook. As a society, we haven't gotten skilled at recognizing these crooks yet.

Along with the fraud, we see problems with the legal rules that are being proposed to govern electronic commerce.[3] Some of the proposals are unfair to consumers.

Be careful about mistakes in filling in order forms. You can be held accountable for any orders that you make online. For example, it can be very easy to accidentally or erroneously submit a form more than once. If you accidentally order 10 copies of a program instead of one, and the publisher downloads the program to your computer 10 times, it can charge you for all 10. It is not clear whether the new laws will give you a right to a refund for the nine extras (perhaps after subtracting the seller's shipping costs). Some companies will do you a favor and give you the refund, but others won't. This will create incentives for customer-insensitive companies to create Web-based order forms that confuse you.

Never use an electronic agent. The agent is a computer program that does your shopping for you. What if you tell your agent to order you a DeskJet 340

---

[3] Kaner has been actively involved in the United States Department of State's Advisory Committee on Private International Law: Study Group on Electronic Commerce and as a participating observer at drafting committee meetings of the National Conference of Commissioners on Uniform State Laws (NCCUSL, a legislative drafting committee funded by the 50 state governments). The NCCUSL committees are drafting the Uniform Electronic Transactions Act, the Uniform Commercial Code Article 2 (Law of Sales), and the Uniform Commercial Code Article 2B, (Law of Licensing). We have both been active on Article 2B, which is a 200–250 page proposed amendment to the UCC that will cover all contracts for the development, sale, licensing, maintenance, and support of software and most contracts involving other types of information (such as books and cable TV). We say more about 2B in the appendix.

printer if the price is $199 or less? Suppose that the agent finds 100 sellers who give that price, and it (oops) orders one printer from each of them. Under the current proposals, you'd have to pay for each printer. You wouldn't even be able to return the 99 extra printers and repay the companies their shipping expenses, unless they let you. The irony here is that these proposals will allow the seller of the agent to disclaim responsibility for known bugs in the software. If your agent goes wild because of a bug that was known to the seller, the loss stays with you.

Never use a digital signature to order merchandise.   You might have obtained a "Digital ID" or a "Driver's License for the Information Superhighway" or some other software that promises to identify you to businesses that you deal with. Unfortunately, if someone fraudulently uses your digital ID, you might discover that you are drastically less well protected than you would have been if you'd used a credit card.[4]

Set the value of your digital ID to zero.   You might be able to get a digital ID that will identify you for some purposes but that you can specify has $0 purchasing authority. When you get a digital ID, ask the certificate authority to set the value of it to zero and to include this zero value in its certificate (the document from the certificate authority that says that you are who you are). This will let you use the digital ID for identification (which some companies may require) but won't let the ID be used for direct purchases.

Exhibit 11.1: FTC Regulations: Part 702 Pre-Sale Availability of Written Warranty Terms

Code of Federal Regulations, available at

www.access.gpo.gov/nara/cfr/index.html

Volume 16, Section:

702.1   Definitions.

702.2   Scope.

702.3   Pre-sale availability of written warranty terms.

> **Authority:** 15 U.S.C. 2302 and 2309.
> **Source:** 40 FR 60189, Dec. 31, 1975, unless otherwise noted.

---

[4] For more details, see Kaner (1998a) or Kaner, Lawrence, and Johnson (1998). Recent drafts of the Uniform Electronic Transactions Act have been revised and no longer pose this problem. However, other current and proposed state laws and proposed international laws still do.

Section 702.1 Definitions.

(a) *The Act* means the Magnuson-Moss Warranty Federal Trade Commission Improvement Act, 15 U.S.C. 2301, et seq.

(b) *Consumer product* means any tangible personal property which is distributed in commerce and which is normally used for personal, family, or household purposes (including any such property intended to be attached to or installed in any real property without regard to whether it is so attached or installed). Products which are purchased solely for commercial or industrial use are excluded solely for purposes of this part.

(c) *Written warranty* means-

(1) Any written affirmation of fact or written promise made in connection with the sale of a consumer product by a supplier to a buyer which relates to the nature of the material or workmanship and affirms or promises that such material or workmanship is defect free or will meet a specified level of performance over a specified period of time, or

(2) Any undertaking in writing in connection with the sale by a supplier of a consumer product to refund, repair, replace or take other remedial action with respect to such product in the event that such product fails to meet the specifications set forth in the undertaking, which written affirmation, promise, or undertaking becomes part of the basis of the bargain between a supplier and a buyer for purposes other than resale of such product.

(d) *Warrantor* means any supplier or other person who gives or offers to give a written warranty.

(e) *Seller* means any person who sells or offers for sale for purposes other than resale or use in the ordinary course of the buyer's business any consumer product.

(f) *Supplier* means any person engaged in the business of making a consumer product directly or indirectly available to consumers.

[40 FR 60189, Dec. 31, 1975, as amended at 52 FR 7574, Mar. 12, 1987]

Section 702.2 Scope.

The regulations in this part establish requirements for sellers and warrantors for making the terms of any written warranty on a consumer product available to the consumer prior to sale.

Section 702.3 Pre-Sale Availability of Written Warranty Terms.

The following requirements apply to consumer products actually costing the consumer more than $15.00:

(a) *Duties of seller.* Except as provided in paragraphs (c) through (d) of this section, the seller of a consumer product with a written warranty shall make a text of the warranty readily available for examination by the prospective buyer by:

(1) Displaying it in close proximity to the warranted product, or

(2) Furnishing it upon request prior to sale and placing signs reasonably calculated to elicit the prospective buyer's attention in prominent locations in the store or department advising such prospective buyers of the availability of warranties upon request.

(b) *Duties of the warrantor.*

(1) A warrantor who gives a written warranty warranting to a consumer a consumer product actually costing the consumer more than $15.00 shall:

(i) Provide sellers with warranty materials necessary for such sellers to comply with the requirements set forth in paragraph

(a) of this section, by the use of one or more by the following means:

(A) Providing a copy of the written warranty with every warranted consumer product; and/or

(B) Providing a tag, sign, sticker, label, decal or other attachment to the product, which contains the full text of the written warranty; and/or

(C) Printing on or otherwise attaching the text of the written warranty to the package, carton, or other container if that package, carton or other container is normally used for display purposes. If the warrantor elects this option a copy of the written warranty must also accompany the warranted product; and/or

(D) Providing a notice, sign, or poster disclosing the text of a consumer product warranty. If the warrantor elects this option, a copy of the written warranty must also accompany each warranted product.

(ii) Provide catalog, mail order, and door-to-door sellers with copies of written warranties necessary for such sellers to comply with the requirements set forth in paragraphs (c) and (d) of this section.

(2) Paragraph (a)(1) of this section shall not be applicable with respect to statements of general policy on emblems, seals or insignias issued by third parties promising replacement or refund if a consumer product is defective, which statements contain no representation or assurance of the quality or performance characteristics of the product; provided that

(i) The disclosures required by Sections 701.3(a) (1) through (9) of this part are published by such third parties in each issue of a publication with a general circulation, and

(ii) Such disclosures are provided free of charge to any consumer upon written request.

(c) *Catalog and mail order sales.*

(1) For purposes of this paragraph:

(i) "Catalog or mail order sales" means any offer for sale, or any solicitation for an order for a consumer product with a written warranty, which includes instructions for ordering the product which do not require a personal visit to the seller's establishment.

(ii) "Close conjunction" means on the page containing the description of the warranted product, or on the page facing that page.

(2) Any seller who offers for sale to consumers consumer products with written warranties by means of a catalog or mail order solicitation shall:

(i) Clearly and conspicuously disclose in such catalog or solicitation in close conjunction to the description of warranted product, or in an information section of the catalog or solicitation clearly referenced, including a page number, in close conjunction to the description of the warranted product, *either*:

(A) The full text of the written warranty; or

(B) That the written warranty can be obtained free upon specific written request, and the address where such warranty can be obtained. If this option is elected, such seller shall promptly provide a copy of any written warranty requested by the consumer.

(d) *Door-to-door sales.*

(1) For purposes of this paragraph:

(i) "Door-to-door sale" means a sale of consumer products in which the seller or his representative personally solicits the sale, including those in response to or following an invitation by a buyer, and the buyer's agreement to offer to purchase is made at a place other than the place of business of the seller.

(ii) "Prospective buyer" means an individual solicited by a door-to-door seller to buy a consumer product who indicates sufficient interest in that consumer product or maintains sufficient contact with the seller for the seller reasonably to conclude that the person solicited is considering purchasing the product.

(2) Any seller who offers for sale to consumers consumer products with written warranties by means of door-to-door sales shall, prior to the consummation of the sale, disclose the fact that the sales representative has copies of the warranties for the warranted products being offered for sale, which may be inspected by the prospective buyer at any time during the sales presentation. Such disclosure shall be made orally and shall be included in any written materials shown to prospective buyers.

[40 FR 60189, Dec. 31, 1975, as amended at 52 FR 7574, Mar. 12, 1987]

Concluding Notes

In the 1970s, many Americans stopped buying American cars. Part of the reason is that the foreign cars were cheaper and more fuel efficient.

But we think that Americans were ready to switch to new car manufacturers because they were sick and tired of dealing with the Big 3. The people who sold these cars had developed a reputation of aggressive dishonesty. The cars themselves were often manufactured poorly, and customers had to argue with their dealers for repairs—often because the dealers had to argue with the manufacturers for warranty repair reimbursements. The car manufacturers seemed willing to risk their customers' lives—our lives—in order to make a few extra bucks.

The success of foreign car companies was an economic nightmare for the United States. It cost jobs and made a mess of our balance of trade. America doesn't need this problem again.

In many ways, we think that the American software industry is too much like the car industry in the mid-1960s. Software is one of America's most important industries. Foreign competition is certainly developing, but we see short-term profit-taking by Americans. We see American consumers getting angry as they buy products that don't work, that the publishers won't stand behind. And, we see publishers demanding new laws that will protect them from these consumers.

We don't see enough customers demanding satisfaction. Too many people take what they get, grumble loudly, but don't raise hell. When foreign companies enter our market, promising higher quality goods, the grumblers will gladly, and justifiably, try their products.

Our best way to protect our software industry isn't with trade tariffs. Our best protection is to strengthen our software industry. This strength won't come from tax breaks, capital gains deductions, subsidies, or laws that create get-out-of-defects-free cards. This strength will come from higher quality products that build customer satisfaction and strong brand loyalty. Better products will come when customers demand them.

This book is about getting your money's worth.

But it's also about protecting a vital industry.

Do your share.

A New Threat to Customers' Rights: Proposed Revisions to the Uniform Commercial Code

 ### Chapter Map

We have referred to this appendix throughout the book. This appendix outlines a proposed new law, Article 2B (which is often called "2B"), a 273-page addition to the Uniform Commercial Code that will govern all software-related contracts and many other kinds of contracts involving information.

This appendix outlines our concerns with Article 2B and asks you to actively oppose 2B as it is currently slanted. We include a sample letter in this appendix. Additional materials are at our Web site, www.badsoftware.com.

About Our Footnotes

As in Chapter 7, "Software Quality and the Law," we're writing to different audiences in this chapter. Please, feel free to read the top of the pages and skip the extensive footnotes. You can get every important point that we make without reading a single footnote. The footnotes are there if you want more detail or specific references to back up our claims. Even if you are experienced in reading legal material, we suggest that you read the main text first. Read the footnotes when (if) you reread the chapter.

For Further Research

We recommend the same materials that we suggested at the overview of Chapter 7. Here are some Article 2B-specific Web sites:

- The Uniform Commercial Code is at www.law.cornell.edu/ucc/2/overview.html.

- Drafts of Article 2B are at www.law.upenn.edu/library/ulc/ulc.htm. Our citations are all to the July 24–31 NCCUSL Annual Meeting draft.

- Carol Kunze's Web site carries a wide selection of downloadable articles on 2B. www.SoftwareIndustry.org/issues/guide/parcom.html.

- Todd Paglia's (Ralph Nader's Consumer Project on Technology) site is at www.essential.org/cpt/ucc/ucc.html.

- Pamela Samuelson organized an eye-opening conference on the intellectual property implications of Article 2B at UC Berkeley. The conference Web site contains pointers to lots of articles on 2B. www.sims.berkeley.edu/BCLT/events/ucc2b/index.html.

- Ed Foster's *Gripe Line* Article 2B forum at www.infoworld.com.

Article 2B Background: A Rich Potential

The *Uniform Commercial Code* (UCC) is being revised to include a special Article on software-related and information-related law. You may recall from Chapter 7, "Software Quality and the Law," that UCC Article 2 is the current Law of Sales. The proposed new law will be called Article 2B (Law of Licenses). The current draft of Article 2B (National Conference of Commissioners on Uniform State Laws, 1998) runs 273 pages.

Article 2B will probably be considered in your State legislature in late 1999 or in 2000.

Uniform laws are good things. The Uniform Commercial Code has been a tremendous asset for the United States. It creates uniformity in the laws across states. Different states have different rules for fair trade practices and consumer protection, reflecting the differences in their cultures. But when a company does business nationally, as many software publishers do, the variations in law create problems and waste. Business is much easier for everyone if there is one law that applies in all states.

We also like the idea of a comprehensive software law, as Article 2B tries to be, because it brings together several tough legal problems, currently governed by different clusters of law, under one conceptual framework. At last, contracts for the development, sale, and support of software and of the content (data) will all be covered by one law. Simplifying and clarifying the law is good for everyone, and Article 2B has done a remarkable job in this respect.

When we reduce uncertainty in the law, either by clarifying the law itself or by resolving differences among different states' laws, we cut down on the opportunities for legal abuse, on the need for huge expenditures on legal research, and on unfair surprises to buyers and sellers. Contracts can be more certain, and software can sell for less money.

Along with favoring the development of a uniform law, we respect the organizations that are working on the law. The Uniform Commercial Code is jointly maintained (written and updated) by two bodies, The *National Conference of*

Commissioners on Uniform State Laws (NCCUSL), and the *American Law Institute* (ALI).

NCCUSL is the main authoring body. This nonprofit, nonpartisan group of senior attorneys who donate their time to the process is funded as a legislative drafting organization by the 50 states. NCCUSL drafts all "Uniform" state laws. The American Law Institute (ALI) is another nonprofit, nonpartisan group of senior attorneys. It publishes the *Restatements* (such as the *Restatement of Contracts* and the *Restatement of Torts*), which are authoritative summaries of the law as it has developed through court decisions across the country. The ALI and NCCUSL work as partners in maintaining the Uniform Commercial Code, jointly running the *Permanent Editorial Board* of the Uniform Commercial Code. NCCUSL and ALI spend more time on draft legislation and on the judicial interpretations of legislation than any legislature and any judge has time for. Their work has been the foundation for much of the best law (legislation and court opinion) in the United States.

Unfortunately, the process hasn't worked this time. The price to be paid for uniformity in Article 2B is the sacrifice of most of your contract-based rights. Uniformity is good, but not when the uniform result for small customers is, "Sorry, you lose."

A POTENTIAL UNFULFILLED

The Article 2B effort started in the American Bar Association several years ago. It became an official UCC task in 1992 and crystallized as the Article 2B project in 1995.

Until late 1995, there was extensive advocacy for publishers and little advocacy for consumers and small customers in the 2B process. Perhaps, this is why the bill has turned out to be so unbalanced.[1] As it stands today, to the best of our knowledge, no advocate for mass-market customers who has studied Article 2B thinks that 2B is even marginally acceptable. We believe that it is a fundamentally unfair draft statute that will result in lower-quality products, lower customer confidence, and a weaker domestic industry.

At its annual meeting in May, 1998, the American Law Institute passed the following motion (Braucher & Linzer, 1998):

> *The current draft of proposed UCC Article 2B has not reached an acceptable balance in its provisions concerning assent to standard form records and*

---

[1] After 2B was seriously criticized at the 1996 annual meeting of NCCUSL, one of the 2B Drafting Committee members wrote, "We have been aided mostly by representatives who *primarily* are suppliers or distributors and enlightened little by those who *primarily* are software and information product and services users. . . . It, therefore, is not, in this light, surprising that some Commissioners [NCCUSL members] questioned the overall balance of the draft." Rice (1996, p. 1)

should be returned to the Drafting Committee for fundamental revision of the several related sections governing assent.

Braucher's and Linzer's supporting memo included the following criticisms of Article 2B:

The Draft reflects a persistent bias in favor of those who draft standard forms, most commonly licensors. It would validate practices that involve post-purchase presentation of terms in both business and consumer transactions (using "shrink-wrap" and "clickwrap"), undermining the development of competition in contingent terms, such as warranties and remedies. It would also allow imposition of terms outside the range of reasonable expectations and permit routine contractual restrictions on uses of information traditionally protected by federal intellectual property law. A fundamental change of approach is needed.

One or both of us has attended all of the Article 2B Drafting Committee meetings since the second one, in February, 1996. (We are participating observers, which means that we speak at the meetings. A typical Article 2B meeting has about 13 Drafting Committee members and about 75 observers, mainly publishers' lobbyists.) We've spent hundreds of unpaid hours and tens of thousands of dollars trying to improve Article 2B. (For example, see Kaner, 1996h, 1996i, 1997a, 1997b, 1997c, 1997d, 1997e, 1997f, 1997h, 1997i, 1997j, 1997k, 1998a, 1998b, 1998c; Kaner and Gomulkiewicz, 1997; Kaner and Lawrence, 1997; Kaner, Lawrence, and Johnson, 1998; Kaner and Pels, 1997, 1998; Kaner and Paglia, 1997).

What's Wrong with Article 2B

In the mass-market, Article 2B changes the law in two fundamental ways.

- First, it adopts a licensing model, saying that when you buy software, you are really buying only a limited right to use the software rather than a copy of the software product.[2] Under Article 2B, you buy a license, not a product.

---

[2]Article 2B accepts the publisher's claim that the publisher is merely granting you a license to use intellectual property when it sells you a software product. Software publishers have been claiming for years that mass-market software sales are licenses and that the pieces of paper inside software packages that call themselves "license agreements" are binding contracts. The original licensing claims were made because American copyright and patent laws didn't protect software. Software developers needed some way to protect their intellectual property investments from being freely copied (Humphrey 1997c; Rice 1997). So, they relied on contracts that declared the software to be full of trade secrets and that committed the buyer of the software to never copying, lending, selling, or renting the software to anyone else. Together, these restrictions provided the same general protection from unfair copying (piracy) as the copyright and patent laws would have. The patent and copyright laws were fixed over the years, but by then, publishers were discovering that the licensing approach gave them additional control—by allowing them to insert restrictive terms in their contracts that they couldn't get, under the Copyright Act, if they simply sold a copy of the software (Rice, 1997).

- Second, it provides publishers with a license-based contracting model that lets them make their terms nonnegotiable, lets them postpone revealing key terms of the contract to you until after the sale is complete, and makes virtually all of those terms enforceable against you.

This is a dangerously powerful combination. Together, these two changes provide the publisher with the ability to avoid almost all liability to you for defects in its products while exercising long-term control over how you use the products.

Publishers' lawyers have repeatedly told us that they need the power of a licensing structure to protect the value of software. The problem they point out is that software is so easy to copy that it requires special protection. This is a genuine and serious problem. We agree that software should be very well protected. But we think that protection has already been developed in the copyright and patent laws. (See our discussion in footnote 2.) But even if licensing *were* the appropriate approach for intellectual property protection, that would not mean that publishers' rights should be as broad as they get under 2B, nor that they should be given a nearly free ride on liability for defective products.

We're going to list a few examples of the terms that publishers will be able to include in their licenses under 2B. First, though, we'll note that proponents of Article 2B have said that some of the terms we describe would not be enforced by courts, because they would be pre-empted by federal intellectual property law (see, for example, Section 301 of the Copyright Act.[3] Article 2B acknowledges this issue in its Section 2B–105.[4]) According to this line of argument, you don't need to worry about the terms that you are confident will be preempted. When you hear that argument, realize that proponents of Article 2B are *also* arguing that contract clauses that would be valid under 2B will *not* be pre-empted by the Copyright Act.[5] If these proponents are right, then the place to fight against overreaching clauses in software contracts is in the Article 2B debates, not in court battles over the interaction between 2B and copyright.[6]

---

[3] United States Code, Title 17, Section 301(a) "[All] legal or equitable rights that are equivalent to any of the exclusive rights within the general scope of copyright . . . are governed exclusively by this title. No person is entitled to any such right or equivalent right in any such work under the common law or the statute of any state."

[4] Article 2B-105 (a) "A provision of this article which is preempted by federal law is unenforceable to the extent of such preemption." This addition to 2B was adopted by the 2B Drafting Committee in September, 1997 and it has since been touted as a concession to customers, especially libraries, as something that somehow protects our rights. But "preemption" means that when there is a conflict between federal law and state law, the federal law wins. As a matter of American constitutional law, whether 2B-105 exists or not, any provision of 2B that is preempted by federal law will be unenforceable.

[5] According to Ray Nimmer, the reporter (lead author) of Article 2B, "There have been no cases in which [Copyright Act] Section 301 preemption was used successfully to challenge and invalidate a term of a contract that was enforceable as a matter of general state contract law." (Nimmer, 1998, p. 20–21.)

Here are *some* examples of the things that a publisher can do in a nonnegotiable, Article 2B-based mass-market contract:

Disclaim the implied warranties. Including the warranty of merchantability, in a post-sale disclaimer.[7] Under 2B, the Magnuson-Moss Act and other state consumer protection laws that specifically protect buyers of goods will no longer apply to mass-market software and so they no longer preserve the implied warranties.[8] (By the way, the Article 2B warranty of merchantability provides less than Article 2's.)[9] Amazingly, a warranty disclaimer can even be achieved by *usage of trade,* so if it is traditional for software publishers to disclaim liability, a disclaimer might be binding even if the contract doesn't even meet 2B's low standards for notice of a disclaimer.[10]

According to the Information Industry Association, the American Medical Association, and the Association of American Publishers (1996), "The Copyright Act does not preempt contract claims" and "Private rights between parties to a contract are not equivalent to property rights under copyright." Therefore, at least according to their reasoning, any contract clause that is valid under 2B will probably not be preempted by the Copyright Act.

[6] Additionally, it costs a lot to take a publisher to court in order to challenge a term of a software license. Even if the term is invalid, it will take a great deal of time, money and work—more than most consumers can afford—to prove it. In contrast, because publishers use the same terms in thousands or millions of contracts (with thousands or millions of customers), they have an incentive and a budget to aggressively defend their contracts (Rubin, 1997).

[7] Section 2B–408. See our discussion in Chapter 7, "Software Quality and the Law," in the section, "Analysis: Warranty Disclaimers." The leading current case that says that warranty disclaimers don't work unless the customer sees them at or before the sale is *Step-Saver*, an opinion that was cited as representative of the majority rule in the United States by the First Circuit (United States Court of Appeal) just last year (*Ionics, Inc. v. Elmwood Sensors, Inc.,*1997, p. 189 and footnote 4). Article 2B is incompatible with *Step-Saver* and so has to get rid of it. Consider the Reporter's Notes to Section 2B-308 (Mass-Market Licenses) of the February, 1996, draft of Article 2B:

"This section reverses *Wyse Technology v. Step-Saver*, where the court used 2-207 to hold that a shrink wrap license in software packages delivered after a prior telephone contract did not become part of the sale contract. See also Arizona Retail Sys., Inc. v. Software Link, Inc., 831 F. Supp. 759, 22 UCC Rep. Serv2d 70 (D Ariz. 1993) (shrink wrap enforceable in transaction where no prior agreement, but not enforceable where there was a prior telephone agreement)."

Gomulkiewicz (1998a) has said that no software publisher can afford to offer the current warranty of merchantability. We don't fully agree with his analysis— we think that businesses in most industries can make arguments about why it's hard for them to sell merchantable products. But compromises are always possible among people of good faith. Kaner and Gomulkiewicz (1997) jointly proposed a modified warranty of merchantability that they felt was reasonably fair to mass market customers while eliminating or modifying terms that would make honest publishers think twice before offering the warranty. This was a viable compromise. Kaner worked it through with other consumer advocates. And, Gomulkiewicz is a senior corporate attorney at Microsoft and knows mass market publishers' licensing practices and concerns quite well. The Drafting Committee rejected this compromise without a vote at its meeting in March, 1998.

[8] We discussed the applicability and value of the Magnuson-Moss Act in Chapter 7, "Software Quality and the Law," in the section, "Analysis: Magnuson-Moss Act and Written Warranties." The federal Magnuson-Moss Act and other state-level consumer protection laws apply to all sales of consumer goods. It is well accepted that products that you can buy off the shelf (including mass-market software) are "goods" governed by UCC Article 2. No published court rulings have settled the question of the applicability of the Magnuson-Moss Act to software, but it is generally believed that courts would rule that the Act applies to consumer software.

Proponents of 2B often claim that 2B does not change consumer protection rules, citing Section 2B-105(c) "In the case of a conflict between this article and a statute or regulation of this State establishing a consumer protection in effect on the effective date of this article, the conflicting statute or regulation controls." Here's the trick that pulls software out of the scope of sales-of-goods law. Under Article 2B, a software product is licensed, not sold. You are buying an intangible, a license, under Article 2B. (As a "senior corporate attorney for Microsoft Corporation" titled a recent article of his (Gomulkiewicz, 1998b), "The License *is* the Product: Comments on the Promise of UCC Article 2B for Software Licensing.") A license is an intangible, not goods. Therefore, the software sale is a sale of an intangible, not a sale of consumer goods and the consumer goods laws must no longer apply.

This point has been made repeatedly in print (for example, Kaner and Paglia, 1997) and in public statements. For example, Kaner laid it out at the recent *Conference on the Impact of Article 2B* at UC Berkeley (in his talk on April 25, 1998). This is Kaner's analysis of this statute, as a practicing attorney familiar with the Magnuson-Moss literature. We have been told by several lawyers familiar with consumer protection laws that our analysis appears sound. We haven't seen any explanation or anything we regard as a serious attempt to explain why we are mistaken about 2B effecting a removal of software sales from the scope of goods-specific consumer protection laws. Instead, what we see and hear is denial. For example, in the Prefatory Note to the Article 2B, the section "Consumer Protection Rules" says, "In the political process that surrounds any new law, many public statements have been made about the effect of Article 2B on consumer protection. Most are political efforts to mislead. The truth is simple. Article 2B retains current UCC consumer protections, preserves existing non-UCC consumer laws, and creates new protections for the digital environment."

Kaner and Paglia (1997, and in several other oral and written remarks) have repeatedly invited the 2B Drafting Committee to clear up the question of applicability of consumer protection laws, if it merely reflects a misunderstanding. All they'd have to do would be to say that, for purposes of determining the applicability of consumer protection laws, licenses of mass-market software products are to be interpreted as equivalent to sales of consumer goods. If they'd done this, we wouldn't be talking about how 2B has made these laws inapplicable to software, because it would be clear in the law that the same laws will still apply in the same way. With such a simple solution at hand, and based on the tone and content of the many 2B Drafting Committee meeting discussions, we can only infer that the Drafting Committee has intended exactly what we believe the bill will achieve: Buyers of mass-market software will no longer be protected by important consumer protection statutes. We'd love to be proven wrong and hope that the Committee does so by clarifying the statute if it doesn't reflect their intentions.

The Article 2B process has developed an increasingly bitter undertone ("political efforts to mislead"). An awful lot of insults have been hurled at consumer protection advocates. But when you get past the sticks and stones and the smoke and mirrors, it comes down to this. If you are a consumer or a small business who buys mass-market software, this law is bad for you.

[9] We thank Gail Hillebrand (1998a, 1998b) for drawing our attention to this. Under Article 2, Section 2-314(2)(c), merchantability requires that goods "are fit for the ordinary purposes for which such goods are used." Under 2B, Section 2B-403(b)(2), merchantability requires that software "be fit for the ordinary purposes for which it is distributed." The difference is that Article 2 focuses on how people use the product; whereas 2B focuses on how the seller defines it. For example, a kitchen chair that is not strong enough for you to stand on, to change a light bulb, would not be merchantable under Article 2 (because everybody uses chairs this way) but it could be merchantable under Article 2B.

Another example discussed involves fungible (equivalent) goods. Under Article 2, section 2-314(2)(b), merchantability requires "in the case of fungible goods, are of fair average quality within the description." There is no comparable requirement in Article 2B, but as Hillebrand notes in her critique, we will probably discover a need for it one of these days. Here's one example that seems clear to us: Under 2B-103(c), the publisher can say that the disks on which a software product is sold are covered by Article 2B, rather than by Article 2. Disks are fungible goods. Under Article 2, the disks would have to be of "fair average quality," and you could return them as defective if you were only able to read from them a few times. (We have bought cheap disks that failed within the first 10 uses.) Under Article 2B, this requirement is gone.

Article 2-314 (3) provides that "other implied warranties may arise from a course of dealing or usage of trade." No comparable section is apparent to us in Article 2B.

[10] Article 2B-406(e) says that "An implied warranty can also be disclaimed or modified by course of performance, course of dealing, or usage of trade." We are aware of no court cases that would allow this in Article 2 implied warranties.

Disclaim virus liability. The publisher is not liable to you for including a virus in its software, even if the cause is its failure to exercise reasonable care to check for viruses before shipping the product.[11]

Sell software that doesn't match its demos. Unlike Article 2, a publisher doesn't automatically create a warranty that a product will live up to a salesperson's demonstration.[12]

Drastically limit the damages it pays you. The publisher can exclude liability for your incidental expenses and consequential losses that were caused by the publisher's defective software.[13] It can limit your recovery to a replacement disk or a refund.[14] The publisher will not be liable even if your losses were caused by a defect that the publisher knew about, and they were exactly what the publisher expected would be caused by the defect.[15] If the publisher charges you $3 a minute to call for support, it doesn't have to refund the charge if your call is about a genuine defect, even one that the publisher knew about when it sold the product.[16] The publisher isn't liable for incidentals or

---

[11] This is disclaimed via the implied warranty of merchantability, because it makes the product unfit for use. Virus disclaimers were discussed in great detail during Article 2B meetings. Most reputable software publishers check thoroughly for viruses most of the time, but there have been some surprising exceptions. What rights does a customer have when she has to rebuild her data because a publisher rushed a disk to manufacturing without a virus check or didn't bother to update its virus check software to the current version? The Drafting Committee considered several proposals to include an implied warranty that the publisher had taken reasonable care to check its disks for viruses and to avoid shipping viruses. Ultimately, these were defeated.

[12] Under Article 2-313(1) (c) Any sample or model which is made part of the basis of the bargain creates an express warranty that the whole of the goods shall conform to the sample or model." In contrast, under Article 2B-402(a) (3) "A sample, model, or demonstration of a final product which is made part of the basis of the bargain creates an express warranty that the performance of the information will reasonably conform to the performance illustrated by the sample, model, or demonstration, taking into account such differences as would appear to a reasonable person in the position of the licensee between the sample, model, or demonstration and the information as it will be used." The difference is Article 2's "shall conform" versus Article 2B's "reasonably conform." The software publisher can demonstrate a product under unrealistic circumstances and create unrealistic expectations without having to live up to them. For example, the Reporter's Notes to section 2B-402 uses the example of "a demonstration of a complex database program running ten files" when "the intended use of the system is to process ten million files." Under Article 2, if speed was important to the customer, and the demonstration makes the product look like a speed demon, the publisher might face a strong argument that the demonstration created an express warranty of fast processing. The publisher who wants to avoid this warranty will find it easier to escape it under Article 2B than 2. In general, we think that unscrupulous publishers will be able to get away with much sharper practices at trade shows and in other demonstration situations under 2B than under 2.

Article 2B Section 2B-402(b) gives publishers another way to show you something during a sales demonstration and then claim that they have not made a warranty that the product will match the demo. They can claim that they showed you that aspect of the product only as a "a display or a description of a portion of the information to illustrate the aesthetics, market appeal or the like." We know of nothing comparable to this in Article 2, in the black letter law or express warranty jurisprudence.

You can always sue the publisher for fraud if it knowingly makes false claims about its product, but why should you have to prove knowing intent to mislead in these cases? The publisher shows you something that is supposed to be what you will get if you pay your money. You should get what you pay for. That seems like simple, fundamental contract law to us, and we see no reason to make it confusing and complicated to prove that there is a breach of warranty under this circumstance.

consequentials even if a remedy that it *did* promise you in its contract with you failed of its essential purpose or was ruled unconscionable by a court.[17] Article 2B drops the Article 2 notion of a "minimum adequate remedy."[18]

---

[13] Article 2B, Section 2B-703 "Contractual Modification of Remedy." Additionally, note that even if a court rules that you are entitled to collect consequential damages, under Section 2B-707, you cannot collect for lost data or work if you would have avoided the loss by regularly backing up your hard disk. In effect, Section 2B-707 says that you have to protect yourself against the publisher's defects even before you have notice of them—this is an unusual requirement. Section 2B-707 is also laying out a standard of behavior that publishers wish was true (people should regularly back up their disks) but that is probably not true in the world. For example, at one session that Kaner attended at the American Bar Association's 1997 annual convention, half of the participants (lawyers who use computers) said that they (and their office staff) did not regularly back up their hard disks. By the way, we agree that it is good practice to back up your hard disk, and we think that people who have critical data on their machines are being very foolish if they don't make regular backups. But a failure to back up should be between the customer and her computer, and should not provide room for excuses by a publisher who sold the product with many (possibly known) defects.

[14] Under Article 2B Section 2B-703(3), the publisher can limit the remedy to "repair or replacement." Under 2B-703(2), the publisher can limit the remedy to "return . . . of copies and refund of the contract fee."

[15] Article 2B does recognize that some defects are known to the seller at the time of sale. In Section 2B-406(d) the customer cannot claim for a breach of implied warranty for a defect that he could have found by inspecting the product unless he did inspect it, didn't find it, and the publisher "knew that it existed at that time." However, 2B does not distinguish between known and unknown defects in its discussions of remedies. The publisher can limit its remedies, period.

In a letter to the 2B Drafting Committee on behalf of the Institute of Electrical and Electronic Engineers, John Reinert (President of IEEE-USA) said that "One should not be able to disclaim incidental or consequential damages in situations where there is a known defect undisclosed, and the damage is of the type reasonably foreseeable." (Reinert, 1998). Kaner and Paglia (1997) raised the same issue. Kaner has spoken of this issue at several Drafting Committee meetings, starting in the February, 1996, meeting. The Kaner/Paglia proposal, intended as a compromise offering, provided that publishers would *not* be liable for consequential damages if they didn't know about a bug (and their lack of knowledge wasn't due to gross negligence) or if they documented the bug. Only if they failed to give the customer fair notice of the defect when they reasonably should have. Further, the proposal suggested a cap on mass-market publisher's liability for consequentials at an amount ($500 or five times the license fee) that would be far less than many customer would suffer. Our idea was to provide a disincentive to ship software with known bugs, but without putting a company at risk of huge damages if it made a dumb decision. Some publishers' lawyers have said privately to us that this is a promising compromise proposal, but the idea has been discussed and rejected by the Drafting Committee without a vote, for example at the Cincinnati, OH, meeting in May 30–June 1, 1997.

[16] Your payments for calls to the support department are incidental expenses. The publisher can, and routinely does, exclude liability for incidental expenses. You might pay $50 for a program and pay $100 for support calls before you finally realize that you're running into a defect that the publisher knows about and will not fix. You get a refund for the $50, but the publisher keeps your $100. We know of no other law that lets a seller profit from its defects. Kaner (1997b) proposed that publishers should not be allowed to keep this money, but to no avail.

[17] Article 2B Section 2B-703(c) "Failure or unconscionability of an agreed remedy does not affect the enforceability of terms disclaiming or limiting consequential or incidental damages if the contract expressly makes those terms independent of the agreed remedy."

[18] Article 2 Section 2-719 allows sellers to limit their consequential and incidental damages, but the Official Comments to 2-719 state that, "[I]t is of the very essence of a sales contract that at least minimum adequate remedies be available. If the parties intend to conclude a contract for sale within this Article they must accept the legal consequence that there be at least a fair quantum of remedy for breach of the obligations or duties outlined in the contract. Thus, any clause purporting to modify or limit the remedial provisions of this Article in an unconscionable manner is subject to deletion and in that event the remedies made available by this Article are applicable as if the stricken clause had never existed. Similarly, under subsection (2), where an apparently fair and reasonable clause because of circumstances fails in its purpose or operates to deprive either party of the substantial value of the bargain, it must give way to the general remedy provisions of this Article."

Article 2B rejects this in favor of Section 2B-703(c), which preserves a clearly written exclusion of incidentals and consequentials no matter what.

Sell you defective software. You still have the "perfect tender" right that we discussed in Chapter 1 *if* you are a mass-market customer.[19] This entitles you to a refund if you discover a defect during your first use of the software. However, Article 2B takes away that right in nonmass-market transactions.[20] If you are buying as a small business, rather than as a "consumer" (and most software customers will *not* be consumers[21]), then it is easy for your purchase to lose its status as "mass-market."[22] If you are not a mass-market customer, or if you are mass-market but you don't discover the defect until a few days after you bought the software (too late to return for imperfect tender), then you are entitled to a refund only if the software's defects constitute a *material breach* of your contract with the publisher.[23] Under Article 2B, it will be harder for a customer to prove a material breach than under current law.[24]

---

[19] *All* customers lost the perfect tender right in early 1996 drafts, but Consumers Union (Gail Hillebrand) protested this so effectively that the Drafting Committee gave mass market customers back perfect tender in the fall of 1996. Article 2B Section 2B-609(b) gives mass-market licensees (only) the right to "refuse tender of delivery of a copy if . . . the tender does not conform to the contract."

[20] Article 2 provides a perfect tender right for all sales, no matter how large. But Article 2B Section 2B-601(d) and 2B-609(a) and (d), a nonmass-market customer can only refuse a product if it materially breaches the contract. A material breach rule requires very significant defects; whereas the perfect tender rule allows refusal of the product if there is any obvious defect.

[21] Under Article 2B Section 2B-102(a)(10) a consumer obtains software or information "primarily for personal, family, or household purposes." 2B excludes use "primarily for profit-making, professional, or commercial purposes, including agriculture." Under 2B, a high school teacher is not acting as a consumer if she surfs the Web for material to bring to class the next day. Nor, is a graduate student who uses a word processor to write research papers. Nor, is an out-of-work secretary who resorts to network marketing in hopes of making *some* money and buys a low-budget desktop publishing program to print flyers. Nor, is someone who takes work home from the office and does it on the home computer. Small businesses, schools, and churches are never consumers under this definition.

[22] Under 2B-102(a)(32), a sale (license) is mass-market if is made to a consumer. Otherwise, the product must be offered "to the general public as a whole." This knocks out products like billing programs for dentists even if they are off-the-shelf and sold with shrink-wrapped, nonnegotiable contracts that the dentist might not see until after the sale. The product also must be sold in "a retail market transaction." There is controversy about whether the Internet is "a retail market." It might be (we don't know) that no nonconsumer purchase on the Internet is a mass-market transaction. (Net-based transactions have been explicitly excluded in some 2B drafts. In this draft, the issue is not raised.) Additionally, the product cannot have been customized. (There are trivially easy ways to customize, such as putting your name on the splash screen.) Additionally, the size of the quantity purchased must be consistent with a retail purchased (which, as the Society for Information Management (1998) notes, might mean no orders bigger than one unit are mass-market), and the purchase must not be as part of a site license. Finally, if you use an Internet Service Provider (ISP) for a non-consumer purpose, your contract with the ISP is not a mass-market contract.

[23] Article 2B Section 2B-601(d).

[24] Under Article 2B Section 2B-109, a breach is material if (2B-109(b)(1)) "the agreement so provides" or (2B-109(b)(2)) "the breach is a failure to perform an agreed term that is an essential element of the agreement" or (2B-109(b)(3)) if the breach causes "substantial harm to the aggrieved party, such as costs or losses that significantly exceed the contract value" or "substantially deprives "the aggrieved party of a substantial benefit it reasonably expected under the contract." This is a high hurdle to jump—for example, you can't ask for a refund unless the product is causing you losses that are *significantly* greater than the price you paid.

Refuse to fix a defect in the software.   Under the Magnuson-Moss Act, a seller of consumer software is required to fix defects unless it isn't commercially practicable.[25] Under Article 2B, the mass-market customer isn't entitled to a repair. Instead, 2B requires sellers to try to cure defects only for nonmass-market (nonconsumer) customers.[26]

The Reporter's Notes to Section 2B-109 points to this section as being derived from the *Restatement (Second) of Contracts* (a leading summary of current law) which, the 2B draft says, lists five significant circumstances:

"(1) the extent to which the injured party will be deprived of the benefit he or she reasonably expected; (2) the extent to which the injured party can be adequately compensated for the benefit of which he will be deprived; (3) the extent to which the party failing to perform or to offer to perform will suffer forfeiture; (4) the likelihood that the party failing to perform or to offer to perform will cure the failure, taking into account all the circumstances, including any reasonable assurances; and (5) the extent to which the behavior of the party failing to perform or to offer to perform comports with standards of good faith and fair dealing."

The *Restatement* factors look to the circumstances, including the seller's conduct and risks, as well as to the harm done to the customer. We can illustrate the difference with an example. Suppose that a publisher sold you a seriously but not devastatingly defective product.

Under Article 2B:

- The shrink-wrapped license won't contain explicit performance standards so the tests of Sections 2B-109(b)(1) and (b)(2) are not met.

- The breach will be material if the defect is too expensive or it deprives you of a substantial benefit. (*How do you prove that?*)

In many cases, such a product will not be defective under the Article 2B standard.

Under the *Restatement of Contracts*:

- The first factor is the extent to which you are deprived of a benefit. A small deprivation counts, just not for much. The deprivation doesn't have to be of a substantial benefit.

- The second factor asks whether you can be adequately compensated without canceling the contract. Sure, but not if all of your incidental expenses and consequential losses are excluded. This question isn't asked under 2B's material breach standard.

- The third factor asks about the possibility that the seller will suffer a forfeiture. If you order custom software and then cancel the order after the seller does a huge amount of work, it suffers a forfeiture. It invested a huge amount and lost everything. This can be too unfair. That's not what's going on in a mass-market situation. There are thousands of sales; yours is just one. Therefore, we don't have to worry that canceling this sale will be unfair to the publisher. This factor is not considered under Article 2B.

- The fourth factor asks whether you will be compensated for the defect. In the mass-market case, we'll assume that the answer is "No"—no partial refund, no reimbursement for losses, and no bug fix. This counts against the publisher under the Restatement but not under 2B.

- The final factor asks whether the publisher's behavior comports with standards of good faith and fair dealing. If the publisher knew about the bug before the sale (as publishers often do), and forgot to tell you about it before you paid your money, then the publisher might not do well at all under this test. Surprise, surprise. This is not a factor under Article 2B's test of materiality.

Customers probably do better under current law (the *Restatement*) than under 2B.

[25] United States Code, Title 15, Section 2301(10): "[T]he warrantor may not elect refund unless (i) the warrantor is unable to provide replacement and repair is not commercially practicable or cannot be timely made, or (ii) the consumer is willing to accept such refund."

[26] Article 2B Section 2B-606(b) requires an effort to cure "in a license other than a mass-market license."

Sell you a service contract but not fix the software's bugs.   Under Article 2B, the publisher is not required to fix all of the software's defects, even if it sells you a service and support contract.[27]

Make your contract noncancelable.   For example, an online service provider could sell you to a five-year Internet access contract, or a software publisher could sell you a five-year software support contract, and the contract could say that the service cannot be cancelled any time over the five years even if the service is poor.[28]

Require you to use a commercially unreasonable security procedure. When you contract with the publisher, and then not reimburse you for incidental and consequential losses that you suffer (such as losses due to identity theft) because of a security failure of that procedure.[29]

Profit from data transmission errors.   The publisher can charge you full price for retransmitting a data file, a program, or a movie to you if the original was corrupted or lost between your Internet Service Provider and your computer.[30]

Profit from your mistakes.   Article 2B gives consumers a limited right to a refund if they make a mistake when ordering software or other information products online. There are several restrictions on consumers' rights here, but nonconsumers don't have this right at all.[31] Under Article 2B, people who we would normally think of as "consumers" will not qualify as consumers and are not entitled to consumer protections.[32] Another way that sellers profit from your mistakes is that you are held fully responsible for any transactions made by your "electronic agent," including mistaken ones.[33] This is a striking illustration of the bias of Article 2B—suppose that you buy "agent" software from a publisher. That publisher will not be liable for the consequences of defects

[27] 2B-616(a)(2)(B) the service provider "does not commit that its services will correct all performance problems unless the agreement so provides."

[28] Article 2B Section 2B-703(a)(1) The agreement (the shrink-wrapped license) may limit your remedies such as by "precluding a party's right to cancel for breach of contract."

[29] Article 2B Section 2B-115, the seller's "liability does not extend to (1) loss of expected benefit; (2) consequential damages."

[30] See Article 2B Section 2B-623 (a) and (d) "Risk of Loss of Copies" and then 2B-102(a)(38) definition of "Receive." As Hillebrand (1998a) puts it, "This section means that the user must still pay for information that he or she cannot receive because of an intervening failure of a third party."

[31] Article 2B Section 2B-118 "Electronic Error: Consumer Defenses."

[32] See the discussion in footnote 21.

[33] An electronic agent is a computer program that can initiate or respond to electronic messages on your behalf. The current draft of the Uniform Electronic Transaction Act (National Conference of Commissioners on Uniform State Laws, 1998b) names this as an "electronic device" instead, which gets rid of all the legal baggage associated with the word "agent." On accountability for the "agent," see Sections 2B-111, 2B-119, 2B-120, 2B-202, and 2B-204(4).

that it put into the product and that it knows about. When you use the software and one of those defects causes a mistaken purchase order, you are fully responsible to the company that you ordered from. Customers get no slack. Sellers get no liability.

Impose a wide range of restrictions on your use of the software.[34] We will list several contractual use restrictions in the next several points. We'll note here that this is an old trick. The restrictions aren't allowed when a product is *sold*, so sellers of copyrighted or patented works have tried to declare a sale to be a "license" by sticking a notice on the product. Historically, the courts haven't bought this.[35] Instead, under copyright law, they declared the

---

[34] These are the *contractual use restrictions* defined in Article 2B Section 102(a)(13) "Contractual use restriction" means an enforceable restriction created by contract on use of licensed information or informational rights, including an obligation of nondisclosure and confidentiality and a limitation on scope, manner, or location of use." Under 2B-102(a)(42) the "scope" of a license is defined partially by the contractual use restrictions. Under 2B-202 and 2B-209(b), a contract is not formed when there is a disagreement about scope, even if (2B-209) the buyer has paid for the product and is using it.

When you buy a book, you have certain rights under the United States Constitution. Article 1, Section 8, Clause 8 of the Constitution gives Congress the power "To promote the Progress of Science and useful Arts, by securing for limited Times to Authors and Inventors the exclusive Rights to their respective Writings and Discoveries." This is the constitutional basis for the Copyright Act and the patent laws. On this basis, American law balances a public interest in making use of these works against a private interest in collecting money for them.

When you buy a copyrighted work, you don't have the right to make unauthorized copies of it, but you can quote short pieces of it, publish a review of it, use the information you get from it to research a paper that the author or publisher would disagree with, let a friend read the book, or analyze the author's writing style. These are examples of "fair use" and "first sale" rights. You don't necessarily have those rights under a license. Licenses can restrict the use of intellectual property. For example, traditional licenses can have nondisclosure provisions (which, for a book, could mean no book reviews), restrictions on how the product is used (no quoting, no use for unapproved purposes) and on who can use it (just you, no friends or family), restrictions on reverse engineering (no analyzing the style), restrictions on transfer of the licensed product (no selling the book as used once you're done with it).

Shrink-wrapped software "licenses" often include all of these provisions. Many are unenforceable under current law, but it appears that they will be enforceable under Article 2B, or at least they will be until (if) they are struck down by federal courts. Everything about a mass-market transaction in software looks like a sale except for the piece of paper in the box. To us, it seems like this is an end-run around the Constitutional balancing of buyers and sellers rights, and that publishers under Article 2B are merely sellers who want the money, but who don't want to give buyers their fair use and first sale rights. Several other attorneys (for example, Karjala, 1997; Lemley, 1995; McManis, 1998; D. Nimmer, 1998; Rice, 1997; Samuelson, 1998b) make essentially this point, with more extensive legal discussion.

[35] See for example, *Authors & Newspapers Association v. O'Gorman* (1906—rejected use restrictions on the inside cover of a book); *Bobbs-Merrill Co. v. Straus* (1908—rejected purported license that required that the book be resold for not less than $1); *Straus v. Victor Talking Machine Co.* (1917—rejected the notion that a license notice on the side of sound-reproducing machines is binding on the customer); *Motion Picture Patents Co. v. Universal Film Manufacturing Co.* (1917—seller cannot create a restrictive license by affixing a notice to a patented machine. Extensive review and discussion of the doctrine of exhaustion.) *Boston Store of Chicago v. American Graphaphone Company* (1918—patent holder cannot extend its rights by contract to control the resale of the product and the form of the license notice on the machine was irrelevant.) *RCA Mfg. Co. v. Whiteman* (1940—on-the-envelope license for sheet music, rejected.) Lemley (1995) reviews more recent cases in many countries.

doctrines of fair use and first sale rights and, under patent law, the doctrine of exhaustion.[36]

Make the sale temporary.   Even if you buy the software in the store, the way you'd buy a book, the publisher can say that you can only use it for a limited period of time.[37]

Limit your right to lend, give, or sell the software.   The publisher can say that you can't lend the software to anyone; you can't give it to anyone; and you can't sell it to anyone.[38]

Limit who can use the software.   For example, the publisher might restrict the use to you and your immediate family, or to you and your *bone fide* employees. Other people can't use the software, even if they come to your house to use it.[39]

Limit where you can use this software.   Use it only on one computer; the hardware you initially installed it on.[40] You can't install it onto a computer that also functions as a network server.[41]

---

[36] The Copyright Act grants the author the exclusive right to make and distribute copies of a book that she wrote, but once she sells a copy of that book, she can no longer control what is done with that copy. The buyer can lend it, resell it, or publicly burn it. This is called the First Sale Doctrine. The author's rights to control use or distribution of a particular copy of her work stop once she has been fairly compensated for that copy. The comparable restriction on inventors' rights in patent is called the Doctrine of Exhaustion. The Institute for Electrical and Electronic Engineers (Reinert, 1998), which represents 220,000 engineers, including software developers, wrote that "Software proprietors should not be able to avoid the impact of the exhaustion doctrine by designating a transaction as a license or bailment rather than a sale when the transaction appears to be a sale" and "Contract terms that frustrate rights otherwise afforded by intellectual property laws should not be enforceable."

[37] Article 2B Section 2B-308, an agreement can specify the duration. Section 2B-310, the publisher can enforce the time limit with a time bomb (electronic restraint that shuts down the program.)

[38] Under Article 2B Section 2B-502(2), "a contractual term prohibiting transfer of a party's interest is enforceable, and a transfer made in violation of that contract term is a breach of contract and is ineffective."

[39] This is a garden variety use restriction. The extreme to which this can go was illustrated in the case of *MAI Systems Corp. v. Peak Computer, Inc.* (1993). MAI restricted the use of its software (the operating system that came with the MAI computer and the system diagnostics) to "bone fide employees" of its customers. These customers would sometimes contract with third-party support organizations to maintain their computers. The support techs would come to the customer site, turn on their MAI computer, thus booting the MAI operating system and then would run the MAI diagnostics that came with the MAI computer. The court ruled that they were making copies (from disk to RAM) of these products, and that this copying was not lawful because they were not bone fide employees of the MAI customers and therefore were not licensed to use the software.

A mass market license that restricted the use of a computer game to you and your bone fide family members could be used in the same way to support a case against your neighbor's kids if they come over and play the game on your computer.

This case illustrates the strangeness of mass-market "licensing." Maybe *MAI* makes sense for big companies, but for neighbor's kids?

[40] This is an example of non-transferability. It is most often seen in contracts involving a multiuser license to run a program on a specific, big computer.

[41] Keeping it off the network server is another use restriction ("limitation on . . . scope . . . or location of use"). The publisher is preventing the program from being made available to several people who have access to the machine's disk.

Limit your ability to repair, modify, or otherwise learn from this software.   The publisher can say that you can't investigate how the product works by reverse engineering it or disassembling the software.[42] You can't modify the software.[43] Only the publisher's staff can fix defects in its software—competing service providers are not allowed.[44]

Tell you how you can use this software.   The publisher can say that you can't create "scandalous, obscene, or immoral works;"[45] that you can't use it to develop a product that competes with this product.[46] Additionally, you may

---

[42] Banning reverse engineering is a controversial contractual use restriction. When someone buys a product, they have a right to reverse engineer it. When someone takes a product under a negotiated license, they can be held to an agreement to not reverse engineer it. The question is, can someone be held to a ban on reverse engineering in a mass-market license?

Most engineers find the idea of a ban on reverse engineering deplorable. Hence, the letters from the IEEE (Reinert, 1998) and participation in the 2B process by the Digital Future Coalition. On the other hand, Gomulkiewicz and Williamson (1996) argue that this should be enforceable. Lande and Sobin (1996) review the literature and conclude that it will probably not be enforceable if it restricts the development of competition (probably the main reason that publishers want to ban reverse engineering). For additional discussion, see Karjala (1997) and Rice (1992).

Reverse engineering and disassembly are also used for investigative purposes. For example, Schulman (1998b) and Russinovich (1998) disassembled SoftRAM in order to examine the basis for Syncronys's (the publisher's) claims about the product. See Chapter 7's section on "The Syncronys SoftRAM95 Cases." Kaner first learned operating system programming by disassembling the Apple II OS. Mass-market restrictions on reverse engineering are banned in Europe. The European Union (1991) Directive on the Legal Protection of Computer Programs allows black box reverse engineering (studying the behavior of the program without decompilation or disassembly) and decompilation/disassembly for the purpose of creating products that will be interoperable (that will work with) this one. These rights cannot be negated between the parties by contract.

Bans on reverse engineering are common in software licenses. If they are enforceable in the United States, but not Europe, we are shooting an important knowledge-gathering component of our competitive ability in the virtual foot.

[43] This is both a use restriction and a reliance on basic copyright that allows a publisher to prevent the creation of derivative works. But it can be applied outrageously these days, to prevent companies who have been stuck with software that has Y2K bugs from reverse engineering the software and fixing it. This software is often mission-critical, and the idea of waiting for an overloaded vendor to get around to repairing its software (for a whopping big fee) is not a comfortable one for many companies. Kaner and Pels (1998) discuss this further. The Y2K literature online, such as at www.year2000.com, has additional discussion.

[44] See our discussion of the *MAI* case in footnote 39.

[45] We pulled this language from one of Corel's licenses. This is just another use restriction under 2B, which allows restrictions on the "manner . . . of use." (2B-102(a)(13)

[46] Noncompetition clauses are common in licenses. Article 2B notes them in the Reporter's Notes to Section 2B-502, where it discusses them as enforceable use restrictions, and in the text of 2B-713. They sometimes appear in shrink-wrap licenses, but if the publisher is too aggressive, it might face federal antitrust laws.

not examine or reverse engineer this product in order to develop products that are compatible with it.[47]

Tell you what you can't publish criticisms of the software. This is dressed up as a confidentiality restriction.[48]

The publisher can impose all these restrictions on mass-market sales of books and movies, too. The publisher can shrink-wrap the product and put a license notice on the shrink-wrap. You're bound to the restrictive terms either because you bought the product with notice of the terms, or because you tore open the package (signifying assent, according to 2B).[49] And, don't think they wouldn't do it. Publishers in a wide range of media have been trying to impose restrictions on mass-market customers for a long time—they just haven't gotten away with it.[50]

---

[47] We discussed the legal controversy surrounding reverse engineering in footnote 42 and noted that Europe gives lawful possessors of software a nonwaivable right to reverse engineer for the purpose of developing interoperable products. The problem of interoperability is important in its own right. Two products are interoperable if they work together. For example, they can read each other's files (or one can read the other's), or a program can properly drive a particular model of printer. We've published many products that had to interoperate in some way with other products, including competitors' products. We know one publishers' lawyer who wants to use Article 2B to try out restrictions on reverse engineering for interoperability. He represents a large publisher and would like to pick and choose which companies can reverse engineer his software's file formats (thus, publishing compatible or competing products). We can understand why he and his company would like this, but we don't understand how it would benefit innovation or any other public purpose.

[48] Article 2B Section 2B-102(a)(13) says that "an obligation of nondisclosure and confidentiality" is just another contractual use restriction. We have one mass-market license from Symantec that says "You agree to hold the Package within your Organization and shall not, without our specific written consent . . . publish or communicate or disclose to third parties any part of the Package." McAfee (now Network Associates) publishes a virus scanner with even more direct confidentiality restriction: "The customer shall not disclose the results of any benchmark test to any third party without Network Associates' prior written approval." Also, "The customer will not publish reviews of the product without prior consent from Network Associates." We obtained the Network Associates license at www.nai.com at a page no longer in service. (We obtained a prior version at www.mcafee.com at a page no longer in service. Copies are on file with the authors.)

Under current law, we don't think that these restrictions are enforceable, and we would violate them without hesitation. We think that they would eventually be tossed out in Article 2B-based contracts, on First Amendment grounds. But in the period between Article 2B's passage and a clear ruling from a federal appellate court, Kaner would be more cautious about advising clients on the effect of these restrictions. At least on the surface, Article 2B makes them valid, enforceable restrictions in a contract. That gives a publisher who wants to sue you for writing a nasty article about its product the right to sue you. The suit almost certainly wouldn't be ruled frivolous by a judge and it would cost you a fortune to defend, even if you finally won.

Some software publishers do threaten some magazines when they hear that an unfriendly review is about to be published. For example, it is reported that Syncronys warned *Dr. Dobbs* magazine that "they would protect their rights for defamatory or misleading statements as well as protect their copyrights and trade secrets" (Cooper, 1996). Syncronys was the subject of a complaint by the Federal Trade Commission over the software discussed in this review. For discussion, see *In the Matter of Syncronys Software*. (1996) and Chapter 7's section on "The Syncronys SoftRAM95 Cases."

[49] Article 2B Section 2B-111(d) "A manifestation of assent may be proved in any manner, including a showing that a procedure existed by which a person or an electronic agent must have engaged in conduct or operations that manifested assent to the record or term in order to proceed further in the use it made of the information or informational rights."

[50] Look at the different types of industries involved in the cases discussed in footnote 35.

Make it nearly impossible for you to sue the publisher.   The publisher gets to choose what country's or state's laws apply to the software.[51] It can choose what courthouse, in what state or country, can hear any complaints filed against it.[52] The publisher can shorten the statute of limitations (how long you have to sue if the product is defective.)[53] You can be required to take your case to arbitration.[54] The publisher can demand a list of bugs from you, and you can't complain later about bugs that you didn't describe accurately or clearly or thoroughly enough.[55] And, the publisher's technical support staff can slip a waiver of liability into an update. When you install the bug fix, you manifest assent (by clicking <OK> during installation) to a term that says you release the publisher from all liability for previous defects.[56]

---

[51] Article 2B Section 2B-107. "The parties in their agreement may choose the applicable law." The only restriction is for consumers (see footnote 21 for a discussion of the narrowness of 2B's definition of "consumer.") That restriction says that if the otherwise ruling (seller's or customer's) state's law has a restriction on choice of law that cannot be varied by agreement, it cannot be varied by the software contract. Some of Corel's licenses specify that they are governed by the law of Ireland. After 2B is passed, this would be enforceable against all customers in most states and enforceable against all nonconsumers (including mass-market customers) in all states that adopt 2B.

[52] Article 2B Section 2B-108 "The parties in their agreement may choose an exclusive judicial forum unless the choice is unreasonable and unjust."

This "unfair and unjust" language might sound like a protection, but it comes from a line of cases starting (in the consumer context) with *Carnival Cruise Lines v. Shute* (1991) (Some of the background facts mentioned here are taken from the 9th Circuit Court of Appeal's overruled opinion, *Shute v. Carnival Cruise Lines*, 1990). This case illustrates the hardship that forum selection clauses can work on consumers. Eulala Shute lived in the State of Washington. In Washington, she bought tickets for a cruise from Los Angeles, California to Puerto Vallarta, Mexico. She was injured on the ship. On the back of the ticket, in fine print, was a forum selection clause that required Shute to file any lawsuit in the State of Florida. This is convenient for Carnival Cruise Lines, which is based in Florida, but Shute would have to fly herself and all her witnesses from the West Coast to Florida. The United States Court of Appeals (Ninth Circuit) noted that this case "would be so gravely difficult and inconvenient that the plaintiffs would for all practical purposes be deprived of their day in court." It then ruled that Shute could sue in Washington. But the United States Supreme Court held that forum selection clauses are enforceable and ruled in favor of Carnival Cruise Lines. Since then, several courts have found that forum selection clauses were not both "unreasonable and unjust," even though they would probably deprive the customer plaintiff of his or her day in court.

We've talked about this repeatedly and at length in the Article 2B meetings. Everybody understands that this will virtually eliminate access to small claims courts and that small customers will be effectively barred from bringing many types of lawsuits by this rule. In the February, 1998, meeting, the committee finally focused directly on the issue of consumer rights. It voted on a motion of David Rice's, based on compromise proposals from Kaner and Paglia (1997) and from the IEEE (Reinert, 1998). The motion provided that when the following conditions are all met, the customer could sue the publisher in small claims court in his home state:

The total amount in dispute must be small enough for Small Claims Court. This effectively eliminates class action suits.

The purchaser must be a consumer (under 2B's very narrow definition of the word "consumer"). Both original proposals specified "mass market customers" here, but Professor Rice changed this to consumer, perhaps in order to make the issue and the discussion crystal clear.

The customer would have to be able to sue the publisher (obtain personal jurisdiction) in his home state if the license agreement was silent on the matter.

Define your liability to the publisher, if you breach the contract.   The publisher owes you very little (no damages, just a refund after you return the product) if it sells you an unusably defective product that breaches its express warranties. But what do you pay the publisher if you breach the contract? Unless the license excludes *your* incidental and consequential liability to the publisher, you are still on the hook for these potentially huge damages. Limitation of liability in Article 2B is determined separately for each party, even though it is defined (in the mass-market contract) by the seller alone.[57]

Exercise "self-help" by shutting down the program.   The publisher can put time-bombs in the code that will stop the program from running after a certain date.[58] Or, the publisher can send a signal to your computer that will shut down the program.[59] (This method of shutting you down without help from a court or sheriff is called *self-help.)* In either case, the publisher can deny you access to the data that you collected or created with the program.[60] This is supposed to be done only if you are in breach of contract (you didn't pay or you're using the software beyond the license), but if the publisher is wrong, it is not liable to you for incidental or consequential damages, even if this shutdown destroys your business.[61]

This was a compromise. It protected individuals (only), who had a claim that would be too small to fly across the country (or the world) to sue for. But it protected businesses strongly by leaving the choice of forum clauses intact in the cases that publishers most fear: lawsuits by all businesses and all class action suits.

Members of the Drafting Committee said that they understood that if consumers have to fly across the country to bring a suit for $100, they really have no power to sue. The Drafting Committee voted down the motion and kept language taken directly from *Carnival Cruise Lines.*

[53] Article 2B Section 2B-705. Our main objection to this section is that the statute of limitations is not tolled while the publisher is supposedly working with you to fix the defect or to help you find a workaround. If you have to file suit (or lose your right to file) within a year after you receive the software, and if the publisher's staff string you along for a few months, you might lose your right to sue just because you were cooperative and unaware of your short time limit.

[54] *Hill v. Gateway 2000, Inc.* (1997). See our discussion of this case in Chapter 7.

[55] Article 2B Section 2B-605 (c).

[56] Article 2B Section 2B-605(a).

[57] Article 2B Section 2B-703 (contractual modification of remedy), 2B-708 (licensor's damages) and 2B-709 (licensee's damages).

[58] Article 2B Section 2B-310.

[59] Article 2B Section 2B-715.

[60] Article 2B Section 2B-310 (c) "Unless authorized by a term of the agreement, this section does not permit a restraint that affirmatively prevents or makes impracticable a licensee's access to its own information in the licensee's possession by means other than by use of the licensor's information or informational rights." On the surface, this sounds like a protection ("does not permit") but it's really a permission. It says that if the seller can get your agreement (click OK to the standard form), then it can prevent your access to your data.

Take advantage of rules governing assent.   We consider these rules un-fair.[62] For example, you agree to the contract merely by doing something that you'd have to do anyway in order to use the product, such as tearing open an envelope that contains the disks (that you paid for) or clicking an <OK> button during installation of software (that you paid for).[63] Your OK to the form license might even override contract terms that you negotiated with the publisher.[64] Terms that are required by law to be "conspicuous" don't have to be available for your inspection until after the sale.[65] Article 2B's rules for assent and conspicuousness override other consumer protection laws' rules.[66] Finally, 2B appears to limit the doctrine of unconscionability.[67]

---

[61] Several proposals have been made to make the publisher liable for damages if it shuts you down wrong-fully, but 2B does not do this. There is no separate damage provision for self-help in Section 2B-715. Instead, the customer will have to look to his basic remedies, as modified under Section 2B-703 (which will mean thatconsequentials and incidentals are excluded). In practice, large customers will demand a war-ranty against self-help, with full damages, and they will refuse to sign contracts without it. Small customers will have less bargaining power and will be at real risk.

[62] Suppose that you bought a refrigerator and took it home. You take it out of the box and try to open the door, but some piece of tape is keeping the door shut. The tape says, "BY BREAKING THIS SEAL, YOU AGREE TO VOTE FOR THE BULLMOOSE PARTY FOR THE REST OF YOUR LIFE." Do you *really* agree to that contract when you break the tape to open the door? Of course not. You are doing something that you have already paid for the right to do—using the fridge. The tape is just something that you have to get past in order to exercise your rights. Breaking it has no legal effect.

Now buy a computer program and take it home. When you open the shrink-wrapped (plastic-wrapped) box, you find that the disks are sealed inside an envelope that says LICENSE AGREEMENT or WARRANTY DIS-CLAIMER. (This is the *shrink-wrapped* or *tear-me-open license.*) The envelope also says "BY OPENING THIS ENVELOPE, YOU AGREE TO THE TERMS OF THIS LICENSE." So, by opening the envelope, are you *really* mak-ing the contract it claims you are making, a contract you never saw before the sale? Of course not. You bought the program. You have the right to open it, install it on your computer, and use it. That's what you paid for. The envelope is just packaging, a piece of trash that temporarily protects your disks during ship-ping. Opening it should have no legal effect.

The new version of the shrink-wrapped "contract" is called the *click-wrap license.* You buy the software, take it home (or download it), and while you are installing the software, a screen interrupts you and says, "BY CLICKING <I AGREE>, YOU AGREE TO WORK FOR BILL GATES FOR THE REST OF YOUR LIFE." (We thank Scott Adams for suggesting this shrink-wrap term in one of his Dilbert cartoons.) You can't proceed with the installation until you click a button on the screen that is labelled, <I AGREE>. When you do click it, are you making this agreement? Of course not. You paid for this software. You have the right to install it and use it. This click is just a nuisance in the way of you doing what you have every right to do. So you click the button to get on with the installation. Clicking should have no legal effect. Students of contract law will recognize this pattern as a classic illustration of *failure of consideration.* Each example runs afoul of the *preexisting duty rule.* The customer already has the right to use the product. The seller inserts a new step inside the task of using the product and says that, because the customer did this task, the customer has agreed to a new contract. The law says, "Humbug!"

If the publisher really wanted to get you to agree to a contract, it could present the contract before the sale and say, "Agree or don't buy." Or, it could offer you an incentive (such as extended technical support) to agree to the contract after the sale. But that's not what the publisher does. Instead, the publisher waits until after you've finished shopping, taken the product home, and tried to use it. At that point, when more shop-ping is probably the last thing that you want to do, the publisher says "Agree to these terms, or we take back the sale. If you don't accept our new terms, you'll have to waste your time going back to the store to get a refund. Then you can buy our competitor's product and take it home to see whether our competitor gives you a better deal." Nice try, but as far as we can tell, the publisher has waited too long. Now that the sale is complete, it is too late to make significant changes to the sales contract.

Prospects for 2B

About 18 months ago, we thought that there was a good chance that Article 2B could be fixed. Nader and Paglia had a surprisingly productive exchange of letters with the Software Publishers Association (SPA) (Nader, 1997; Wasch, 1997). It wasn't very friendly yet, but there was a basis for an important proposal by Paglia that the SPA did not oppose. Kaner, Paglia, and other lawyers (some have asked to remain anonymous) were hashing through details of compromise proposals (ultimately brought together in Kaner and Paglia, 1997). We've mentioned most of these already, but here's a short list:

Warranty for documentation.   Paglia proposed that statements of fact in user documentation that comes with the software should be express warranties. This was partially based on (Software Publisher Association President) Wasch's (1997) reaction to Nader's (1997) claim that publishers wanted to avoid taking responsibility for statements in their documentation. Wasch denied this. Paglia said at a 2B meeting that he was encouraged and that he would propose that publishers be held accountable for factual claims about their products in their documentation. An attorney for the SPA said that the SPA would not oppose this, and when the proposal actually came before the Drafting Committee (meeting of May 30–June 1, 1997), he did not oppose the motion. Several of us, on several sides, thought that this could be the foundation of a successful 2B that recognized a limited but actual responsibility of the publisher to the customer. Unfortunately, the Drafting Committee considered the proposal and rejected it without a vote.

Damages only for known and undocumented bugs.   Kaner proposed (see also Kaner and Paglia, 1997 and Reinert, 1998) that consequential damages be eliminated except when the publisher knew about a bug and chose not to document it or failed to know about the bug only because of gross negligence. Kaner and Paglia also proposed that the amount of consequential damages could be capped. This protected publishers from unpredictable liability and

---

[63] Article 2B Section 2B-111(d).

[64] We think this is the effect of Article 2B Section 2B 203(d)(2).

[65] Article 2B Section 2B-102(a)(9) definition of conspicuous.

[66] Article 2B Section 2B-105 (c), 2B-105(d)(3) and 2B-105(d)(4). Consumers Union has repeatedly protested these provisions, expressing its concern that these changes reduce consumer rights in ways that will have genuine effects. See Hillebrand (1997, 1998a, 1998b).

[67] White and Summers (1995) and many others talk about unconscionability as having two components, procedural unconscionability and substantive unconscionability. Procedural unconscionability involves unfair contracting process, and substantive unconscionability involves outrageously unfair terms. Several courts require both types of unconscionability before they will rule a contract as unconscionable. Article 2B prescribes a method for the publisher to obtain all of its terms without telling the customer the terms in advance and without allowing for negotiation. We might consider this procedurally unconscionable, but how could we argue unconscionability to a judge when this is the method specifically approved by a statute? After Article 2B passes, we suspect that all publishers' contracts will conform to the specified method, and therefore, that no contracts will be provable as unconscionable under the current two-factor test.

exposed them to liability only under situations that they could manage in the normal course of engineering the product. (For additional detail, see footnote 15.) Variants of the proposal have been discussed a few times and have been rejected by the Drafting Committee without a vote.

Virus liability.   Kaner proposed a compromise on virus liability that made publishers liable only when a virus that they shipped was there because they failed to exercise reasonable care to detect it before shipping the product. Additionally, under four circumstances, publishers would be exempt from a duty of care to check for viruses (they gave the file to the recipient for free; they had genuine consent from the recipient to send an untested file that the recipient would test; the file received its virus during transmission, not from the publisher; the licensor was merely passively redistributing the software and did not know of the virus). The Drafting Committee voted down the proposal in its meeting of April 11–13, 1997.

Forum Selection.   Kaner and Paglia (1997) and the IEEE (Reinert, 1997) proposed that mass-market customers would have a right to sue in small claims court in their own state under a narrow set of circumstances. In all business-critical cases (suits by businesses for significant damages and class action suits) the publisher's choice of forum clause would be enforced. Professor David Rice reframed the proposal even more narrowly for the Drafting Committee, restricting it to consumers. We discuss this motion in more detail in footnote 52. The Drafting Committee voted it down.

Warranty of merchantability.   Kaner and Bob Gomulkiewicz (from Microsoft) set out to revise the implied warranty of merchantability. Our goal was to develop something that publishers such as Microsoft would be willing to offer that would be fair to consumers. (If you don't have to disclaim the warranty, arguments about whether the disclaimer should be given presale or postsale become academic.) After a lot of work, we developed Kaner and Gomulkiewicz (1997), which was further discussed by Gomulkiewicz (1998a). The Drafting Committee considered and rejected it without a vote. For more details, see footnote 7.

Self-help.   Susan Nycum and the Society for Information Management (SIM) have made several proposals to try to reach a compromise on this issue. They want self-help (the publisher can send a message to your computer and shut your software down) banned because of the devastating effects of a shut-down of corporate critical systems. The mere threat of a shut down can force a customer company to pay off the publisher (Society for Information Management, 1998). The compromise proposals have allowed some form of self-help but require extra care from the publisher, such as advance notice (so the customer can go to court and get an emergency injunction if that's appropriate) or assumption of the risk of consequential damages if the publisher wrongfully shuts down the customer's system. To our astonishment, all of these proposals have failed. Nycum is one of the brightest and most respected computer lawyers in the United States, and SIM represents huge businesses (big businesses are customers too). Self-help has to be fixed or (we think) these businesses will spend whatever it takes to kill a bill that allows companies to turn off their core data processing capability. But even this basic compromise hasn't happened yet.

We just don't get it. The Drafting Committee are good people. We *like* them. They are doing this work as volunteers. They're working very hard. They want a successful end product that is adopted across the United States. But instead of seeing progress, *when progress is possible*, we see reassurances that Article 2B is really OK for consumers and accusations that we are just being political. It isn't. We aren't. Progress is possible. We can all do better than current law provides, but we have to make more room for each other's legitimate needs, or we won't achieve it. We think that the current Drafting Committee is stuck in a conceptual framework and style of meeting that isn't helping them make progress. We are losing hope that enough progress will be made.

Article 2B Isn't Bad Just for Consumers

The people who will lose the most under Article 2B will be small businesses who don't qualify as mass-market customers. They lose the perfect tender rule. They are subject to the less favorable definition of material breach, so they'll have to prove significant losses to be entitled to cancel a contract for bad software. They still won't have the power to negotiate terms in what is probably still a shrink-wrapped (or standard form) license. They aren't entitled to conspicuous notice of warranty disclaimers. Damage limitations will more likely be held against them (less chance of success at arguing that terms are unconscionable.) Time limits and other use restrictions in their licenses will be more enforceable against them. They don't have any protection against unfavorable choice of law or choice of forum clauses. None of the few consumer protections in Article 2B apply to them. Article 2B provides these customers with no protections and with fewer than they have today under Article 2.

Representatives of small business (doctors, dentists, convenience store owners, and so on) simply haven't been coming to Article 2B meetings. Their interests haven't been considered at any meeting that we've attended (at least, we don't recall any discussions). The results are, or should be, alarming.

What To Do

Our three main suggestions are these:

1. Write a letter to your governor and your state legislator. We provide a suggested form in Exhibit A.1.

2. Check out our Web site, www.badsoftware.com and Todd Paglia's Web site, www.essential.org/cpt/ucc/ucc.html. If you are a writer, check www.nwu.org, the Web site of the National Writers Union.

3. Post your reactions to 2B at Carol Kunze's Web site, www.SoftwareIndustry.org/issues/guide/parcom.html.

If you have additional suggestions or can volunteer time to help make software laws fair to customers, please contact us via www.badsoftware.com.

Exhibit A.1 Sample Letter to Your Governor

Dear Governor:

I am deeply concerned about the proposed new addition to the Uniform Commercial Code, Article 2B.

Include any of the following:

- This draft law is unfair to customers.

- It is unfair to independent software developers.

- It is unfair to freelance writers.

- It expands intellectual property rights in ways that will limit competition and interfere with the growth of small software startups.

- It expands intellectual property rights in ways that will make research much more expensive and drive the costs of public and university libraries much higher.

- It will result in lower quality software and will weaken our international competitive position.

Please let me know what you are doing to oppose the enactment of this law in our state and what I can do to help you in that.

Yours truly

We suggest that you copy the letter to Gene Lebrun, President, NCCUSL, 211 E. Ontario Street, Suite 1300, Chicago, IL 60611, and to Geoffrey Hazard, Executive Director, American Law Institute, 4025 Chestnut Street, Philadelphia, PA 19104.

Action Plan

Regarding Article 2B, we urge you to check our Web site, www.badsoftware.com for more information and to write your state's governor and your state legislator to express your concern about Article 2B. Please send us a copy of your letter.

And, because this book is sold (rather than licensed), you have the right to lend it to your friends. Spread the word.

References[1,2]

21st Century Properties Co. v. Carpenter Insulation and Carpeting Co. (1988) Federal Supplement, *vol. 694*, p. 148 (United States District Court, Maryland).

Adler, R.S. (1994) "The last best argument for eliminating reliance from express warranties: 'Real-world' consumers don't read warranties." *South Carolina Law Review, vol. 45*, p. 429.

Accusystems, Inc. v. Honeywell Information Systems (1984) Federal Supplement, *vol. 580*, p. 474 (United States District Court, Southern District of New York).

Advent Systems Ltd. v. Unisys Corp. (1991) Federal Reporter, 2nd Series, *vol. 925*, p. 670.

Alloy Computer Products, Inc. v. Northern Telecom, Inc. (1988) Federal Supplement, *vol. 683*, p. 12 (United States District Court, District of Massachusetts).

Alm v. Van Nostrand Reinhold (1985) North Eastern Reporter, 2nd Series, *vol. 480*, p. 1263 (134 Ill. App.3d 716; 89 Ill. Dec. 520) (Appellate Court of Illinois).

Altronics of Bethlehem, Inc. v. Repco, Inc. (1992) Federal Reporter, 2nd Series, *vol. 957*, p. 1102 (United States Court of Appeals, 3rd Circuit).

AMF Inc. v. Computer Automation, Inc. (1983) Federal Supplement, *vol. 573*, p. 924 (United States District Court, Southern District Of Ohio).

American Bar Association's Section on Science and Technology, Subcommittee on Proposed UCC Article 2B (1998, January 21) "Mass Market Licenses and UCC Article 2B." (unpublished) *Meeting of the NCCUSL Article 2B Drafting Committee*, Dallas, TX, February 20–22, 1998. Available at www.webcom.com/software/issues/guide/docs/abast.html.

---

[1] If you are an attorney, you'll note that our main citation for each case avoids the traditional, terse, legal-reference style. We agree that once you know the system, **423 F.2d 15** is easier to work with than **Federal Reporter, 2nd Series, *volume 423*, page 15**. Our interest is in making these materials as easy for a consumer to understand as possible.

[2] Many of our references are to section numbers rather than to page numbers.

We do this for law books because they are frequently updated and the page numbers change. Many of these books are loose leaf bound. When you get the update, you throw away old pages and insert new ones. A quote that was on page 40 last year might be on page 42 today. Other books are updated with a separate "supplement"—a soft covered booklet that lists all the changes in the law since the main volume was written. To determine what the law is today, you might read Section 4.01 in the book (the main volume) and then read the corresponding Section 4.01 in the supplement.

We refer to statutes by section because they don't have official page numbers. The Uniform Commercial Code has been reprinted in dozens of books. The page layout and page numbers change. The numbers of the sections of the Code stay the same.

American Medical Association (1912) *Nostrums and Quackery*, 2nd Edition. As quoted by Lee (1992).

Anton, J. (1996) *Customer Relationship Management*, Upper Saddle River, NJ: Prentice-Hall.

Archeluta v. Kopp (1977) Pacific Reporter, 2nd Series, *vol. 562*, p. 834 (90 N.M. 273) (Supreme Court of New Mexico).

Arizona Retail Systems, Inc. v. The Software Link (1993) Federal Supplement, *vol. 831*, p. 759. (United States District Court, Arizona).

Arizona Retail Systems, Inc. v. The Software Link: Response to Plaintiff's Motion for Partial Summary Judgment and Defendant's Cross-Motion for Partial Summary Judgment, August, 1992.

Arthur, W.B. (1994) *Increasing Returns and Path Dependence in the Economy.* Ann Arbor, MI: University of Michigan Press.

Associated Press (1995) "After Sizzling '94, Gleeful Electronics Execs Gather at Trade Show" (January 5). Association of Support Professionals (1997) *1997 Technical Support Cost Ratio Survey*, Association of Support Professionals.

Authors & Newspapers Association v. O'Gorman (1906) Federal Supplement, *vol. 147*, p. 616 (United States District Court, District of Rhode Island).

Bach, J.S. (1995a) "Process management in a mad world," Software Test Labs, downloaded from www.stlabs.com/bach.

Bach, J.S. (1995b) "What happens to bug reports you file with the company?" *Bug Net version 2.7* (August), p. 16.

Bach, J.S. (1996) "The Challenge of 'Good Enough' Software," Software Test Labs, downloaded from www.stlabs.com/bach/good.htm.

Barazzatto v. Intelligent Systems, Inc. (1987) North Eastern Reporter, 2nd Series, *vol. 532*, p. 148 (Court of Appeals of Ohio).

Barden v. HarperCollins Publishers, Inc. (1994) Federal Supplement, *vol. 863*, p. 41 (United States District Court, Massachusetts).

Barlow, J., and C. Moller (1996) *A Complaint is a Gift,* Berrett-Koehler Publishers.

Beeck v. Kapalis (1981) North Western Reporter, 2nd Series, *vol. 302*, p. 90 (Supreme Court of Iowa).

Belcher v. Versatile Farm Equip. Co. (1983) Southern Reporter, 2nd Series, *vol.* 443, p. 912 (Supreme Court of Alabama).

Bergman, P., and S.J. Berman-Barrett (1998) *Represent Yourself in Court: How to Prepare and Try a Winning Case.* 2nd Ed., Berkeley, CA: Nolo Press.

Bernacchi, R.L., Frank, P.B., and Statland, N. (as updated June 1995) *Bernacchi on Computer Law*, Boston: Little, Brown & Co.

Bertolucci, J. (1996) "PC reliability and service: Good-bye to good support," *PC World,* (December) p. 143-152.

Better Business Bureau (1996) *Annual Inquiry and Complaint Summary (1995).* Available at www.bbb.org.

Better Business Bureau (1997) *Calls To Better Business Bureaus Soar In 1996: Rapid Rise In Inquiries and Complaints On Telephone-Related Services.* Available at www.bbb.org.

Bevard v. Howat Concrete Co. (1970) Federal Reporter, 2nd Series, *vol. 433*, p. 1202 (United States Court of Appeals, District of Columbia Circuit).

Bevine v. Ballard (1982) Pacific Reporter, *vol. 655*, p. 757 (Supreme Court of Alaska).

Biakanja v. Irving (1958) Pacific Reporter, *vol. 320*, p. 16 (Supreme Court of California, *en banc*).

Bily v. Arthur Young & Co. (1992) Pacific Reporter, 2nd Series, *vol. 834*, p. 745 (Supreme Court of California, *en banc*).

Birmingham v. Fodor's Travel Publications, Inc. (1992) Pacific Reporter, 2nd Series, *vol. 833*, p. 70 (Supreme Court of Hawaii).

Black, Johnson & Simmons Insurance Brokerage, Inc. v. IBM (1982) North Eastern Reporter, *vol. 440*, p. 282 (Appellate Court of Illinois).

Blackwell, C.A. (1995) "A Good Installation Guide Increases User Satisfaction and Reduces Support Costs." *Technical Communication, vol. 42, #1*, p. 56.

Blumberg, D.F. (1991) *Managing Service as a Strategic Profit Center.* New York: McGraw-Hill.

Bobbs-Merrill Company v. Straus (1908) United States Reports, *vol. 210*, p. 339 (United States Supreme Court).

Bonura, L.S. (1994) *The Art of Indexing*, New York: John Wiley & Sons, Inc.

Boston Store of Chicago v. American Graphophone Company (1918) United States Reports, vol. 246, p. 8 (United States Supreme Court).

Bowdoin v. Showell Growers, Inc. (1987) Federal Reporter, 2nd Series, *vol. 817*, p. 1543 (United States Court of Appeals, 11th Circuit).

Braucher, J. & Linzer, P. (1998) "Assent Issues in Proposed UCC Article 2B." *Motion and supporting memo submitted to the American Law Institute for consideration at its Annual Meeting.* Available at www.ali.org/ali/braucher.htm.

Brown, D (1996) *Optimizing Support Center Staffing*, Superior, CO: Service Management Institute.

BugNet. For information on this magazine about bugs, email BugNetMag@aol.com or write BugNet at P.O. Box 393, Sumas, WA 98295.

Bultema, P. & Oxton, G. (1997, March) "Emerging Standards for the Support Industry," *Software Services Conference East,* Nashville, TN.

Burroughs Corp. v. Hall Affiliates, Inc. (1982) Southern Reporter, 2nd Series, *vol. 423,* p. 1348 (Supreme Court of Alabama).

Byrd, R.G. (1992) "Misrepresentation in North Carolina." *North Carolina Law Review, vol. 70,* p. 323.

Calamari, J.D., and Perrillo, J.M. (1987) *The Law of Contracts* (3rd Ed.) St. Paul, MN: West Publishing Corp.

California Civil Code (1998 supplement) *Deerings California Codes Annotated.*

California Department of Consumer Affairs (1996) *Consumer Law Sourcebook for Small Claims Court Judicial Officers, vols.* 1-3.

Campanella, J. (Ed.) (1990) *Principles of Quality Costs,* 2nd Ed. Milwaukee, WI: ASQC Quality Press.

Carmody, W.C., and Anderson, M.A. (1994) "Deceptive Trade Practices Act." *Southern Methodist University Law Review, vol. 47,* p. 1033.

Carnival Cruise Lines v. Shute (1991) *United States Reports, vol. 499,* p. 585 (United States Supreme Court).

Cates v. Morgan Portable Building Corp. (1985) Federal Reporter, *vol. 780,* p. 683 (United States Court of Appeals, 7th Circuit).

Centon Electronics, Inc. v. Bonar (1993) Southern Reporter, 2nd Series, *vol. 614,* p. 999 (Supreme Court of Alabama).

Central Point Software, Inc. v. Global Software & Accessories, Inc. (1995) Federal Supplement, *vol. 880,* p. 957 (Eastern District of New York).

Chatlos Systems v. National Cash Register Corp. (1980) Federal Reporter, 2nd Series, *vol. 635,* p. 1081 (United States Court of Appeals, 3rd Circuit).

Cherovsky, I. (1992) *Competent Counsel.* New York: John Wiley & Sons.

Christopher, E.L. (1997) "Desktop strategies for success: Maximizing service opportunity within industry trends" (February 3) *Dataquest* (available at www.dataquest.com).

Clancy, S. (1996,) "Service Opportunities in the Home PC User Market" (February 5), *Dataquest* (available at www.dataquest.com).

Clarke Auto Co. v. Reynolds (1949) North Eastern Reporter, 2nd Series, *vol. 88,* p. 775 (Indiana Appellate Court).

Clark, B., and Smith, C. (1984, supplemented 1994) *The Law of Product Warranties,* St. Paul, MN: Warren Gorham & Lamont.

Clement v. Smith (1993) California Appellate Reports, Fourth Series, *vol. 16,* p. 39 (California Court of Appeal).

Colonial Life Insurance Co. of America v. Electronic Data Systems Corp. (1993) Federal Supplement, *vol. 817*, p. 235 (United States District Court, District of New Hampshire).

Computer Systems Engineering, Inc. v. Quantel Corp. (1984) Federal Reporter, 2nd Series, *vol. 740*, p. 59 (United States Court of Appeals, 1st Circuit).

Commerce Clearing House (1990) "Computer Company Agrees Not to Advertise Unavailable Software." *CCH Guide to Computer Law*, *23*, (April 27).

Consolidated Data Terminals v. Applied Digital Systems (1983) Federal Reporter, 2nd Series, *vol. 708*, p. 385.

Cooper, C. (1996) "Syncronys Warns Dr. Dobbs Over Upcoming Review", *PC Week Online* (June 21). Available at www.zdnet.com/pcweek/news/0617/21esync.html.

Council of State Governments (1970) "Uniform Deceptive Trade Practices Act (1966)." *Suggested State Legislation, vol. 26*, p. 141.

Cox v. Lewiston Grain Growers, Inc. (1997) Pacific Reporter, 2nd Series, *vol. 936*, p. 1191 (Court of Appeals of Washington).

Creative Labs, Inc. v. Cyrix Corp. (1997) United States Patents Quarterly, 2nd Series, *vol. 42,* p. 1872 (United States District Court, Northern District of California).

Cringely, R.X. (1996) "Where has loyalty gone? Users grow weary of vendors' cheating ways" *InfoWorld* Notes from the Field column (March 4). Available at www.infoworld.com.

Crowley, T.E. (1994) *Settle it Out of Court.* New York: John Wiley & Sons.

Cumming, E. (1992) "Balancing the Buyer's Right to Recover for Precontractual Misstatements and the Seller's Ability to Disclaim Express Warranties." *Minnesota Law Review, vol. 76*, p. 1189.

Customer Care, Institute. (1993) *Customer Care Survey 1993: Service & Support Practices in the Software Industry.* Available from Customer Care Institute., 235 Martling Ave., Tarrytown, NY 10591.

Customer Care Institute (1994) *Customer Care Survey 1994: Service & Support Practices in the Software Industry.* Available from Customer Care, Institute., 235 Martling Ave., Tarrytown, NY 10591.

Dataquest (1997) "1996 Begins Era of 'Warranty Take-Back," press release for Christopher (1997), available at www.dataquest.com.

Daughtrey v. Ashe (1992) South Eastern Reporter, 2nd Series, *vol. 413*, p. 336 (Supreme Court of Virginia).

Diamond Fruit Growers, Inc. v. Krack Corp. (1986) Federal Reporter, 2nd Series, *vol. 794*, p. 1440 (United States Court of Appeals, 9th Circuit).

Desmond, M. (1997) "Software speed-ups: Bold claims and dubious promises", *PC World* (April). Also available at www.pcworld.com/software/utility/articles/apr97/1504p058.html.

DiCarlo, L. (1996) "Support Woes Still Dog Gateway", *ZDNet* (February 23). Downloaded from www4.sws.uiuc.edu/Pcpage/o23pgtw.html.

Dively, M.J., Schumm, B., & Cohn, D. (1995) *An Overview of Proposed Revisions to UCC Art. 2 Dealing with the Commercial Aspects of Software and other Intangibles Licensing*, Presented to the Computer Law Association on April 27, 1995. Printed in the course materials for *The 1995 Computer and Telecommunications Law Update*, Computer Law Association & Federal Communications Bar Association. Available from the Computer Law Association, 3028 Javier Road, Suite 402, Fairfax, VA 22031.

Dobbs, D.B. (1993) *Law of Remedies: Damages—Equity—Restitution.* (2nd Ed.) St. Paul, MN: West Publishing Corp.

Driscoll, D.P. & Henley, W.M. (1996) *Class Action Complaint for Fraud and Breach of Warranty.* (Defendant: Syncronys and several retailers) ftp.uni-mannheim.de/info/Oreilly/windows/win95.update/complain.txt.

Driscoll, D.P. (1998) *Complaint for Unfair Competition* (Defendant: Blizzard Entertainment). www.gamespot.com/news/news/98_05/01_lawsuit/index.html.

D'Ulisse-Cupo v. Board of Directors (1987) Atlantic Reporter, 2nd Series, *vol. 520*, p. 217 (Supreme Court of Connecticut).

Duncan, R. (1996) *How to Sue for Up to $25,000...and Win! Suing and Defending a Case in Municipal Court Without a Lawyer.* 2nd Ed. Berkeley, CA: Nolo Press.

Dykas, P.L. (1991) "Opinion v. Express Warranty: How Much Puff Can a Salesman Use, if a Salesman Can Use Puff to Make a Sale?" *Idaho Law Review, vol. 28*, p. 167.

Eddington v. Dick (1976) New York Supplement, 2nd Series, *vol. 386*, p. 180 (Geneva City Court).

Einhorn, D.A. (1992) "Box-Top Licenses and the Battle-of-the-Forms." *Software Law Journal, vol. 5,* p. 401.

Eisen, C.R. (1991) "Don't Confuse Us with the Facts?: The Relevance of the Buyer's Knowledge of a Written Exclusion of an Implied Warranty Which is Inconspicuous as a Matter of Law (U.C.C. S 2-316(2))." *Seton Hall Legislative Journal, vol. 15*, p. 297.

Erdman v. Johnson Bros. Radio & TV Co. (1970) Atlantic Reporter, 2nd Series, *vol. 271*, p. 744 (Maryland Court of Appeals).

Essenburg v. Russell (1956) North Western Reporter, 2nd Series, *vol. 78*, p. 136 (Supreme Court of Michigan).

European Community (1991) "Council Directive 91/250 on the Legal Protection of Computer Programs." *Official Journal of the European Communities* (L. 122).

Family Drug Store of New Iberia, Inc. v. Gulf States Computer Services, Inc. (1982) Southern Reporter, 2nd Series, *vol. 563*, p. 1324 (Louisiana Court of Appeal).

Federal Trade Commission v. Hare (1998) Complaint available at www.ftc.gov/os/9804/compl3.htm. News release, "FTC Halts Internet Auction House Scam" available at www.ftc.gov/opa/9804/hare.htm.

Feist Publications, Inc. v. Rural Telephone Service Co. (1991) United States Reports, *vol. 499* p. 340 (United States Supreme Court).

Ferguson, P., Humphrey, W.S., Khajenoori, S., Macke, M., and Matuya, A. (1997) "Results of applying the Personal Software Process," *IEEE Computer* (May) p. 24.

First Equity Corp. of Florida v. Standard & Poor's Corp. (1987) Federal Supplement, *vol. 670*, p. 115.

First United Financial Corp. v. United States Fidelity & Guarantee Co. (1996) Federal Reporter, 3rd Series, *vol. 96*, p. 135 (United States Court of Appeals, 5th Circuit).

Fisher, R., Ury, W., and Patton, B. (1991) *Getting to Yes*, New York: Penguin Books.

Fisher, R. & Ertel, D. (1995) *Getting Ready to Negotiate: The Getting to Yes Workbook*, New York: Penguin Books.

Flamme v. Wolf Insurance Agency (1991) North Western Reporter, 2nd Series, *vol. 476,* p. 802 (Supreme Court of Nebraska).

Flory, J. (1997) "Web Self-Support Works! 6 Surprising New Case Studies", Support Management, *vol. 1*, #5, p. 46.

Foonberg, J. G. (1995) *Finding the Right Lawyer.* American Bar Association.

Forbes v. Par Ten Group, Inc. (1990) South Eastern Reporter, 2nd Series, *vol. 394*, p. 643 (North Carolina Court of Appeal).

Ford, W., and Baum, M.S. (1997) *Secure Electronic Commerce*, Upper Saddle River, NJ: Prentice-Hall.

Foster, E. (1997) "BACs hearken back to product-specific user groups of days gone by." *InfoWorld* (May 26). Gripe Line column available from www.infoworld.com.

Foundation Software Laboratories, Inc. v. Digital Equipment Corporation (1992) Federal Supplement, *vol. 807*, p. 1195 (United States District Court, Maryland).

Friedman, M. (1998) "Coping with Consumer Fraud: The Need for a Paradigm Shift," *Journal of Consumer Affairs, vol. 32,* p. 1.

Frank M. Booth, Inc. v. Reynolds Metals, Co. (1991) Federal Supplement, *vol. 754*, p. 1441 (United States District Court, Eastern District of California).

Freund, J.C. (1992) *Smart Negotiating: How to Make Good Deals in the Real World*, New York: Simon & Schuster.

Froomkin, A.M. (1996) "The Essential Role of Trusted Third Parties in Electronic Commerce," *Oregon Law Review, vol. 75*, p. 49.

Fundin v. Chicago Pneumatic Tool Co. (1984) *California Appellate Reports, 3rd Series, vol. 152*, p. 951 (California Court of Appeal).

Garman, E.T. (1996), *Consumer Economic Issues in America,* 4th Edition, Houston, TX: Dame Publications.

Glovatorium v. NCR Corporation (1982) Federal Reporter, 2nd Series, *vol. 684*, p. 658 (United States Court of Appeals, 9th Circuit).

Glyptal, Inc. v. Engelhard Corp. (1992) Federal Supplement, *vol. 801*, p. 887 (United States District Court, District of Massachusetts).

Goldman, L. (1993) "The World's Best Article on Competitor Suits for False Advertising." *Florida Law Review, vol. 45*, p. 487.

Goldstein, N. (1994) *The Associated Press Stylebook and Libel Manual*, Reading, MA: Addison-Wesley.

Gomulkiewicz, R.W. (1998a) " The Implied Warranty of Merchantability in Software Contracts: A Warranty No One Dares To Give And How To Change That." (to be published). Available at www.webcom.com/software/issues/guide/legart.html

Gomukiewicz, R.W. (1998b) "The License *is* the Product: Comments on the Promise of UCC Article 2B for Software Licensing." *Proceedings of the Conference on the Impact of Article 2B*, UC Berkeley, April 23-25, 1998.

Gomulkiewicz, R. W., and M.L. Williamson (1996) "A Brief Defense Of Mass Market Software License Agreements," *Rutgers Computer & Technology Law Journal, vol. 22*, p. 335.

Goodman, J., Malech, A., and Adamson, C. (1988) "Don't Fix the Product, Fix the Customer," *The Quality Review* (Fall).

Goodman, J. (1997) "Utilizing customer feedback to measurably improve the value of support." Presented to the *Support Services Conference East*, Nashville, TN, March, 1997.

Gray, D., and A. Lyons (1996) *How Not to Get Screwed by Your Attorney.* Citadel Press.

Grech, C. (1992) "Computer documentation doesn't pass muster." *PC Computing, vol. 5* (April) p. 212.

Grech C. (1992) "Shelfware Secrets: The programs you never use—reader survey on software owned but not used." *PC-Computing, vol. 5* (August) p. 270.

Gryna, F. M. (1988) "Quality Costs" in Juran, J.M., and F. M. Gryna (1988, 4th Ed.), *Juran's Quality Control Handbook*, New York: McGraw-Hill.

Hackos, J. (1994) *Managing Your Documentation Projects*, New York: John Wiley & Sons, Inc.

Hackos, J. (1997) "Online Documentation: The Next Generation", *Conference Proceedings of the 15th Annual International Conference on Computer Documentation*, Salt Lake City, UT, October, 1997.

Hadley v. Baxendale (1854) English Reports, *vol. 156*, p. 145.

Hahn v. Ford Motor Company (1982) North Eastern Reporter, 2nd Series, *vol. 434*, p. 943 (Court of Appeals of Indiana).

Hancock, W.A. (Ed.) (1994a; supplemented November 1997) *Corporate Counsel's Guide to Software Transactions*, Chesterland, OH: Business Laws, Inc.

Hancock, W.A. (Ed.) (1993; supplemented November 1997) *Corporate Counsel's Guide to Warranties*, Chesterland, OH: Business Laws, Inc.

Hancock, W.A. (Ed.) (1990; supplemented April 1998) *Data Processing Agreements* (2nd Edition), Chesterland, OH: Business Laws, Inc.

Hawaiian Telephone Co. v. Microform Data Systems, Inc. (1987) Federal Reporter, 2nd Series, *vol. 829*, p. 919 (United States Court of Appeals, 9th Circuit).

Help Desk Institute (1997) *Help Desk and Customer Support Practices Report: October, 1996 Survey Results.*

Hill v. Gateway 2000, Inc. (1997) Federal Reporter, 3rd Series, *vol. 105*, p. 1147 (United States Court of Appeals, 7th Circuit).

Hill v. Gateway 2000, Inc. (1997b) *Petition for Writ of Certiorari of Rich Hill and Enza Hill.* Filed with the United States Supreme Court, May 5, 1997.

Hillebrand, G. (1997) "Comments on draft of UCC Article 2B" (unpublished) *Annual Meeting of the National Conference of Commissioners on Uniform State Laws,* Sacramento, CA, July 25 – August 1, 1997.

Hillebrand, G. (1998a) "Comments on the February 1998 Article 2B Draft (in the order in which they arise in the draft.)" (unpublished) *Meeting of the NCCUSL Article 2B Drafting Committee*, Cincinnati, OH, March 27-29, 1998.

Hillebrand, G. (1998b) "Opposition to UCC Article 2B" (unpublished) *Annual Meeting of the National Conference of Commissioners on Uniform State Laws*, Cleveland, OH, July 24-31, 1998.

Hoffman, J.M. (1991) "Soldiers of Misfortune: A Survey of Claims by Victims of Negligent Publishing and Broadcasting." *The Brief, vol. 20* (Summer) p. 23.

Holdych, T.J. (1994) "Standards for Establishing Deceptive Conduct Under State Deceptive Trade Practices Statutes That Impose Punitive Remedies." *Oregon Law Review, vol. 73*, p. 235.

Humphrey, W.S. (1997a) *Introduction to the Personal Software Process,* Reading, MA: Addison-Wesley.

Humphrey, W.S. (1997b) "Comments on Software Quality." (unpublished) *Annual Meeting of the National Conference of Commissioners on Uniform State Laws,* July 25–August 1, 1997, Sacramento, CA. Available at www.webcom.com/software/issues/guide/docs/whsq.html.

Humphrey, W.S. (1997c) "Software Contracts[md] An Historical Perspective." (unpublished) *Meeting of the NCCUSL Article 2B Drafting Committee,* Cincinnati, OH, May 30-June 1, 1997. Available at www.webcom.com/software/issues/guide/docs/hist.html.

Hunter v. Up-Right, Inc. (1993) Pacific Reporter, 2nd Series, *vol. 864*, p. 88 Supreme Court of California, *en banc*).

InfoTech (an international multimedia market research firm, based in Woodstock, VT), (1995, February) *Optical Publishing Industry Assessment*, 7th Edition, as cited in Steinberg & Sege (1995).

Information Industry Association, American Medical Association, & Association of American Publishers (1996) *ProCD, Inc. v. Matthew Zeidenberg, and Silken Mountain Web Services: Brief of Amici Curiae.* Manuscript on file with the authors.

In re Pentium Processor Litigation, Master Case Number CV745729, 11 volumes on file at the Santa Clara County Superior Court, San Jose, California.

In the Matter of America Online, Inc. (1998) Docket No. C-3787. Complaint at www.ftc.gov/os/9803/9523331.cmp.htm. Decision and order at www.ftc.gov/os/9803/9523331.d&o.htm.

In the Matter of Apple Computer, Inc. (1997) Docket C-3763. Complaint at www.ftc.gov/os/9708/c3763cmp.htm. Decision and order at www.ftc.gov/os/9708/c3763ord.htm.

In the Matter of Compuserve, Inc. (1998) Docket No. C-3789. Complaint at www.ftc.gov/os/9803/9623096.cmp.htm. Decision and order at www.ftc.gov/os/9803/9623096.d&o.htm.

In the Matter of Prodigy Services Corporation (1998) Docket No. C-3788. Complaint at www.ftc.gov/os/9803/9523332.cmp.htm. Decision and order at www.ftc.gov/os/9803/9523332.d&o.htm.

In the Matter of Syncronys Software. (1996) Docket C-3688. Complaint atwww.ftc.gov/os/9610/c3688cmp.htm. Decision and order at www.ftc.gov/os/9610/c3688d&o.htm.

Internal Revenue Service (1985) "Revenue Ruling 85-189: Return preparers; sale of computer program. A person who prepares a computer program and sells it to a taxpayer to use in preparing the tax-payer's income tax return may be an income tax return preparer." *Cumulative Bulletin, vol. 1985-2*, p. 341.

Internal Revenue Service (1986, May 6) "IRS announces that companies who sell return preparation computer software and programs may be considered return preparers subject to penalties." *I.R.S. News Release, IR-86-92.*

Ionics, Inc. v. Elmwood Sensors, Inc. (1997) Federal Reporter, 3rd Series, *vol. 110*, p. 184 (United States Court of Appeals, 1st Circuit).

J'Aire Corp. v. Gregory (1979) Pacific Reporter, 2nd Series, *vol. 598*, p. 60 (Supreme Court of California).

Johnson v. Compaq (1997) Class action complaint filed against Compaq Computer in North Carolina. For the text, see users.aol.com/Cclass450/index.htm. This is a remarkable series of documents, and it is kept updated.

Johnson, B. (1995) "Electronic Services: What Do Users Think?", *Software Support '95 Conference Report*, San Francisco, CA, December 1995.

Johnson, B., and Gately, A. (1996) "SystemSoft to Develop Products to Automatically Identify and Resolve PC Users' Most Common Problems," *Dataquest* (March 12). (Access this through www.dataquest.com.)

Judicial Council of California (1994) *1994 Annual Report of the Judicial Council of California to the Governor and the Legislature.*

Kaner, C. (1995a) "Software Negligence and Testing Coverage", *Software QA Quarterly, Volume 2*, #2, p. 18. An updated version of this paper was presented at the *Proceedings of STAR 96 (Fifth International Conference on Software Testing, Analysis, and Review)*, Orlando, FL, May, 1996, p. 313.

Kaner, C. (1995b) "Liability for Defective Documentation", *Software QA Quarterly, vol. 2*, #3, p. 8. Available at www.badsoftware.com/baddocs.htm.

Kaner, C. (1996a) "Uniform Commercial Code Article 2B: A new law of software quality", *Software QA, vol. 3*, #2, p. 10.

Kaner, C. (1996b) "Warranty and Liability Hypotheticals for UCC Article 2B," (unpublished.) *Meeting of the NCCUSL Article 2B Drafting Committee*, Philadelphia, PA, April 26-28, 1996. Available at www.badsoftware.com

Kaner, C. (1996c) "Liability for Defective Content", *Software QA, vol. 3,* #3, p. 56. Available at www.badsoftware.com

Kaner, C. (1996d) "Liability for Bad Software and Support", presented to *the Software Support Professionals Association Executive Briefing*, San Diego, CA, October, 1996. Also in the *Proceedings of the Support Services Conference East*, Nashville, TN, March, 1997. Available at www.badsoftware.com.

Kaner, C. (1996e) "Negotiating testing resources: A collaborative approach", presented to the *Ninth International Software Quality Week Conference*, San Francisco, CA, May, 1998. Available at www.kaner.com.

Kaner, C. (1996f) "Privacy Problems in Article 2B", (unpublished.) *Meeting of the NCCUSL Article 2B Drafting Committee*, Tampa, FL, November 22-24, 1996. Available at www.badsoftware.com.

Kaner, C. (1996g) Quality Cost Analysis: Benefits and Risks. *Software QA, vol. 3*, #1, p. 23. Available at www.badsoftware.com/qualcost.htm.

Kaner, C. (1996h) Uniform Commercial Code Article 2B: A new law of software quality. *Software QA, vol. 3*, #2, p. 10. Available at www.badsoftware.com/uccsqa.htm.

Kaner, C. (1996i) Warranty and Liability Hypotheticals for UCC Article 2B. (unpublished.) *Meeting of the NCCUSL Article 2B Drafting Committee*, Philadelphia, PA, April 26-28, 1996. Available at www.badsoftware.com

Kaner, C. (1997a) What is a Serious Bug? Defining a "Material Breach" of a Software License Agreement. (unpublished.) *Meeting of the NCCUSL Article 2B Drafting Committee*, Redwood City, CA, January 10-12, 1997. (abbreviated version, *Software QA*, 3, #6.) Available at www.badsoftware.com/uccdefect.htm.

Kaner, C. (1997b) Remedies Provisions of Article 2B. (unpublished.) *Meeting of the NCCUSL Article 2B Drafting Committee*, Redwood City, CA, January 10-12, 1997. Available at www.badsoftware.com/uccrem.htm.

Kaner, C. (1997c) Proposed Article 2B: Problems from the Customer's View: Part 1: Underlying Issues. *UCC Bulletin*, January, p. 1. Available at www.badsoftware .com/uccpart1.htm.

Kaner, C. (1997d) Proposed Article 2B: Problems from the Customer's View: Part 2: List of Key Issues. *UCC Bulletin*, February, p. 1. Available at www.badsoftware .com/uccpart2.htm.

Kaner, C. (1997e) Not Quite Terrible Enough Software. (unpublished.) *Annual Meeting of the Software Engineering Process Group*, San Jose, CA, March 1997. Available at www.badsoftware.com/sepg.htm.

Kaner, C. (1997f) "The impossibility of complete testing", *Software QA, vol. 4*, #4, p. 28.

Kaner, C. (1997g) Liability for Bad Software and Support. *Proceedings of the Support Services Conference East,* Nashville, TN, March 12, 1997. Available at www .badsoftware.com/support1.htm.

Kaner, C. (1997h) Article 2B is Fundamentally Unfair to Mass-Market Software Customers. (unpublished.) Circulated to the American Law Institute for its Article 2B review meeting, October 1997. Available at www.badsoftware.com/ali.htm.

Kaner, C. (1997i) Status Report: New Laws that will Govern Software Quality. *Proceedings of the 15th Annual Pacific Northwest Software Quality Conference*, Portland, OR, October 28, 1997, p. 269.

Kaner, C. (1997j) Restricting Competition in the Software Industry: Impact of the Pending Revisions to the Uniform Commercial Code. Proceedings of Ralph Nader's conference, *Appraising Microsoft*, Washington, DC, November, 14, 1997. Available at www.badsoftware.com/nader.htm.

Kaner, C. (1997k) Legal Issues Related to Software Quality, *Proceedings of the Seventh International Conference on Software Quality.* Montgomery, AL, October 8, 1997, p. 2. An expanded version appears in *Software Quality*, #2, 1997-98, p.1.

Kaner, C. (1998a) Speedbump on the information superhighway: The insecurity of digital signatures. *UCC Bulletin* (February) p.1.

Kaner, C. (1998b) "Bad software—Who is liable?" Proceedings of the American Society for Quality's 52nd Annual Quality Congress, Philadelphia, May, 1998. Available at www.badsoftware.com.

Kaner, C. (1998c) "Article 2B and Quality/Cost Analysis," *Conference on the Impact of Article 2B*, UC Berkeley, April 23-25, 1998.

Kaner, C., Falk, J., and Nguyen, H.Q. (1993) *Testing Computer Software*, 2nd Ed., International Thomson Computer Press.

Kaner, C. & Gomulkiewicz, B. (1997) *Moving Toward a Usable Warranty of Merchantability.* Proposal circulated at the *Meeting of the NCCUSL Article 2B Drafting Committee*, Cincinnatti, OH, May 30-June 1, 1997.

Kaner, C. & Kurtz, M. (1997, March), *Software contracting: Proposed revisions to the UCC*, MCLE seminar sponsored by the High Tech Law Section of the Santa Clara County Bar Association.

Kaner, C., and Lawrence, B. (1997) "UCC changes pose problems for developers", *IEEE Software* (March/April) p. 139.

Kaner, C., B. Lawrence, and R. Johnson (1998) "SPLAT! Requirements Bugs on the Information Superhighway", *Software QA*, vol. 5, #1, p. 18.

Kaner, C., and T. Paglia, (1997) Letter to American Law Institute outlining the consumer community's priorities for its Executive Council meeting, December, 1997. *In press, UCC Bulletin.* Available at www.badsoftware.com/alidec.htm.

Kaner, C. & Pels, D. (1996) "User documentation testing: Ignore at your own risk", *Customer Care, vol. 7*, #4, p. 7.

Kaner, C., and D. Pels (1997) Article 2B and Software Customer Dissatisfaction. (unpublished) *Meeting of the National Conference of Commissioners on Uniform State Laws' Article 2B Drafting Committee*, Cincinnati, OH, May 30, 1997. A shorter version of this paper, for the software community, was published as Software Customer Dissatisfaction, *Software QA, vol. 4*, #3, p. 24. Available at www.badsoftware.com/stats.htm.

Kaner, C., and D. Pels (1998) "Copyright Laws and Y2K Maintenance." *Innovations in Software Support: Journal of the Software Support Professionals Association* (April) p. 2.

Karjala, D.S. (1997) Federal Preemption of Shrinkwrap and On-Line Licenses, *University of Dayton Law Review, in press.*

Katz, P.R. (1994) "Caveat Vendor: Limitation Clauses in Software Agreements May Not Withstand Judicial Scrutiny." *The Computer Law Association Bulletin, vol. 9, #2*, p. 12.

Keeton, W. P., Dobbs, D. B., Keeton, R.E., and Owen, D.G. (1984, supplemented 1988) *Prosser and Keeton on Torts* (5th Edition), St. Paul, MN: West Publishing Corp.

Kelso, J.C. (1995) *Unfair Trade Practices Litigation*, Charlottesville, VA: The Michie Company.

Keup, E.J. (1993) *Mail Order Legal Guide*, Grants Pass, OR: The Oasis Press.

Khandpur, N. & Laub, L. (1997) *Delivering World-Class Technical Support*, New York: John Wiley & Sons.

Kubey, C. (1991) *You Don't Always Need a Lawyer.* New York: Consumer Reports Books.

Kutten, L.J. (1987, Supplemented 1998) *Computer Software: Protection / Liability / Law / Forms.* Volumes 1-4. St. Paul, MN: West Publishing Corp.

Kwestel, S. (1992) "Freedom From Reliance: A Contract Approach to Express Warranty." *Suffolk University Law Review, vol. 26*, p. 959.

Landau, T. (1997) *Sad Macs, Bombs, and other Disasters*, Berkeley, CA: Peachpit Press.

Lande, R.H., and S.M. Sobin (1996) Reverse Engineering of Computer Software: The Antitrust Issues. *Harvard Journal of Law & Technology, 9, #2*, p. 237.

Lanning v. Sprague (1951) Pacific Reporter, 2nd Series, *vol. 227*, p. 347 (Supreme Court of Idaho).

Lawyers Co-operative Publishing Co. (1995, including the supplementary material) "Annotation: What Constitutes False, Misleading, or Deceptive Advertising or Promotional Practices Subject to Action by Federal Trade Commission." *American Law Reports, 2nd Series, vol. 65*, p. 255.

Lee, D. B. (1992) "The Colorado Consumer Protection Act: Panacea or Pandora's Box?" *Denver University Law Review, vol. 70*, p. 141.

Lemley, M.A. (1995) Intellectual Property and Shrinkwrap Licenses, *Southern California Law Review, 68*, p. 1239.

Lengyel v. Lint (1981) South Eastern Reporter, 2nd Series, *vol. 280*, p. 66 (West Virginia Supreme Court of Appeals).

Leveson, N.G. (1995) *Safeware: System Safety and Computers*, Reading, MA: Addison-Wesley Publishing Co.

Levin, S. (1986) "Examining Restraints on Freedom to Contract as an Approach to Purchaser Dissatisfaction in the Computer Industry." *California Law Review, vol. 74*, p. 2101.

Levy, L. B., and Bell, S.Y. (1990) "Software Product Liability: Understanding and Minimizing the Risks." *High Technology Law Journal, vol. 5*, p. 1.

Livingston, B. (1997) "My latest Windows mystery is solved: at least, I think it is." InfoWorld, *vol. 19*, #21, p. 36.

Logan Equip. Corp. v. Simon Aerials, Inc. (1990) Federal Supplement, *vol. 776*, p. 1188 (United States District Court, District of Massachusetts).

Long Leaf Lumber, Inc. v. Svolos, Southern Reporter, 2nd Series, *vol. 258*, 121.

Long Island Lighting Co. v. Transamerica Delaval, Inc. (1986) Federal Supplement, *vol. 646*, p. 1442 (United States District Court, Southern District of New York).

Louisiana AFL-CIO v. Lanier Business Products (1986) Federal Reporter, 2nd Series, *vol. 797*, p. 1364 (United States Court of Appeals, 5th Circuit).

Mahler, J. (1994) "Pentium flaw raises eyebrows at FDA; Agency action uncertain." Dow Jones News Service.

Magnuson-Moss Warranty—Federal Trade Commission Improvement Act, United States Code, *Title 15*, Section 2301.

MAI Systems Corp. v. Peak Computer, Inc. (1993) *Federal Reporter, 2nd Series*, vol. 991, p. 511 (United States Court of Appeals, 9th Circuit).

Marable, L. M. (1995) "Better Business Bureaus are a Bust." *Money* (October) p. 106.

MasterCard International & National Fraud Information Center (undated) *Schemes, Scams & Flim-Flams—A Consumer's Guide to Phone Fraud*. MasterCard 1-800-999-5136.

Maxwell, P.K., and Labadie, T. (1993) "Deceptive Trade Practices and Antitrust." *Southern Methodist University Law Review, vol. 46*, p. 1325.

McCrimmon v. Tandy Corp. (1991) South Eastern Reporter, 2nd Series, *vol. 414*, p. 15 (Georgia Court of Appeals).

McKenna, J.A. (1994) "Consumer Protection and the Maine Unfair Trade Practices Act." *Maine Bar Journal, vol. 9*, p. 78.

McManis, C. (1998) "The Privatisation (or 'Shrink-wrapping') of American Copyright Law". *Conference on the Impact of Article 2B*, UC Berkeley, April 23-25, 1998.

Meighan v. Shore (1995) California Appellate Reports, *vol. 34*, p. 1025 (California Court of Appeal).

Metropolitan Life Ins. Co. v. Noble Lowndes Int'l, Inc. (1993) Appellate Division Reports, Second Series, *vol. 192*, p. 83 (New York Supreme Court, Appellate Division).

Microsoft Corp. v. Manning (1995) South Western Reporter, 2nd Series, *vol. 914,* p. 602 (Texas Court of Appeals).

Microsoft (1993) *User's Guide: Microsoft MS-DOS 6.*

Mid-State Homes, Inc. v. Startley (1979) Southern Reporter, 2nd Series, *vol. 366*, p. 734 (Alabama Court of Appeals).

Minasi, M. (1993) *Troubleshooting Windows*, Alameda, CA: Sybex.

Minasi, M. (1996) *The Complete PC Upgrade and Maintenance Guide*, 7th Ed., Alameda, CA: Sybex.

Mirken v. Wasserman (1993) Pacific Reporter, 2nd Series, *vol. 858*, p. 568 (Supreme Court of California).

Miron v. Yonkers Raceway, Inc., (1968) Federal Reporter, 2nd Series, *vol. 400*, p. 112 (United States Court of Appeals, 2nd Circuit).

Mitchell v. Dahlberg (1996) Northwestern Reporter, 2nd Series, *vol. 547*, p. 74 (Michigan Court of Appeal).

Model Penal Code (1962) Official Draft, American Law Institute.

Moore, G.A. (1991) *Crossing the Chasm*, New York: HarperBusiness.

Moore, G.H. & Hadden, J.D. (1996) "On-Line Software Distribution: New Life for 'Shrinkwrap' Licenses?" *The Computer Lawyer* (April).

Mossberg, W. (1994), "Intel isn't serving millions who bought its Pentium campaign," *Wall Street Journal* (December 15), p. B1.

Motion Picture Patents Co. v. Universal Film Manufacturing Co. (1917) United States Reports, *vol. 243*, p. 502 (United States Supreme Court).

Mueller, S. (1996) *Upgrading and Repairing PCs*, 6th Ed., Indianapolis, IN: QUE.

Mulvany, N. (1994) *Indexing Books*, Chicago: University of Chicago Press.

Murtagh, S. (1993) *Staffing, Scheduling and Workforce Planning*, Colorado Springs, CO: Help Desk Institute.

Murtagh, S.J. (1994) *An Analysis of Cost of Calls in the Customer Support Industry*, Colorado Springs, CO: Help Desk Institute.

Myers & Chapman, Inc. v. Thomas G. Evans, Inc. (1988) South Eastern Reporter, 2nd Series, *vol. 374*, p. 385 (North Carolina Supreme Court).

Nader, R. (1997) *Re: Shrinkwrap Licenses and Uniform Commercial Code Article 2B*, Letter to Bill Gates, dated March 31, 1997. Available at the web site of the Consumer Project on Technology (a Nader organization), at www.cptech.org/ucc/nader.html.

National Conference of Commissioners on Uniform State Laws (1997) *Uniform Commercial Code Article 2B, Law of Licensing*. Draft of September 22, 1997. Available at www.law.upenn.edu/bll/ulc/ulc.htm.

National Conference of Commissioners on Uniform State Laws (1998) *Uniform Commercial Code Article 2B, Law of Licensing.* Annual Meeting Draft of July 24-31, 1998. Available at www.law.upenn.edu/bll/ulc/ulc.htm.

National Conference of Commissioners on Uniform State Laws (1998b) *Uniform Electronic Transactions Act.* Annual Meeting Draft of July 24-31, 1998. Available at www.law.upenn.edu/bll/ulc/ulc.htm.

National Fraud Information Center & MasterCard International (undated), *Schemes, Scams, & Flim-Flams.* For a copy, call NFIC 1-800-876-7060.

New England Foundation Co. v. Elliot A. Watrous Co. (1940) North Eastern Reporter, 2nd Series, *vol. 27*, p. 756 (Supreme Judicial Court of Massachusetts).

Nimmer, D. (1998) "The Metamorphosis of Contract into Expand." *Conference on the Impact of Article 2B*, UC Berkeley, April 23-25, 1998.

Nimmer, R.T. (1997, 2nd supplement 1998) *The Law of Computer Technology: Rights, Licenses, Liabilities* (3rd Edition), St. Paul, MN: West Group.

Nimmer, R.T. (1998) "Breaking Barriers: The Relation Between Contract and Intellectual Property Law", *Conference on the Impact of Article 2B*, UC Berkeley, April 23-25, 1998.

Occidental Chemical Corp. v. Elliott Turbomachinery Co. (1996) Federal Reporter, 3rd Series, *vol. 84*, p. 172 (United States Court of Appeals, 5th Circuit).

Orthopedic & Sports Injury Clinic v. Wang (1991) Federal Reporter, *vol. 922*, p. 220 (United States Court of Appeals, 5th Circuit).

Osborn v. Wills (1931) North Western Reporter, *vol. 236*, p. 197 (Supreme Court of Minnesota).

Ott v. Alfa-Laval Agri, Inc. (1995) California Appellate Reports, *vol. 31*, p. 1439 (California Court of Appeal).

Oxton (1997) "Multivendor support challenges", *Software Services Conference East, Nashville,* TN, March, 1997.

Paul v. Cameron (1934) North Western Reporter, *vol. 256*, p. 11 (Supreme Court of Nebraska).

Pawelec v. Digitcom, Inc. (1984) Atlantic Reporter, 2nd Series, *vol. 471*, p. 60.

PC Week (1994) "Testing reveals that Intel's and IBM's claims both exaggerate the magnitude of problems, risks", *PC Week, vol. 11*, #50 (December 19), p. 1.

Peterson, I. (1995) *Fatal Defect*, New York: Random House: Times Books.

Plauger, P.J. (1990, November) "Shelfware." *Computer Language, vol. 7*, p. 17.

Powers, D. (1994) *Legal Street Smarts: How to Survive in a World of Lawyers.* New York: Plenum Press.

Pratt v. Thompson (1925) Pacific Reporter, *vol. 233*, p. 637 (133 Wash. 218) (Supreme Court of Washington).

Princeton Graphics v. NEC Home Electronics (1990) Federal Supplement, *vol. 732,* p. 1258 (United States District Court, Southern District of New York).

ProCD, Inc. v. Zeidenberg (1996) Federal Reporter, 3rd Series, *vol. 86*, p. 1447 (United States Court of Appeals, 7th Circuit).

ProCD, Inc. v. Zeidenberg (1996b) Federal Supplement, *vol. 98,* p. 640 (United States District Court, Western District of Wisconsin). *Note: This decision was overruled by ProCD, Inc. v. Zeidenberg (1996).*

Raritan River Steel Co. v. Cherry, Bekaert & Holland (1988) South Eastern Reporter, 2nd Series, *vol. 367*, p. 609 (Supreme Court of North Carolina).

Raysman, R. & Brown, P. (1984, updated 1998) *Computer Law: Drafting and Negotiating Forms and Agreements*, New York: Law Journal Seminars-Press.

RCA Mfg. Co. v. Whiteman (1940) Federal Reporter, Second Series, *vol. 114*, p. 86 (United States Court of Appeal, Second Circuit, opinion by Learned Hand). *Certiorari denied* United States Reports, *vol. 311*, p. 712 (United States Supreme Court).

Reda v. Sincaban (1988) North Western Reporter, 2nd Series, *vol. 426*, p. 100 (Wisconsin Court of Appeals).

Reinert, J. R. (1998) Letter to the National Conference of Commissioners on Uniform State Laws, February 23, 1998, Available at www.webcom.com/software/issues/guide/docs/ieee2b.html.

Resolution Trust Corp. v. Mooney (1991) Southern Reporter, 2nd Series, *vol. 592*, p. (Supreme Court of Alabama).

Restatement (2nd) of Torts (1965) American Law Institute.

Rice, D. (1992) "Public Goods, Private Contract and Public Policy: Federal Preemption of Software License Prohibitions Against Reverse Engineering." University of Pittsburgh Law Review, *vol. 53*, p. 543.

Rice, D. (1996) "Committee Review of General Balance and Related Issues." (unpublished.) *Meeting of the NCCUSL Article 2B Drafting Committee*, Minneapolis, MN, September 25-27, 1996. Available at www.SoftwareIndustry.org/issues/guide/parcom.html.

Rice, D. (1997) "Digital Information as Property and Product: UCC Article 2B." *University of Dayton Law Review, vol. 22,* p. 621.

Richard v. A. Waldman & Sons, Inc. (1967) Atlantic Reporter, 2nd Series, *vol. 232*, p. 307 (Supreme Court of Connecticut).

Riley Hill General Contractor, Inc. v. Tandy Corp. (1987) Pacific Reporter, 2nd Series, *vol. 737*, p. 595 (Supreme Court of Oregon).

Rio Grande Jewelers Supply, Inc. v. Data General Corp. (1984) Pacific Reporter, 2nd Series, *vol. 689*, p. 1269 (New Mexico).

Ritchie Enterprises v. Honeywell Bull, Inc. (1990) Federal Supplement, *vol. 730*, p. 1041 (United States District Court, Kansas).

Robertson, R.J., Jr. (1994) "A Modest Proposal Regarding the Enforceability of 'As Is' Disclaimers of Implied Warranties: What the Buyer Doesn't Know Shouldn't Hurt Him." *Commercial Law Journal, vol. 95,* p. 1.

Rodau, A. (1986) "Computer Software: Does Article 2 of the Uniform Commercial Code Apply?" *Emory Law Journal, vol. 35*, p. 853.

Roome v. Sonora Petroleum Co. (1922) Pacific Reporter, *vol. 208*, p. 255 (Supreme Court of Kansas).

Rose, B. (1990) *Managing Software Support*, San Diego, CA: Software Support Professionals Association.

Rose, B. (1996) "Email: Software Support's Secret Weapon" downloaded from www.sspa-online.com/publications/email.html.

Roto-Lith, Ltd. v. F.P. Bartlett & Co. (1962) Federal Reporter, 2nd Series, *vol. 297*, p. 497 (United States Court of Appeals, 1st Circuit).

Rubin, E.L. (1997) "The Code, the Consumer, and the Institutional Structure of the Common Law," *Washington University Law Quarterly*, *vol. 75*, p. 11.

Russinovitch, M (1998) "Reverse-Engineered Disassembly of SoftRAM 95 - Windows 95 Version." (original publication date unknown). Downloaded from http://ftp.uni-mannheim.de/info/Oreilly/windows/win95.update/softdiff.asm.

Rustad, M., E. Martel, and S. McAuliffe (1995) "An Empirican Analysis of Software Licensing Law and Practices (Part 2)." *Computer Law Association Bulletin, vol. 10*, number 4, p. 3.

Sacramento Regional Transit District v. Grumman Flexible (1984) California Appellate Reports, *vol. 158*, p. 289 (California Court of Appeal).

Salahutdin v. Valley of California, Inc. (1994) California Appellate Reports, *vol. 24,* p. 555 (California Court of Appeal).

Saloomey v. Jeppesen & Co. (1983) Federal Reporter, 2nd Series, *vol. 707*, p. 671 (United States Court of Appeals, 2nd Circuit).

Samuelson, P. (1998a) Intellectual Property and Contract Law for the Information Age: Foreword to a Symposium." Introduction to the *Conference on the Impact of Article 2B*, UC Berkeley, April 23-25, 1998. Available at sims.berkeley.edu/~pam/papers/clr_2b.html

Samuelson, P. (1998b) "Legally Speaking: Does Information Really Want To Be Licensed?", *In Press, Communications of the ACM*. Available at sims.berkeley.edu/~pam/papers/acm_2B.html.

Sanco, Inc. v. Ford Motor Corp. (1985) Federal Reporter, 2nd Series, *vol. 771*, p. 1081 (United States Court of Appeals, 7th Circuit).

Schreiber, R. (1997, March) "How the Internet Changes (Almost) Everything," presented at the Association for Support Professionals' *Internet Support Forum*, San Jose, CA.

Schulman, A. (1998) *SoftRAM95: "False and Misleading."* http://ftp .uni-mannheim.de/info/Oreilly/windows/win95.update/softram.html

Schulman, A. (1998b) Analysis of SoftRAM 95 SOFTRAM1.386. (original publication date unknown.) Downloaded from http://ftp.uni-mannheim.de/ info/Oreilly/windows/win95.update/softram1.txt

Schurtz v. BMW of North America, Inc. (1991) Pacific Reporter, 2nd Series, *vol. 814*, p. 1108.

Schwartz (1994) "Louisiana's Unfair Trade Law: An Elusive Remedy and Uncertain Threat." *Louisiana Bar Journal, vol. 41*, p. 522.

Schwartz v. Electronic Data Systems, Inc. (1990) Federal Reporter, 2nd Series, *vol. 913*, p. 279 (United States Court of Appeals, 6th Circuit).

Shambaugh v. Lindsay (1983) North Eastern Reporter, 2nd Series, *vol. 445*, p. 124 (Indiana Court of Appeals).

Seekings v. Jimmy GMC (1981) Pacific Reporter, 2nd Series, *vol. 638*, p. 210 (Supreme Court of Arizona).

Sengstack, J. (1996) "Anniversary PC Owners Fight Gateway—And Win", *PC World online* (from the June, 1996, issue of PC World), available at www.pcworld.com.

Sheldon, J. & C.L. Carter (1997) *Consumer Warranty Law*, National Consumer Law Center. *This book seems to be hard to get or overpriced on Net-based bookstores. Contact NCLC directly at www.consumerlaw.org.*

Sheldon, J., and C.L. Carter (1997b) *Unfair and Deceptive Acts and Practices* (4th Edition), National Consumer Law Center.

Sherkate Sahami Khass Rapol v. Henry R. Jahn & Son, Inc., (1983) Federal Reporter, 2nd Series, *vol. 701*, p. 1049 (United States Court of Appeals, 2nd Circuit).

Shute v. Carnival Cruise Lines (1990) Federal Reporter, 2nd Series, *vol. 897*, p. 377 (United States Court of Appeals, 9th Circuit).

Smith v. Linn (1989) Atlantic Reporter, 2nd Series, *vol. 563*, p. 123 (Superior Court of Pennsylvania).

Smith v. Reynolds Metals Co. (1986) Southern Reporter, 2nd Series, *vol. 497*, p. 93 (Supreme Court of Alabama).

Snell v. Cornehl (1970) Pacific Reporter, 2nd Series, *vol. 466*, p. 94 (Supreme Court of New Mexico).

Smedinghoff, T.J. (1993) *The SPA Guide to Contracts and the Legal Protection of Software.* Washington, DC: Software Publishers Association.

Society for Information Management (1998) Letter to the Article 2B Drafting Committee, March 23, 1998 (unpublished) *Meeting of the NCCUSL Article 2B Drafting Committee*, San Diego, CA, March 27-29, 1998.

Software Publishers Association (1993) *Model PC Software License Agreement (and Explanatory Comments)*, Washington, D.C.

Software Publishers Association (1995) *1995 Technical Support Survey Report*, Washington, D.C.

Software Publishers Association Software Packaging SIG (1995a) *Recommended Practices & Guidelines for Desktop Software Packaging*, Washington, D.C. (www.spa.org/sigs/package/guide.htm)

Software Publishers Association Software Packaging SIG (1995b) *Recommended Practices & Guidelines for Jewel Case and Jewel Case Alternative Software Packaging*, Washington, D.C. (www.spa.org/sigs/package)

Software Publishers Association (1996) *The Retail Consumer Software Market: Category Management and Beyond*, Washington, D.C.

Software Publishers Association (1996b) *ProCD, Incorporated vs. Matthew Zeidenberg and Silken Mountain Web Services, Brief of Amicus Curiae Software Publishers Association in Support of Plaintiff-Appellant.* Available at http://www.ggtech.com/spabrief.html.

Software Support Professionals Association (1997, "document number"). This is a members-only database of the SSPA's best estimates of several support statistics. The SSPA Support Center document number is the number of the specific document available from the database that provides the quoted statistic.

Spencer, C.J., and Yates, D.K. (1995) "A Good User Guide Means Fewer Support Calls and Lower Support Costs." *Technical Communication, vol. 42, #1*, p. 52.

Starnes, T. (1996) *Mad at Your Lawyer? What to do when you're Overcharged, Ignored, Betrayed, or a Victim of Malpractice.* Berkeley, CA: Nolo Press.

Stein v. Treger (1950) Federal Reporter, 2nd Series, *vol. 182*, p. 696 (District of Columbia Circuit Court of Appeals).

Steinberg, R., and Sege, A. (1995, May) *The Joy of Licensing: The Multimedia Lawyer's Cookbook,* paper presented at the Sixteenth Annual Computer Law Institute, Los Angeles, California.

Step-Saver Data Systems, Inc. v. Wyse Technology and The Software Link, Inc., (1991) Federal Reporter, 2nd Series, *vol. 939*, p. 91 (United States Court of Appeals, 3rd Circuit).

Sterne, J. *(1996) Customer Service on the Internet*, New York: John Wiley & Sons.

Straus v. Victor Talking Machine Company (1917) United States Reports, *vol. 243*, p. 490 (United States Supreme Court).

Stuessy v. Microsoft Corp. (1993) Federal Supplement, *vol. 837,* p. 690 (United States District Court, Eastern District of Pennsylvania).

Sullivan v. Allegheny Ford Truck Sales (1980) Atlantic Reporter, 2nd Series, *vol. 423*, p. 1292 (Pennsylvania Superior Court).

Swisher, K., (1995, April 28) *Georgetown Software Firm, Fox Sign Pact*, Washington Post at F2.

Tarter, J. (1993) "Benchmark report: Technical support cost ratios," *Soft-letter, vol. 10*, #10, p. 1.

Tarter, J. (1996) "Is there a payoff for service quality?", *Soft*Letter, vol. 12*, #18, p. 1.

The 10th Anniversary Club (1998) *What is the 10th Anniversary Club?* www.hal-pc/~mose/10thclub/te01000.html.

Tidrow, R. (1996) *Windows 95 Registry Troubleshooting*, Indianapolis: New Riders Publishing.

Tolmie Farms, Inc. v. Stauffer Chemical Company, Inc. (1992) Pacific Reporter, 2nd Series, *vol. 124*, p. 613 (Court of Appeals of Idaho).

Tourniare, F., and R. Farrell (1997) *The Art of Software Support.* Upper Saddle River, NJ: Prentice Hall PTR.

Townsend, C. (1992) *1-800-HELP! With Windows 3.1*, Indianapolis: Sams.

Trust Co. of Norfolk v. Fletcher (1929) South Eastern Reporter, *vol. 148*, p. 785 (Supreme Court of Virginia).

United States v. Dell Computer Corporation (1998) Consent decree at www.ftc.gov/os/9804/consent5.htm.

The United States Code (updated to 1997) law.house.gov/usc.htm. Also at www.law.cornell.edu/uscode.

The United States Code of Federal Regulations (updated to 1997) www.access.gpo.gov/nara/cfr/index.html.

Uniform Commercial Code www.law.cornell.edu/ucc/2/overview.html

United States Federal Trade Commission (1998) *Fighting Consumer Fraud: New Tools of the Trade.* Available at www.ftc.gov/reports.

United States Fidelity & Guaranty Co. v. Black (1981) North Western Reporter, 2nd Series, *vol. 313*, p. 77 (Supreme Court of Michigan).

United States Federal Trade Commission (1995) *A Business Guide to the Federal Trade Commission's Mail or Telephone Order Merchandise Rule.* Available at www.ftc.gov/bcp/conline/pubs/buspubs/mailordr/index.htm

United States Government Printing Office (1998) *Code of Federal Regulations.* Available at www.access.gpo.gov/nara/cfr.

United States Office of Consumer Affairs (1997) *Consumer's Resource Handbook.* Available at www.pueblo.gsa.gov/1997res.htm.

United States Postal Service (1994) A Consumer's Guide to Postal Crime Prevention. For the same information on the net, go to www.usps.gov/websites/depart/inspect.

Van Bennekom, F. (1994) *The Boundary Spanning Activities of the Customer Support Organization: Hearing and Articulating the Customer's Voice to Improve Software Product Quality.* Doctoral Dissertation, Boston University Graduate School of Management. Available from University Microfilms International. Synopsis available at www.smiweb.com/publications.

Vault Corp. v. Quaid Software Ltd. (1987) Federal Supplement, *vol. 655*, p. 750 (Eastern District of Louisiana), affirmed in *Vault Corp. v. Quaid Software Ltd.* (1988).

Vault Corp. v. Quaid Software Ltd. (1988) Federal Reporter, 2nd Series, *vol. 847*, p. 255 (United States Court of Appeals, 5th Circuit).

Wall Street Journal (1994) "Humble pie: Intel to replace its Pentium chips" *Wall Street Journal* (December 21) p. B1.

Warner, R.E. (1997) *Everybody's Guide to Small Claims Court* (7th Ed), Berkeley, CA: Nolo Press.

Wasch, K. (1995) Testimony of the President of the Software Publishers Association to the Federal Trade Commission during its Hearings on Global and Innovation-Based Competition. Available at www.spa.org/gvmnt/kentest.htm

Wasch, K. (1997) *Re: Response to Your Letter to Bill Gates, dated April 7, 1997.* Available at the web site of the Software Publishers Association, at www.spa.org.gvmnt/finance/Rnader.htm. The letter is listed on the SPA, page, *Testimony and Official Statements,* www.spa.org/gvmnt/tos/default.htm.

Waukesha Foundry, Inc. v. Industrial Engineering, Inc. (1996) Federal Reporter, 3rd Series, *vol. 91*, p. 1002 (United States Court of Appeals, 7th Circuit).

Weng v. Allison (1997) North Eastern Reporter, 2nd Series, *vol. 678*, p. 1254 (Illinois Appellate Court).

Westlye v. Look Sports, Inc. (1993) California Appellate Reports, Fourth Series, *vol. 17*, p. 1715 (California Court of Appeal).

West Publishing (1995) *Selected Commercial Statutes,* St. Paul, MN: West Publishing Corp.

West Side Federal Savings & Loan Association v. Hirschfeld (1984) New York Supplement, 2nd Series, *vol. 476,* p. 292 (New York Supreme Court, Appellate Division).

Whipp v. Iverson (1969) North Western Reporter, 2nd Series, *vol. 168*, p. 201 (43 Wis.2d 166) (Supreme Court of Wisconsin).

White, J.J. , and Summers, R.S. (1995, Supplemented 1998) *Uniform Commercial Code* (4th Edition), Practitioner Treatise Series, St. Paul, MN: West Publishing Corp.

Wiener, L.R. (1993) *Digital Woes*, Reading, MA: Addison-Wesley Publishing Co.

Wilson v. Jones (1932) South Western Reporter, 2nd Series, *vol. 45*, p. 572 (Texas Court of Civil Appeals).

Winter v. G.P. Putnam's Sons (1991) Federal Reporter, 2nd Series, *vol. 938,* p. 1033 (United States Court of Appeals, 9th Circuit).

Winson, R. (1991) *Help! The Art of Computer Technical Support,* Berkeley, CA: Peachpit Press.

Wolf & Klar Co. v. Garner (1984) Pacific Reporter, 2nd Series, *vol. 679*, p. 258 (101 N.M. 116) (Supreme Court of New Mexico).

Wood, J.B. (1996, October) "Linking customer loyalty to the bottom line," *Software Support Professionals Association Executive Forum,* San Diego, CA.

Wright, B. (1997) The Law of Electronic Commerce: EDI, E-mail, and Internet—Technology, Proof, and Liability. 2nd Ed., Aspen Law & Business.

Yanase v. Automobile Club of Southern California (1989) California Appellate Reports, 3rd Series, *vol. 212,* p. 468 (California Court of Appeal); *reprinted and analyzed in* American Law Reports, Fifth Series, *vol. 2*, p. 1084.

Yourdon, E. (1996) *The Resurrection and Rise of the American Programmer*, Englewood Cliffs, NJ: Yourdon Press.

Zimmerman v. Kent (1991) Northeastern Reporter, 2ndSeries, *vol. 575*, p. 70 (Massachusetts Appellate Court).

Index

About the Authors

Cem Kaner practices law, usually representing individual developers, small development services companies, and customers. His focus is on the law of software quality. He is also actively involved in legislation affecting the law of software quality. He attends, as a participating observer, Drafting Committee meetings for Uniform Commercial Code Article 2B and for the Uniform Electronic Transactions Act. He has also served pro bono as a Deputy District Attorney and as an investigator/mediator for a California county's Consumer Affairs Department.

Kaner consults on technical and software development management issues and teaches about software testing at UC Berkeley Extension, UC Santa Cruz Extension, and at several software companies. He founded and hosts the Los Altos Workshops on Software Testing. His book, *Testing Computer Software*, received the *Award of Excellence* in the Society for Technical Communication's 1993 Northern California Technical Publications Competition. Kaner began working with computers in 1976, while a graduate student of Human Experimental Psychology. He came to Silicon Valley in 1983 and has worked as a programmer, human factors analyst, user interface designer, software salesperson, associate in an organization development consulting firm, technical writer, software testing technology team leader, manager of software testing, manager of technical publications, software development manager, and director of documentation and software testing.

Kaner holds a B.A. (Arts & Sciences, concentrating in Math and Philosophy), a J.D. (law degree), and a Ph.D. (Experimental Psychology) and is Certified in Quality Engineering by the American Society for Quality Control.

David Pels is a native Californian who grew up in Silicon Valley. He has worked in computer and software support and sales since 1981. His positions have included management of sales administration and customer operations (including product support) for a publisher of automotive diagnostics; director of client support and services for a financial application publisher; group manager of product support for a large mass-market maker of computer peripherals and software applications; director of world-wide client support and services for a maker of high-end color copy and printing systems; manager of product support for a mass-market productivity software publisher; supervisor of product support for a publisher of game and productivity/small-business software; and retail sales of consumer electronics. He has attended, as an observer, several meetings of the Uniform Commercial Code Article 2B Drafting Committee. David is member of the Association of Support Professionals. He is also a scout leader in the Boy Scouts of America and a member of the National Eagle Scout Association.